Education for Empire

Education for Empire

AMERICAN SCHOOLS, RACE, AND
THE PATHS OF GOOD CITIZENSHIP

Clif Stratton

UNIVERSITY OF CALIFORNIA PRESS

University of California Press, one of the most distinguished university
presses in the United States, enriches lives around the world by advancing
scholarship in the humanities, social sciences, and natural sciences. Its
activities are supported by the UC Press Foundation and by philanthropic
contributions from individuals and institutions. For more information, visit
www.ucpress.edu.

University of California Press
Oakland, California

Library of Congress Cataloging-in-Publication Data

Stratton, Clif, 1980– author.
    Education for empire : American schools, race, and the paths of good
citizenship / Clif Stratton.
        pages   cm
    Includes bibliographical references and index.
    ISBN 978-0-520-28566-8 (cloth : alk. paper)
    ISBN 978-0-520-28567-5 (pbk. : alk. paper)
    ISBN 978-0-520-96105-0 (ebook)
    1. Racism in education—United States—History.   2. Racism in
education—United States—Case studies.   3. Education and state—United
States—History.   4. Race relations in school management—United States—
History.   5. Nationalism and education—United States—History.
6. Minorities—Education—United States—History.   7. United States—
Territorial expansion—Social aspects.   I. Title.
    LC212.2.S77   2016
    370.89—dc23   2015032356

Manufactured in the United States of America

24   23   22   21   20   19   18   17   16
10   9   8   7   6   5   4   3   2   1

In keeping with a commitment to support environmentally responsible and
sustainable printing practices, UC Press has printed this book on Natures
Natural, a fiber that contains 30% post-consumer waste and meets the
minimum requirements of ANSI/NISO Z39.48–1992 (R 1997) (*Permanence
of Paper*).

For Kristen, Inman, and Livie

And in memory of Cliff Kuhn

CONTENTS

ACKNOWLEDGMENTS

The acts of research and writing often involve long periods of solitude. Yet, this book bears the mark of conversations and interactions with many people who have helped me to find my own voice and to think more deeply about the place of schools in society and the meanings of citizenship.

I had the privilege of working with an incredibly collegial and sharp group of scholars at Georgia State University. They have all left indelible marks on this book and on me as a teacher, a writer, and a person, including Jared Poley, Cliff Kuhn, Michele Reid-Vasquez, Charles Steffen, Isa Blumi, Rob Baker, Michelle Brattain, Brian Ingrassia, Carolyn Biltoft, and Larry Youngs. Ian Fletcher invited me to join the Trans-Empire Research Cluster. There, he, Shannon Bontrager, Carrie Whitney, Abu Bamba, Andy Reisinger, Masako Racel, and several others offered constructive comments at the earliest stages of this project, as well as much-needed commiseration. Veronica Holmes opened her home to many of us for delicious meals, great wine, and rich conversation. Christine Skwiot offered unparalleled mentorship and insight into the ways empire has shaped American thought and life. She has encouraged me to be bold and clear in my assertions and reminded me when necessary that formal schooling also did good things, like increase literacy. Casey Cater read drafts, shared countless stretches of bar, and talked Braves baseball. He remains a damn fine historian and friend.

Archivists and librarians at a range of public institutions have offered their expertise and guided me through sometimes large, overwhelming bureaucratic school board collections with patience and kindness. At the New York Municipal Archives, David Ment's vast knowledge of the Board of Education Records made my work efficient and my afternoon rides in the city that much more enjoyable. Thanks to Jonathan Scott for the couch and the loaner bike.

After my lovely morning walks from Waikiki, I never encountered such a precision team effort as I did among the staff at the Hawaii State Archives. Melissa Shimonishi was most helpful with images. At the San Francisco History Center, the staff was also very helpful, pointing me toward parts of the SFUSD records I hadn't considered but that turned out to be fruitful. Thanks to Jeff Thomas and Yael Schwartz for help with images and scans. I owe a great debt to the unnamed early twentieth-century scrapbooker who compiled seemingly every scrap of local press coverage of the San Francisco School Exclusion Crisis. In Atlanta, Andrea Jackson at the Robert W. Woodruff Library at the Atlanta University Center and Traci Drummond and staff at the Southern Labor Archives at Georgia State University were incredibly attentive, accommodating, and knowledgeable.

Far-flung scholars have offered a variety of insights, constructive critiques, and encouragement along the way. Many of them will not remember, but I do, and I remain grateful, especially to Stephen Berrey, Gary Gerstle, Alecia Long, Nayan Shah, Doug Sackman, Kat Cleland, and the anonymous reviewers at the University Press of Mississippi and the University of California Press. Yong Chen offered timely encouragement in the early stages of peer review. Lorrin Thomas was painstakingly meticulous in her reviews of the manuscript. Her attention to detail, substantive critiques, and constructive and usable suggestions about framing, readability, and clarity of argument have ultimately made this a much better book than the draft she was first delivered. Eiichiro Azuma graciously offered his expertise with regard to Japanese language sources and ambiguous demographic data. Solsiree del Moral saved the day by sharing a critical and elusive primary source at the last hour. Many, many thanks to Niels Hooper at University of California Press for taking a chance on this project and for his keen insights. Thanks to Bradley Depew for his fastidious and timely attention to detail and to he, Niels, and Kate Hoffman for helping me navigating the publication process. I also am forever indebted to Drew Nelson for pushing and inspiring me to become a scholar and teacher.

I am fortunate to have joined a wonderful community of scholars and friends at Washington State University. Jenny Thigpen, Jeff Sanders, and Matt Sutton helped shape book proposals and craft reader responses. Ray Sun and Steve Kale have supported my research above and beyond the call of duty. Thanks to the College of Arts and Sciences and the Converse Endowment for their generous completion funding, to Pat Thorsten-Mickelson and Sue Allen for facilitating that support, and to Robert Franklin for offering his scanning skills. Jesse Spohnholz read chapters and shared bike rides, including one in a snowstorm. Conversations with Katy Fry about immigration and about teaching have proven most fruitful. This project never would have reached completion without the camaraderie and astute suggestions of Emily Anderson and Lawrence Hatter. Our year of coffee, dessert, and draft chapters was a time of utmost productivity.

Lastly, thanks to my family, immediate and extended, for their unwavering support in ways so varied and numerous I cannot do them justice here. My parents David and Ginny and my brother Mark provide strong foundations and models for a life of inquiry and exploration. With Kristen Stratton, I have the great pleasure of sharing a home, a life, and two sweet children, Inman and Livie. This book is dedicated to them.

Introduction

GOOD CITIZENS

AFTER CONGRESS DECLARED COLUMBUS DAY a national school holiday in June 1892, California superintendent of public instruction James W. Anderson called upon schools across the state to prepare to celebrate "the system of free education which has been so powerful a factor in the progress and prosperity of the great American people." On October 21, schoolchildren across the United States gathered in patriotic displays of flag waving, saluting, singing, and pledges of allegiance to dedicate the grounds of the World's Columbian Exposition in Chicago.[1] The festivities seemingly bound children of all races, creeds, and national origins together under a banner of equal American citizenship. But at the fair, "tropical settlements" of exotic Filipinos, fierce Negroes, stoic Indians, and "Chinese bazaars"—arrayed along the exposition's Midway Plaisance for the educational amusement of its white patrons—contrasted sharply with the White City's celebration of Western institutions and technology.[2] Both schools and the fair arranged peoples according to hierarchies of their value and contributions to civilization. The path to citizenship that led to "progress and prosperity" as articulated by Anderson was in fact not open to all schoolchildren.

Education for Empire argues that American public schools created and situated children along multiple unequal paths to "good citizenship."[3] These paths both reflected and created broader institutional patterns of subordination and exclusion at work in American society—patterns intimately tied to hierarchies of race and national origin and to US imperial ambitions and practices. Citizenship operated in a highly fluid and contested manner in which the nation's inhabitants, native- and foreign-born alike, were subject

1. To introduce the differences of schools in regards to race to perpetuate a process in which political gain is evident.

2. Preparing U.S. children to become citizens in a racially bias world. How does this effect today?

1

to a range of historically informed assumptions about who is and is not citizen material, no matter what legal claims to citizenship one might have. Though always within specific local or regional contexts, school boards, superintendents, textbook authors, and teachers collectively created a range of competing and unequal hierarchical possibilities for and narratives about participation and inclusion in American political, economic, and cultural life—what Elizabeth Cohen has called "semi-citizenship" common in modern liberal democracies. In this sense, the paths to citizenship on offer in American schools were as uneven and contentious in what they bestowed upon those that trod them as the interpreted meanings of citizenship that underscored the political economy and civic discourse.[4]

This book brings together subjects in American history usually treated separately. In particular, I argue that the distension of public schooling for the purpose of crafting degrees of citizenship at home and the proliferation of American economic power through empire-building projects both at home and abroad were more intimately intertwined than is usually recognized.[5] Central to these projects, to borrow from Paul Kramer, were "modes of exceptionalizing difference" in order to "enable and produce relations of hierarchy, discipline, dispossession, extraction, and exploitation."[6] Imperialism offered not simply the chance to exercise authority over foreign markets, resources, and labor pools, but also the opportunity to reinforce, reshape, and reorder the relations of power at home, including in the nation's growing public school systems. As such, imperial ambitions were not only the concern of territorial governors, capitalists, and missionaries in far-flung colonial outposts. Public school administrators, teachers, and textbook authors (most of whom were teachers themselves) promoted and shared in the benefits of commercial and territorial expansion, and in both territories *and* states, they applied colonial forms of governance to the young populations they professed to prepare for future citizenship.[7] Moreover, local concerns and anxieties about assimilating certain kinds of foreigners and outsiders into a community's political, social, and economic fabric via public education manifested on national and international stages, sometimes with consequences for American diplomatic and international economic interests. Textbooks, segregated schools, Americanization campaigns of varying degrees of coerciveness, and policies and narratives of colonialism forged a variegated schooling experience in which certain common threads emerged, especially preparation for different and unequal forms of citizenship.

Ultimately, the paths of citizenship available to many students, particularly foreign-born and nonwhite, were incongruent with the promises of
public education as the institutional mechanism of equal social opportunity
and as the vehicle of economic mobility heralded by many school reformers
at the turn of the twentieth century and beyond.[8] Nor was there a single ideal
citizen to which schoolchildren were supposed to aspire, despite claims by
many educators to the contrary. Rather, citizenship functioned as a "gradient
category" composed of myriad and shifting "statuses, actions, institutions,
and rights."[9] While school history textbook authors like Waddy Thompson,
for example, claimed to send students down a singular "path of good citizenship," the broader intellectual and institutional project in which Thompson
participated recognized as absolutely imperative competing, complementary,
and unequal forms of "good" citizenship.[10] Framing points of study
→ 35 year imm.

The 1882 Chinese Exclusion and 1924 National Origins Acts frame the
majority of the narrative. These two pivotal immigration laws entangled in
US quests for empire in and across the Pacific, Caribbean, and Atlantic call
greater attention to how the debates, stakes, and contests over belonging and
exclusion were of central concern to white nationalists, Americanizers,
expansionists, and anti-imperialists. Making "good" citizens was as much
about excluding or subordinating certain kinds of people as it was about
including, regenerating, and reshaping others. Myriad Americanization
movements, including both coercive and more pluralistic forms of citizen
making in public schools, drew strength from increasingly exclusionary
immigration laws. These two statutes and others passed in the years intervening were in turn often conditioned by the decisions and actions of administrators, teachers, parents, and children.[11]

During this period, schools forged disparate paths to citizenship in the
mutually sustaining arenas of textbooks and curricula on the one hand and
school politics and policy on the other. Paths tracked divisions of labor
and the economic imperatives of US empire that frequently precipitated and
overlapped with constructions of race and nationality. In this sense, schools
within the bounded national space often served as domestic colonial institutions, espoused narratives that projected American power onto both foreign
and domestic geographies and populations, and created distinctive paths to
citizenship that many native-born and indeed many naturalized whites
hoped would strengthen the boundaries of race and nation. For white children, notably native-born or immigrants from northern and western Europe,

schools usually opened a path to full citizenship that included uncontested voting rights (for males), potential managerial and professional status in expanding public and private bureaucracies, and full acceptance in the national community of citizens. Through Americanization projects, many school officials also hoped to shape both native- and foreign-born children of dubious whiteness into hard-working, patriotic, white Americans, even as some of those same administrators welcomed the 1924 National Origins Act. Through the enactment of annual quotas, the act impeded flows of migrants from southern and eastern Europe—a move that school professionals believed would accelerate the twinned tasks of Americanization and cultural whitening they argued had either stalled or reversed in the 1910s.

In contrast, schools aimed to reform and subordinate foreign- and native-born children of color for future industrial, domestic, and agricultural work. This colonial path frequently led to either full exclusion from national belonging, particularly for foreign-born nonwhites, or citizenship bereft of legitimate and secure suffrage rights or upward social and economic mobility. But schools and the rhetoric of liberty and democracy so frequently touted as unique to the American system of free education also offered space for parents and students to claim a greater share of the economic and social capital that public education supposedly made available with its promise of "progress and prosperity." By contesting and resisting efforts to subordinate them and by blazing alternative paths to "good" citizenship, marginalized people destabilized the boundaries of race and nation that white nationalists worked so hard to erect and maintain.[12]

Immigration and empire gave immediacy to the bureaucratic revolution that, in the late nineteenth century, translated from corporations to social and municipal institutions including schools. This period was marked by an economic reorganization increasingly geared toward efficient mass industrial production and consumption, and the new economy permeated politics, social institutions, and culture. Scientific management and assembly lines not only transformed the factory system but also created the need for an educated, obedient, and reliable workforce capable of producing, transporting, and consuming the goods that underpinned American economic and geopolitical expansion. The forceful opening of Latin American, Caribbean, and Asia-Pacific markets for the extraction of raw materials and marketing of American goods animated movements to order American society along lines of race and class as the civilizing process folded into the new corporatized structures of industry and empire. Public schools helped define and reinforce acceptable social, economic, and political habits and roles for all those who lived within the republic and its overseas empire. Schools educated a new managerial class of white-collar workers and channeled millions of others into jobs on factory assembly lines, and on plantations and farms increasingly reliant on mechanization and emerging national and international supply chains headquartered in urban centers.[13]

In seeming contradiction to the exclusionary nature of segregation and immigration restriction that reflected white desires to maintain racial homogeneity, the growth of industrial capitalism advanced US imperial claims to incorporate new places and peoples into its economy, if not its polity. And the scale of industrialization hastened the confluence of labor migrations and market expansions. Thus, white Americans' anxieties about the corrosion of national character collided with aspirations for American-led global capitalism and international greatness. The architects of school curricula responded with support for a new corporate imperial model through historical narratives of progress and celebrations of the free market. Like American colonial schools in the Philippines that taught selected native elites to uphold and promote the new class boundaries created by foreign industrial investment and redefinitions of property ownership, schools in other colonial territories and on the US mainland supported emergent hierarchical social structures that both shaped and were shaped by corporate culture and the new imperialism that global capitalism afforded.[14]

This book's primary concern is to locate—in more meaningful and concrete ways—formal public education within the complex web of race consciousness, immigration restriction, and empire building spun during the Gilded Age and Progressive Era. It pays more careful attention to the specific ways that school officials, textbook authors, and teachers bolstered racial nationalism and both contested and promoted overseas empire and immigration restriction. It also allows us to see post-Reconstruction reunion as a truly transnational project in which white supremacy pervaded Asiatic exclusion in the West and imperial expansion in the Pacific and Caribbean as much as it did the acceptance of the Jim Crow order by white Northerners and Southerners in the East. Likewise, the creation of a white ethnic workforce in the Northeast and Midwest demanded not only immigrants from Europe and national expansion through the creation of transcontinental railroads, but also labor pools, export markets, and the extension of American power in the Pacific and in Latin America, its presumed "backyard." Industrial projects like railroad and canal building required and made possible certain kinds of subordinated laborers, compressed space and time, and connected the United States to the world. A focus on schools and citizenship compels us to insert transnational questions about belonging and exclusion, race and nation, and republic and empire into the story of reunion, industrialization, and the rise of mass democracy.[15]

Education for Empire also urges a rethinking of the temporal and geographic anchoring of the period. European migrations and immigrants have enjoyed a privileged status in Gilded Age and Progressive Era historiography of US industrialism, assimilation projects, and state building. But Chinese exclusion opened new debates about what constituted a good immigrant, and it preceded the groundswell of European migrations from southern and eastern Europe and subsequent Americanization and restriction campaigns aimed at winning hearts and minds while also limiting immigration to newcomers from northern and western European states. The Chinese Exclusion Act also anticipated federal Jim Crow policies that were enshrined into national law in 1896, the culmination of the violence, disenfranchisement, and segregation directed at African Americans during and after the collapse of Reconstruction. *Plessy v. Ferguson* officially joined African Americans with Chinese Americans as second-class citizens in the eyes of the nation's highest court, three decades after hard-won emancipation.

As nation and empire reciprocally shaped one another, movements in the West animated policies promulgated in Washington, DC, and the myriad rigid and more flexible hierarchies of race in the New South and Northeast. In the 1880s, national concerns over immigration initially arose not on the Atlantic seaboard but on the western edge of US continental holdings and in Hawai'i, where the nation's much-desired transpacific empire seemed to move eastward in the form of Asian field hands, rail workers, miners, settlers, and entrepreneurs. In California, Oregon, Washington, and intermountain western states and territories, white policymakers, unions, and some sympathetic capitalists attempted to impede the flow of Asian immigration, and then in 1917 and 1924, shut off the valve altogether. The National Origins Act did not just assign exceptionally low immigration quotas to southern and eastern European nations—primarily an Atlantic imperative. It simultaneously reaffirmed Chinese Exclusion and Congress's 1917 Asiatic Barred Zone in support of white California's ongoing campaign to rid the state of Asians. 1924 was as much about Pacific concerns as it was about Atlantic ones, and that year European Americans also completed the centuries-long "internal" conquest of Native Americans by imposing citizenship and expectations of patriotism while suffrage remained elusive and tribal sovereignty was further weakened.[16] Notably though, the National Origins Act imposed no quotas on nations in the Western Hemisphere, and in the years and decades following its passage, restrictionists cast Mexico and Latin America more broadly as sources of undesirables to be documented and inspected, Americanized or deported.[17]

In this context, schooling was as much about empire building as it was about nation building. While educators imparted lessons in good citizenship to wide varieties of children, they simultaneously reinforced the racial hierarchies formed by continental European settler colonialism and transformed by extensions of American commercial and state power in the Caribbean and Pacific. The entanglement of education in US imperial projects at home and abroad often rendered mercurial the categories of citizen, subject, and foreign national. An emergent social studies curriculum that included geography, history, and civics made meaning out of American empire by contrasting it with the decadence and tyranny of European colonialism, infusing its logic with the language of liberty, civilization, and commerce, and consciously avoiding the application of the imperial label to the United States at all. Most of all, US colonial peoples were not just Hawaiian, Puerto Rican, and Filipino. Imperial subjects included Native Americans, the descendants of slaves, Mexican immigrants and Mexican Americans, and until inculcated with Anglo-Saxon cultural norms, ambiguously white immigrants from southern and eastern Europe. Either through overt legal segregation or less obvious but no-less-constructed residential patterns, many of their children attended public schools, often but not always separately from native-born whites. In this sense, the projects of creating colonial subjects abroad and that of opening ascriptive paths to citizenship at home paralleled and shaped each other in important ways. Should colonial peoples overseas migrate to the United States, as many Filipinos and Puerto Ricans did, they were usually subordinated alongside native-born racial minority groups that had long been regarded as "foreigners within."[18]

Rather than treat colonialism as a process tangential to or apart from public schooling in the United States, it needs to be understood as a central ideological, narrative, and organizational force in schools at home as well as abroad. Administrators, teachers, and textbook authors actively imagined and institutionalized a hierarchical social order that transcended the walls of classrooms and informed debates about immigration, racialized forms of citizenship, and US international power. But this order rested precariously on identities of white and nonwhite, native-born and foreign, citizen and subject, patriot and dissident—binaries that were not nearly so stable as native-born whites sought to make them. As such, empire allows us to see familiar narratives and policies, including black-white segregation, Americanization campaigns targeting arrivals from Europe, or Asiatic exclusion, with fresh eyes.[19]

In addition, a national textbook market forged a cohesive pedagogy of racial geography, national exceptionalism, and patriotism and had the effect of a top-down national education system less locally driven than is generally recognized.[20] Despite the absence of a European-style centralized national education ministry and bureaucracy tasked with administering schools across the country, many local school administrators and teachers occupied themselves with creating American patriots and defining and policing boundaries of morality, race, civilization, and national belonging. Local and state superintendents and school boards set policy, adopted textbooks, and attempted to establish cultures of loyal citizenship and patriotism for teachers and schoolchildren that emphasized hierarchies of race and nation and promoted US global commercial interests. A handful of large publishing houses in Boston, New York, and Philadelphia published the vast majority of textbooks distributed to schools through integrated national supply chains. These included MacMillan, Ginn, and the conglomerate American Book Company—formed at the end of the nineteenth century as the distribution point for five major publishers, including Harper Brothers, D. Appleton, and A. S. Barnes. American Book controlled 80 percent of the textbook market at one point. School administrators, like their white-collar counterparts in corporations and publishing houses, considered themselves invested in the mission of producing good citizens and maintaining the economic and social structures that had afforded them jobs as managers and as empowered social actors. And despite sectional differences over the legacies of Confederate leaders, Abraham Lincoln, and Reconstruction, most authors writing during this period stressed reconciliation and reunion, the inevitability of American liberty, and valor on the battlefields of the continental American West, Cuba, the Philippines, and later France. All the while, the efficacy of non-white citizenship remained volatile.[21]

Yet school administrators and their allies in civic government could not impose either inclusive or exclusive Americanization at will. Asians, Asian Americans, and Hawaiians in the transpacific US West, blacks in the New South, southern and eastern Europeans in the urban Northeast, Mexican Americans in the Southwest, and Puerto Ricans in both the Caribbean and New York City, as case studies reveal, responded to public schools in ways neither uniform nor in keeping with the desires of white nationalist professionals at the helm of curricula and policy. They often challenged in sometimes subtle but no less meaningful ways the paths to citizenship allotted to them in order to share in and shape the "progress and prosperity" described by Superintendent Anderson. In this sense, this is also a story of ordinary people, many engaged in transnational struggles against empire and global capitalism, pursuing access to education and its prospects for full citizenship and socioeconomic opportunity equal to that of native-born whites in the United States and other self-described "white men's countries."[22]

Education for Empire first demonstrates how authors and educators leveraged both ideas and policies to proclaim the beneficence of free public education and its inclusive paths to citizenship. These same people, though, preferred that many nonwhites and immigrants not embrace the full meaning of citizenship, and they often implemented restrictive policies in accordance with that goal. In chapter 1, I argue that authors and the school administrators in charge of vetting and adopting textbooks crafted and selected narratives of race hierarchy, empire as national destiny, and patriotism that often masked and almost always reinforced the deep inequalities and exclusionary school policies that are the subjects of the five chapters that follow. There, I contend that proponents of immigration exclusion, manual training, segregated schools, and Americanization and English-only schemes forged separate and subordinate paths to citizenship for nonwhites, foreign-born, the native-born children of immigrants, and colonial subjects even as they expected these children to become as ardent patriots as their native-born white counterparts and to support America's imperial endeavors at home and abroad.

In the decades surrounding the turn of the twentieth century, a symbiotic curriculum of world geography, American history, and community civics emerged to organize race, empire, and citizenship at global, national, and local levels. World geographies commanded an understanding and acceptance of the world's racial divisions and the place of the United States in that global racial order. New "scientific" and "objective" narratives of American history heralded the United States and its European American population as an exceptional nation and people in ways that reinforced the divisions of race and civilization taught in world geography. As Elmer Miller of the California State Normal School wrote in the American Bureau of Geography's inaugural 1900 bulletin: "[Geography] is an aid to most subjects, but to no other subject is it so valuable as to history. It tells us at least in part why various peoples are in different stages of advancement; why the Esquimo and central African are more backward than Europeans."[23] In turn, the architects of civics courses stressed productivity and patriotism and sustained an exceptionalist historical narrative in order to mold good citizens within the context of their local communities and for citizenship in a nation with growing imperial clout.

If schoolbook authors imagined and narrated a nation and empire imbued with global racial hierarchies; an exceptionalist, anticolonial, democratic ethos; and civic-minded, patriotic political and economic actors, administrators and teachers attempted to create this world through specific policies. The case studies that follow chapter 1 emerged from specific local and regional circumstances and unfolded unevenly over this period. Yet collectively they prescribed similar paths to citizenship along lines of race, national origin, and imperial desire even as local circumstances dictated variegated tactics. In chapters 2 through 5, I examine how school administrations in four locales—San Francisco, Hawai'i, Atlanta, and New York City—engaged in localized identity politics of inclusion and exclusion that in turn guided the currents of racial nationalism and power relationships at the centers of industrial and imperial America between 1882 and 1924. Chapter 6 offers comparative and "relational" frameworks for understanding the experiences of Mexican Americans and Puerto Ricans in schools after the passage of the National Origins Act. Since the act had not applied quotas to any nations in the Western Hemisphere and since Puerto Ricans possessed US citizenship, restrictionists swiftly called attention to what they perceived as "the racial problems involved in immigration from Latin America and the Caribbean."[24]

California representative Everis A. Hayes's lucid 1906 association of West and South best illustrates the transnational Atlantic, Pacific, and Caribbean connections among race, immigration, and empire. On the heels of the decision of San Francisco's school board to segregate Japanese children, Hayes warned that "the race problem on the Pacific Coast is rapidly taking on a character similar to the race problem in South Carolina and it will be only a course of a few years till [sic] the Japanese predominate in California."[25] Hayes's connection suggested that racially exclusive measures extended from South to West. However, the San Francisco school exclusion incident continued a longer struggle by white nationalists to purge the American West of Asian immigrants—a movement that won its first major victory with the 1882 Chinese Exclusion Act and reaffirmed its efficacy among the national populace with the 1892 Geary Act, the restrictions of which proved even more onerous for Chinese laborers, previously exempt Chinese residents, and Chinese American citizens than those of the 1882 statute.

But like Chinese before them, Japanese parents and students did not passively accept the school board's decision. As parents petitioned the school board, the Japanese ambassador, and President Theodore Roosevelt, Japanese students in Denver, Colorado, refused to pledge alliance to the flag in a show of solidarity with San Francisco students denied equal educational opportunity. The press seized on the protest as an act of disloyalty out of touch with the rituals and values of citizenship that Japanese students should have learned in civics class. The 1907 Gentlemen's Agreement between the United States and Japan restored integrated public schooling for Japanese in San Francisco, but it also set the agenda of exclusionists that culminated in the 1924 National Origins Act.[26]

In response and contrast to white California's call for a more robust restriction regime, Hawaiian-born white (haole) school officials, newspaper editors, and politicians heralded the territory as a model for racially tolerant communities in which representatives from diverse nations lived, worked, and learned free from the divisive nature of race relations on the mainland. However, as chapter 3 demonstrates, the realities of Hawaiian cosmopolitanism were in fact far from the amicable picture painted by some haole, who attempted to reconcile visions of racial harmony with practices of colonial oppression.

Native Hawaiians and diverse cohorts of immigrants from Asia and southern Europe met haole efforts with resistance at every step. Following the 1909 cane workers' strike, students at Waiale'e Boys' Industrial School resisted the forced labor and corporal punishment of the school's superintendent by eschewing work, escaping to Honolulu, or retreating into the nearby cane fields, where the boys' labor provided revenue for the grossly underfunded public reform school. Attempts to strengthen the manual training model of the missionary era floundered in the face of constant defiance by students who refused to remain subordinate to colonial authority. As school officials on the mainland increased their Americanization efforts during and immediately after World War I, haole attempted to regulate Japanese language schools that many argued impeded the Americanization of children of Japanese ancestry. In response, Japanese community leaders petitioned their haole employers, engaged in vehement protest, and by 1927, successfully pressured the US Supreme Court into striking down a law that placed foreign language schools under the control of the Department of Public Instruction.[27]

While white Californians and haole moved to create racially stratified societies, Atlanta's all-white school board worked to enshrine Jim Crow segregation and a colonial curriculum that attended US continental and overseas expansion. The politics of white supremacy, in the case of schools, was also a politics of empire, as the bonds of racial nationalism broken during the Civil War reasserted themselves on new frontiers in Cuba and the Philippines. Meanwhile, African Americans challenged the inadequacies of black schooling in the city and the curriculum prescribed by white school officials. Black intellectuals at Atlanta University often claimed the same rhetoric of "higher appreciation for the meaning of American citizenship" in promoting the expansion and funding of Atlanta's black schools, but they also pushed back against attempts to make industrial training the bulwark of black education—a colonial model pioneered by Hawaiian-born Samuel Chapman Armstrong at the Hampton Institute in Virginia and used in schools run by the Bureau of Indian Affairs.[28] Instead, students at Atlanta University, many of whom became teachers in Atlanta and throughout the South, maintained "co-education of the races" as the proper path to good citizenship and rejected claims that industrial education constituted the only appropriate form of training for the New South economy. Atlanta's first black high school opened only in 1924 after persistent grassroots political efforts organized by the National Association for the Advancement of Colored People (NAACP), Atlanta's leading black citizens, and Atlanta University graduates. However, black schools remained mostly separate and inherently unequal well after the *Brown v. Board of Education* decision in 1954. As an "alien race"—described as such by University of Georgia chancellor William Boggs before the Georgia Legislature in 1889—African Americans fared in ways similarly discriminatory to San Francisco's Japanese students, the racially diverse school population in Hawai'i, and as I argue in chapter 5, certain kinds of European immigrants.[29]

The children of the "new" European immigration to New York entered an urban public school system whose administrators were similarly anxious about and devoted to managing the city's racial and ethnic heterogeneity. The dubious whiteness of southern and eastern European immigrants in particular prompted both native-born and allied naturalized whites to pursue with vigor campaigns of Americanization. The campaign in New York City's public schools began in the 1880s with an English-only movement. By the turn of the century, schooling and whitening in a cultural sense became twinned projects as school boards and superintendents attempted to remake foreign children in the image of republican Anglo-American patriots and workers. During and after the Great War, school authorities hoped to alleviate the threats of Bolshevism and anarchism they were sure lurked in the city's ethnic enclaves and immigrant homes. Despite competing efforts to achieve either "100 Percent Americanism" or a more culturally inclusive assimilation that recognized the historical and cultural contributions of some of the new immigrants, schoolmen and civic leaders were satisfied only after 1924, when the National Origins Act severely curtailed the arrival of southern and eastern Europeans. With the tide of immigration effectively stemmed, the city's school officials believed that they could now fashion good young "Caucasian" citizens who, if afforded greater upward mobility and privileged status as whites, could be counted on to defend and participate in US imperial policies abroad and to buy into its myriad racially restrictive covenants at home.

Chapter 6 explores how the education of Mexican Americans and Puerto Ricans shaped debates about US imperial and immigration policies beyond 1924. After the passage of the National Origins Act, prospective immigrants from Mexico became more visibly contentious as foreigners in the American imperial imagination. Following the implementation of quotas for all nations outside of the Western Hemisphere, hard-line restrictionists looked south and agitated for heftier and more expansive security apparatus in order to regulate the movement of goods and people across the southwestern border. These initiatives, while successful only to certain degrees, served to underscore and promote images of Mexican Americans as foreigners in the United States, even if native-born. Anglo educators throughout the region weighed in on the immigration issue, and many argued that despite or in fact because of the effects of nativism and racism, restriction and segregation were the only practical ways to assimilate and Americanize those already attending public schools in the United States. As the more "flexible enforcement" of the border in the early 1920s gave way to tighter control and "repatriation" measures, immigration officials made little effort to distinguish between citizens and noncitizens. In their eyes, all Mexicans were deportable. Those who remained and those who navigated a more robust physical and bureaucratic border to reach the United States contended with historically inferior and segregated public schools for their children. In most "Mexican" schools throughout the Southwest, administrators and teachers employed the mechanisms of English-only instruction and manual training to create unequal paths to citizenship reinforced by US imperial power over Mexico.[30]

If Mexican Americans were deportable in the eyes of Anglos in the Southwest, Puerto Ricans represented a similarly marginal kind of Latin American "immigrant." After almost two decades of US imperialism, in 1917 the United States imposed citizenship on Puerto Ricans born on the island. Despite the Jones Act, restrictionists in the 1930s and 1940s largely disregarded Puerto Rican rights of citizenship, often citing the innate intellectual inferiority of Puerto Rican schoolchildren as a reason to place limits on freedom of movement between island and metropole. But education also served as a mechanism through which Puerto Rican administrators, teachers, parents, and children claimed their rights as US citizens and fashioned new notions of colonial citizenship that ultimately forced the United States to reform the colonial relationship between itself and Puerto Rico.

Congress repealed the racial restrictions of Chinese Exclusion in 1943 and replaced the discriminatory quotas of the National Origins Act with a more colorblind system in 1965. It granted Hawaiian statehood in 1959, and ultimately responded positively, albeit slowly, to the civil rights movement's demand to end legal segregation. But political, social, and economic opportunity and equality have not necessarily followed, nor has American imperialism abated. Moreover, public schools remain at the center of the cultural politics of nationalism, race, and empire. The recent history wars signal the continued need for deeper historical reckoning with the entanglements of race, citizenship, and empire in the United States. Several state legislatures and local school boards have attempted to amend, restrict, and in some cases abolish history lessons that, in the words of one Jefferson County, Colorado, school board member, do not "promote citizenship, patriotism, essentials and benefits of the free enterprise system, respect for authority, and respect for individual rights" or that "encourage or condone civil disorder, social strife, or disregard for the law." In response, hundreds of suburban, mostly white high school students walked out of class in protest in September 2014.[31]

The more recent controversy in Colorado followed on the heels of one of the most nationally visible attempts to suppress historical knowledge and thinking. In June 2011, Arizona superintendent John Huppenthal announced the elimination of Tucson's highly successful Mexican American Studies program, claiming that it violated a new state law that prohibits courses that "promote resentment toward a race or class of people" and are "designed primarily for pupils of a particular ethnic group." The school board followed with a decision to ban seven critical histories with radically different interpretations than the celebratory and uncritically patriotic histories of a century before. The banned books, which include *Pedagogy of the Oppressed* (1970), *Occupied America* (1988), and *Rethinking Columbus* (1998), also depart from consensus histories currently predominant in public schools that have similarly failed to challenge in critical ways the underlying assumption of the inevitability of the supposed exceptional American virtues of freedom, liberty, and the stated support of the United States for democratic movements around the world.[32]

Together, these decisions to limit access to certain kinds of historical interpretations that might cast the United States in a negative light have kept alive the culture wars so prevalent from the 1920s onward, when liberals and conservatives struggled over the place of religion, patriotism, and pluralism in public school curricula and policy.[33] But Arizona's laws targeting Latinos also compel us to revisit the imperial dimensions of public schooling and to consider the ways in which schools became critical institutions of American empire at home and abroad. It is my desire that this book engage a broad readership of teachers, policymakers, and education reformers who, in the era of Tucson's book banning policy, "show me your papers" statutes, voter ID laws, and sustained commitments to the US free-trade agenda, will encounter, debate, and decide issues of citizenship, national belonging, and imperial expansion that have historical precedent in an earlier age of race making, immigration, and empire.

Geography, History, and Citizenship

These subjects are really three phases of one, namely, human life
.... Geography treats the earth as the home of man. History is
the story of the past life of man. Civics has to do with the present
social, industrial, and political relations of man.[1]

CALVIN KENDALL AND GEORGE MIRICK, *How to Teach
the Fundamental Subjects,* 1915

The social studies of the American high school should have for
their conscious and constant purpose the cultivation of good citizenship. We may identify the "good citizen" of a neighborhood
with the "thoroughly efficient member" of that neighborhood;
but he will be characterized, among other things, by a loyalty
and a sense of obligation to his city, State, and Nation as political
units.[2]

US BUREAU OF EDUCATION, *"The Social Studies in Secondary
Education,"* 1916

IN 1900, THE NEW YORK DEPARTMENT OF EDUCATION sent a collection of student work to the Paris Exposition Universelle. Among the submis-
sions were the geography transcriptions of thirteen-year-old Italian-American
Charles Digennaro, a student at Public School 26 in Brooklyn. In his account
of North America, Digennaro reported: "the most important [country] is the
United States. This is because ... it has [a] temperate climate.... It is just the
kind of place for people to work in .... The people of the United States have
made more progress than any other nation in the world." Digennaro contrasted the climate of the United States with that of Canada, where "the
people cannot work because it is too cold," and Mexico and Central America,
"where it is so warm, the people are lazy." In addition to favorable climate,
Digennaro recounted the racial makeup of the United States: "Most of the
inhabitants are white, but there are also Chinese, Negroes, and Indians."[3]
Digennaro's commentary on the preeminence of the United States in the
Western Hemisphere mirrored contemporary geographical and historical

interpretations that filled the pages of the most widely assigned schoolbooks at the turn of the twentieth century. And while he wrote about geography and historical "progress," the tropes Digennaro offered aligned his assertions with the kinds of nationalist and racial thinking only good white citizens and ardent patriots could muster. His civics teacher would have likely approved.

Together, these three subjects—geography, history, and civics—brought into focus a world in which race and empire were paramount in shaping the contours of national citizenship. The authors of school geography textbooks and curricula opened for schoolchildren the widest possible lens through which to see themselves and the United States in the world. Lessons emphasized three key threads of racial and imperial thought. First, they proved a critical means through which schoolchildren "[learned] to divide the world" into metageographical and racial categories. Undergirded by the science of evolution and by social Darwinism, authors offered continental and national schematics of human development that relied on the language of civilization, barbarism, and savagery.[4] Cartographies of climate provided absolution for modern forms of empire and carried with them a host of economic and sociological arguments that validated Herbert Spencer's "survival of the fittest" theory of human inequality. Authors further claimed that geographic determinism did not apply to Anglo-Saxon settlers in the world's tropical and semitropical regions. To this end, they presented imagined reserved, open, and abundant landscapes where Europeans and Americans carried out the business of civilization at the expense of "barbarous tribes," according to one author.[5]

Schoolbook histories in turn cast the United States and white Americans as an exceptional nation and people within the broader scope of world nations and races imparted through geography lessons. The Monroe Doctrine, the US War with Mexico, and the Spanish-American War provided explanations for America's ascendancy to global and industrial power. Critical to these imperial narratives were the discourses of race and civilization. But most importantly for this study, despite in many cases the denial of American forms of imperialism by most authors of the day, empire punctuated and buttressed historical narratives used in schools. Its language of civilization, economic imperatives, and implications for national allegiance made empire a far more usable and animated historical framework than is generally ascribed to the otherwise boilerplate US histories published after about 1890.

If geography and history normalized for students the "natural" hierarchies of the world and nation in which they lived, civics offered approved ways to think and act as citizens of an exceptional nation and ascendant global power. Emerging in the curriculum in the 1890s, community civics intended to create patriotic citizens, deferential managers, docile workers, and for those with the franchise, predictable voters for a two-party system through active, localized participation in the national community of citizens, workers, and consumers. Courses and texts stressed cleanliness, industriousness, and loyalty and pitted capitalism against the radicalism of striking immigrant workers, a subject of utmost concern for school officials in New York City for example, subjects of the book's fifth chapter. After the US entrance into World War I and the outbreak of the Bolshevik Revolution in 1917, civics lessons commanded greater political and ideological conformity in efforts to dissolve the threats of collective organization by working-class nonwhites and immigrants. By the early 1920s, the American melting pot of races of the early twentieth century gave way to more rigid racial lines and an emphasis on cultural homogeneity and unquestioned loyalty to the state. But challenges to the postwar conformity of Americanism and the restrictionism of immigration debates emerged in tandem, transforming curricula from the 1920s onward.[6]

Despite a spike in the sheer number of schoolbook titles published in the late nineteenth century to meet the demands of rapidly expanding public school bureaucracies throughout the country, a relatively small number of titles in each discipline made significant impacts or had longevity. That is, few books made it into large numbers of classrooms in the largest urban school districts or were reissued for multiple editions. These narratives were either written by or directly descended from some of the leading practitioners of the period, who steadfastly believed they imparted to schoolchildren geographical, historical, and political truths derived from objective science. In geography, books authored by Harvard's William Morris Davis, Cornell's Ralph Tarr, Colgate's Albert Perry Brigham, and Alexis Everett Frye, first school superintendent of the US occupation of Cuba, among several others, became the "leading" and "definitive" geographical texts of the period. They offered, according to their publishers, "definite science instead of the haphazard way" typical of earlier books that emphasized description over explanation. Ginn & Company, which operated seven national distribution houses, argued of its author Frye that his "books have a national use and are endorsed by the leaders of educational thought and methods as the most logical, the most practical, and the most suggestive text-books on the subject." The emphasis on logic and practicality informed how school geographers came to see their mission by 1900: to provide students with a worldview organized "according to principles of race, environment, and nationalism."[7]

In history, Harvard's Albert Bushnell Hart, Penn's John Bach McMaster, and Columbia-trained Charles Beard, for example, fashioned themselves professionals who claimed the mantles of objectivity and historical truth but also regarded schools and school history as engines of "legitimating the social and political order."[8] In 1910, Hart charged professional historians with seeking a "genuinely scientific school of history . . . which shall dispassionately and moderately set forth results." At the close of World War I, American Book Company confirmed this methodological claim, arguing that Hart's school histories gave "young people a new and broader understanding of our true relations, both past and present, with other countries" in ways that were "decidedly patriotic . . . yet devoid of 'spread-eagleism.'" While some professional historians began to question their closely held "faith in [historical] progress" after the war, Hart's optimistic ideological outlook, evident in his *School History of the United States* (1920) and *New American History* (2nd ed., 1921), seemed to persist. The consensus schoolbook historians of the period claimed to wield an "authentic and sound" patriotism, in the words of historian Peter Novick, and an "intelligent, tolerant patriotism," according to the American Historical Association's 1899 Committee of Seven.[9]

Civics then served as a kind of applied social science that extended from the presumed objective nature of geographical and historical study. In more intentional and overt ways, civics celebrated patriotism and national exceptionalism, at times seemingly as ends in themselves. Because civics courses and textbooks were rather novel in the late nineteenth century, their architects tended to come from the ranks of school administrations and teaching forces instead of the faculties of leading colleges and universities. Indeed in many school districts throughout the country, civics was simply part of the American history curriculum. But by 1915, the National Education Association endorsed community civics, what Julie Reuben has called a "radical departure from earlier forms of citizenship education," because it de-emphasized political participation in favor of more benign and undefined acts of community engagement. Thus, school civics sought to carve out ways for all citizens to actively contribute to American economic and social progress, even if legal statute or local white resistance barred many newcomers and racial minorities from political activism, especially voting. So while on the surface the new community civics seemed to run counter to the kinds of rigid racial hierarchies taught in geography or the Anglo-Saxonism of school histories, in practice the three reinforced each other. In the early twentieth century, despite the rhetoric of "community" and of "active and intelligent" cooperation, civics was still about national conformity to the hierarchies of race, the imperatives of empire, and the politics of immigration.[10]

METAGEOGRAPHIES OF RACE AND EMPIRE

In their 1899 _Complete Geography_, which Werner School Book Company pedaled as "in full harmony with the most advanced ideas on the 'New Geography,'" Horace and Martha Tarbell asked primary school children about presumed novelties: "Have you ever seen a negro? An Indian? A Chinaman?" The authors' use of the interrogative revealed several assumptions about audience. That students may have yet to lay eyes on a "negro" or an "Indian" or a "Chinaman" in their own lives certainly affirmed that the Tarbells believed their readership to be overwhelmingly and unequivocally white. It followed then that other races provided imperial spectacle for inquisitive, curious, and racially and culturally homogeneous schoolchildren whose daily interactions rarely or never transgressed racial lines. The authors continued: "The Caucasian or white race is the most intelligent and most powerful of all the races." Schools were in fact much more racially heterogeneous if not necessarily integrated than the Tarbells assumed, but the authors' ignorance or denial of the realities of racial diversity accompanied by a commonly constructed racial hierarchy helped shape and reinforce visions of the United States as a white republic for its neophyte citizens.[11] While geography lessons underscored American whiteness as an essential lesson for schoolchildren, the study of the Earth, its continental and national divisions, its climatic variations, and the racial varieties of its human inhabitants reinforced this consciousness and served as spatial justification for an expansive US empire.[12]

School geographers repackaged for schoolchildren three major tenets of American racial and imperial thought that affirmed the centrality of race and geographic origin to questions of citizenship, national belonging, and empire building. First, textbook authors drew on Darwinian theories of evolution to outline and detail three stages of human development, most commonly described as savagery, barbarism, and civilization. Not merely descriptions but instead analytical scientific frameworks through which to understand humans and their relationship to the natural world, school geographers argued that to the trained eye, these stages presented themselves among contemporary racial groups, including "Philippine savages," "naked [Japanese] natives," and "dark-eyed, languid [Mexican] women," at one end of the spectrum, and "intelligent" and "powerful" whites at the other end.[13] William Morris Davis, "the father of American geography," saw the new physical geography of the late nineteenth and early twentieth centuries as a critical window into "the progress of mankind from the savage to the civilized state ... largely made by taking advantage of favorable geographic conditions."[14] Evolution then served as scientific evidence of the privilege of white citizenship in the United States and the nation's rightfully endowed position as a burgeoning global power by the early twentieth century. Its allegedly common racial heritage with strong European empires, especially Great Britain, further confirmed the distinction.

Lessons then mapped these grand divisions of race onto the Earth's climate zones. The scientific and anthropological debates among European and American intellectuals, most of whom occupied distinguished positions at leading colleges and universities, including Ellen Churchill Semple (University of Chicago), Ellsworth Huntington (Yale University), and Charles Henry Pearson (Trinity, later University of Melbourne, Australia), found simplified form and resonance among colleagues that in turn narrated these arguments for primary and secondary schoolchildren. Despite disagreement over factors including blood purity, miscegenation, and global migration, these intellectuals agreed that differences in physical environment produced racial and cultural differences. The frigid, temperate, and torrid zones served as the cartographic framework to arrange and understand varied human racial typology—critical foundations for the justification of modern forms of imperialism that employed race as a primary marker of subjecthood, belonging, and power. Environment determined, according to climatological arguments, not only skin color, but also degrees of intelligence, industriousness, and the likelihood of one's economic and social status and survival. The imperatives for educational policy could not have been more immediate. As subsequent chapters demonstrate, administrators used the kinds of claims about climate and race found in the pages of geography readers to argue that nonwhite children throughout the United States and its territories should receive manual training for agricultural and domestic work in lieu of an academic education. Because many white educators regarded Hawaiians, Puerto Ricans, Mexicans, and African Americans, for example, as members of "tropical races," their natural environments made them innately lazy and immoral but also well suited to toil in fieldwork. As a remedy, they needed lessons in productivity and morality.

Finally, geography textbooks conveyed the exceptionalism of the United States so crucial to its national historical narrative by embedding its people, climate, resources, landscapes, and political institutions within metageographical constructs of the world and its populations. But to do so, school geographers had to sidestep, qualify, or in some cases challenge the orderly schematics of climate, continents, and evolution that rendered Native Americans savages in the temperate zone, African Americans tropical races flourishing in the US South (though ostensibly under white tutelage), and white Europeans and Americans industrious empire-builders in the semi-tropical and torrid zones. The end results were at times twinned racial and national exceptionalisms that either avoided evolutionary and environmental explanations altogether or in other cases challenged them head-on.

It is perhaps ironic that Herbert Spencer, a vigorous opponent of state-supported education, found his "survival of the fittest" principle's most basic articulation in geography readers used in publicly funded schools. According to the authors of most school geographies published from the 1800s through the 1920s, dispossession and disappearance was easily explained using the increasingly powerful science of evolution. By such rationale, the eradication of Native Americans or Australia's "oceanic Negroes," as the Tarbells described the continent's indigenous population, occurred not because of malicious American or European imperial policies, the proliferation of technological warfare, or settlerism and forced removal, but through processes inherent in nature. Indeed, most school geographers argued that colonialism could alleviate the trappings of backwardness and racial inferiority. For Colgate University geographer and editor of the Annals of the Association of American Geographers Albert Perry Brigham, Europeans were to be commended for integrating Africa into the global economy through a painstakingly slow struggle to overcome the "character of the native people": "Fanaticism and intolerance prevailed in the north, and dark and ignorant savagery in the center and south, until far into the nineteenth century." Only the commercial nations of Europe "served as the [forces] which [have] given Africa the beginnings of commercial life." For Brigham, global capitalism imposed through European imperialism could ostensibly save the continent from its twinned states of Arab barbarism and African savagery.[16]

Mytton Maury provided perhaps the starkest endorsement of Euro-American imperialism and racial genocide in his 1893 *Physical Geography*. A clergyman who proselytized to the Crow Creek tribe of South Dakota, Maury also served as editor of his late cousin Matthew Fontaine Maury's children's geographical series, primarily during the 1890s. For Maury, contact between whites and nonwhites yielded not amalgamation and degeneration of the higher type but rather the extinction of the lower: "Wherever the white man establishes himself he speedily becomes dominant; while the communities of other races into which he introduces himself are commonly subjected to a gradual process of extinction."[17] Though he grounded human difference in fixed stages of evolution, Maury also advocated, in some cases, limited self-government to presumed barbarous and savage races, usually under the watchful eye of colonial administrators or advisors. He praised the Japanese for adopting Western governmental institutions and the Chinese for the competitive nature of the civil service examination. These advances, according to Maury, were relatively recent phenomena contingent on contact with European and American science and government: "[The Chinese] remained for the ages just where their ancestors had been." That is, "in the past, they have displayed the mental activity which marks the Mongolian in general." He recognized potential in contemporary Chinese and Japanese society because of their interest in or embrace of constitutional government and global commerce and, most importantly for Maury, adopting "many important features of European civilization [which] entitle[d] them to rank among the progressive nations of the world." Only through the intervention of Western-approved forms of government and economic activity could non-white societies inch closer to the high mark of Caucasian civilization.[18]

By the 1890s, immigrants from eastern and southern European began to present American geographers with an intellectual dilemma: What would be the place of American racial Anglo-Saxonism in the genre of school geography? Would the white/nonwhite binary withstand the strong currents of racialization of European nationalities crucial to the more extreme wings of the Americanization movement?[19] By situating gradations of whiteness within a broader metageography of race, Maury placed greater emphasis on similarities between nonwhites and dark-skinned, non-European Caucasians rather than on differences among European ethnicities. He noted the extremes of Caucasian physiognomy, offering Germans with "flaxen hair, blue eyes, and fair skin," and accompanying intelligence, ingenious, thrift, and "scientific and literary attainments" as the most favorable appearance and "Hindoos with raven locks, black eyes, and olive-brown or brownish, black skin" as less desirable on the Western beauty aesthetic. According to Maury, South Asians shared more in common physically with "Mongolians" displaying "olive-yellow" skin and "straight, course, black" hair than they did with European Caucasians, even people possessing ostensibly darker complexions and tropical sensibilities in Spain, Portugal, or Italy.[20]

Future president of the board of directors of the American Eugenics Society and, along with Davis, arguably one of the most famous American geographers of the early twentieth century, Ellsworth Huntington shared in the relative collective silence over European racial variety and the potential danger unfit European migrants posed to American citizenship. In his 1920 *Principles of Human Geography*, co-authored with Sumner Cushing of the Massachusetts Normal School, Huntington mapped "very high" civilization onto "most of Europe," while "high" civilization blanketed the rest of the continent—hardly a warning about degraded or semibarbarous immigrants that might undermine the character of American liberty or the population's capacity for self-government. While Huntington acknowledged that factors including race, religion, institutions, government, and education collectively determined a nation's degree of civilization, his interest lay primarily in the historical and contemporary influence of physical environment on race and civilization: "The agreement between regions of stimulating climate and high civilization means that the health and energy imparted by such a climate are among the conditions necessary for progress."[21]

Like the science of evolution, the imperial desires of myriad Europeans and their far-flung settlers, found on all habitable continents by the nineteenth century, informed geographic explanations of the inequalities of the physical and mental character of races. Though authors seldom used climate zones as the preeminent organizational framework for their narratives of human development, opting primarily for racial schematics, they meticulously embedded the study of continents, nations, and races within global representations of "isotherms and heat belts," as Ellen Churchill Semple described in her 1911 *Influences of Geographic Environment,* where she attested that climate "helps determine [people's] efficiency as economic and political agents."[22] Representations of the frigid, temperate, and torrid zones offered a global framework on which to hang racialized assertions about human character, constitution, and productive energy. William Swinton's 1881 illustrations and descriptions of the Earth's climate zones offered typical evidence of the effects of heat and cold on race. Bands stretching across both

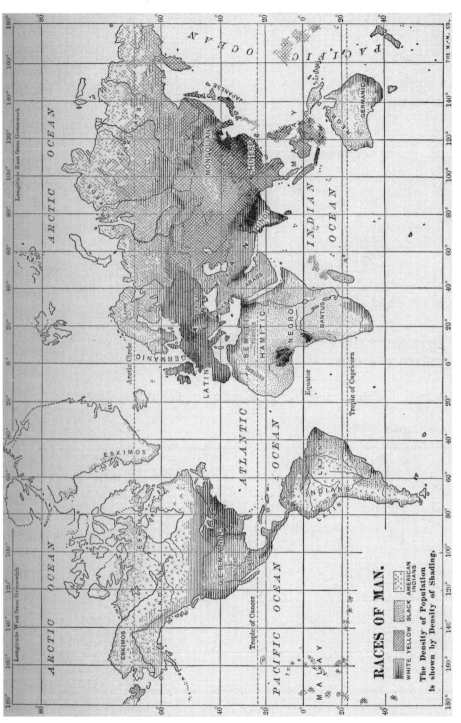

FIGURE 1. Races of Man. Ralph Tarr and Frank McMurry, *Advanced Geography* (New York: Macmillan, 1907), fig. 275, black-and-white insert between pp. 244 and 245.

hemispheres mapped Anglo and other European expansions and settlements rather neatly into the temperate regions of North America, South Africa, South America, and Australia. Meanwhile, largely nonsettler imperial holdings in Latin America, Oceania, Africa, and Asia straddled the equator.[23] Though Swinton's accompanying textual description did not directly implicate race, separate lessons on continents joined race and climate to make claims about the relative advancement and productivity of each continent's inhabitants. With the "greater part of South America . . . in the Torrid Zone," Swinton noted, "the people are in general uneducated and unprogressive," having "given to the rest of the world little except its tropical products." In contrast, Europe's position in the temperate zone and the "influence of warm ocean currents and warm winds" produced a "great number of powerful civilized nations."[24]

High school geographies often joined preeminent climatic explanations with warnings about blood mixture and miscegenation. Cornell's Ralph Tarr and Frank McMurry of Columbia Teachers' College offered a multilayered explanation for why the British and their North American progeny, rather than the French or Spanish, managed to colonize the vast majority of the North American continent. Despite leaving only a "narrow strip" along the Atlantic coast in the wake of their early colonial successes, the French and Spanish soon lost most of their North American possessions to the "English-speaking race," save "Mexico, Central America and a few small islands." The authors offered "good reasons for this strange result," including racial differences among the English, French, and Spanish. But the combination of imperial desire and North America's climatic variation together constituted the primary cause of the Anglo victory. In particular, "after robbing and enslaving [the Indians]," the Spanish then "married them freely, so that, in time, half-breeds came to make up more than half the population . . . an ignorant class, far inferior to the Spaniards themselves, and so backward that they still follow many of the customs of the Aztecs." Climate offered the other half of the explanation: "in a large part of [Spanish] territory the weather is too warm to produce energetic people . . . . So little energy is required to find sufficient food that the people do not need to exert themselves, and hence do not." Though Tarr and McMurry located a more favorable climate in French North America, ignoring important historical and cartographic overlaps with Spanish territories, the French too had "intermarried with the Indians and adopted some of their customs." In contrast, the "temperate climate of [the English] section is the best in the world for the development of energy.

The warm summers allowed abundant harvests; but the long, cold winters forced the settlers to exert themselves to store supplies." "Reasonable" expenditure still left energy and time for "improvement."[25]

If the Earth's hot, steamy regions were "nowhere inhabited by a vigorous race of men," and "reasonably dry climates" remained the "most salubrious for the people of the Caucasian race," then it followed that European designs on Africa's interior or America's island empire in the south Pacific and Caribbean were also subject to geographic determinism.[26] Likewise, temperate climate could invigorate nonwhite races and lift them to the level of Euro-American civilization. This is where arguments tended to break down. Darwinian schematics of race and civilization and deterministic lessons about climate and coastline operated within a neat framework that treated continents as the natural homes of distinct races and oceans more as boundaries rather than conduits for human locomotion and commercial activity, industrious white Europeans excepting. Yet the entire foundation of these scientific claims had emerged from Europe's imperial projects, of which migration to and settlement of North America figured prominently in US school lessons in geography and history. How did school geographers reconcile settler colonialism, racial hybridity, the spread of European religion and civilization, and other episodes of empire with the tidy narratives of race, climate, and continent? Where did indigenous North Americans fit into the racial hierarchies of human energy and into the temperate climate that supposedly produced active and industrious subjects and citizens? What role did geography play in the expansion of the US continental and overseas tropical empire and in the multiethnic and multiracial landscapes of America's coastal urban centers? Answers to these questions varied, but a common tactic involved treating nonwhite natives and immigrants within the United States as inexplicable aberrations to the idea that favorable climate yielded intelligent, energetic, and productive commercial actors and citizens. In many cases, authors seemed willing to abandon their geographic arguments altogether. Likewise, white superiority often trumped the tropic's allegedly negative influence on racial fortitude.

For school geographers, the history of imperial conquest had proven whites adaptable to climate variation, primarily through technological ingenuity, while weaker races remained subject to geographic determinism. Brigham's numerous treatments of US geography omitted any explanations as to why indigenous peoples, living in the same temperate climate, had not developed agricultural methods or modes of life on par with European settlers, opting instead for a mysterious historical ponderance: "What has become of the Indians?"[27] Maturin Ballou, author of a geography textbook that employed a travel narrative style, also reconciled Indian poverty with American prosperity in racial, not climatic terms. Other authors, though, took into consideration the logical problems that would inevitably rise in the minds of young students who might struggle to reconcile the myth of the open continent with what their history textbooks told them about European encounters with Native Americans. Davis, one of Brigham's earliest mentors at the 1889 Harvard Summer School of Geology, argued that race, as much as geography, had influenced US history: "the aboriginal inhabitants of this great land were savages who did not know how to develop its riches."[28] Yet even in this meeting of savagery and civilization, Europeans—the "original discoverers"—represented still only a stage in the progression of civilization. The struggle against British imperial and monarchical tyranny had culminated in a successful revolution that in turn secured for newly minted American citizens the freedom to realize the continent's agriculture, mineral, and commercial potential.[29]

Narratives like Davis's established the United States as a nation *above* other nations. Not Europeans, but instead their descendants in the United States possessed the racial fortitude and heritage appropriate for and capable of establishing themselves as the preeminent carriers of human progress. Davis identified three factors—favorable geography, racial superiority, and republican government—that gave to the "young nation a giant's strength."[30] The dichotomy of empire and republic also obscured the racialized imperial activities of the United States both at home and abroad. And in a republic, technological imperatives and a system of free enterprise, argued Wallace Atwood, had enabled Americans to "overcome many of the difficulties that physical features once presented." Accompanying the more recent "industrial and commercial prosperity of the United States" were "our demands from foreign lands," as Atwood noted, which primarily consisted of "certain foods and various other raw materials which . . . we cannot produce in this country or which we can secure more economically from foreign countries for our exports."[31]

Even if he had not named it as such, Atwood's discussion of the United States and its new foreign trading partners cast the Caribbean, Latin America, and the Pacific as natural fields of tropical empire for a nation no longer a European colonial outpost but instead a world power in its own right: "We shall look more to the countries of the tropics" with trade "expected to increase more rapidly along north-and-south lines than along the east-to-west routes across the Atlantic." Atwood also forecast "with confidence . . . the great increase in the trade across the Pacific Ocean," where the inhabitants "are sure to want some of the wonderfully useful articles invented and manufactured in the United States" in exchange for "raw materials, foods, and many articles from their factories that we enjoy having in our homes." Atwood's long accompanying list of foreign imports underscored temperate appetites for tropical products.[32] Written in 1920, the year he assumed the presidency of Clark University in Worchester, Massachusetts, Atwood's description was as much an account of recent imperial history as it was a forecast of the coming American Century, and it was embedded in a much deeper understanding of North American geography and European empire, as the author came to acknowledge in his concluding remarks. Unlike many of his contemporaries, Atwood failed to provide an explicit racial hierarchy for his readers, instead opting for the more idyllic representation of the United States as a nation where hard work and "difficult conditions" yield "greater freedom for the inhabitants." In this interpretation, climate and race carried less weight than individual aspirations served well by the republic's manifestly favorable political and economic conditions.

But if making good citizens could proceed irrespective of the grand divisions of race, a notion that many of Atwood's colleagues rejected, the project of overseas empire came with a tremendous sense of responsibility and mission that extended from white supremacy, temperate climate, technological prowess, and republican virtue. "In time, we came into possession of foreign lands. We assumed new responsibilities in caring for those lands and in governing, or helping to govern, other people. We now have a great responsibility, with other nations, to maintain peace and freedom in the world," Atwood concluded.[33] The authors of myriad school histories of the United States built on this providentially, geographically, and racially endowed sense of exceptional place and purpose in order to further bound the paths of good citizenship by race and national origin as the United States exercised imperial power at home and abroad.

AMERICAN HISTORIES OF IMPERIAL EXPANSION

In the immediate aftermath of the 1898 US invasion of Cuba, Harvard historian Albert Bushnell Hart commented on the role of historians in what he called the "up-building of the nation" and on the condition of historical study in the United States. He argued that Americans possessed a profound reverence and interest in current events, yet when it came to thinking historically about those events, Americans—including academics, policymakers, and citizens—displayed a woeful ignorance. As an example, Hart scorned the popular notion that the insurrection in Cuba existed in isolation from the history of colonialism in the Americas—that it somehow appeared at the end of a relatively "quiet and uneventful decade" to awaken the United States to its task of policing the Western Hemisphere. He placed most of the blame for America's collective historical disregard on historians themselves—for failing "to set clearly before their countrymen the course of our diplomatic policy"—and on history teachers "who have not imbued their students or pupils with the sense of the sequence of historical events." But what Hart had in mind was not a historical account of *American* expansion, which history textbooks covered quite thoroughly if usually in a celebratory fashion. Rather, students needed to comprehend the deep history of *Spanish* conquest and colonial rule in the Americas in order to situate the Cuban revolution within its proper historical context. Only then would it vindicate American action against Spain in the Caribbean and Pacific and alleviate concerns and tensions over the course of both historical and contemporary American empire.[34]

The word *empire* and iterations of it figured rather subtly in most school histories of the United States published from the 1880s through the 1920s, precisely the period in which the United States officially became an overseas imperial power and completed its conquest of the American West. When it appeared, empire was almost always in reference to other nations' empires that were despotic and tyrannical (like Spain) or at the very least antithetical or indifferent to American republican values (like Britain). Exceptions, of course, existed. Hart's 1923 *We and Our History* provided one of the few direct references to American empire, but Hart's reasons were of a geographical nature. The sheer and "immense" size of the United States—forty-eight states, three organized territories, and far-flung island possessions in the Caribbean and Pacific—produced an "Empire of the United States." And Hart's American empire was diplomatic. It asserted power in the interest of stable global trade, not to subjugate supposedly lesser races or nations.[35] In other words, it did not think or act as its European equivalents.

But empire's career within those historical volumes was in fact lively, discordant, and central—not peripheral—to the framing of an American historical narrative for schoolchildren. It manifested as international trade agreements, extensive transportation networks, industrious homesteaders, brave and daring explorers, transformed natural environments, subdued or civilized Indians, subordinated Negroes, docile and hardworking immigrants, and the expansion of continental and transoceanic frontiers. Between lines espousing the virtues of the republic and Washington's warnings against entangling alliances lay ideological and historical foundations for American imperial power. Moreover, the framing of American histories closely informed the kinds of people school officials hoped to render good citizens and those who they worked to subordinate or exclude. Using historical accounts purportedly informed by objective, "scientific" truths, authors explained, for example, the reasons why African and Native Americans, among others, required industrial training instead of an academic education. They offered "evidence" of Chinese and Japanese inferiority and thus the need for Asiatic exclusion in the US West. And they legitimated colonial rule and education in Hawai'i, Cuba, Puerto Rico, and the Philippines.[36]

Imperial narratives relied on a framework of four interdependent categories of people that overlapped with and confronted one another in both in the past and in the decades surrounding the turn of the twentieth century: settlers, natives, immigrants (or more appropriately, would-be immigrants), and colonial subjects (who were very seldom, if ever, labeled as such). In school histories, settlers were white, more often than not explicitly Anglo-Saxon, and endowed by both Providence and racial fortitude to forge on western frontiers a special democracy to be revered and emulated but never fully achieved by others. On continental and overseas frontiers, white settlers confronted both natives and potential immigrants. Authors cast Native Americans as historical threats to national security and the extension of American enterprise at precisely the time in which federal policy and popular imagination sought the incorporation of remaining Indians into the community of citizens by dismantling the reservation system, educating native children to white norms, and extending limited rights. And yet Indians remained integral to school histories even as notable authors, including Charles Beard, disavowed their role in shaping American character.[37]

So too did colonial subjects and prospective immigrants serve to juxtapose white citizenship with those kinds that potentially changed, endangered, or polluted it. This was particularly true after 1848 for Mexicans in the Southwest against whom Anglo-Texans and shortly thereafter the United States waged war in the 1830s and 1840s to extend American sovereignty and power. It was also the case for myriad peoples and nations of Latin America and the Caribbean over which the United States claimed a special protection vis-à-vis the Monroe Doctrine and its subsequent evocations in the service of "Open Door" liberalism. But by 1898, protection gave way to direct colonial rule over Puerto Ricans and Cubans in the Caribbean (and Filipinos and Hawaiians in the Pacific), who all held the potential for migration to the United States in the wake of conquest. In response to overseas empire, authors projected their anxieties about incorporating racial inferiors into the polity by recasting the Monroe Doctrine as a policy tool that while originally wise and benevolent had, over time, imperiled American international standing by shielding the democratic claims of inferior peoples not yet ready to govern themselves.

An unwavering commitment to self-determination and republicanism in the Western Hemisphere underscored most schoolbook treatments of the Monroe Doctrine and its subsequent applications. In particular, sympathy, integrity, and danger served as a common vocabulary set on which to hang arguments about the benevolence of American foreign policy and the complementary toxicity of European colonialism.[38] But after 1898, schoolbook historians projected their anxieties about US interventions onto historical applications of the Monroe Doctrine. US entry into World War I further heightened the skepticism of historians about the efficacy of the Monroe Doctrine in the twentieth century.[39] For example, authors cast potential Spanish recolonization after the revolutions of the 1820s and 1830s as a threat to the national security of the United States, not simply an affront to Bolívarian revolutionary republics. European monarchical alliances necessitated an active American foreign policy that at times required expansive measures, however reluctantly, in order to protect national sovereignty and the integrity of republicanism at home. In particular, the Holy Alliance between Austria, Russia, and Prussia, created "for the purposes of suppressing in Europe just such revolution as had happened in South America," as historians Charles Beard and William Bagley argued, prevented "the rule of the people" everywhere. But more importantly, an alliance between Russia, with ambitions in the Pacific Northwest, and the Spanish, with colonies in the Caribbean, had "imperiled" American freedom. Confronted with encroaching monarchical colonialism from the south and west, "the future of the [United States] would have been in peril." A policy tool of "imperial anticolonialism," as historian William Appleman Williams has described the Monroe Doctrine, was in this formulation not only a matter of commitment to national values but also an imperative of national security that legitimated a robust military presence on land and at sea.[40]

In the wake of national reconciliation after Reconstruction, new perceived threats to American liberty and sovereignty arose, and a collective dedication to republicanism did little to abrogate the political and racial hierarchies that characterized US involvement in Latin America. Authors often undermined their claims that self-government should serve as the standard for all nations in the Western Hemisphere with anxieties about the ability of the younger republics to govern themselves. Though an important "tenet of American national policy," the Monroe Doctrine was fraught with "increasing difficulty of application" in Yale historian Emerson Fite's estimation. The "vagueness of the doctrine," and the backing of American naval power, Fite asserted, invited "the southern republics to be reckless in their foreign relations, upon the almost certain knowledge that the United States will step in to protect them from too vigorous action on the part of outside [European] powers." He and other authors, including John Latane of Johns Hopkins University, likened the relationship between the United States and its southern neighbors to that of a parent and a child. The United States was steadfast, omniscient, and evenhanded, while Latin American nations were immature, ill behaved, and rash. Under the assumption that the United States had finally fulfilled Monroe's desire to achieve equal imperial footing with European powers, it had come to occupy an authoritative position charged with restoring order among chaotic and ungrateful southern peoples. For Latane, Monroe's declaration thwarted domestic opposition to an imperial agenda and ultimately proved effective in arbitrating international conflict between unequal nations. Moreover, Latane argued that the proclivity of presumably inferior Latin and African races to endanger law and order required the guiding hand of Anglo-Saxon rule.[41] Fite too was deeply concerned with the implications and responsibilities of overseas empire. Yet despite his ideological reservations about direct control over the Philippines, for example, he nonetheless regarded American colonial policy as in keeping with racial and civilizational order.

US entrance into World War I yielded sharper criticism of the expansionism and deepening involvement fostered by liberal internationalist statesmen who justified many of their actions using the Monroe Doctrine. For schoolbook critics writing during and after the war, Monroe's message became an idyllic symbol of righteous and benevolent hemispheric and international policy that had, over the decades, descended into a questionable and wrongheaded foreign policy contrary to national interests. In particular, detractors deplored the foray into the affairs of continental Europe and argued that President Wilson had betrayed the fair-minded policies of Monroe and Adams, who adhered to George Washington's warnings against entangling alliances. In *An American History,* first published in 1911 and reprinted again in 1920, David Saville Muzzey, a Columbia-educated left-leaning historian at Barnard College, Anglophile, skeptic of corporate power, and arguably one of the most widely distributed schoolbook authors of the entire first half of the twentieth century, offered such skepticism to growing US internationalism:

> Our statesmen have gradually stretched the [Monroe] doctrine far beyond its original declaration . . . . It has even been invoked as a reason for annexing territory to the United States . . . . With the entrance of the United States into the great World War . . . that part of the Monroe Doctrine which regards the world as divided into two separate and remote halves has been rendered obsolete. If we still maintain that our interests are "paramount" in the Western hemisphere, we no longer refrain from interfering in the political and territorial questions of the Eastern hemisphere.[42]

Despite a relatively sustained critique of overseas American empire and an expanded role in international politics by schoolbook historians of the early twentieth century, few if any connected Monroe's 1823 message to the continental expansions of the mid-nineteenth century. The Monroe Doctrine, they argued, did not apply to disputes over contiguous territory that, after about 1850, had become part of the nation with paths to statehood, even when the United States wrestled those lands away from a Latin American state whose sovereignty the United States claimed to honor and protect. Authors extricated the Mexican War of 1846–48 from historical treatments of American foreign policy and instead folded the annexation of Texas and subsequent war of questionable legality into a national narrative insulated from questions of international relations. Though deeply embedded in the imperial experience, historical accounts denied the culpability of the United States in a key exercise in territorial conquest. In this view, the American Southwest was destined to become part of the United States, and war with Mexico was simply the means by which settlers, soldiers, and policymakers fulfilled that destiny.[43]

Assumptions of Anglo-Saxon supremacy and complementary theories about Mexican racial inferiority injected inevitability into historical narratives that authors used either to cast Mexico as shortsighted in its policy of open Anglo settlement or, in critiques, to render the War with Mexico unnecessary in the context of Anglo-Saxon destiny. As Fite argued, "not realizing the inevitable result, [Mexico] freely invited the citizens of the United States . . . . Only after it was too late did the Mexicans attempt to stem the tide. It was like the irresistible march of settlers across Ohio, Indiana, and Illinois, or through Georgia, Alabama, and Mississippi." While he certainly implicated Mexican settlement policies in Texas in the ensuing conflicts, manifest destiny trumped any preventative action or foresight on the part of Mexican officials: "It could not be expected that citizens of the United States, with Anglo-Saxon blood in their veins and with the independent spirit of frontiersmen, would feel loyalty to a weak and shifting government in Mexico."[44] Similarly, Beard and Bagley interpreted the Southwest as a vast resource hitherto untapped by "the descendants of the men who had despoiled Mexico and Peru" and who "had no bent for hard or steady labor. These pleasure-loving idle soldiers became owners of vast stretches of land which they had no inclination to till or develop."[45]

Race and manifest destiny rendered the Mexican War at once unnecessary but justified given the trajectory of a presumed and foregone Anglo-Saxon right to inhabit the Southwest and to spatially and culturally displace racialized aliens in the name of progress. In doing so, Anglo-Saxons would usher into these regions the structures of republican citizenship and government they believed ultimately to be in the service of other races—a kind of citizenship and identity to emulate but never fully achieve. The notion even allowed critics like Haverford College historian Allen C. Thomas to assert that "while it has been far better that that large territory acquired should be under Anglo-Saxon control, there is little reason to doubt that it would soon have come under the rule of the United States through settlement, or purchase, or in some way less questionable than that which was followed." Confident in the assured completion of continental expansion, Thomas endowed the violence of territorial conquest with an extrinsic quality. War, he argued, was lamentable given what he and others believed to be the providential certainty of Anglo-Saxon expansion.[46]

Thomas and Hart offered what seem to be two of the few dissenting historical opinions, drawn from Whig criticisms of American bellicosity, but stopped short of questioning the efficacy of Anglo-Saxon destiny.[47] In the second edition of *History of the United States,* published in the midst of the American conquest of the Philippines, Thomas argued that the United States had "little reason for glory, for her successes were won in a questionable war against a weak and divided [Mexican] enemy." Likewise, Hart condemned President James K. Polk's dubious claims of Mexican aggression in his 1920 *School History of the United States:* "[Polk] forced war upon Mexico, on the plea that the Mexicans had begun it."[48] But the vast majority of authors blamed Mexico for the outbreak of hostilities, described the embattled Anglo-Saxon settlers as the rightful occupants of the Southwest, and rendered the military campaign a crucial and consequently justified episode in the fulfillment of America's manifest destiny. Perhaps no author defended the Mexican War more boldly than Muzzey, who described the annexation of Texas as a "perfectly fair transaction." As he revised *An American History* at the height of the Red Scare, his justification fit neatly within a framework of American foreign policy that sought to extend American military power, acquire territory, and pursue economic markets under the auspices of national defense against aggressive enemies abroad and subversive elements at home. Muzzey positioned his argument squarely against the consensus of school historians like Thomas and Hart who offered open if not entirely firm critiques of American foreign policy that extended from the southwestern frontiers to overseas campaigns in Hawai'i, the Philippines, Puerto Rico, and Cuba. Muzzey took his fellow historians to task: "The Mexican War has generally been condemned by American historians as 'the foulest blot on our national honor' .... But Mexico had insulted our flag, plundered our commerce, imprisoned our citizens, lied to our representatives, and spurned our envoys."[49] While Muzzey may have departed from his colleagues on the issue of initial aggression (though more sympathized with his view than he disclosed), authors shared a racialized understanding of the longer arc of American expansion in which the Mexican War was but an episode among many. Ironically, in 1925, a former Army director targeted Muzzey's alleged pro-British interpretation of the American Revolution and led an unsuccessful campaign to remove *An American History* from schools in Washington, DC. Muzzey's bellicose defense of American continental expansion in the 1840s was, in the 1920s, apparently not enough to withstand conservative charges of subversion and unpatriotic historical writing.[50]

Schoolbook historians described the Mexican War as having served two primary functions: to complete the project of continental manifest destiny and in turn to place the United States on the road to settling the issue of slavery that in hindsight reciprocally elevated US standing as a world power. Fite argued that the eradication of slavery in the United States, which he applauded, "happily" united North and South America in the 1860s after a decade of distrust following the American acquisition of the Southwest. Furthermore, the two peoples found "a sense of common danger following the French invasion of Mexico [in 1861]." In Fite's estimation, the Monroe Doctrine, the sincerity of which he acknowledged had been in jeopardy following the War with Mexico, resumed its rightful place as the tie that bound the United States to its southern neighbors.[51] One of the few to explicitly connect the continental conquests of the 1840s to the overseas extensions of the 1890s, Fite concluded his section titled "Mexican Annexations and Phases of Expansion" with a quote from Richard Dana, who visited Hawai'i in 1860 and who "paid the following tribute to the labors of these pioneer [American missionaries]": " 'They have established schools, reared up native teachers . . . and whereas they found these islanders a nation of half-naked savages . . . abandoned to sensuality, they now see them decently clothed . . . going to schools and public worship with more regularity than the people at home.' "[52] Those penning their school histories following 1898 engaged what many considered to be new epochs in American expansion, disconnected from the continental expansions that swept away Mexican sovereignty as well as the imperial claims and aspirations of European rivals. Yet many accounts of the Spanish-American War echoed the historical narratives that rendered the Monroe Doctrine benevolent and nonaggressive and the War with Mexico justifiable by racial theories of Anglo-Saxonism, even if authors injected these new imperial forays with a tone of reluctance infrequently applied to continental empire-building projects of the nineteenth century.

Though Anglo-Saxonism remained paramount in accounts of American empire, school histories of *overseas* expansion seldom featured the kind of bombastic defense present in Muzzey's interpretation of the War with Mexico. Instead, authors trotted out the paternalism that accompanied treatments of the Monroe Doctrine to ultimately claim that despite the sometimes questionable means of imperial acquisition and its detriment to democratic rule at home, the globalization of American republican values and free enterprise was ultimately a force for good. The United States did not *want* to become an empire, schoolbook authors claimed. The republic was *forced* into its "new role" by a combination of Spanish tyranny, native savagery, and a perceived obligation of American Anglo-Saxons to extend the guiding hand of civilization to oppressed peoples abroad as they had done and were doing among Native Americans, blacks, Mexicans, and immigrants at home.

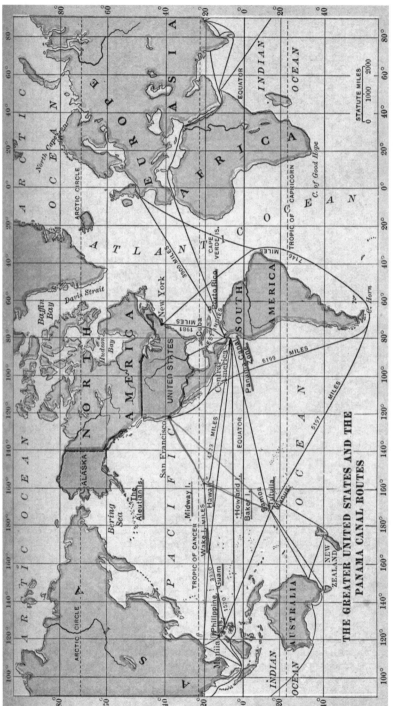

FIGURE 2. The Greater United States and the Panama Canal Routes. David Saville Muzzey, *An American History* (Boston: Ginn, 1911), color map insert between pp. 602 and 603.

School historians writing after the American victory in 1898 attested that Spanish colonialism in Cuba, Puerto Rico, and the Philippines had reaffirmed an inherent Iberian tyranny at work in Mexican-ruled Texas that had necessitated earlier interventions in the Southwest. The brutality of "the Butcher," as Fite described General Valeriano Weyler, in reference to the earned notoriety of the Governor-General of Cuba and the Philippines, "made it harder for the sympathetic neighboring [United States] to keep her hands off." On the eve of US entry into World War I, when Fite penned *History of the United States,* Prussian aggression was proving equally irresistible.[53] Syracuse University historian William Mace agreed that "harsh things done [by Spain] in an attempt to break the spirit of the Cubans filled the American people with bitter indignation."[54] Muzzey too described American intervention in Cuba as one of deliberate hesitation that ultimately proved futile in light of calls to end Spanish repression. He argued that "corrupt officials squandered [Cuba's] revenues, raised by heavy taxation, and Spanish soldiery ruthlessly quelled the least movement of rebellion." Adding that Spanish colonialism had endangered "large amounts of American capital" invested in sugar and tobacco, Muzzey, in the end, justified what had come to commonly define the American way of empire by the early twentieth century—conquest in the protection of liberal capitalism.[55]

If postwar Cuban independence, secured by the "promise" of self-government laid out in the Teller Resolution (1898), was preferable though not necessarily required, the Platt Amendment, a 1901 congressional act that granted the US military unilateralism on the island, extended the protection of American military power to Cubans struggling for liberty, argued several authors. Boston-based David Henry Montgomery, whose *Leading Facts of American History* went through seven editions between 1890 and 1920, noted that following formal US recognition of the new republic in 1902, "Cuba had occasion to ask for our assistance. An insurrection broke out [in 1906]."[56] Hart likewise listed the benefits of these "occupations" for his readers, including modern schools, sanitation campaigns, and the suppression of yellow fever epidemics—advances he believed negated any threats to liberty afforded by continued military rule. "The United States did much to help the people before it withdrew . . . in 1902 and left the Cubans to rule themselves," declared Mace.[57] The benefits of empire extended to Puerto Rico and the Philippines too, argued Hart, who noted that Puerto Rico received "the great advantage" of free trade with the United States. Montgomery likewise hailed the "many excellent public schools" established for the benefit of Filipinos;

Beard and Bagley offered new highways, railroads, agricultural methods, and industries as evidence of American progress in the Philippines; and Fite described the proliferation of public education in Puerto Rico in the first fifteen years of "[prosperous]" American rule. His account corroborated what US school officials and local elites in Puerto Rico touted at the time. American colonialism, these authors claimed, was for the benefit of the colonized, as Fite so vividly relayed regarding American influence in Hawai'i.[58] As Mace unequivocally declared: "This [Spanish-American] war was fought for the sake of humanity and freedom and not for gain or glory. The United States had taken the side of an oppressed people struggling for independence but she did not claim these countries as the spoils of war."[59]

Despite authors' faith in the efficacy of Anglo-Saxon superiority, school histories of the Spanish-American War also revealed the wider debates and disagreements over US colonialism among policy makers, academics, and the American public.[60] This was especially true in the case of the Philippines, which historians singled out as too savage, too foreign, and too unfit for self-government to enter into congress with the United States in any other fashion but as a subordinate colony. Echoing the rhetoric of Senator Albert Beveridge, whose 1900 defense of the war against the Philippine Republic pitted the "just, humane, civilizing government" of the United States against the "savage, bloody rule" of the Spanish, schoolbook authors—to borrow from Paul Kramer—"[sublimated] conquest into liberation."[61] The experience of the war against the insurgency offered evidence of Filipino savagery for imperialists and anti-imperialists alike. The former were certain that they could subjugate inferior races. The latter were wary of the future implications for American democracy should Filipinos become assimilated into the republic as either distant citizens or migrants to North America. Ultimately, school historians concluded, American racial ideology necessitated the suppression of the insurgency followed by the "admirable moderation and wisdom" of American imperial rule that characterized the "strong and sympathetic administration of the Islands."[62]

In the closing pages of the 1921 edition of *New American History,* Hart offered a concise recap of US expansion in a chapter titled "What America Has Done for the World." After a brief chronological summary of continental and overseas expansion, Hart listed the myriad freedoms that he argued extended from international power. Personal freedom; freedom of the mind, of labor, of business; and popular government—the "largest contribution that America has made to the world"—contained the essential lessons of the

American past, argued Hart, in a rework of earlier conclusions that "westward movement was in part an application of one of the greatest lessons which America has taught mankind, the right of personal liberty."[63] But Hart, like most of his fellow authors, believed that no matter how far the United States might extend its authority over distant lands and peoples, liberty had its limits among both colonial subjects and nonwhite immigrants until they deem themselves capable and worthy of its exercise. In the case of immigrant children and the children of immigrants—white, nonwhite, and of questionable whiteness—public school officials attempted to accelerate this process by crafting a third subject to complement the racial architecture of world geographies and historical narratives of US expansion. Civics emerged in the 1890s as a form of explicit instruction in American loyalty and patriotism designed to transform young citizens into supporters of US imperialism and of the racial and class hierarchies that underscored its logic, execution, and outcomes.

CIVICS AND THE POLITICS OF PATRIOTISM

On the eve of the US entrance into the Great War, Jasper McBrien charged schools with what he deemed to be "the prime and vital service of amalgamating into one homogeneous body the children alike of those who are born here and of those who come here from so many different lands." The former Nebraska state superintendent and US Bureau of Education official argued that only the "right material on which the American youth may settle their thoughts for a definite end in patriotism" would eradicate divided loyalties in times of both peace and international conflict. McBrien drew on the authority of President and professional historian Woodrow Wilson who, in a 1915 address to the Daughters of the American Revolution, called on citizens and noncitizens alike to make clear their national loyalties. McBrien stressed the need for "study and reflection along patriotic lines" in America's schools.[64] His call for a clearly defined program of civics and patriotism in the public schools was not novel in 1916. In the late nineteenth and early twentieth centuries, administrators, teachers, and schoolbook authors debated and crafted the "right material" by which to bind an increasingly heterogeneous school-age population to the ideals of the nation, the policies of the state, and the demands of burgeoning corporate power attached to each. Writing in the *California School Review* in 1891, Amherst College president Merrill Edward Gates argued that the "supply of new citizens" came from two primary sources: "immigration and the growing up of American children. We are all keenly alive to the dangers that threaten our government when ignorant and immoral foreigners are made citizens by hundreds and thousands."[65] For the children of nonwhite or dubiously white lineage, Americanization frequently came with subordination and exclusion.[66]

Between 1898 and 1917, civics lessons expanded the meaning of patriotism and the paths of good citizenship by infusing disciplined support for the nation's expansive military power with a sense of civic responsibility to a national community of citizens. During and after World War I, many school officials, particularly those presiding over schools populated with "new" immigrants from southern and eastern Europe, embarked on programs of "100 Percent Americanism" that demanded sharply drawn lines between patriot and dissident. Wartime and postwar Americanization stressed not only cultural conformity but also strict and active adherence to the political ideology of anticommunism.

At every step, the paths of citizenship forged in America's expansive imperial ambitions both reimagined and reinforced established boundaries of race and national origin. One potential solution to the perceived problem of increased heterogeneity was a fresh civics curriculum. Community civics emerged in the 1890s and gained widespread acceptance by the 1910s as the primary method for imparting lessons in civic duty. The new curricula, developed in large part as a response to the dramatic social and economic transformations of the late nineteenth century, offered a redefinition of citizenship. Progressive supporters of community civics argued that political activism was unsafe given the dramatic changes wrought by industrialization, urbanization, and immigration. Southern and eastern Europeans, Asians, Mexicans, and African Americans made up increasingly larger proportions of urban school populations.[67] Should these children—who according to prevailing pseudo-scientific and social theories of human development did not constitute the kind of democratic citizens the founders had supposedly envisioned—be encouraged to strive for full participation in the American democratic process? Or, should civics instruction open alternative spaces for these future workers and citizens to contribute to national discourse and economic progress?

Advocates of the new curricula tended to favor the alternatives. Rather than emphasize a partnership between individuals and the republic through voting, the new civics model stressed membership in a larger community of citizens and workers. Patriotic citizens were not concerned with elections necessarily, though the right kinds of citizens (white males) were certainly encouraged to participate in the electoral process. The individual, reified as hard working, loyal, obedient, and unquestionably patriotic, continued to enjoy symbolic meaning within the school curriculum. Rather than eradicate the individual's role in favor of mass loyalty to the state, the individual citizen simply became, in theory and symbol, the most ardent supporter and pillar of the national community of citizens.[68] The embrace of community civics did not signal the immediate demise of more traditional notions of civic participation. But a focus primarily on voting and a knowledge of the branches of government seemed out of place to many progressive educators, whose female, black, and foreign-born students would likely be excluded from such participation once of voting age. So while older definitions of civic engagement persisted, they did so amidst a groundswell of change in the nature of school civics and the broadening of its scope to include a culture of patriotic loyalty to both the state and its free market ideological underpinnings.[69] The community civics model at once opened new spaces to marginalized citizens and reinforced the inequalities of white-only primaries and male suffrage.

A sizable body of pedagogical material appeared in support of the recharged mission of the nation's public schools. While geography and history often remained confined to the pages of books, compositions, and exams, civics could not, argued many educators, succeed unless schools emphasized an active and ritualistic participation in American patriotic life. To this end, exposition exhibits, daily pledges of allegiance, patriotic songs and exercises, war commemorations, and active support for America's war efforts became the hallmarks of community civics. These activities often transcended the walls of schoolrooms and pages of books and gave schoolchildren a visible and prominent presence in local communities and national life. The new civics model de-emphasized political activities like voting in favor of a more open patriotism among individuals who were to see themselves as part of a national community of citizens. As Michael Kammen has observed, "every conceivable mode of education was viewed as a potential contribution to solving the nation's pressing social problem of extreme heterogeneity."[70]

One of the most common and public forms of patriotism was participation in national commemoratory celebrations, where patriotic sentiment translated into active nationalism. In October 1898, San Francisco school

FIGURE 3. Kindergarten Flag Drills. Manhattan Public School 21, ca. 1905. Courtesy Milstein Division of United States History, Local History and Genealogy, New York Public Library, Astor, Lenox, and Tilden Foundations.

board president Charles Barrington requested the presence of students and their families at a Drill Competition between three US volunteer regiments—a benefit to "[obtain] funds for our boys in Manila."[71] The city held similar events on Memorial Day to commemorate those who died serving in the US military, events that by 1903 included those who had died in America's wars for overseas empire. The city's Memorial Day committee appealed to public school children: "In your daily routine you salute the flag, and in that way show your love for the principles for which our Comrades fought and died .... Will you not join with us in this beautiful tribute to heroic deed, and thus testify a gratitude to those who participated under God, in the maintenance of this glorious Union, now a leader of Nations?"[72] The committee's plea not only recognized schoolchildren as potential participants in national rituals, but also as a group upon which to impress the notion of the United States as an exceptional nation—one that fought just wars of liberation in order to extend freedom abroad while also serving as a model to other nations. While the subsequent brutal suppression of Emilio Aguinaldo's Philippine nationalists suggested otherwise, schoolchildren were instead to concentrate their efforts on honoring fallen American soldiers and glorifying death in military service. By providing time and space for the performance of these rituals outside of the classroom, the committee hoped that at young ages, students would find value in national remembrance and in demonstrating patriotism, particularly during times of war. They supposedly developed strong faith in a government intent on expanding US influence abroad despite the sovereignty and desires of other nations and cultures. Schoolchildren who recognized national "purity through fatality" could be counted on as adults to actively support and serve in the nation's wars of expansion.[73]

War mobilization joined commemoration rituals as a primary vehicle of patriotism at century's end. School officials attempted to transform schools into community centers to foster support for the nation's geopolitical endeavors and to directly involve local communities in war efforts. Wars of empire in the Pacific and Caribbean, which demanded virulent nationalism, had the power to rejoin North and South in the common cause of American global leadership, the expansion of US commercial interests, and an imagined anti-imperialism that claimed to prevent European powers from meddling in the affairs of free peoples in the Western Hemisphere. So too did wars to make the world "safe for democracy" demand such nationalism. In 1917, the Georgia Department of Education declared "each school house should be a community center to teach patriotism and to give proper information as to the cause and real meaning of this [World] War to every citizen." It encouraged increased agricultural production, conservation, the purchase of Thrift Stamps, and envisioned the state's schools as the centers of activism. "It will not make [schools] less efficient but transform many a pale anemic institution into a throbbing center of life and learning as well as of patriotic activity," the department claimed. Teachers and students were to become the bearers of patriotic sentiment and activism to their communities.[74]

Financial commitment to the US war economy also formed part of schools' multidimensional projects of creating patriots. New York district superintendent William O'Shea, who was in charge of War Service Work for the city's superintendent's office, asked all principals to invite parents and any other adult relatives of the schools' students to a meeting regarding the logistics and benefits of buying US war bonds. In 1918, the National War-Savings Committee in Washington beseeched "every school teacher in the land" to organize "War-Savings societies" among students. This, they hoped, would mobilize the nation's youth to educate their parents about active patriotism in the form of economic assistance.[75] "A very good way of advertising the Liberty Loan in the home is to get the school children to talk about it ... by the assignment of compositions or by giving them ... questions ... and asking them to bring their answers to school after they have conferred with their parents." O'Shea hoped that by having children educate their own parents on the benefits of patriotic almsgiving, both parent and pupil would develop and maintain vested interests in the nation's military and economic expansion.[76] Board president William Willcox appealed to principals and teachers to purchase Liberty Loans themselves. He argued that in doing so, school employees could help to "demonstrate the loyalty, patriotism, and interest of the personnel of the public school system," further solidifying the role of public schools in the support of the state's foreign military endeavors.[77]

By 1917, patriotism had become synonymous with Americanization in many schools that took on the responsibility of assimilating European immigrants. As the fear of Bolshevik infiltration escalated in the years after the US entry into World War I, the more tolerant Americanization of the century's first decade—the "Melting Pot"—gave way to more coercive, militant calls for patriotism.[78] Public education stood on the front lines of the ideological battle against Bolshevism, and school officials seized on the perceived necessities of anticommunism to increase their influence in states and local communities by pushing for an expansion of public support for schools. Moreover, appeals to taxpayers for public education were not confined to urban centers with large populations of immigrants. In its annual report to the General Assembly, the Georgia Department of Education argued that "taxation for schools is just as much a part of the American scheme of government, just as much in accord with democratic principles, as taxation for courts, for police protection, for roads." Should the state's taxpayers neglect their duties to support education and thus neglect to protect the Republic, they "ought to move into the jungles of Africa where [they] would be called upon to pay no taxes, where [their] road would be a path through the wilderness, 'zigzagged' by some denizen native to the wild." The department's chosen imagery was certainly befitting its white Southern audience, but threats posed by the "denizens" in the "jungles of Africa" to "American government" and "democratic principles" permeated white racial thinking throughout the nation. In its appeal, Georgia's leading educators bound together the projects of Southern economic growth, national expansion, the growth of state power, and the preservation of rights to liberty and property.[79]

The state's black intellectuals and progressives challenged the paradoxical patriotism imposed on African Americans during times of international conflagration. Atlanta's Neighborhood Union, founded in 1908 by Lugenia Burns Hope, wife of Morehouse College president John Hope, addressed the president, cabinet, and Congress of the United States in March 1918. The Neighborhood Union, which took up the improvement of black schooling as one of its primary campaigns, wrapped the nation's failure to address the lynching of African Americans into the immorality and hypocrisy of wartime patriotism: "We accordingly regard lynching as worse than Prussianism which we are at war to destroy." In particular, the Neighborhood Union questioned the efficacy of the tacit promotion of lynching given the willingness and eagerness of black Americans to fight in the name of the nation's founding principles: "What thinks you will be the effect on the morale of black men in the trenches when they reflect that they are fighting on foreign fields on behalf of their nation for those very rights and privileges which they themselves are denied at home? We appeal to you in the name of our American citizenship!" [80]

On the West Coast, at a special school bond election in November 1922, city superintendent Alfred Roncovieri and school board president F. Dohrmann, Jr. echoed the Georgia Department of Education's sentiment in an open letter to the citizens of San Francisco. The schoolmen appealed to taxpayers' sense of civic duty, patriotism, and economic self-interest:

> Be generous—not only to the children of your city, but to yourselves in this matter .... [C]onsider that school taxes are the insurance premiums ... to protect ... persons and their property against anarchy. Lack of proper education is the basic cause of the crimes being committed by the Reds and fanatics of Europe .... WHAT WOULD YOUR PROPERTY BE WORTH WITHOUT AN EDUCATED DEMOCRACY? For your answer look to Mexico, to Russia, to Turkey, to India and to all lands where dense ignorance prevails. [81]

By educating schoolchildren about the perceived evils of socialism, labor unions, and anarchism, the nation's leaders could rest assured that the next generation of workers, teachers, professionals, and policy makers would in turn protect democracy and capitalism. Drawing an ideological line between democratic capitalists and socialist despots allowed Roncovieri and Dohrmann to remind white citizens of the social and political perils of immigration. Their acute emphasis on Mexico, Turkey, and India, three decidedly nonwhite countries, rather than the more generalized "Reds and fanatics of Europe," implied both ideological *and* racial dangers. While German and Russian immigrants might become white through Americanization, Indians, Mexicans, and Turks met social and legal resistance to any desires for naturalization or national belonging. [82]

From the 1890s through the early 1920s, civics education shifted from an emphasis on voting to a process of Americanization to meet the perceived challenges of immigration, racial diversity, social revolution, and global military conflict. During the prelude to the war mobilization and propaganda of 1917–18, school authorities generally upheld a commitment to a more inclusive Americanization. Even the most coercive attempts to win over immigrant children to American ways and values were usually tempered by sympathy for abhorrent slum conditions. But with the outbreak of the Bolshevik Revolution, Americanization became for the most part a totalizing, immediate, and coercive effort to purge the nation of foreignness and radicalism. Consequently, charges of anti-Americanism, Bolshevism, and radicalism bore racial implications. And despite the tireless efforts of school reformers, many still doubted the overall effectiveness of schools in Americanizing the nation's foreigners and regarded immigration restriction as a more definitive solution. As popular anxieties and fears about a socialist takeover pervaded American social discourse, school authorities, in the service of national security, set aside their liberal and civic Americanization responsibilities in favor of a more militant antiradical and racial nationalism.[83]

In 1924, Harvard professor Robert Ward lauded Washington representative Albert Johnson's Immigration Act for its "definite numerical limitation" and, in particular, its racial exclusivity. The National Origins Act of 1924, signed into law by President Calvin Coolidge on May 26, limited the overwhelming majority of future immigration to "the same racial stocks as those that originally settled the United States." Ward's *Foreign Affairs* article recounted what, in his opinion, amounted to important but ultimately ineffective attempts to stem the tide of unwanted and inassimilable aliens before 1924. Ward singled out schools for perpetuating the myth of the American Melting Pot: "It was believed that sending alien children to school, teaching them English, giving them flag drills, letting them recite the Gettysburg Address and read the Declaration of Independence, would make thoroughgoing Americans of them, similar in all respects to the native-born or the traditional type." Instead, he argued that the Melting Pot had become corrupted with inferior races and thus provided "no hope of producing a superior or even of maintaining a homogeneous [American] race." According to Ward, "the public consciousness awakened to the realization that . . . education and environment do not fundamentally alter racial values [or] . . . offset the handicap of ancestry." In the late 1920s and 1930s, restrictionists like Ward directed their energy at new groups of immigrants and colonial subjects, Mexicans and Puerto Ricans in particular, that they believed to be biologically and culturally unassimilable.[84]

After 1924, schools continued to carve out paths to good citizenship, but did so within the context of immigration restriction. The next two generations of European-American schoolchildren would learn that "nations" and "races" were not coterminus. Myriad European nationalities, including Irish, Armenians, Italians, Greeks, Sicilians, and Poles who were naturalized as "free white persons" under the 1790 Naturalization Act, became *Caucasians* only after legal restrictions effectively sealed the borders in the mid-1920s. The transition in terminology from *white* to *Caucasian* was neither precipitous nor totalizing, and 1924 represented more of a high point of Anglo-Saxonism than an abrupt end to whiteness as a category or an identity. *Caucasian* lent the authority of science and anthropology to the process of liberating European immigrants from racial ambiguity and reforging Americanism along the lines of the major racial divisions. From 1924 until the post–World War II civil rights movement, *Caucasian* and *white* were often interchangeable. Though the division of humanity into white and non-white never disappeared in American society during the first decades of the twentieth century, the dubious whiteness of certain European "races" had no doubt complicated its centrality in educational and popular discourse.[85]

Yet even as proponents of "100 Percent Americanism" and immigration restriction couched radicalism and Bolshevism as biologically ingrained cultural and political proclivities, new strains of progressive civics emerged to counter the totalizing and racializing effects of patriotism and restrictionism. In fact, the extremism of Americanization, anticommunism, and exclusion potentially undermined the efforts of school geographers and historians to explain contemporary inequalities through the lens of objective science. If hierarchies of race and nation were natural, why did restrictionists and Americanizers expend so much energy to maintain them? The intolerance that crested from 1917 to 1924 also galvanized rather than demoralized leftists and minorities, and from the edges, they continued to formulate alternative and more inclusive visions of American citizenship.[86] The case studies that comprise the following five chapters explore not only the mechanisms through which immigration policy and imperial power on the one hand and school policy on the other reciprocally shaped each other in specific local and regional contexts, but also how marginalized communities, parents, and children challenged the forces of imperialism and inequality so central to American public education.

Visions of White California

Even distant China, disturbed by war and rebellion, sent some 25,000 of her poverty stricken laborers to our Pacific coast, where their low standards of living and their strange Oriental habits caused economic and social friction.[1]

DAVID MUZZEY, *An American History,* 1920

An anarchist, a polygamist, a person guilty of a crime or a member of a society which does not believe in organized government, cannot become a citizen. Japanese, Chinese, Koreans, and Hindus cannot become citizens.[2]

NEW YORK DEPARTMENT OF EDUCATION,
Course of Study, 1922

ON APRIL 1, 1886, SAN FRANCISCO SCHOOL SUPERINTENDENT ANDREW MOULDER gave direct orders to his charges "that no Principal, Teacher, or employé [*sic*] in the Public School Department of this city employ, patronize and or encourage the Chinese in any way, but do all in their power to legally promote their removal from this Coast and to discourage further immigration." Though Moulder did not prescribe specific penalties should one challenge or violate this policy, his official statement directly implicated educators in enacting and strengthening what he apparently deemed a national Chinese Exclusion Act that did not extend far enough. Moulder claimed simply to concur with the "feeling" of "the Taxpayers of San Francisco by whose liberality and cheerful contributions our Public Schools are supported," but the superintendent also stressed that he was acting nobly and in the best interest of the students: "The duty which the teachers owe to the children . . . should prompt them to active efforts to save the rising generation from contamination and pollution by a race reeking with the vices of the Orient, a race that knows neither truth, principle, modesty nor respect for our laws. The moral and physical ruin already wrought to our youth by contact with these people is fearful."[3]

While it is difficult to assess how teachers and principals received such orders from on high (the school board registered no formal protests in its records), Moulder's vehement opposition to the presence of Chinese in his city, state, and nation attests to how official San Francisco hoped to order the country's most heterogeneous urban center of the late nineteenth century. Moulder, whom the California State Department of Public Instruction described *In Memoriam* as "the highest type of American gentleman," envisioned a community in which white workers were afforded appropriate wage protections from the "gigantic evil production of great wrong to the laboring men and women of the community" and one in which racial hierarchies structured social and institutional relationships. The superintendent found these propositions absolutely compatible with San Francisco's idealized image as an American city.[4]

But other school officials also hoped to actively prepare students for participation in the expansion of American capitalism and empire in the Pacific and Asia, ventures that brought Americans in contact with wildly diverse peoples, languages, religions, and cultures. In a 1913 budget preamble, the school board recommended foreign language teaching "throughout the department instead of being confined to a limited number of schools." While it regarded the ability to speak and read German, French, Spanish, or Italian as skills that "will add greatly to the culture and happiness of the people and be of material value in fostering the extension our trade with foreign countries," the board also recommended "with wisdom" that schools offer instruction in Chinese language. The board's reasoning was commercial and pragmatic: "The opening of the Panama Canal and the modernization of China will make San Francisco the commercial capital of the world." The board projected that trade with Asia would soon outstrip Atlantic trade with Europe, and it intended to ready its students to reap the benefits of San Francisco's centrality in an American-dominated Pacific economy. "If our merchants could send great numbers of our young men to China able to speak the language of the people they there do business with we should obtain a practical monopoly of the Chinese trade."[5] In this sense, some members of the school board saw themselves fostering a true cosmopolitan spirit among the future ambassadors of American capitalism by equipping young San Franciscans with basic cultural navigation skills with which to establish commercial ties. Though a far cry from the openly racist policies of Moulder, whose tenure as superintendent ended in 1887, the board's embrace of Chinese language instruction signaled how the twinned processes of racial exclusion at home and commercial imperialism abroad informed local school decisions.

Though seemingly incompatible, the "broader logic of 'civilization'" and the national borders that defined it, as Adam McKeown notes, bound exclusion and extraterritoriality together in complementary ways. At the turn of the twentieth century, American-born Chinese in San Francisco and elsewhere in the United States seldom enjoyed the full benefits of American citizenship because of a presumed cultural inferiority that drew intellectual authority from scientific racism. Chinese immigrants, of course, were denied naturalization under the 1790 law restricting naturalization to "free white persons." At the same time, school officials sought to increase white students' exposure to the Chinese language for the purposes of commerce that was to take place not in California with visits from Chinese merchants, but in Asia and on American terms.[6]

Chinese immigrants and Chinese Americans were not the only targets of exclusion, subordination, and segregation in California. The state's admission to the Union in 1850 both followed and furthered the American conquest of Californios, Mexicans, and Indians. In the decades that followed, they joined African Americans, Hawaiians, Irish, Germans, Italians, Scandinavians, and native-born whites in a heterogeneous society that initially functioned more through fluidity and mobility than established or rigid hierarchies. As the urban epicenter of the astounding growth that attended the 1849 gold rush, San Francisco attested to how the urban West's racially and ethnically polyglot populaces served as crucibles in which national immigration policies and racial statutes were forged. The city's diverse mix of races and nationalities occasioned its self-appointed elites to claim to have created harmonious, cosmopolitan social order out of a disorderly frontier town and critical Pacific port of transit for both immigrants and commercial goods. Though it certainly incorporated national norms of race, gender, and class into its myriad political, social, and cultural institutions, including schools, San Francisco continued to function as an urban frontier in which identities of race, ethnicity, and national belonging remained contested and in flux into the early twentieth century. Simultaneously, the city's elites worked to create and normalize ordered legal and institutional hierarchies that challenged and undermined the mutability of social relations and cultural practices. They were, at convenient times, prone to heralding the cultural diversity of the city even as they implemented policies of subordination and exclusion based on race and national origin. The cosmopolitanism of nineteenth-century white Californians was not based on the concept of a global community of equals, but instead on global hierarchies of race and nationality offered by school geographers and historians.[7]

As formal civic institutions that incorporated and reframed local and national social norms, San Francisco's schools stood at the fore of the twinned projects of nation making and empire building. Administrators and teachers tried to order race, ethnicity, and national origin in order to carve out multiple and uneven paths to American citizenship. As school board members developed and implemented sets of policies designed at once to enforce the exclusion or segregation of nonwhites and to actively promote a curriculum intended to further US imperial interests abroad, they sought complicity in a transnational process of American orientalism that, in the words of Lisa Lowe, "displaced expansionist interests in Asia onto racialized figurations of Asian workers within the national space."[8]

The precedents furnished by San Francisco offered points of collusion and approval, critique and rejection, and adaptability and utility for other school boards in the United States and its overseas territories. Most notably, Hawai'i's territorial school board cloaked its economic imperatives of cheap plantation labor in the language of cosmopolitanism and tolerance, claiming to have created a harmonious racial order in which all islanders knew their place. In late 1906, the Hawai'i Board of Education explicitly critiqued San Francisco's segregation of Japanese schoolchildren. But as school officials in San Francisco sought a near complete rejection of the possibilities for Americanization and good citizenship for its Asian students, demographic realities and economic interests fostered a Hawaiian curriculum meant to raise a new generation of deferential and earnest plantation workers whose rights of American citizenship amounted to little more than strong patriotic feeling and loyalty. Despite white claims of Hawaiian cosmopolitanism, the politics of racial segregation and exclusion so central to the development of San Francisco's schools pervaded the formal Pacific empire as well.

CONTINENTAL EMPIRES AND THE ORIGINS OF ASIAN EXCLUSION

White California's leadership at the vanguard of anti-Asian racism and exclusion in the United States was not foreordained. In 1849, 325 Chinese gold prospectors inaugurated what would become a decades-long migration of Chinese to and from California, especially San Francisco, and elsewhere in the American West, Northeast, and South. Flocking to California in increasingly larger numbers after mid-century—nearly 50,000 between 1851 and 1855 alone—Chinese migrants joined native-born and other foreign sojourners and settlers in goldfields, urban centers, and fertile valleys throughout the former Mexican territory. When authorities officially celebrated statehood in 1850, Chinese immigrants joined in the ceremonies alongside whites, and in 1852, Governor John McDougal heralded Chinese immigrants as "one of the most worthy classes of our newly adopted citizens." But McDougal was either oblivious or willfully ignorant to a growing nativism among white gold miners, who claimed special access to goldfields and charged that Chinese miners undermined wages and refused the conditions and obligations of American citizenship. White protests found traction in the state assembly and with a new governor, John Bigler, who in May 1852 signed into law a foreign miners' license tax designed to make Chinese immigration cost-prohibitive. The law granted exemptions for noncontract laborers who endeavored to become citizens, but 1790 national law allowed only "free white persons" to naturalize, denying aspiring Chinese Americans the very option of citizenship that whites accused them of eschewing. Subsequent measures placed further economic burdens on Chinese residents, produced sizable sums of money for state and local authorities, and despite lucrative revenues, ultimately furthered the goal of exclusion.[9]

State authorities may have directed the foreign miners' tax toward the Chinese, but they were by no means the only native or adopted Californians subject to exclusionary laws and practices in the second half of the nineteenth century. Instead, the Chinese Exclusion Act of 1882 was part of a broader set of attempts after 1850 to create a white California, and schools served critical functions in both furthering and undermining this proposition. *Plessy v. Ferguson* set a national precedent for legalized segregation in 1896, but litigation over unequal schools for San Francisco's African American children established "separate but equal" in California as early as 1874 in the face of black legal challenges to the board's unofficial 1854 precedent of segregated schools for black and white children. Despite the relatively high cost of maintaining separate institutions for small numbers of black students—only 247 statewide by 1866—whites initially appeared willing to bear the tax burden. The court's decision in favor of the school board, which frequently boasted about the quality of its Negro schools, followed earlier state statutes regulating interracial marriage, legal testimony, the franchise, and holding public office, and it also precipitated the expansion of segregationist school policies throughout the state.[10] Only disagreement over the wording of a proposed exclusion law banning free black immigration jettisoned attempts to isolate and ultimately eliminate California's African American population.

During the 1860s, authorities amended school laws to prohibit local superintendents and principals from denying minority students access to education altogether. But if the 1855 school law failed to require local school boards to provide segregated schools for nonwhites, the amended 1863 statute additionally denied "Negroes, Mongolians, and Indians" access to (white) public schools without demanding districts provide separate schools. Though the legislature revised the law the following year to require local boards to honor the request of "ten or more parents or guardians of ten or more colored children" for a schoolhouse, it made no such requirement in districts in which fewer than ten nonwhite children resided. In 1866, the legislature permitted but did not require such districts to admit nonwhite children to nominally white schools if white parents did not formally object. But in 1874, the California State Supreme Court upheld the 1872 decision of principal Noah Flood to deny Mary Frances Ward enrollment at Broadway School in San Francisco because the city already provided a "colored school." Twenty-two years before *Plessy,* California enshrined "separate but equal" into its school laws. For San Francisco's African American schoolchildren, however, *de jure* school segregation did not outlast the decade. A combination of persistent black organizing in the wake of *Ward v. Flood* and a thin tax base resulting from national economic depression eroded the board's support of the *Ward* decision, and by 1880, the state legislature temporarily removed all mention of race from the school code.[11] Many districts, including San Francisco, nevertheless continued to practice forms of exclusion and segregation, especially against Asian students. As Chinese immigrants and their children became the most visible minority group, they began to bear the brunt of white racism, segregationist policies, and calls for exclusion. Yet at the same time, city officials in San Francisco found it necessary to devote at least some public resources to evening schools for adult Chinese immigrants. From 1861–70, the city operated a separate adult evening school, but it folded under growing pressure from exclusionists unwilling to entertain the idea that Chinese immigrants might become good naturalized citizens.[12]

Though no exact local or national census statistics exist and though both English and Chinese language sources range wildly from 25,000 to upward of 75,000 for a single year, the most reliable figures suggest that from 1870 to

1900, San Francisco's Chinese population remained around 30,000 even as it declined as an overall percentage of the city. In part because of racist hostility but mostly because of opportunities for employment, social camaraderie and familiarity, and the maintenance of transpacific ties to family and commercial contacts in China, Chinese San Franciscans built and maintained a vibrant, dynamic, and expansive ethnic community in the heart of the city. White observers described Chinatown differently. First *Boston Globe* editor and geography textbook author Maturin Murray Ballou, for example, posited that with only a "slight stretch of the imagination," a white American could "believe one's self in Canton or Hong Kong" once having transgressed into San Francisco's Chinatown, an enclave "at total variance with the general surroundings." Ballou located "poor abandoned men and women of other nationalities" who sought cover "from the shame and penalty of their crimes" amidst an "Oriental atmosphere" marked by "grotesque signs," connected only to the urban spaces beyond by the "broad streets after the American and European fashion, open to the sky." Chinatown represented for Ballou's readers an Oriental outpost on the West Coast, as foreign as Asia in a cultural sense, but also situated strategically in California's best deepwater port, an important geographical feature of the civilized world, as Ballou and other geography textbook authors argued.[13]

While white tourists patronized and championed Chinatown as a window into a wickedly foreign, timelessly antiquated, and morally corrupt civilization, its residents in fact participated in a modern manufacturing, commercial, and service economy that was at once local and global. Young adult men indeed comprised the majority of the population and over one thousand women were listed as prostitutes in 1870, but Chinatown's demography was more complex and variegated than white observers typically allowed. Though many Chinese men worked as laborers, others operated laundries, cigar shops, or barbershops. Shopkeepers, grocers, and restaurateurs offered both imported and domestic products, and women worked as domestics, lodging-house operators, and in garment production.[14]

US- and Chinese-born children constituted important elements of the social landscape of San Francisco, even as virulent anti-Chinese crusaders claimed that "[the Chinese] bring no children with them, and there is, therefore, no possibility of influencing them by our ordinary educational appliances," as California senator Creed Haymond declared in 1877.[15] In 1860, forty-two Chinese children, defined as such by a lack of employment and dependency on one or more adults, resided in the city. By 1870, that number jumped to 390, and California-born increased from half to nearly three-quarters of the overall number of Chinese children in the state. Indeed, native Californians of Chinese descent born between 1861 and 1870 comprised an astounding 94 percent of all California-born Chinese by the 1870 census. Despite high sojourn rates during the 1850s and contrary to the claims of Haymond and other exclusionists that the Chinese in California amounted to nothing more than coolies and prostitutes, the steady increase in the number of children, especially those born in California, attested to a growing familial stability in Chinese San Francisco.

Chinese parents sought social and economic opportunities for themselves and their children in America even as they maintained ties to China.[16] Yet this reality did not stop anti-Chinese orators from claiming that "the Chinese, as a rule, have no families .... Submitting to the same conditions as the Mongolian has established," G. B. Densmore argued in 1880, "means that the Caucasian must abandon the family relation as it exists among us, to compete with men who have no families."[17] These assertions revealed a willful ignorance among state legislators and local observers about the implications of Chinese settlement. But instead of openly denying the increasing permanency in Chinatown like elected officials in Sacramento, San Francisco's school bureaucrats hoped to constrain Chinese integration into the broader society of which the city's schools claimed a central and increasingly important role in creating paths to citizenship. In the minds of most late nineteenth-century school officials, Chinese children born in the United States still lacked the racial fortitude and moral capacity to become good Americans.

Chinese parents initially requested and successfully secured access to public schooling for their children within the existing legal and social framework of segregation. In September 1859, the school board opened a single Chinese school on the edge of Chinatown. During the next decade superintendents and board members oscillated between nominal support and outright contempt for the school and its patrons. As superintendent James Denman remarked, "there is none other [than Chinatown], having in its midst a heathen temple, established and used for the worship of idols, whose worshippers may also enjoy the blessings of the free Common Schools."[18] In particular, administrators questioned the efficacy of public tax expenditure on a facility with such low attendance rates when, in the words of Denman, "we have not the means to furnish suitable accommodations for the large numbers of our own children." In 1870, the legislature dropped the word

"Mongolian" from the state's school segregation law, which the superintendent took to mean that he was no longer required to provide a separate school for Chinese children, but only for African and Native American children.

The school board accepted Denman's interpretation and promptly closed the school in spite of the 1868 Burlingame Treaty that accorded Chinese subjects living in the United States access to public education. However, the treaty had not explicitly protected children born in the United States to Chinese parents from statutory or practical discrimination, and the board's closure of the school disproportionately offended the rights of American citizens of Chinese descent, by then the overwhelming majority of Chinese children in San Francisco. The school board did not reopen the Chinese school for fifteen years, and in the interim, Denman and subsequent superintendents argued that Christian missionary and Chinese language schools in Chinatown met the Chinese population's basic educational needs. Even though the majority of Chinese children in the city were by birthright American citizens, the board showed no inclination to prepare them even for second-class citizenship on par with segregated and underfunded African American schools in the New South or Mexican schools in California and elsewhere in the Southwest.[19]

The closure of the Chinatown school and continued exclusion from white public schools ironically fueled arguments that California's Chinese refused to assimilate despite several decades of steady immigration and settlement. Moreover, national economic crises fanned the flames of the most vitriolic wings of the anti-Chinese movement in the West and intensified intellectual and popular expressions of American orientalism that long predated the arrival of the first Chinese immigrants in California.[20] The Panic of 1873 generated long-term unemployment and wage cuts among both skilled and unskilled industrial workers, as capitalists attributed the problems of the working class to an alleged proclivity for idleness instead of the structural unsoundness of a largely unregulated capitalist system. What emerged was an uneven but momentous industrial working-class consciousness among native-born whites and northern and western European immigrants, usually to the exclusion of African Americans, Mexicans, Chinese, and southern and eastern Europeans.

In the West, as transcontinental railroad work dried up, Chinese and other non-whites competed in larger numbers with semiskilled and skilled white workers in the manufacturing and service economies in and around San Francisco and other western towns and cities. While the 1875 Page Act restricted the importation of contract laborers, prostitutes, and other "unde-sirables" from Asia, in July 1877, Denis Kearney's San Francisco–based Workingmen's Party, ostensibly founded in solidarity with striking Central Pacific Railroad workers, consolidated under its umbrella numerous anti-Chinese organizations decades in the making. The party's infamous slogan, "The Chinese Must Go," became the rallying cry of many white Californians. With labor protectionism as their cover and racism as their guiding ideology, bands of working-class whites including Germans and Irish who might have been scorned by Anglos in the East vandalized Chinese businesses, murdered Chinatown residents, clashed with police, and set blazes in a city with few fireproof structures. Later that year, white ethnic induction into the Anglo–San Franciscan mainstream became official with the establishment of a local branch of the Order of Caucasians. The order fused established tropes of scientific racism with a sense of moral and economic urgency to exclude Chinese from the United States. It employed not only incendiary rhetoric but also discriminate violence indicative of the Ku Klux Klan.[21] As the order charged in its constitution, members were to "meet all enemies within and without, calm, cool, and firm as rocks meet waves, and dash them back, bro-ken by their own fury and rottenness, from when they came; or crush them to nothingness beneath the world of Caucasian civilization and American intelligence, progress, and will."[22]

But anti-Chinese racism was not simply a pastime of working-class white Californians, nor were they the sole inventors and purveyors of it. The campaign found resonance among middle-class professionals and bureaucrats including state legislators, city council members, and school administrators. At the second California constitutional convention in 1878, the Workingmen's Party claimed a third of the delegate seats, and the delegation attempted to write a host of anti-Chinese articles into the new constitution. Though the strategy was mostly unsuccessful in the face of sound resistance by Colonel C. V. Stuart, who implored his fellow delegates to abandon the platform of "a few insane foreign and alien leaders of a party in San Francisco," voters cut across class and party lines and overwhelmingly approved a ban on Chinese immigration in a September 1879 statewide referendum that underscored the two anti-Chinese sections ultimately included in the revised constitution. Moreover, the conven-tion sought an abrogation of the Burlingame Treaty should Congress fail to modify the treaty's terms to restrict free Chinese migration to the United States. In a prelude to the alarmist eugenic arguments of Madison Grant and others that contributed to the passage of the 1924 National Origins Act, Joseph W.

Winans of California's first congressional district concluded that a failure on the part of Congress to halt Chinese immigration amounted to race suicide, and he implored his fellow delegates to prevent whites from suffering the same fate as Native Americans:

> Before the advancing march of civilization the red man ... receded, until now the relics of that fated race are swiftly passing to those happy hunting grounds which lie beyond the boundaries of time .... And now, as in the past, when the uncounted and innumerable hordes of Asia are pouring in upon us, there is no compatibility and no power of assimilation. The stronger will absorb the weaker, and the result may follow, if relief is not obtained, that the white race will succumb to their Mongolian invaders.[23]

What followed was an intensive and sustained effort by California politicians and labor leaders to create and implement national Chinese exclusion legislation. Arguments often included an alleged Chinese resistance to public education in a longer list of civilizational deficiencies and divides. In a memorial to the US Senate, Creed Haymond declared that

> during their entire settlement in California they have never adapted themselves to our habits, modes of dress, or our educational system, have never learned the sanctity of an oath, never desired to become citizens, or to perform the duties of citizenship, never discovered the difference between right and wrong, never ceased the worship of their idol gods, or advance and step beyond the musty traditions of their native hive. Impregnable to all the influences of our Anglo-Saxon life they remain the same stolid Asiatics that have floated on the rivers and slaved in the fields of China for thirty centuries of time.[24]

By the early 1880s, such arguments echoed with frequency in the chambers of the US Congress. Checked only by a veto from President Rutherford B. Hayes, an 1879 bill limiting the number of Chinese passengers aboard any ship bound for US ports to fifteen enjoyed bipartisan support in both chambers of Congress. Maine senator James G. Blaine, twice secretary of state for the Garfield, Arthur, and Harrison administrations and one of the leading American imperialists of the Gilded Age, emerged as the foremost champion of Chinese Exclusion at the national level. In 1882, Congress authorized the Chinese Exclusion Act, which placed a ten-year moratorium on virtually all Chinese immigration (the law exempted those approved as nonlaborers). Congress renewed the legislation in 1892, 1902, and 1904, and in 1917 expanded its provisions to create the Asiatic Barred Zone that stretched from Turkey in the west to the Solomon Islands in the east. The 1924

National Origins Act further reaffirmed the US commitment to Asian exclusion.

California's campaign against the Chinese could not, on its own, account for national legislation. Nor do racism or national white working-class solidarity adequately explain its broad support, particularly in regions of the country where few if any Chinese settled by the 1880s. Historian Andrew Gyory contends that the Chinese Exclusion Act was an unprecedented piece of American legislation that condemned an entire national group to racial exclusion. Though akin to the antebellum Fugitive Slave Act in the power of its racism, postbellum Chinese exclusion enjoyed wide-ranging support that cut across class, partisan, regional, and sectional lines in ways that the Fugitive Slave Act did not and in doing so inaugurated a new era in which top-down legislation legitimized racism, segregationist policies, and restrictive immigration measures.[25] Though this final point is convincing to a degree, national politicians could not have conjured and implemented the Chinese Exclusion Act without a sound canon of forerunning racist law, social practice, and popular rhetoric condemning the Chinese as inevitable outsiders, the architecture of which was primarily assembled on the West Coast. White California and its national allies became partners in realizing federal immigration law that stood to disproportionately impact in practical ways the varied social and cultural landscapes of the US West. Yet Californians were apt to point out its national importance. In a defense of the Geary Act, which renewed and strengthened the original act in 1892 and was immediately yet unsuccessfully challenged in federal court, Senator George C. Perkins exclaimed that "though the Pacific coast of our country is probably the most interested as yet, it is important to all sections, for unless the tide was stopped [in 1882] it might not be long before it took a turn and affected other sections as disastrously."[26]

In San Francisco's school system, the Chinese Exclusion Act and subsequent renewals lent national approval to what the board, principals, and teachers had already been doing. But demands by Chinese parents forced the board to reopen the Chinatown school. In October 1884, the Imperial Chinese Consulate in San Francisco took up the cause of Joseph and Mary Tape, self-described Americanized and Christianized Chinese and fifteen-year San Francisco residents, to enroll their eight-year-old daughter Mamie at Spring Valley School. Principal Jennie Hurley refused to admit Mamie, a native-born American, on the grounds that her racial status, and not her citizenship, ultimately precluded her from public schools. Consulate General

Frederick A. Bee challenged Hurley's decision, which superintendent Moulder unsurprisingly supported, on the grounds that it violated both constitutional law and international accords. In January 1885, the California superior court ruled in favor of the Tapes by citing the Fourteenth Amendment's equal protection clause. In his condemnation of the lower court's decision, state superintendent William T. Welchel questioned whether or not "a Federal Court has the power to condemn the State of California to undergo the expense of educating the children of Chinese when the presence of such foreigners is declared by the Constitution 'to be dangerous to the well-being of the State.'"

Though the California Supreme Court ultimately refused the school board's appeal, state legislators and city school officials prevented integration by reopening and relocating the Oriental school, reviving "separate but equal" in the absence of outright exclusion.[27] With sympathy for the school board, the legislature amended Article X, Section 1662 of the state school law to grant "Trustees" the power "to exclude children of filthy or vicious habits, or children suffering from contagious or infectious disease, and also to establish separate schools for children of Mongolian or Chinese descent. When such schools are established Chinese or Mongolian children must not be admitted to any other schools."[28] Under the more liberal tenure of state superintendent John Swett (1863–67), versions of the statute had excluded specific mention of race but still allowed principals and teachers broad authority to interpret "filthy or vicious habits" in racialized ways and shielded them from accusations of discrimination by virtue of the individualized nature of the language. In the wake of the Chinese Exclusion Act, the legislature made race an explicit reason for school segregation or exclusion.

In a 1903 decision, a federal court affirmed the school board's decision when it denied Wong Kim the right to attend Clement Street School instead of the Oriental School in Chinatown. The amended school code mostly affected San Francisco and smaller Chinese communities on the Sacramento River delta where school authorities administered combined Chinese-Japanese schools. In other municipalities, small numbers of Chinese children, most of them American-born, attended regular public schools. Even in San Francisco, a 1905 boycott by Chinese parents forced the board to allow Chinese children to attend regular public schools, while enrollment at the Chinatown school increased.[29] Yet despite its acquiescence, the superintendent's office continued to monitor the numbers of Asian children and other nonwhites in order to safeguard against system-wide integration and assimilation. Regular calls for census reports on Chinese, Japanese, and occasionally Korean and African American students reveal attempts by the board to privately manage or control the city's Asian constituents and their calls for integration while publicly demonstrating tolerance.[30]

As tens of thousands left Japan for the US west coast, often via Hawai'i in the first decade of the twentieth century, San Francisco's school administrators renewed their attempts to guard access to public education and informed citizenship along lines of race and national origin. The school exclusion crisis of 1906–7 was in many respects an extension of the anti-Chinese movement that achieved its first national victory in 1882. Exclusionists would also win a series of legal and political battles that restricted the prospects of citizenship and national belonging for immigrant and native-born Japanese alike.[31]

COMPETING PACIFIC EMPIRES AND
THE SCHOOL EXCLUSION CRISIS OF 1906–1907

On November 1, 1906, *San Francisco Bulletin* editor Fremont Older charged President Theodore Roosevelt with meddling in local politics: "A good deal is being said about the exclusion of the little brown children from the public schools in San Francisco. Certain agitators are . . . trying to make an international issue out of a local condition which has no significance . . . [other] than that the Japanese children have been put in separate schoolhouses as a matter of expediency, owing to our overcrowded condition." Older referred specifically to Roosevelt's attempt to mend strained diplomatic relations with Japanese diplomats following the passage of a city ordinance that excluded Japanese and all other Asian children from San Francisco's mainstream public schools and forced them to attend a single Oriental Public School in Chinatown. Japanese authorities regarded the segregation of its subjects in American schools as a direct affront to their right to migrate, settle, and work—the very same afforded to citizens and subjects of Western nations. Many white San Franciscans, on the other hand, the constituency for which Older presumably spoke, considered school segregation a vital measure in defending California from the "yellow peril" that had been averted but not eradicated by the Chinese Exclusion Act.[32] While Older vehemently denied that "heated race prejudice" motivated school exclusion, many of his fellow Californians made clear their intentions to guard against "Oriental invasion" and to protect jobs for white workers.[33]

Japanese on both sides of the Pacific fought back in response to racist threats to both individual and national sovereignty. For many Issei (first-generation immigrants) and their Nisei children born in America, school segregation, or exclusion from the schools that they would otherwise attend by virtue of their residence, exposed in very stark ways the institutional and social power of racial identity and racialization in the United States—a modern Western nation Japan tried to emulate in many ways. Taken within the myriad contexts of race, migration, and diplomacy, school exclusion was anything but a "local condition." Instead, it generated new questions for US policymakers about the racial imperatives of Japanese transnational labor, US-Japanese imperial competition in the Pacific, and the contested meanings and parameters of American citizenship.[34]

From 1885 to 1907, *kaigai dekasegi,* defined in the post-1868 Meiji period as the intention to travel abroad for temporary work and then to return to Japan, characterized most male Japanese migration to the United States. Despite the objective of sojourn, many Issei settled in the US West and Hawai'i. The 1890 US census counted 1,147 Japanese out of a total California population of over 1.2 million. Most were *dekasegi-shosei,* or student-laborers between the ages of fifteen and twenty-five who, because of limited financial means, were compelled to work in order to finance their educations in America. Many lived with and worked for wealthy white families in San Francisco and its environs. Language barriers often created obstacles to understanding the terms of employment, and many student-laborers failed to secure wage guarantees, suitable living quarters, or time off to attend school. Some attended classes only after working as a domestic for a number of years and saving enough money to finance their educations. At the same time, the Japanese government issued just over two thousand passports to women bound for the United States between 1868 and 1900. Though there were certainly exceptions, the first female Issei were primarily prostitutes.[35] In response, student-laborers appealed to the Foreign Ministry to cease the exportation to America of "women [who] are a blot on our national prestige," lest white exclusionists condemn alleged Japanese immorality in ways similar to Chinese immigrants before them.[36]

The Issei were anything but disparate migrants haphazardly bound for new lands in search of economic opportunity. Rather, Japanese transpacific migration emerged as a sustained effort to project national prestige, particularly in the face of an increasing European and American presence in East Asia and the Pacific. The collective transnational movements of Japanese in the late nineteenth and early twentieth centuries comprised a "blurring of the boundaries between emigration and colonization," as Eiichiro Azuma has convincingly argued.[37]

Eager to garner international respectability and economic clout on par with the Western powers engaged in new forms of imperialism in Africa, Southeast Asia, and the islands of the Pacific, Japanese state officials and intellectuals began to imagine the migration and subsequent settlement of its people as critical components of state-building and security. In *Jiji Shimpō,* the scholar and teacher Fukuzawa Yukichi urged his countrymen to "go to foreign lands without hesitation and select suitable places to live . . . . The more emigration flourishes, the further our national power will expand."[38] Following the Meiji restoration of 1868, imperial expansion unfolded both internally and externally as workers and settlers left for Hokkaido, Okinawa, Taiwan, Hawai'i, British Columbia, California, Oregon, Washington, and elsewhere. Between 1891 and 1900, the United States admitted 27,440 mostly laboring Japanese, and between 1901 and 1907 they were followed by 42,457 directly from Japan and an additional 38,000 from recently annexed Hawai'i. By 1910, over 72,000 Japanese lived in the continental United States.[39] For the imperial Japanese state, this exodus served two purposes. In a similar conceptual framework proposed by American historian Frederick Jackson Turner in 1893, some Meiji elites contended that these new frontiers served as safety valves for an overpopulated Japan. Second, voluntary migration and colonization afforded the Japanese state the opportunity to realize its own ambitions for modern industrial capitalist expansion. Like the transoceanic Anglophone connections forged by Britain and its settler societies, Meiji state officials supported entrepreneurial emigration. As James Belich has said of Great Britain, Japan too aspired to become a "transcontinental, transnational entity" through settler colonialism.[40]

Though relatively quiet following the passage of the Geary Act in 1892, the leaders of California's Asian exclusion movement renewed calls to arms at the turn of the twentieth century and this time directed the brunt of its vitriol at Japanese immigrants. In May 1900, Walter MacArthur of the Sailor's Union and San Francisco mayor James Duval Phelan led a rally whose speakers mostly trotted out the same economic arguments so salient during the anti-Chinese campaigns of the late 1870s and early 1880s. Phelan also charged Issei with refusal to assimilate and a general lack of character indicative of good citizenship: "They are not the stuff of which American citizens can be made . . . . Personally we have nothing against Japanese, but as they will not assimilate with us and their social life is so different from ours, let them keep at a respectable distance."[41]

But since the majority of Issei in America lived in San Francisco, the calls of Phelan, MacArthur, and other labor leaders often fell on deaf ears throughout the rest of the state, particularly in rural areas. Only when Japan shocked Western powers with its successful military campaign against Russia in early 1905 did those outside of the city and state begin to take notice. In February of that year, John P. Young, editor of the *San Francisco Chronicle,* initiated a barrage of anti-Japanese articles that by virtue of the paper's conservative readership cut across class lines to unite white workers and white ownership against Issei. Young's history of exclusionist activism undergirded a movement in San Francisco that no longer primarily catered to labor interests but employed with full force the cultural and scientific racism that soon after came to characterize anti-immigrant campaigns throughout the United States.

As the state legislature passed a series of anti-Japanese measures designed to persuade Congress to restrict immigration, local delegates from sixty-seven organizations in and around San Francisco formed the Asiatic Exclusion League (AEL), that drew support from broad swaths of California's white population from its inception through World War II.[42] At its first national annual convention in Seattle in 1908, the league protested to the president, House of Representatives, and Senate the continuance of Asian immigration "upon the exalted grounds of American patriotism," claiming that "the introduction of this incongruous and non-assimilable [Asiatic] element into our national life will inevitably impair and degrade, if not effectually destroy, our cherished institutions and our American life." Particularly in the wake of the San Francisco school crisis, the seeds planted by white San Franciscans would bear fruit at the regional and national levels.[43]

Yet the exclusion crisis itself was initially a matter of local politics. Superintendent Alfred Roncovieri and school board president Aaron Altmann were close friends and political allies of the new Union Labor mayor Eugene Schmitz, who reconstituted the board in 1902 and had run in part on a platform of school segregation. In May 1905, the board announced its intentions to expand the school in Chinatown and send all Asian students there, but did nothing in this regard for a year. Then, following the successive earthquake and fire of April 1906 that destroyed large sections of the city, systematic anti-Japanese violence exploded in San Francisco. The AEL threatened white customers of Japanese businesses with public shaming,

FIGURE 4. Oriental School. December 1, 1908. Courtesy San Francisco History Center, San Francisco Public Library.

demanded that the unions enforce penalties for such patronization, and began an official boycott in October that ended only when police successfully extorted Japanese restaurant owners for protection money paid to prevent vandalism.[44]

In the midst of the boycott, the school board fulfilled its promise of racial segregation. On October 13, the board's secretary instructed principals to send all "Chinese, Japanese, and Korean children to the Oriental Public School . . . on and after Monday, October 15" in accordance with a resolution passed two days earlier. The fires had destroyed the original school building, but the board opened a new facility on the same site by early October and ninety-three Japanese, twenty-three Chinese, three Korean, and one Alaskan who previously attended integrated neighborhood schools were now required to attend the lone segregated school in the city.[45]

Not only did families face logistical dilemmas with forced segregation, but this was also the first case in which local school officials, in congruence with Article X, Section 1662 of the state school code, segregated or excluded Japanese and Korean children because of a presumed "Mongolian" racial identity. While the statute conflated Mongolian and Chinese (and therefore race and national origin), the San Francisco resolution broadened the scope of Mongolian to subsume within a single racial category multiple Asian nationalities in order to justify the segregation of each of them. Moreover, its proponents fused race and culture in order to project established and relational anti-Chinese prejudices rooted in assumed moral depravity and cultural stagnation onto the newest substantial groups of immigrants from Asia. If Chinese exclusion was already firmly grounded in the national immigration statute, then the Japanese too must ultimately become subject to its provisions, exclusionists argued.

The school resolution stood at a crossroads of intellectual and legal discourse on the meanings and measures of national citizenship. While the arguments for Japanese exclusion put forth by school officials, labor leaders, newspaper editors, and others articulated a kind of cultural nationalism that pitted American values against Asian social decay and degraded wage labor, the employment of Mongolian as a *racial* category that included multiple nationalities and that contrasted with the "free white persons" permitted to naturalize under 1790 law signaled a shift toward a particularly virulent brand of American nationalism increasingly prevalent and decidedly underscored by race. Though the architects of subsequent immigration statutes, including the authors of the National Origins Act, attempted to obscure or de-center race in order to feign nondiscrimination, the anthropological categories of race and the designations *white* and *nonwhite* continued to constitute the primary organizational framework within which policymakers determined whether one's nation of origin was either productive or prohibitive in offering good American citizens.[46]

DEBATING RACE, NATION, AND LAW

Some detractors of segregation challenged the language of the state school code and the racial classifications inherent in the board resolution by pointing out the "scientific error" in categorizing the Japanese as Mongolian. In doing so, they sought to reframe the debate as one about race to one about culture and civilization. In a test suit, attorneys Charles Fickert and Matsuji Miyakawa challenged the legitimacy of the school resolution in the US Circuit Court and asked the school board to provide justified cause as to why K. Yasuhara should be barred from Pacific Heights School. Though the judge dismissed the proceedings and forced subsequent challengers of the law to rely solely on the merit of international treaty rights rather than the courts, Miyakawa posed historically grounded challenges to the board's actions in "light of modern ethnological and anthropological research." According to Miyakawa, a former law lecturer at Indiana University, "it was the Japanese who crushed the tide of Mongol invasion and saved Europe by slaughtering 100,000 of them in 1281. It is still customary in Japan . . . to stop children from crying by telling them that the Mongolians will get them." The argument not only articulated a racial and cultural distinction and division between Japanese and Asian mainlanders; it also heralded Japan as the savior of Western civilization. According to this historical logic, Article X, Section 1662 did not apply to Japanese children. Not only were the Japanese not Mongolian, but past Japanese resistance to and subsequent cultural notions about the Mongols held the nomads of the steppe to be enemies of Japan, Europe, and by extension, the United States—a nation that defined itself as the inheritors of Anglo-Saxon civilization in popular and academic discourse.

Furthermore, the attempt by many Issei to disassociate themselves from other Asian immigrant communities in the United States, particularly the Chinese, underscored the contested nature of the racial categories and language employed by school officials. Mongolian was not a racial category, Miyakawa argued. Or if it was, the Japanese were not Mongolian. The *Call*, which carried the story, opined that "all this and other data which this Japanese Daniel and former college don has up his sleeve to bowl over the legal sharps of the white man in San Francisco is deadwood in view of the new color lent to the dispute since it has been made a matter of diplomatic negotiation."[47] Upon the November arrival in San Francisco of Victor Metcalf, a former Republican congressman from Oakland and President Roosevelt's secretary of commerce and labor, the *Call* dismissed Metcalf's agreement with Miyakawa as a "rather silly technicality." The debate hinged on the mutability of the meaning, categorization, and terminology of race. The daily argued that "such discrimination as may exist is justified by the facts, and if the term 'Mongolian' is not broad enough the law can and probably will be widened by the Legislature to include all Asiatics."[48]

Others critical of the school board resolution operated within the prevalent categories of color and race that largely organized contemporary human geography lessons, including those taught in San Francisco, but questioned whether the Japanese were Mongolian (yellow) or were instead Malay (brown).[49] Metcalf asserted that the school board likely misrepresented the

Japanese as Mongolian because of "local prejudice" against the Chinese (who by implication Metcalf considered yellow) and as a consequence the race of the Japanese "must be determined in Washington." In its retort, the *Examiner* explained to its readers that *Lippincott's Gazetteer* "boldly declare[d] that 'the Japanese are of the Mongolian race,' though [described] Mongolia as a part of China." As the daily concluded: "The Brown people are Malaya and the Japanese are brown, and so Secretary Metcalf seems to be worried as to whether the Japanese pupils may be legally classed as Mongolians within the meaning of Section 1662." Following a conference with board president Altmann, Metcalf cabled Washington for official clarity as to which nationalities could be considered Mongolian and therefore subject to the California school law. He received no definite response, much less one that would satisfy white San Franciscans, and the secretary's assumption that the national government could determine race and thus define exclusion and inclusion sparked resentment from Californians who felt that the federal government had undermined the court-affirmed right of states to segregate schools according to race and by implication determine the racial categories appropriate for such statutes. More importantly, the struggle to classify the Japanese by race undergirded complicated legal and cultural movements that on the one hand defined the United States as a white nation and on the other resisted such a description and framework for citizenship in part or entirely.[50]

But the immediate concern of Metcalf, Roosevelt, and many legal observers was not whether or not the Japanese were Mongolian. They were at the very least nonwhite and thus ineligible for naturalization as citizens. The official diplomatic, legal, and scholarly debate that unfolded between late 1906 and early 1908 hinged first on whether the exclusion of Japanese students from San Francisco's regular public schools effaced the most favored nation agreement between Japan and the United States, and second, on whether international treaties usurped the prerogatives of states when the Constitution did not explicitly grant such powers to Congress. Writing in the *Michigan Law Review* in March 1907, Theodore Ion of Boston University Law School argued that the theoretical and historical diplomatic relations between "civilized nations" failed to provide precedent in which any nation "granted to foreigners all civil rights without exception." Should Japanese treaty rights ultimately trump the school board's decision, Ion posited, students of Chinese parentage could also claim access to the regular public schools under the provision of the Burlingame Treaty. Ion further underscored his defense of the school board with a host of case law affirming the principles of "separate but equal" and an alleged impotence of the law in abating "racial instinct," an ironic argument given the racialized motivations and underpinnings of the school code. But Ion's most paradoxical argument concerned the protection of equal rights of minority citizens of the United States from the overprivileging of aliens covered under international treaty: "the Mongolian citizen of the United States by birth ... or the people of African descent and Indian citizens, would be excluded from such schools for white people by virtue of a State law or an act of Congress, and aliens ... or colored subjects of Great Britain, France, and other States, or Mexican Indians, would have free access." [51]

Ion's defense of states' rights seemed a retort to Edwin Maxey who, in the *Yale Law Journal,* defended the absolute authority of the United States to abrogate state codes that contradict or undermine its international treaties and thus to project its commercial imperial agenda in the Pacific free of the image problem of domestic racial conflict. He called on Congress to "make offenses against the treaty rights of foreigners domiciled in the United States cognizable in federal courts" primarily to avoid appearing weak to its international partners and adversaries. Though he predicted a swift resolution to the school exclusion crisis in light of its assumed unconstitutionality, Maxey feared that if the Roosevelt administration continued to prolong the debate with the school board, California's labor unions, and state politicians, "it is hardly fair to expect that the Japanese people will understand that our federal government which is entrusted with the making of treaties cannot also secure obedience to their provisions upon the part of its subordinate divisions." [52]

After two weeks of meetings in San Francisco with school board representatives, Metcalf returned to Washington in late November and released his report that President Roosevelt then promptly relayed to Congress on December 4. Metcalf's indictment of the school board and Roosevelt's subsequent demand that Japanese students return to regular public schools rested primarily on the assertion that the local school code and the state school law violated the treaty agreement between Japan and the United States. The president warned of "lawless violence" among local whites that could "plunge [the United States] into war" and also condemned school segregation of Japanese children as a "wicked absurdity." He also asked Congress to provide Issei with a path to naturalized citizenship. It was the only time he would do so, and as prior scholars have rightly suspected, Roosevelt likely spoke to appease concerned Japanese and Japanese Americans and to advance the debate well beyond the point at which he knew he could negotiate with Californians in order to play the role of compromiser. The strategy revealed Roosevelt's pragmatism and careful attention to civic nationalism, not his sensitivity to the plight of racial minorities. An aggressive racial nationalist, Roosevelt firmly believed that white Americans could achieve national strength and cohesion through the expulsion or subordination of those they deemed racially inferior. Ever the imperialist, Roosevelt both participated in and praised the conquests of 1898, arguing that the campaigns, like those against Native Americans in "the winning of the West," strengthened bonds of race and nation. And while Roosevelt certainly regarded Asians as a subordinate race, he also admired imperial Japan's recent stunning military victory over Russia in 1904–5 and its adoption of allegedly Western institutions, including constitutional monarchy and industrial technology and development. In the case of the school exclusion crisis, Roosevelt seemed willing to set aside his racial nationalism in order to preserve amenable relations with another emerging Pacific power.[53]

Whites in California, however, failed to comprehend the gravity of international diplomacy. The local press promptly berated the president in the first round of what became a yearlong political battle over race, citizenship, school segregation, and states' rights. The *Chronicle* claimed that Roosevelt acted in a manner "evidently insincere" and "degraded" the executive office by demanding integrated schools and naturalization for Japanese. The paper highlighted Roosevelt's statement earlier that year about the "frightful barbarity" with which Japanese seal hunters conducted their "raids" as evidence of his contradictory position: "And those are the savages whom the President recommends Congress to admit, by special law, to American citizenship!" The *Chronicle*'s editorial staff claimed that should the president seek the exclusion of Japanese "coolies . . . the school question will disappear."[54]

Yet Metcalf's report also revealed critical demographic findings that the ensuing diplomatic debate quickly subsumed and rendered irrelevant but that underscore the centrality of race and citizenship to the school exclusion crisis. Metcalf reported that among the 93 Japanese students required to relocate to the Oriental school, 25 of them were Nisei, and thus native-born American citizens.[55] Moreover, the data compiled by the Japanese Consulate in San Francisco shortly thereafter suggests that there were far more than 25 school-age Nisei in the city, and Metcalf had simply not included them in his analysis. As of December 1907, only a year after the school crisis and near the end of the diplomatic exchange that would become the Gentlemen's Agreement, the consulate reported that there were 439 American-born Nisei children (199 boys and 240 girls) to complement the 268 Issei children (145 boys and 123 girls) in San Francisco. Even if a noticeable number of older Issei teenagers stood out among the grammar school population—outlying examples on which the local press and school board seized—it is far more likely that the majority of the city's school-age children of Japanese descent were in fact native-born American citizens.[56] Yet with the exception of Metcalf's passing comment in his official report, no sustained debates seemed to have emerged either locally, nationally, or internationally as to their rights. As Roger Daniels has noted in his comprehensive study of the anti-Japanese movement in California, the state and national precedents of "separate but equal" schools virtually eliminated public tolerance for a challenge on behalf of Nisei children, who were "in no way a diplomatic problem."[57]

The fluctuating tensions between the imperial Japanese state and its subject-settlers throughout the Pacific diaspora, however, defy or at least should offer pause over the simplistic explanation that Nisei children were somehow not integral to the diplomatic debate. Over the previous decade or so, Japanese *and* Issei elite argued that the moral reformation of *dekasegi* migrants in the West would elevate national prestige and ameliorate white–Japanese relations. Social elites in Tokyo hoped to limit and reform an individualistic strand of emigrant nationalism that paradoxically allowed the second or third sons of modest farming families to immigrate but that loosened the reigns of the state over its colonists. As entrepreneurial laborers sojourned between Japan, Hawai'i, and the American West they obscured the identities of individual and imperial subject, sometimes to the disapproval of the imperial state. In the US West, emergent progressive programs among a core Issei elite leadership mimicked the demands by elite and middle-class whites for the social transformation of the white ethnic working class into one that was at once productive, obedient, and respectable. Leading Issei, including Abiko Kyūtarō, through his *Nichibei Shimbun,* promoted the rejection of *dekasegi* labor, the embrace of permanent settlement, farming, marital order, and the transformation of Japanese abroad into model immigrants and by extension ideal imperial subjects.

In this context, Nisei were the fruits of Japanese settler colonialism, even if individual Issei parents and their children might have eschewed or remained ignorant of such imperial constructions of social order and family. From the perspective of some Japanese state officials and other elites, Nisei constituted important figures in the diplomatic debate and resolution. Empire, not simply immigration, revealed the American citizenship of Nisei as a point of contention lost in the diplomatic exchange between Tokyo and Washington and between Washington and San Francisco.[58]

Still, at the end of 1906, Roosevelt and Secretary of State Elihu Root hoped to appease both nativist Californians who advanced calls for outright prohibition against the immigration of male Japanese laborers, and the Japanese government, consulate, and likely many Japanese in America who regarded restriction on par with Chinese Exclusion as not only conflicting with diplomatic agreements but as a blow to the transnational service economy that relied to a great degree on the relatively free flow of laborers. Roosevelt tried to entice the school board and the state legislature to rescind the segregation code and to refrain from further restrictive legislation at the state level with assurances of a forthcoming congressional-approved Executive Order restricting Japanese immigration to the continental United States and the isthmian Canal Zone via Mexico, Canada, and Hawai'i. Yet despite Roosevelt's compromise, exclusionists in California proved insatiable and sustained campaigns against local Japanese and his administration.

RACE AND DOMESTICITY IN THE POPULAR PRESS

Nowhere was the barrage of rhetorical attacks more prominent and outspoken than in the popular local and state press. Following the initial school board resolution in October 1906, anti-immigrant vitriol filled the pages of widely distributed San Francisco dailies. The *Bulletin* countered the supposed attacks of Roosevelt and other federal officials, who argued that school segregation was a begrudging attempt to bar hard-working and "efficient" Japanese laborers from competition with American workers: "The Japanese are not good workers. In point of intelligence, skill and industry they rank far below American workingmen. If the American workingman will descend to the Japanese plane of living he can meet the Japanese competition in the labor market." The *Bulletin* appealed to eastern critics of exclusion by arguing that just as tariffs protect American-made goods, so too would exclusion protect wages for white workers: "Why not an exclusion law to protect our flesh and blood? Are men and women worth less than goods and chattels? Is not a mechanic's family worth protecting as well as a capitalist's factory?"[59]

But the press argued most forcefully against coeducational schools, where white boys and especially white girls would presumably sit beside and perhaps even play with Japanese children. The *Sacramento Union* maintained: "Our schools are our own . . . . We have no thought of turning them into establishments for the Americanization of Orientals . . . . We will provide for their education in separate schools, but we will not consent that our little ones shall suffer infection in mind, in morals or in manner."[60] The *Call* too opined: "We regard the public schools as part of the home, and we are not willing that our children should meet Asiatics in intimate association. That is 'race prejudice,' and we stand by it." As both the familial household and domestic national space, the home, in this formulation, was to be ordered and defended.[61] William Richardson, editor and manager of the *Berkeley Daily Gazette,* also adamantly opposed the "promiscuous association" of white and Asian children in the public schools. "Our public schools are for our own children and not for the scum of the earth," Richardson exclaimed. "It is mere courtesy on our part when we give them separate schools for their use and . . . it is presumptuous of them to demand a full share of our facilities which are maintained on our own. Then, again, the moral code of Asiatics does not harmonize with our high standards and we have no idea of lowering ours to conform to theirs. Beggars should never be choosers."[62]

Missing from the domestic constructions of both the *Call* and the *Gazette* was the process of domesticity itself, which in the case of schools figured into the intentions of board members and administrators to Americanize foreign children and the children of foreigners. The absence of any distinction on the part of the California press between Issei and Nisei students marked a stark contrast to the ways in which the children of immigrants from southern and eastern Europe were treated in the public schools of major metropolitan centers in the Northeast and Midwest. Eager to sever the linguistic and cultural ties that linked the children born to immigrants in the United States to their parents' homelands, school officials actively promoted campaigns of Americanization with the goal of producing loyal, patriotic, hard-working citizens. And though some like Miyakawa challenged the underlying assumptions about the racial categorization and identity of Asians, even those school officials most directly implicated in the production of good citizens failed to distinguish between native- and foreign-born Japanese in America.[63]

In January 1907, a delegation of the school board and Mayor Schmitz agreed in Washington to alter the parameters of the local school code so as to soften but certainly not eliminate its strictures along lines of both race and national origin. Though there was no intention of enforcing the new requirements in the case of European immigrants, the board placed age restrictions of up to two years above the normal age for each common school grade and delegated to principals the task of determining the "educational qualifications" of the "children of alien races who speak the English language." But the board and Roosevelt failed to explicitly define what they meant by "alien race." It almost certainly included Japanese and other children of Asian parentage, but the conflation of one's status as a noncitizen (alien) with one's membership in a particular race left open legal as well as cultural questions about the mutually sustaining relationship among race, national origin, and citizenship. In theory, the revised code returned most Nisei and some Issei students to the regular public schools, but in practice, the school board and principals retained broad power to determine the fitness of individual "aliens" for regular attendance. Far from achieving the stated goal of protecting Japanese schoolchildren, including native-born Americans, from discriminatory segregation, Roosevelt's compromise with the San Francisco board (and through the terms of the agreement, other school boards in California) recognized as local the privilege of determining the parameters of national belonging and citizenship.[64]

To this end, whites expressed particular concern over encounters between Japanese boys and white girls. As in the postemancipation South, white womanhood represented a sacred bond of the nation against outsiders both foreign and domestic. Whites cast Japanese boys in popular racist images of freedmen whose animism prompted sexual violence against innocent white women. The age of some of the Japanese boys attending San Francisco schools often served as a guise for cultural and racial prejudice. *Gazette* editor Richardson asked whether the influence of Japanese boys, apparently much older than their racial stature as "little folk" suggested, was "wholesome" for white girls. "They do not look up on our girls with the same eyes of purity and admiration that *we* do," warned Richardson. In doing so, he conjured up frightful racial images in the minds of whites of free black men ravaging virtuous Southern white women—a crime often punishable by lynch mob. To be sure, the association of Asians and African Americans in white discourse was nothing new in early twentieth-century California. In 1862, for example, California physician Arthur B. Stout warned that just as the creation of inferior hybrids among Caucasians, Africans, and indigenous Americans threatened the purity of the white race, so too would the infusion of "Chinese, Japanese, Malays, and Mongolians" impose degraded racial types on the national community of citizens. For Stout, exclusionary law was the only answer. As white Americans had done to Chinese immigrants in the mid-nineteenth century, the Japanese became the subjects of "Negroization," further strengthening the bonds of white nationhood fractured but not broken during the Civil War.[65]

One week after the school board and Mayor Schmitz struck an unofficial deal with Roosevelt's administration that readmitted Japanese students under the age of sixteen in exchange for the exclusion of Japanese migrant laborers, editors appealed to white parents' trepidation about reintegration. According to the *Call* and the *Examiner,* eighteen-year-old Frank Mukai, a Japanese student at Mill Valley Grammar School, sent an "indecent letter" to fourteen-year-old classmate May Havlock. Following Mukai's arrest, the *Examiner* printed a facsimile of the "vile" letter along with Mukai's picture, which the dailies intended as reminders to white parents of the moral and sexual dangers of school integration. Though the new agreement barred students of Mukai's age from attending regular grammar schools, the *Examiner* exclaimed that the story "[emphasized] the evil of permitting the young men of the Oriental race, with their different standard of morals, free access to the public schools." Reintegration meant access to white girls for Japanese boys.[66]

The Mukai incident, seemingly isolated and insignificant in the much larger discussion about school integration, prolonged the battle between California and the federal government over the state's right to enforce racial apartheid in public schools. State officials, school board members, and editors decried the tyranny of the Roosevelt administration for continuing to meddle in state affairs and by implication to promote cultural and racial pollution by alien Japanese students. California governor George Pardee already agreed with the San Francisco school board that separate Oriental schools were "as good" and thus complied with the 1894 treaty. In a statement akin to Southern charges of Northern bullying, Pardee argued that "if Californians decide to segregate the Japanese students it is nobody's business but ours, and we shall not be moved . . . by abusive language, based on ignorance" from the East.[67] The unofficial agreement reached between the White House and the school board did not satisfy California lawmakers either. On March 8, 1907, the California state senate passed George Keane's resolution following the re-entry of Japanese children to San Francisco's public schools. The legislature sought restriction of all Asian immigration and what they regarded as the completion of the unfinished 1882 legislation that excluded Chinese. Only then, the legislature argued, could native-born whites thoroughly assimilate the state's foreign population: "Instead of extending the

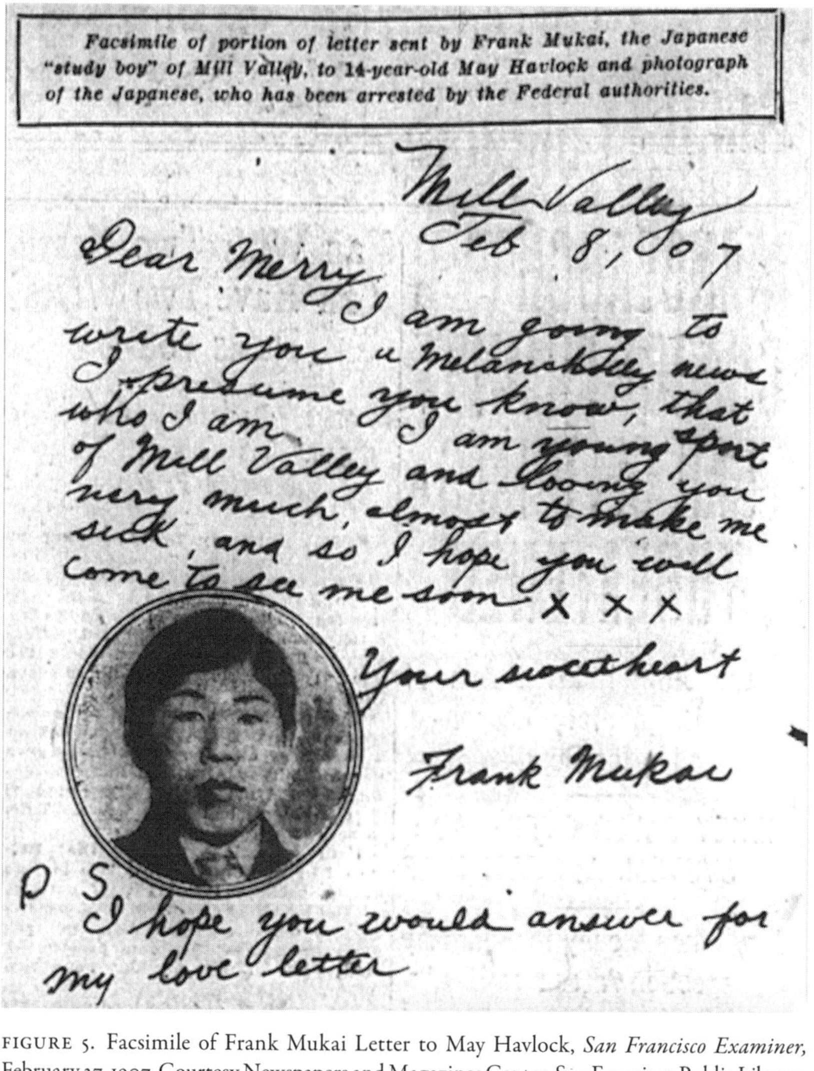

Facsimile of portion of letter sent by Frank Mukai, the Japanese "study boy" of Mill Valley, to 14-year-old May Havlock and photograph of the Japanese, who has been arrested by the Federal authorities.

Mill Valley
Feb 8, 07

Dear Merry
I am going to write you a Melanchkelly news
I presume you know, that who I am. I am young sport of Mill Valley and looving you very much, almost to make me sick, and so I hope you will come to see me soon X X X

Your sweetheart

Frank Mukai

P S
I hope you would answer for my love letter

FIGURE 5. Facsimile of Frank Mukai Letter to May Havlock, *San Francisco Examiner*, February 27, 1907. Courtesy Newspapers and Magazines Center, San Francisco Public Library.

elective franchise by adding a large and undesirable element to our voting population, our endeavor should be to thoroughly Americanize our already large foreign population and safeguard and elevate our citizenship by all reasonable restriction."[68]

Supporters of the resolution spoke of the apocalyptic and inevitable destruction of white America should Asian immigration remain unchecked. Andrew Furuseth, a Norwegian immigrant and head of the Sailors' Union of the Pacific, argued that "absolute exclusion" was the only course of action amenable to Californians: "All I know is that the Japanese are coming. Anything that temporizes this issue is wrong. California should accept nothing but absolute exclusion on the lines laid down in the Chinese act. Anything short of that will make California a yellow man's country." If debate still existed as to whether or not the Japanese belonged to the same racial group as the Chinese (Mongolian), Furuseth and others sought to make clear through the application of law the distinctions between whites and Asians.[69]

Though no single measure debated during 1907 ever passed both state houses, representatives well outside of San Francisco buttressed anti-Japanese legislation and demonstrated that like Chinese exclusion, Japanese exclusion enjoyed broad support. Nor did the Gentlemen's Agreement, brokered from late 1907 through early 1908, appease exclusionists, particularly once they realized that the language of the accord permitted returning Japanese laborers and women to emigrate. As Issei men sent for wives, anti-Japanese violence escalated in California and elsewhere in the American West. In response to what they saw either as Roosevelt's failure to honor his promises or the president's foolish and misplaced trust of the Japanese government, exclusionists experimented with new tactics to deprive Japanese in America of the cultural and historical foundations of national belonging rooted in the land itself. Sometimes at the behest of Meiji elites but more often in pursuit of familial and economic stability, Issei often invested capital in agricultural land, either in the form of outright ownership or cash tenancy. The result in California and other western states was a rapid escalation of Japanese farming activity between 1905 and 1920 and near monopoly of niche crops including asparagus, berries, melons, and onions. While white landholders continued to possess the majority of arable land under cultivation in California, they and their urban allies sought to dispossess Issei of their modest farm holdings, thwart efforts to secure economic autonomy, and create a dependent class of rural Japanese field laborers.[70]

In 1913, California lawmakers passed the Alien Land Law, dictating that eligibility for citizenship prefigured eligibility for land ownership. The statute, followed by its more stringent 1920 successor, stripped Japanese Californians of nearly 300,000 acres of land, forced many into contractual relationships with paternalistic whites who dictated the terms of leases, anticipated a similar measure in Washington state, and paved the way for licensure restrictions that prohibited aliens ineligible for citizenship from becoming members of an expanding urban professional class. Opponents of Japanese landownership framed their actions in anti-imperial terms as they contended that Issei land ownership and upward economic mobility circumscribed white mobility and would facilitate a reversal of the dependency bred by the alien land laws. In short order, exclusionists argued, California and the US West would become a veritable Japanese colony. The State Board of Control cited "strong social race instinct" among the Japanese that resulted in "large colonies of Japanese, the population in many places even exceeding the white population." The San Francisco school exclusion crisis had precipitated more pervasive economic and legal measures to make difficult residence, mobility, and assimilation for Issei, Nisei, and others of Asian descent in the American West.[71]

EMPIRE AND EXCLUSION

By the 1910s, the visionaries of white California who initially sought the segregation of Asian schoolchildren in San Francisco and those who resisted were now at the vanguard of national debates and contestations over the legal and ethnological meanings of race and eligibility for citizenship. In particular, California's exclusion movement made real for white mainlanders the contours of the US overseas empire and the implications of incorporating into the national framework places like Puerto Rico and the Philippines presumed to harbor backward and uncivilized races. Moreover, as the full scope of American military and economic power came into sharper relief following turn-of-the-century colonial wars and the rapid industrialization and integration of the national economy, some, including a majority of 1918 congressional members, predicated individual eligibility for citizenship not simply on race but on national loyalty. Calls for "100 Percent Americanism" and assimilation guided efforts to determine either the fitness for citizenship or need for exclusion of individual immigrants and entire ethnic and racial groups. Varying degrees of emphasis on English language proficiency, knowledge about and affinity for democratic values and capitalism, and general health and hygiene pervaded Americanization efforts. The same year that California prohibited aliens ineligible for citizenship from owning land, the state also created the Commission of Immigration and Housing (CSCIH) and charged it with making acceptable Americans out of the state's growing, heterogeneous foreign population. Initially an antidote to nativist calls for strict conformity to Anglo-Saxon norms, the CSCIH utilized sympathetic schoolteachers and administrators as assimilative actors both among school-age children and during evenings and weekends among immigrant adults. In some cases, CSCIH teachers made considerable efforts to assimilate Nisei, Chicanos, and others in the face of state-sanctioned and popular racism directed at them.[72]

But the National Origins Act of 1924 that formally ended Asian immigration to the United States did not abate anti-Asian racism in the American West. The work not only of exclusionists in Washington but also of the newly constituted California Joint Immigration Committee, the 1924 law placed an indefinite moratorium on Asian immigration and, for Issei, sealed their political disenfranchisement and social subordination in the United States until after World War II. While Nisei maintained the right to attend integrated schools in California per the Gentlemen's Agreement, the rise of Japanese militarism in the 1930s caused many whites to question the allegiance of American-born Japanese.[73] Indeed as early as 1920, exclusionists, including the likes of *Sacramento Bee* owner V. S. McClatchy charged the Japanese, Issei, and Nisei with imperial collusion and antagonism toward the United States. "The Japanese have determined to colonize favorable sections of the United States," McClatchy reported in a hearing before the House Committee on Immigration and Naturalization. In particular, McClatchy expressed alarm that "American-born Japanese on whom we confer citizenship are being trained here and in Japan to use their American citizenship for the glory of the Mikado and the benefit of the Japanese race." Professor Kuno Yoshisaburō of the University of California "confirmed" McClatchy's "evidence of a startling character" in the ensuing months, when he collaborated with white exclusionists to claim that the Japanese government and emigrants waged a "skillful propaganda campaign" in America to "[establish] plantations of their own" and to introduce "their peculiar civilization and government, as well as educational institutions, right in the midst of American civilization." Two developments most alarmed Kuno and his exclusionist partners: "that remarkable birth rate" among Japanese in America and separate Japanese language schools. Kuno predicted that the Japanese population in California would double by 1930 and reach an astounding ten million by the end of the century through a combination of natural increase and "'restricted' immigration . . . under violations of the intent of the Gentlemen's Agreement as now practiced," especially the importation of picture brides.

Moreover, Kuno argued that Japanese language schools instilled in Nisei children "two codes of morality and two loyalties." Rather than serving as a "bridge of understanding" in a historically constructed and emerging "Pacific civilization," as some Issei intellectuals began to imagine by the 1930s, Nisei exposed the "dangers of dual citizenship," exacerbating domestic racial conflict and potential Pacific conflagrations between the United States and Japan. While only a minority of Issei in the American West condemned community-based educational programs for Nisei that fused reverence for Japanese national heritage with the imperatives of American citizenship and loyalty to the state of their birth, most Issei parents and community leaders favored such attempts to create an "eclectic" curriculum that eschewed Japanese state militarism, rejected the claims of white nativists about the unassimilative nature of the Japanese race, and emphasized the compatibility of Japanese morals and ethics with Judeo-Christian traditions in America.[74] Despite such aims, many Nisei and their Issei parents continued to battle economic, political, and social marginalization in the American West along with other Asian immigrant communities.

In 1921, a California state law censored the content of textbooks and lessons taught in Japanese language schools and required teachers to pass examinations in American history and institutions and to demonstrate proficiency in English. Though a high percentage of applicants passed certification thanks to preparation classes sponsored by the Japanese Association of America and the Central Japanese Association of Southern California, exclusionists continued to charge language schools with un-Americanism, and in 1923, the legislature passed a measure banning language schools by July 1, 1930. Only intervention from the US Supreme Court in a 1927 suit against the Hawai'i Department of Public Instruction nullified the 1921 California law. But as right-wing militarists ascended to political power in Japan in the 1930s, Japanese in America endured even more intense scrutiny over their national loyalty than during the debates that culminated in the National Origins Act.[75]

For its part, the San Francisco school board never made good in the short term on its 1913 stated intention to offer Chinese language classes for the purposes of preparing a rising generation of American businessmen to reap the benefits of the China trade and to establish San Francisco as the commercial capital of the world. In a 1917 survey of the city's public schools, the US Bureau of Education reported only foreign language courses in French, German, Italian, and Spanish in the regular public schools. A private Chinese school offered language instruction but catered only to the city's Chinese American population. The bureau suspected that the Chinese school and similar schools for Spanish, French, and German instruction did "nothing to promote a better Americanism." Subsequent courses of study and annual superintendents' reports in the 1920s and 1930s made no mention of Chinese language instruction save Mandarin and Cantonese courses for adult Chinese immigrants enrolled in evening courses.[76] Debates about un-American activities, alleged Japanese colonization of the American West, and immigration restriction subsumed the cosmopolitan language training envisioned by the board in 1913 that would have ostensibly served the city's commercial and imperial interests.

Years of struggle against school segregation, alien land laws, and racialized immigration restriction continued to rouse the well-grounded suspicions of some Japanese elites and intellectuals who came to see the United States as an unfaithful partner in Pacific peace and commercial prosperity. In contributions to publications of the Japan Society of America, Juichi Soyeda and Tadao Kamiya, honorary members of the Tokyo Chamber of Commerce, commented on the imperial meanings and lessons of exclusion in California. The authors situated the school exclusion crisis within the broader context of American expansion in the Pacific and, even as they heaped compliments on the founding ideals of the United States, argued that the motivations of exclusionists and imperialists were intimately bound together:

> If, contrary to her traditional faithfulness to justice and humanity, contrary to the high and noble principles laid down by her illustrious forefathers, and above all, contrary to the teaching of the Christian faith, the great Republic of the United States of America is going in for militant imperialism, and some of her statesmen are looking forward to worldly ambitions and territorial aggrandizement, and are even ready to kindle the fire of race hatred and world-wide consternation, then what would be the disappointment of her trusting friend on the other side of the Pacific, and with it that of the teeming populations of the Orient?[77]

Soyeda and Kamiya offered both condemnation and warning to American imperialists that eschewed faithful diplomacy in favor of expansion predicated on racial exclusion at home and in its territories. Expansionists, they charged, sought not commercial partners but instead colonies. And how would hundreds of millions of Asians greet American Pacific interests undergirded by racial exclusion and national exceptionalism? As the next chapter demonstrates, American colonial officials in Hawai'i denied collusion with more virulent racial exclusionists on the mainland and instead promoted visions of a multiracial society free of the political divisiveness over integrated schools. In rhetoric, it claimed to welcome the thousands of Japanese immigrants, Filipinos, and those from the Asian mainland to its schools and neighborhoods. Yet in part because so few students under the Department of Public Instruction's supervision were either white Americans or of direct European ancestry, schools instead became the focus of manual training curriculum designed to sustain the islands' plantation labor force and to remain true to its nineteenth-century oligarchic roots. Despite claims of cosmopolitanism and international, multiracial cooperation, Hawai'i became deeply implicated in the politics of empire and territorial aggrandizement charged by Japanese critics of the United States and San Francisco.

3

Hawaiian Cosmopolitans and the American Pacific

[T]he whole school population . . . in Hawaii is of an industrial rather than of an academic cast. Manual training it is felt should form an important part of public instruction in Hawaii. It is peculiarly adapted to this country.[1]

ERNEST A. MOTT-SMITH, *Report of the Minister of Public Instruction*, 1899

Were [Chinese and Japanese children] not to become citizens and voters I should advise saving the expense of educating them, but as they will be it is a prime necessity to educate them, so that they will vote intelligently . . . . We must make Americans.[2]

ALATAU T. ATKINSON, *Report of the Superintendent*, 1903

IN JUNE 1881, PRINCIPAL WILLIAM WOODWELL of the Government English School at Pahala, Hawaiʻi inquired of his superior J. W. Leavitt at the kingdom's Department of Public Instruction (DPI) as to whether he was required to submit the standard detailed report before September 30. He reminded Leavitt that the school had only opened in June to what Woodwell described as a "decidedly cosmopolitan" student body of thirty-five pupils, and a later report estimated approximately sixty children of school age in the vicinity. "Therefore," he said, "my labors will be somewhat arduous."[3] Woodwell did not simply intend his statement to help him escape his bureaucratic duties. Nor was his use of "cosmopolitan" a celebration of Hawaiʻi's multiracialism or a tolerant iteration of a "global political consciousness" committed to inclusive notions of citizenship and to cultural openness.[4] Instead, Woodwell's version of cosmopolitan order spoke more to Immanuel Kant's economic articulation of "cosmopolitan unity," whereby states (or in Woodwell's case inhabitants of Hawaiʻi) worked together to maintain order and prevent violence in the interest of economic prosperity. And racial hierarchy was central to the maintenance of that order. Woodwell shared with many fellow haole—whites born in Hawai'i—and white Americans the perception of native Hawaiians and nonwhite immigrants as inferior in intelligence, questionable republican citizens, and appropriately suited for training as unskilled but reliable and docile workers. In this context, colonial imperatives of race took on the guise of cosmopolitanism. This imperial worldview and social arrangement, underpinned by geographical and historical understandings of race and civilization, strengthened Hawai'i's central role in a burgeoning transpacific economy over which Britain, the United States, and later Japan competed. And as Woodwell intimated, haole educators, most of whom possessed dual US citizenship and Hawaiian subjecthood, regarded the task of Americanizing the islands as difficult but essential to the US colonial project in the Pacific.

Twenty-six years later, as San Francisco attempted to segregate its public schools—a move that precipitated further entrenchment of the US commitment to Asiatic exclusion and white nationhood—*New York Evening Post* correspondent E. G. Lowery accompanied a congressional party to the then US Territory of Hawai'i. In his letters, reprinted later in the *Hawaiian Gazette,* Lowery expressed bewilderment over San Francisco's earlier exclusion of Japanese students: "Why San Francisco raised such an uproar over the presence in her public schools of half a score of Japanese children is more of a mystery than ever after visiting the public schools of Honolulu and the chief cities of the other islands. Here red, yellow, brown, and white children are taught side by side in one room." Though Lowery underestimated the number of children excluded in San Francisco by at least eighty-three, his juxtaposition exposed tensions among workers, managers, newspaper editors, school administrators, and politicians in Hawai'i and California over access to public education, upward economic mobility, and national belonging. Lowery further illustrated the apparent divergences on schools and race and touted Hawaiian public schools as bastions of interracial cooperation and understanding: "A little Chinese boy occupies the same seat with a bullet-headed lad who answers to the name McTavish. On another bench one finds a Korean and a Scandinavian studying from the same book; again the Japanese and the Portuguese share their luncheons and playthings."[5]

Lowery also failed to acknowledge that white students attending Hawai'i's schools constituted a small minority of the overall school population. In 1906, the year before Lowery's visit, white students numbered 1,009 American, 187 British, 273 German, and 82 Scandinavian, out of a total of

21,890, or about 7 percent. If, as some haole suggested, only when politically expedient, the children of Portuguese cane workers were white, then the percentage climbed significantly to twenty-seven. But many nonplanter haole frequently questioned the character and capacity for self-government of Portuguese. To Anglo and American haole, they were Caucasians of an inferior variety. Many were Azoreans possessed of "swarthy skins" and mixed Euro-African ancestry, and most hailed from the peasant class in contrast to Hawai'i's elite and middle-class haole. But their European origins entitled Portuguese to the possibility of naturalization under US law. At times, they were also willing to participate in anti-Asian rhetoric and demonstrations, even as haole distinguished them as "non-Anglo-Saxon." If one includes only public schools, the figures for white students drop to 5 and 24 percent, respectively, as fully half of American haole children attended private schools. So Lowery's notion that Hawai'i's public school system had somehow managed to carve out equal space for nonwhite students in ways that mainland schools did not, ignored the reality that white children *were* the minority.[6]

While Woodwell's ideas about the arduousness of educating a "cosmopolitan" school-age population predated the overthrow of the Hawaiian monarchy and US annexation, they also presaged the mutually sustaining tasks of creating citizens and training workers that haole educators upheld as unique to Hawai'i. Haole teachers and school administrators implementing and setting policy in the DPI regarded modernization, Americanization, and schooling as civilizing obligations that furthered Hawai'i's development allegedly begun under the guidance of New England missionaries and advanced through constitutional reforms at mid-nineteenth century.

What is more, potential US annexation was hotly contested both in the islands and on the mainland, mostly because of Hawai'i's large nonwhite population. The year before annexation, Anglo and American whites in Hawai'i constituted only 6 percent of a population that included full-blooded (31,000) and mixed-race (8,400) Hawaiians, Chinese (21,600), Japanese (24,400), and Portuguese (15,100). Though annexationists attempted to fold Portuguese settlers and laborers into the mix of white inhabitants of Hawai'i in order to inflate their numbers and further the goal of an agreement with the United States, the multiracial populace, especially the Asian majority, presented a significant obstacle. The desire to establish a white republic modeled after the US continental expansions and Britain's settler societies in Canada, New Zealand, Australia, and South Africa and premised on the threat or use of military force to displace, subordinate, or exclude racial pariahs required but also potentially prevented annexation.[7]

But annexationists did win out in 1898, and in the first two decades of the twentieth century, as California's anti-Asian fervor reached fever pitch with the San Francisco school crisis, many haole resolved that the white settler colonialism they had promoted was a fleeting fantasy. While some continued to envision Hawai'i as a white settlers' and workers' paradise, many turned increasingly to the language of cosmopolitanism and Americanization to show skeptical white mainlanders that despite Hawai'i's monarchical past, majority Asian populace, and presumed nonwhite inferiority, the territory deserved its place within the imperial republic.

Annexationists placed schools at the forefront of this public relations makeover. School officials, newspaper editors, politicians, and other leading haole heralded the territory as a model for racially tolerant communities in which representatives from diverse nations lived, worked, and learned free from the divisive and violent racism in California and elsewhere in the United States. In response to San Francisco's segregation of Japanese students, acting governor of Hawai'i and former education minister Ernest A. Mott-Smith claimed: "in this country, with mixed races, sound and sane counsel and moderation should prevail." In this sense, haole understandings of citizenship appeared to complicate if not outright oppose racialized notions of white republican citizenship so powerful in mainland discourses on national belonging.[8]

But despite the rhetoric of haole like Woodwell and Mott-Smith and mainland observers like Lowery, schooling in territorial Hawai'i was more about Americanizing natives and immigrants and limiting socioeconomic mobility than it was about acculturating diverse peoples into society on their own terms. In the two decades after annexation, haole recognized that similar posturing by nativist Californians on integrated schools would little serve their own interests as the self-proclaimed economic and political leaders of Hawai'i. Instead, they employed myriad strategies to promote the education of the islands' overwhelmingly nonwhite school-age population as a purported experiment in multiculturalism long before the term garnered meaning or use. However, their primary instructional strategy drew on the principles of educating nonwhites established at Hilo Boarding School, other missionary institutions in the islands, and later at the Hampton and Tuskegee Institutes in the American South. Basic literacy and arithmetic and a focus on deferential patriotism and English-only instruction attended a program of manual training meant to create subordinate worker-citizens in an economy dominated by sugar and pineapple production.

After the 1908 Gentlemen's Agreement, no group became more clearly marked targets of school Americanization than the Nisei generation of Japanese in Hawai'i. As second-generation immigrants from southern and eastern Europe and elsewhere used public schools across the United States to achieve upward economic and social mobility, albeit not without resistance from white nationalists, haole oligarchs hoped to limit the aspirations of Nisei and the children of other plantation workers who also struggled against curricula and policy that checked their designs on middle and upper socioeconomic status. Ultimately, Nisei in Hawai'i left plantations and successfully entered American middle-class life, and not necessarily on the terms dictated by white Americanization crusaders. As haole at the DPI attempted to wrestle control of and ultimately abolish Japanese language schools, organizing, petitioning, and protest culminated in a 1927 US Supreme Court decision to vest authority with local Japanese communities in Hawai'i and not with the DPI.[9]

Japanese students and parents were not the only ones to challenge the oligarchy's grip on education. Haole investments in manual training and the racial ideology that served it met resistance from students and parents of diverse backgrounds. At Lahainaluna School, Hawaiian parents protested a curriculum focused almost exclusively on preparation for cane work. At the Boys' Industrial School at Waiale'e on O'ahu, students—referred to by the administration as "inmates"—defied the manual training and forced labor programs by refusing work, protesting conditions at the school, acting out, and escaping. Ultimately, haole visions of an oligarchic society undergirded by nonwhite labor and sugar profits had to contend with alternate visions of a republic founded on principles of free labor and equal citizenship.

NEW ENGLAND ORIGINS

Hawai'i's public school system was born of New England missionary roots. Richard and Clarissa Armstrong arrived in Honolulu in May 1832 from New Bedford, Massachusetts. Two months before their departure, Princeton theologian Archibald Alexander wrote of his star student that Richard "has been induced by a pure zeal for the glory of God and desire for the salvation of the heathen," and their granddaughter would later describe the couple as "the pioneer type, fitted to enter into unbroken fields and prepare them for later fruitfulness." During the 1830s, the Armstrongs devoted themselves to what Richard regarded as the "exceedingly difficult" work of establishing Christian schools among a Hawaiian population that he later described as "poor creatures" unable to "shake off the low wretched habits of their former state."[10]

In that decade, most mission schools shifted focus from adult literacy to the common education of children. In 1836, Armstrong's colleague David Lyman founded Hilo Boarding School with the purpose of funneling the most promising aspiring native missionaries into Lahainaluna Seminary. Hilo soon emerged as the exemplar for manual training curriculum later employed at other mission schools funded by the American Board of Commissioners of Foreign Missions (ABCFM), in the public schools of the Hawaiian kingdom, and at schools established for former slaves and Native Americans in the United States. Though Lyman's decision to employ scholars in agricultural and industrial work was likely born out of necessity and lack of funds, he nevertheless advertised manual labor as an attractive feature to potential benefactors. Couched in the language of self-sufficiency, the Hilo model, when infused with white attitudes about what kinds of citizens and subjects nonwhites made, served as the launching point for a curricula that carved out marginalized political and economic spaces for its pupils.[11]

The Hawaiian monarchy assumed formal control over education in 1840, a change brought about in part by the depression of 1837 that drained the coffers of the ABCFM and left many American missionaries in Hawai'i without sufficient funds. But not until the 1845–46 Organic Acts established ministries to govern the interior, foreign affairs, treasury, and public education did the government, now a self-declared constitutional monarchy, grant itself the necessary economic and political authority to establish a unified school system. Haole served in three of the four original ministry positions, including William Richards as the first minister of public instruction. Their presence sparked resentment and suspicion among Maka'āinana (people of the land), who questioned their elected representatives' abilities to counter and limit an increasing haole influence over political, economic, and cultural affairs.

Land dispossession presented a particularly grave problem for Maka'āinana. In the 1840s, they submitted dozens of petitions expressing criticism of the government for either ignoring or failing to understand the threat posed by haole. Despite the representative nature of the 1840 constitution, which theoretically included Maka'āinana in the legislative process, the Organic Acts bestowed upon ministers advisory roles that gave them exclusive access to the Mō'ī (paramount chief or monarch). These connections allowed haole to affect changes in land distribution. The monarchy abandoned the ancient tenure system, which haole argued had oppressed Maka'āinana, to a system of private holdings in which capitalized haole secured far more acreage than Maka'āinana. When, in 1850, an "Act to Abolish the Disabilities of Aliens to Acquire and Convey Lands in Fee Simple" appeared before the legislature, public instruction minister and Privy Council member Richard Armstrong vehemently defended the bill in the face of the Maka'āinana protest. The bill's passage resulted in the swift dispossession of the commoners en route to what haole and their native allies in the government regarded as a modern and civilized society rooted in private property.[12]

The concentration of land in the hands of private and royal hands markedly shaped a school system that privileged industrial and agricultural training for boys and homemaking for girls, and Armstrong promoted such a curriculum from the time of his appointment as education minister in 1848. By all accounts, the reorganized public school system of 1855 took on new administrative features including a board of commissioners, strengthened the financial base for schools through a specific school tax, and expanded teacher training, but ultimately held to a system of manual training and rudimentary literacy conducive to an expanded laboring class that served haole planter interests, especially in the infant but prosperous sugar industry.[13]

Armstrong's emphasis on manual training in the government schools predated concerted efforts in the United States, and when such efforts did unfold, they often extended directly from Hawai'i.[14] In 1868, the sixth son of Richard and Clarissa, Samuel Chapman, transplanted the "fruitfulness" of moral and manual training described later by his daughter Edith Armstrong Talbot to Virginia, where he founded the Hampton Normal and Agricultural Institute after commanding an African American Union regiment during the American Civil War.[15] His childhood among the O'ahu mission schools, his father's leadership as the minister of public instruction, and his intimate association with Hilo Boarding School motivated Armstrong to pursue a career as an educator of the "weak tropical races" of the American South.[16] Decades earlier, Samuel and his brother Baxter accompanied their father on an 1851 school inspection tour, "visiting nearly every hamlet . . . and being entertained not only at the various missionary houses, but more often in the huts of the natives." Armstrong would later recall: "the [Hilo] school was always a labor school, simple, homelike and elementary, which attracted chiefly the country lads, and fitted the best teachers and missionaries that the Islands have produced. Their students were among the solid men of the country, and their experience has been of not a little help to me at Hampton."[17]

In the aftermath of the American Civil War, with Cuba's sugar plantation economy on the brink of complete collapse by 1868 and Louisiana's prosperous sugar economy already in shambles, Hawai'i's sugar industry exploded. Increasing tenfold between 1874 and 1891, its dominance of Hawaiian commodity export markets hinged on favorable trade agreements and cheap labor. The Reciprocity Treaty of 1875 abrogated tariff barriers between the Hawaiian kingdom and the United States and attracted additional American sugar investments that joined political forces with established haole planters. With the decline in native numbers due in large part to the ravages of Euro-American microbes, haole planters operating within the Hawaiian government hastily embraced Chinese contract labor and visions of transforming the islands into a veritable plantation regime granted free and open access to American sugar markets.[18] In his representations of what he regarded as Hawai'i's magnificent capitalist potential as both a peripheral American plantation economy in the age of emancipation and a gateway to Asian markets, Mark Twain described for his mainland readership "peaceable, obedient" imported Asian laborers who were "steady, industrious workers when properly watched."[19]

In the twelve years following reciprocity, Chinese numbers in Hawai'i reached approximately 15,000, with a peak at 22.2 percent of the total population in 1884. Though approximately half worked as free, day laborers, most were men, and many nonplanter haole elite cast the islands' Chinese population as gamblers, thieves, and opium addicts—exigencies seen by contemporaries, in Sally Engle Merry's interpretation, as "threatening to the fragile moral capacity of Native Hawaiians."[20]

The Hawaiian and American anti-Chinese movements of the 1870s and 1880s fed off of each other. Nonplanter haole and native Hawaiian elites followed the 1882 Chinese Exclusion Act with an unofficial end to Chinese immigration in 1886, possible only through a deal struck between Prime Minister Walter Murray Gibson and planter elites to replace the flow of Chinese labor with Japanese cane workers. While Chinese labor imports declined briefly between 1886 and 1890, a revival followed an 1892 constitutional amendment that allowed field hands to stay for no more than five years. Coupled with the import of Japanese workers—30,000 by 1894 and increasing nearly 400 percent during the 1890s—Chinese and Japanese male migrants, their wives, and children constituted 20 and 22 percent respectively of the entire population by 1896, bested only for a short time by native Hawaiians then at a mere 28 percent.[21] By the time of Queen Liliʻuokalani's overthrow in 1893 and the forced establishment of the "revolutionary republic," sugar, reciprocity, and disease had wrought dramatic demographic changes that transformed the culture and politics of schooling.

SCHOOLS IN A DECADE OF DISPOSSESSION AND ANNEXATION

The death of King Kalākaua in January 1891 followed his forced approval of what native Hawaiians termed the Bayonet Constitution. Foisted upon the monarchy through the consolidated efforts of haole businessmen and missionary sons, known then as the "missionary party," the constitution of 1887 protected powerful political influence to which haole perceived threats from the remaining descendants of King Kamehameha I, including Liliʻuokalani. The Bayonet Constitution stripped Kalākaua of his executive authority and placed it instead with his haole cabinet ministers, made those ministers voting members of the House of Nobles, granted haole the right to vote without naturalized status, and created a privileged sector of the electorate through property and income requirements.[22]

The new constitution aligned well with nonplanter haole intentions of white settlerism in the islands. As Jonathan Osorio observes, the Bayonet Constitution was the first Hawaiian constitution to prescribe race as a qualification for voting, essentially granting the franchise to any immigrant able to meet the new language requirements of Hawaiian, English, or any European language. Consequently, the new republican constitution effectively disenfranchised Hawaiʻi's large Asian minority, some of whom had been naturalized citizens under the monarchy. For native Hawaiians, birth and subjecthood now meant little, as Kalākaua, under threat of violence, became no more than a figurehead in his own government. Power was now firmly vested with the ruling haole minority.[23]

The 1893 overthrow of Queen Liliʻuokalani and the establishment of the Republic of Hawaiʻi formalized the earlier takeover of government institutions and economy by the sons of missionaries and other haole. But questions of citizenship remained. During the constitutional convention debates of

1894, many native Hawaiians protested and refused to take the oath required to cast a ballot. Japanese and Chinese merchants and officials petitioned the conventioneers to grant their settlers and workers the rights of franchise in an ostensible democracy. In response, haole oligarchs wrote language requirements into the naturalization clauses in order to curtail Asian political participation without admitting to overtly racist restrictions.[24]

Though the administration of schools changed little and manual training remained a central curricular component, new ways of talking about educational missions in Hawai'i emerged in light of oligarchic republicanism and the constitutional and annexation debates. Schools now became central to the task of creating citizens as well as workers, and even before annexation, haole educators recognized the practicality of embracing rather than rejecting Hawai'i's cosmopolitanism. But doing so did not mean providing space for all present nationalities to teach their own languages, values, and cultures. Instead, haole intended to mold nonwhite schoolchildren into English-speaking, patriotic workers who would continue to serve the economic interests of the islands' white establishment.

After 1893, the DPI initiated further consolidation of the islands' schools under its supervision. The board of education reported that it had finally been able to enforce compulsory attendance laws in Chinese schools, which it administered as government schools beginning in 1895. Board president William D. Alexander projected that the DPI could no longer "continue them as distinctively race schools." Alexander touted their success under haole supervision as a testament to "the gradual emancipation of our Chinese residents from inherited prejudices." At a time when many whites in California and other western states sought to exclude Chinese altogether through national legislation, haole hoped to incorporate them into Hawaiian society by stripping Chinese communities of local school control and administering instruction in English. Similarly, Alexander paused briefly to regret the passing of instruction in the Hawaiian language, having "virtually ceased to exist . . . probably never [to] appear again in a Government report." But he chalked up regret to "sentimental reasons," arguing that "it is certainly in the interest of the Hawaiians themselves."[25]

The following year, statute rendered English the only legally permissible language of instruction in government schools, and by 1898, proficiency in English became the standard measure of qualification for grade-level promotion. Education minister Ernest Mott-Smith described the place of English language instruction in terms of race and foreignness: "The solution of this problem of nationalization has been suggested in the expedient of educating a part of our alien population, the part most amenable to education to act as a barrier against the rest . . . . All classes should be brought to the realization of their duties to each other and to the state. The state is Anglo-Saxon and its institutions must be Anglo-Saxon all through." As a prelude to twentieth-century attempts to control and eventually phase out Japanese language schools, Mott-Smith reported an earlier decision of the education commissioners to deny Japanese children early dismissal from government schools in order to attend Japanese language schools. He framed the decision in terms of national security: "The security of the state is to be found in the intermingling of children in the schools common to all."[26] While Hawai'i's government schools were open to all children and would be administered in English, only haole and a small number of nonwhite parents had the choice and means of sending their children to private institutions.

Annexation immediately disenfranchised almost 60 percent of Hawai'i's population as US law denied naturalized citizenship to Asian immigrants, and the passage of the Organic Act in 1900 insured that oligarchic rule would not abate simply because Hawai'i was now a formal US colony. In particular, the few that owned and controlled the sugar industry and its supporting banking, insurance, shipping, and wholesale firms in many ways wielded more political power than the elected legislature. Territorial Hawai'i then remained a society with a vast underclass of largely nonwhite industrial agricultural laborers that purportedly served the economic interests of a white elite. In the first three decades of the twentieth century, that elite would increase their use of the islands' schools to feed the plantation system. They met myriad forms of resistance every step of the way.[27]

MANUAL TRAINING IN TERRITORIAL HAWAI'I

In May 1901, the Young Men's Research Club convened a meeting that filled the "pretty parlors and spacious lanais" of a Honolulu home. Prominent haole gathered for an address by O'ahu College President Walter Maxson Smith on the state and goals of public schooling. Smith waxed eloquent about the "organic social whole" created by the symbiosis of the school and the community: "The development of the school type, in general, has naturally proceeded along lines parallel with the development of civilization." He drew clean, direct historical lines from modern institutions of "original research and intellectual endeavor," to medieval Catholic monasticism, New England Protestant schools, and American common schools. And while Smith celebrated what he considered to be natural developments inherent in Euro-American civilization, he also noted limitations in its extension to the foreign, if cosmopolitan population of Hawai'i.[28]

Smith gleaned his arguments from the rich body of educational theory and research of the late nineteenth century and, in particular, stressed that pedagogy coincide with the natural mental abilities of students afforded by biology and environment. "The student too often looks upon the school as a retreat into which he may escape from the world," Smith accused. "A [Hawaiian] school system very largely American in character and methods, is maintained in a community which is really very largely non-American." What Smith recommended to fuse this disconnect was not unique among haole, who, beginning with Lyman and Armstrong, believed strongly that manual training was the most useful pedagogical approach to educating nonwhites. "The idea of WORK, the use of one's own powers for some useful end—that is the secret of the great power and value of Manual Training," announced Smith.[29]

If Smith's blunt racialization of schooling paralleled the Christian civilizing mission of the mid-nineteenth century, he departed, in 1901, from both the antagonistic racism of US politicians that steered annexation debates in the 1890s as well as the whites-under-siege narrative espoused by pro-annexationist haole. Smith's willingness to re-engage racial discourse and to highlight Hawai'i's large nonwhite population constituted a reorientation of the stated goals of schooling within the US empire. Most striking was Smith's overt description of the social and economic disparity between haole and both US whites and nonwhite Hawaiians: "Here the majority of white school children," only 9 percent of all students, "do not now feel and do not look forward to the necessity of having to exercise their own powers in order to exist: work does not stare them in the face as it does the average American school boy or girl. But the very great majority of nonwhites in Hawaiian public schools differ very much in the other direction, i.e., they will be compelled even more than the average American child to work for a living."

Smith's reframing of the imperial discourse at this early juncture—just one year after official transfer of the republic to the United States—forecast a transformation in US overseas imperialism, particularly in respect to Hawai'i. A decade later, haole and their brethren in the United States realized the futility of creating a white settler society in Hawai'i and began to reimagine the islands as European-style colonial societies where a privileged white elite ruled the dark masses that had fueled anti-annexationist arguments. As Christine Skwiot has recently argued of Hawaiian tourism, promoters "made decadent pleasure rather than republican virtue central" in the decades after annexation. Smith's support of manual training for nonwhite children bolstered this narrative: "The Hawaiian white child will need to do less, the Hawaiian nonwhite will need to do more."[30]

Post-annexation school officials heeded Smith's call. In 1905, Superintendent Atkinson reported to Governor George Carter "eagerness" on the part of himself and school commissioners to expand manual training in the public schools. Atkinson assured Carter that both male and female graduates of the Normal School "are all capable of giving instruction in sewing, knife work, weaving, agriculture, and drawing.... There is not a school under government control which does not instruct in some portion of manual training." And though Atkinson lamented his financial inability to submit to the 1904 St. Louis Exposition an exhibit of "the most interesting examples of manual work," he assured the governor that his department was creating capable and docile workers, including over 6,100 students training for agricultural jobs.[31]

A later committee on industrial and vocational training regretted that they could not report "greater progress" but assured the board of education that "no retrogression" had stifled manual training. The committee also touted the normal school as a place where "the foundation is being laid among the future teachers of the public schools for a corps of teachers who will be able to develop the 'practical side' of education when assigned to positions in the public service." In other words, the DPI was planting the seeds that would spring forth a malleable workforce that, with the rights of citizens, would also theoretically attend the interests of the oligarchs at the ballot box. While the committee reported excellent manual training in the primary schools, they strongly recommended the expansion of vocational high schools, one for each county "for the pupils who may not be quick in 'book learning' but are apt in some branch of the trades not excluding agriculture."

Yet in the same report, the committee also cited unrest among the parents of children at Lahainaluna School, a Maui vocational high school and in 1913 the only one of its kind in the territory. Native Hawaiian parents objected to Lahainaluna's regular program of placing boys in the service of cane cultivation, and some had already removed their children from the school: "There is among many Hawaiian-Americans of the Territory a well defined prejudice against having boys taught to grow cane, because they feel that this is 'Not Education' but rather training their boys for the work of 'coolies'. This is an interesting side light on the effect of coolie labor on the native citizens of the islands and its tendency to degrade the dignity of agricultural labor as performed on the large plantations of the Territory. It is a most unfortunate state of affairs."[32]

In the minds of the committee members, "an interesting side light" seems all that the protest of Hawaiian parents constituted. In keeping with gendered dichotomies of manual labor, the committee recommended the appointments of county supervisors of sewing and domestic science and supervisors of agriculture who would routinely visit government schools, instruct students in appropriate industrial work, and correct any problems with such instruction as currently deployed by teachers. The committee argued that traveling supervisors could inject "more life and enthusiasm" into the "preliminary preparation" of "children who will find in [manual training] an opportunity to perfect themselves for taking up an occupation for which they are especially adapted." Though a 1914 report indicated that vocational training lacked the pervasiveness desired by many haole—primarily because many were unwilling to match their rhetoric with funding—Superintendent Henry Kinney reported in 1915 "exceedingly marked" progress that included self-sustaining kitchens, carpentry shops in all large Honolulu city schools, and certification of ten normal school graduates "to teach along vocational lines."[33]

The entry of the United States into World War I demanded a heightened commitment among DPI administrators to manual training. Kinney hoped to replace departed male teachers serving as soldiers with female normal school graduates equipped to instruct students in agriculture and domestic work. And while Kinney praised the current system of rotating vocational instructors on each of the islands and normal school training in vocational instruction, he solicited the legislature for an additional $50,000 annually for manual training, a 100 percent increase in the budget. He hoped to staff each school with one male teacher devoted entirely to shop and garden work and a female teacher to conduct classes in "cooking, sewing, and other domestic arts." Kinney appealed to economic arguments affecting all of Hawai'i: "The Department believes that it should aim to educate the rising generation so as to equip it for the work which will come to its hands when it leaves school, rather than to train it to measure up to certain arbitrary academic standards.

The Territory will not long be able to carry on its wasteful policy of import-ing from abroad laborers to do its agricultural work."[34]

In the century's second decade, the legacies of Richard and Samuel Chapman Armstrong loomed large as the board of education hoped that domestic and agricultural training would increase the "value" of nonwhite students "as a community asset for good citizenship." The vocational com-mittee assured board members that it remained proactive, "rather than com-mit the unpardonable sin of doing nothing."[35] More importantly, if Hawaiian parents and children objected to industrial agricultural training at Lahainaluna, the DPI already had other means at their disposal through which to institutionalize manual work for at least a portion of the territory's youth. Yet this program too, which relied on the criminalization of nonwhite children and adolescents and the parsimony to spend as little public money as possible on basic health and sanitary needs, met forceful resistance from those most affected by the strictures of reform school and the subordinate paths to citizenship allotted them.

WORK AND CRIMINALITY AT WAIALEʻE BOYS' INDUSTRIAL SCHOOL

On April 21, 1912, school superintendent Hugh Tucker reported to his supe-rior, Superintendent Willis T. Pope, at the DPI the escape of six inmates from the Boys' Industrial School at Waialeʻe. Four of them "ran away as the boys were coming up from the laundry to breakfast and went inward the Kahuku cane fields," remarked Tucker in his correspondence. In a series of letters, Tucker detailed the events that unfolded over three days, including the apprehension of Joseph Huli, one of the original escapees, who according to Tucker was "captured in *our* cane after a long hunt" (emphasis mine) and was allegedly "armed with a heavy club made from a sledge hammer handle." Upon Huli's capture, Tucker ordered him to wear "hobbles" (shackles) for an unspecified amount of time, a practice later condemned by a commission of local legislators sent to inspect conditions at the school. The other three origi-nal escapees, Mike Hapai, Peter Pacheco, and George Telles, all made it to Waialua plantation camp, a distance of about eight miles, where they were tracked down three days later, an event that gave Tucker "great pleasure." Two other boys, Martin Telles and Palea Poe were part of the original search party that led to Huli's capture, but fled the grounds later that evening.

Willie Lininoe, John Kahumia, and Harry Sam Ku also escaped two days later, and Tucker suspected the involvement of at least three other boys in the "plot." Exhausted and no doubt frustrated with all of the excitement, Tucker could not "understand what has taken possession of . . . the boys. I know about the bad ones"—likely referring to Hapai, Huli, and Martin Telles who escaped earlier that year—"but why the good ones want to run off when their time is so near out I cannot understand." [36]

A year earlier, Pope granted permission to Tucker to continue contracting the boys' labor out to the Kahuku Plantation Company that bordered Waiale'e estate, this in defiance of the legislature's recommendation that the work program stop. Many of the boys worked full days at Kahuku, and the school enjoyed a half share of their wages. Pope's decision was based on Tucker's assertion that Kahuku's manager Andrew Adams had pleaded that without the boys the plantation would be in a "pretty bad fix." "As we are indebted to the plantation in more ways than one, I told [Mr. Adams] I would leave the boys there until some other arrangement could be made," replied Tucker. A year later, neither Pope nor Tucker grasped the irony—that the boys forced to work the Kahuku cane fields would use that landscape as cover for their flight from Waiale'e. Whether aware of it or not, in attending their own personal desires for freedom, the escapees challenged haole visions of a racialized economic order that served the interests of sugar planters and political oligarchs. [37]

In 1903, Waiale'e officially became part of the US imperial project in the islands, when seventy boys at the Honolulu Reform School were relocated to the new site on a 700-acre estate, seventy miles north of Honolulu. The DPI quickly opened a girls' reform school at the old Honolulu location for girls from the "lowest and most vicious classes" to learn "house work, sewing, washing, ironing, cooking, and lace making." Superintendent Alatau Atkinson reported that after a few months their "physical condition is very much improved," and in 1905, his successor James Davis described the facility as "quite sufficient and comfortable for the girls." [38] But in a scathing 1910 report, the school's superintendent Sadie Sterritt described many of the fifty-three girls as "anemic, badly nourished, and in poor physical condition"—hardly a portrait of a productive domestic workforce. Sterritt cited deplorable health and sanitation, including improper ventilation of the workroom, "infection of tuberculosis," "no provision for hot water," and a "supper ration [of] dry bread and water." Girls worked "continuously from early morning til dark, and some few on certain days after dark," leading Sterritt to describe "cramped prison-like surroundings [as] depressing mentally, morally, and physically." Most girls remained in the workroom all day—"a veritable sweat-shop"—and the school had few provisions for agricultural work and allowed "very few books." By April 1910, the schoolroom had exceeded capacity by nearly 50 percent.[39] Sterritt tendered her resignation from the school in November 1914 after the DPI refused to dismiss members of the faculty that she described as incompetent, insubordinate, incompatible, and cruel. In particular, Sterritt charged a Miss Evans with "stirring up race hatred" among Hawaiian teachers against her. While the administrators and teachers squabbled over the relations of power, the school continued to operate as a *de facto* juvenile prison facility.[40]

If the Girls' Industrial School intended to reform and release into the local workforce docile domestic workers, the DPI used the Boys' Industrial School to raise an army of field hands. By 1904, the new site at Waiale'e boasted all of the necessary implements and machinery for manual training: "a barn, a blacksmith shop, a carpenter shop, a poi house, and . . . gasoline engine." Additionally, the boys, whose numbers more than doubled from 47 to 110 between 1902 and 1903, cultivated sweet potatoes, bananas, sorghum, and "minor vegetables," raised dairy cattle and pigs, and employed plow horses and mules.[41] The DPI assumed jurisdiction over Waiale'e that year and maintained authority over it until 1916, when it was transferred to the Board of Industrial Schools. Like all other schools under the DPI's authority, Waiale'e was technically "free and open to all . . . regardless of color or race"—this a description by Atkinson. Though theoretically true, the superintendent's claim requires a bit more nuance, especially in regards to Boys' Industrial School.[42]

Inmates at Waiale'e were overwhelmingly Hawaiian, part Hawaiian, and Portuguese (dubious whites), with smaller numbers of Japanese, Chinese, Filipinos, and Puerto Ricans. For example, in 1902, the school, then located in Honolulu, had only one inmate defined as a white American in a class of 63. Native Hawaiians topped the list that year at 34; part Hawaiian, 7; Portuguese, 9; Puerto Rican, 10; American (colored), 2. Subsequent DPI and governors' reports did not always quantify racial identity, but in 1910, very few fully Anglo-American names appeared in the enrollment records of a school that averaged 174 students annually by 1918. In 1919 Governor Charles McCarthy again reported just one lone white inmate.[43]

As a way of ensuring the continued supply of docile nonwhite labor for the territory's sugar economy, especially after the largest producers collectively known as the Big Five successfully waited out the 1909 strike by evicting cane

FIGURE 6. School Grounds with Buildings. Waialeʻe Boys Industrial School, 1900–10. Courtesy Hawaiʻi State Archives.

workers from their camps and employing scabs, the Boys' Industrial School and the broader school system of which it was a part labeled young Hawaiians and children of nonwhite immigrants as inclined to petty larceny, vagrancy, gambling, homelessness, incorrigibility, disobedience, and leading "idle and dissolute" lives. But despite referring to the boys as inmates in official correspondence and other documents, officials like industrial school superintendent Thomas Gibson paradoxically also regarded Waialeʻe as an institution for training and second tries, not one for penance: "If a boy is sent to jail that is punishment and a disgrace, while if a boy is sent to this school it is not for punishment but for training and to be given a chance."[44]

Upon sentencing by a Honolulu judge, adolescents and teenagers were sent to Waialeʻe for nonviolent and often vaguely defined offenses. Attendance records compiled and submitted to the DPI sometime after February 1911, about a year before the big escape into the cane fields, listed 145 boys as inmates at Waiale'e. At the time of printing, Keo Kai had been at the school the longest, committed in January 1904 at the age of ten for truancy. His "sentence" was set to expire in September 1914. Kai's stint at Waiale'e was typical. The enrollment list indicates that many of the boys were handed sentences expiring sometime between their eighteenth and twentieth birthdays regardless of how old they were at the time of commitment. For example, David Namalu was committed on June 21, 1907, at age thirteen for leading an "idle and dissolute life." His sentence was set to expire on March 7, 1915, at the age of twenty or possibly twenty-one. Despite what Atkinson described as a "regular system of parole," Tucker made a habit of keeping boys beyond their parole dates. In a letter to Pope, he admitted "there are some who should be allowed out on parole provided there is work for them to do." Prospects for release appeared unofficially contingent on the availability of low-wage unskilled jobs, particularly cane work.[45]

While the school did in fact have high parole rates, sometimes turning over two-thirds of the population in a school year, Waiale'e and the Department of Public Instruction were no doubt in the business of contracting laborers out to the Kahuku Plantation Company, other O'ahu plantations, and allied Honolulu businesses, all under the auspices of reform, uplift, and industrial training. Correspondence records reveal that Honolulu business owners used Tucker and the Boys' Industrial School as a resource for acquiring workers for low-wage menial tasks. For example, a plumbing company requested a "bright boy of 14 or so who could make himself generally useful—Portuguese or other nationality," while Soichi Imamoto was paroled in April 1913 to cut cane at Kahuku. By ascribing criminal status to young would-be field hands *and* by training them in such work, the Boys' Industrial School upheld the visions of the sugar regime and other haole to enshrine white authority over subordinate nonwhite labor.[46]

The racialization and criminalization of a segment of the youth population in turn had consequences for the island's tropical environment. With sugar profits driving the decisions of the Big Five and their allies in the territorial legislature and in the US government, Waiale'e furthered the abandonment of centuries-old preservation laws upheld under the monarchy aimed at conserving the island's natural resources. Many Native Hawaiians mourned and challenged the ecological transformations wrought by expanded haole influence in the nineteenth century and decidedly Western claims over the natural world as a commodity of unlimited economic potential. Haole took note of such resistance and, in true paternalistic form, assumed the burden of agricultural and manual instruction, especially among the island's youth. In his 1906 report to the secretary of the interior, Governor George Carter argued that "agriculture is practically the exclusive basis of Hawaii's wealth, and so long as the rising generation, in large proportion, is not being bred to cultivation of the soil, thus far a serious lack in the educational system will be perpetuated." The consolidation of the Big Five sugar planters in 1909 signaled the further extension of such claims, and as noted earlier, haole educators renewed commitments to manual and agricultural training in the century's second decade.[47]

At Kahuku plantation, Waiale'e inmates were expected to contribute to these changes in the land. Work reports confirm that Joseph Huli and John Kahumia worked twenty and eighteen days respectively for seventy-five cents a day at Kahuku in July 1910 and were among twenty-four boys who worked in the cane fields at least fifteen days that month. Harry Sam Ku worked nineteen days that month for sixty cents a day. Mike Hapai and Martin Telles each put in one day's worth of work cutting cane that month. At least five of the seven escapees of May 1912 worked at Kahuku at some point prior to their escapes. While seventy-five cents a day was in fact slightly above the average earned by full-time Japanese cane cutters on the eve of the 1909 strike, the school's share cut the boys' pay in half.

Only three hours per day were actually devoted to "school" and Kahuku's profits were not meager. A report from Waiale'e to the DPI reveals that the boys' labor produced 1,329 tons of raw cane, 119 tons of sugar, and $3,758.11— all of this over a period of seven days. The curriculum at Waiale'e offered a more entrenched version of what haole argued was the destiny of nonwhites in Hawai'i. In an apparent bid for appointment as superintendent of the DPI by Governor Lucius Pinkham, an anonymous haole citizen argued that "most of [the pupils] should be trained for a practical life as workers" and offered Lyman's Hilo Boarding School as "the most successful institution of its kind in the islands" that might offer "the solution to our local problem." If Hilo represented missionary assumptions about the dignity of free labor and its particular suitability to nonwhite populations in an era of black slavery, Waiale'e emphasized criminality as the pretense for renewed regimes of forced labor in the age of emancipation.[48]

On the heels of Sadie Sterritt's whistle-blowing at the Girls' Industrial School, Tucker came under fire in 1915 from the territorial legislature for abhorrent conditions at Waiale'e, particularly the use of iron leg shackles as

FIGURE 7. Inmates Wearing White Uniforms Standing in Formation on School Grounds. Waialeʻe Boys Industrial School, 1900–10. Courtesy Hawaiʻi State Archives.

punishment. A grand jury investigation commenced. In November of that year, fifty-four inmates escaped while Tucker was away in what the *Honolulu Star-Bulletin* described as a "mutiny." The next month, Superintendent Henry Kinney sent to the county attorney the names of fifteen boys who had taken part in a "riot."[49] Five months later the school was transferred to the jurisdiction of the newly created Board of Industrial Schools, which sought to expand manual training in order to increase the pool of low-wage labor for haole planters and allied service industries, including the growing pineapple canning industry.

The school seems to have severed its connections to the Kahuku sugar plantation by mid-decade, but by 1920, 226 of Waialeʻe's 700 acres were devoted to pineapple production under lease to "an outside party." That same year, a federal survey on education in Hawaiʻi reaffirmed the curriculum at Boys' Industrial and recommended its expansion in the islands: "It must be clear that the vocational needs as well as the vocational opportunities in the islands are in large part connected directly or indirectly with the sugar industry, and in a less degree with pineapple growing," stated the authors. Though the corruption of Hawai'i's industrial schools seemed to discredit the stated goals of manual training, it did little to abate haole support of the plantation regime. And while alleged proclivities for criminality among the school's students made Waiale'e exceptional, its mission of creating a docile, malleable nonwhite labor force for mono-agriculture was not.[50]

The school board and DPI conveniently cast the industrial reform schools as extreme examples and continued to centralize manual training in its broader educational mission of creating worker-citizens. By the 1910s, Nisei schoolchildren and their Issei parents had become the demographic majority, and it was to this group that the DPI turned most of its attention. As the anti-immigrant bluster of 100 Percent Americanism proliferated throughout schools and other institutions in the United States during and after World War I, Japanese in Hawai'i fell under the increased scrutiny of haole educators who hoped to strip Japanese communities of local school control in an effort to fully and forcefully Americanize the Nisei generation whose birth in Hawai'i legally entitled them to the rights of American citizenship. The DPI would attempt to funnel Nisei down paths of good citizenship defined by Americanization and that featured plantation labor and limited social mobility.

NISEI ASPIRATIONS AND THE LIMITS OF AMERICANIZATION

As Japan and the United States negotiated the Gentlemen's Agreement in 1907, *Post* correspondent Lowery heralded Hawai'i's schools for making suitable citizens out of people one daily reporter called "kimono-clad aliens." But Lowery also detected emerging and problematic differences among the territory's diverse Asian population.[51] In particular, he described the Japanese as unwilling to embrace American political and social institutions in ways that Hawai'i's Chinese seemed to accept quite readily: "The Chinese are much better liked than the Japanese in Hawaii, because they have shown themselves much more susceptible to the genius of American institutions." He also recognized similar prejudice among haole against the Japanese to that on open display among nativist whites in California. Bishop Henry Restarick reported to Lowery that Chinese children become "impregnated with . . . American ideals" and, more importantly, take those ideals with them to

China, effectively "Americanizing the Orient." Conversely, Japanese parents saw to it that their children received instruction in the Japanese language each day before attending Hawai'i's public schools. Restarick, rather evangelically, remained optimistic that "we have an opportunity of teaching the Orientals something which they could not gain in their own lands. It will all tell, and is telling, in the uplifting of the race."[52]

The schooling of Japanese children in Hawai'i hinged on two entwined haole goals that directly conflicted with the aspirations of the Nisei generation for upward social and economic mobility in the American Pacific. First, haole hoped to keep young citizens of Japanese ancestry on the sugar plantations that their Issei parents worked, in low-wage, unskilled positions in other agricultural industries, and out of the small business economy and professional class then dominated by nonplanter haole. To this end, administrators renewed efforts to strengthen what some internal administration critics considered by 1920 to be a fledgling manual training curriculum. Administrators repackaged the *dignity of labor* argument in terms of the prescribed duties of citizenship. Not only did educational leaders partner with sugar planters to ensure a reliable native labor supply, they also hoped to eliminate autonomous schools which served that labor force. The nativist hysteria so central to Americanization campaigns on the mainland found its complement in Hawai'i. In the 1920s, the DPI sought complete control over Japanese language schools, where haole believed Nisei children learned subversive ideas and cultivated divided national loyalties that threatened American national security in its Pacific empire. Both efforts ultimately failed.

By 1900, Japanese immigrants and their families constituted a plurality of cane workers in Hawai'i. Their numbers remained between 26,000 and 28,000 from 1909 to 1920, even as many Japanese sought work outside the plantation regime and as planters increasingly recruited cane cutters and field hands from the American-ruled Philippines. Between 1885 and 1924, approximately half of the Issei sojourners, who may have originally intended to return to Japan after saving enough money, chose instead to remain as settlers. Some did so after 1907 in response to the Gentlemen's Agreement, which barred male laborers from re-entry to the territory if away for more than three years. Limited economic prospects in Japan also prompted many Issei to remain in Hawai'i, even under oppressive conditions on sugar plantations, or to pursue work on the US mainland. After 1910, the migration of Japanese women to Hawai'i as picture brides delivered greater gender balance

FIGURE 8. Arrival of Japanese Contract Laborers at Honolulu Harbor, 1893. Courtesy Hawai'i State Archives.

to a Japanese immigrant population hitherto composed heavily of male laborers. Traditional Japanese family units in Hawai'i began to proliferate. While haole welcomed this shift in theory, particularly planters who saw familial bonds among workers as an intervention in labor transience, most worried that the Nisei generation, guaranteed the right to vote via birthright citizenship, would eventually dominate territorial politics.[53]

In the cane fields, Issei and Nisei workers formed the vanguard of union activism. Their struggle for and relative success in obtaining from plantation owners higher wages, improved housing, and financial support for Japanese language schools drew the ire of nonplanter haole who, fearing competition, hoped to limit the entry of upwardly mobile Japanese into skilled positions and independent business. After the Hawaiian Sugar Planters' Association (HSPA) refused to even recognize the existence of the Japanese-led Higher Wages Association, much less its demands for fair pay, reduced hours, and improved living conditions, 7,000 cane workers were on strike by the end of May 1909. Planters responded in solidarity with camp evictions, loss sharing, legal harassment of strike organizers, and the employment of scabs. Though the strike lasted only through the summer, Japanese workers demonstrated that if the plantation regime wanted to profit from their labor, it must recognize Asians, under US immigration law, as potentially permanent settlers instead of transient workers quickly replaced by regular influxes of cheap contract laborers.

Planters responded by recruiting US colonial subjects and foreign nationals, including Filipinos, who numbered 20,000 in Hawai'i by 1920 and 75,000 by 1930, and smaller numbers of Portuguese and Puerto Ricans. They too protested abhorrent plantation conditions and frequently left for the US west coast.[54] Planters also oscillated between anti-recruitment statutes that restricted the movement and choice of workers and "welfare capitalism"— a form of "necessity paternalism" that pedaled the promise of conditions that would turn labor camps into communities as a way to stifle the ability of free laborers to improve their economic conditions through strikes or threat of transience. The 1920 strikers, primarily Hawaiian-born Nisei and far more organized at the ground level than in 1909, triggered four main reactions by the HSPA, some of which had ensued after 1909 with limited success and implementation. First, the association supported antilabor legislation that rendered legal the harassment and prosecution of strikers. Second, planters hoped that ethnic and racial segregation of the workforce would prevent class solidarity among cane workers. Had Japanese and Filipino strikers collaborated more during the 1920 strike, the outcomes may have been different. Third, the HSPA pledged to improve the living and working conditions on plantations in order to retain workers in the absence of liberal US immigration laws. Fourth, the HSPA appealed to the DPI to cease their alleged policy of overeducating Hawai'i's youth and to further entrench manual training.[55] This last approach, planters hoped, would ensure a steady supply of homegrown docile laborers with the stability of American citizenship.

Labor shortages—no doubt exaggerated by the HSPA and the Hawai'i American Legion as they lobbied the territorial legislature and President Warren Harding for more favorable labor recruitment policies—nonetheless promised to affect dramatic changes in Hawai'i's tropical economy if unaddressed. By 1910, Chinese and Portuguese proportions of the plantation workforce dropped to 7 percent each after respective representation of 25 and 17 percent in the 1890s. Though Japanese workers maintained a plurality from 1910 to 1920, their numbers too declined from 64 to 44 percent. By 1930, Issei and Nisei workers constituted only 18 percent of the workforce, and as Congress threatened to shut off the flow of colonized Filipino labor to the United States, planters turned to the DPI for homegrown unskilled labor.[56] But in the absence of an emergency labor bill that would grant Hawai'i exceptions to racialized US immigration codes—a move that J.K. Butler, a representative of the American Legion, argued rather paradoxically would realize "a more diversified alien population ... as a necessary step toward our Americanization plan"—and faced with transformations and potential shortages in the workforce, planters sought stability.[57]

In the early 1920s, they obtained a mutual partnership with the DPI to limit the academic prospects of its cosmopolitan and Nisei-dominated school-age population. Acting as an unofficial liaison between the HSPA and the DPI, Governor Wallace Farrington implored the "mental engineers" of the DPI to stress to public school teachers the importance of "dignifying agriculture." Farrington later relied on anecdotal evidence that plantation work would precipitate either homestead opportunities or managerial status on sugar plantations. But nonwhites, Farrington failed to acknowledge, were ineligible for the latter, and the limited prospects for upward mobility were not lost on Nisei, who remained committed to using public education to escape the menial labor conditions that their parents endured.[58] Efforts to produce docile workers clashed with the desires of Nisei for full exercise of the rights of citizens, and if haole hoped that an emphasis on industrial and agricultural training in the public schools would keep Nisei on plantations, they also hoped to strip worker communities of autonomous language schools that the DPI believed promoted un-Americanism among the fastest-growing sector of the electorate.

In the 1910s and certainly by the early 1920s, the Americanization of Hawaiian Nisei rested in large part on questions of English instruction and private language schools. The DPI denied a request in June 1911 to use public school buildings for after-hours Japanese language instruction, describing the decision as "in the best interest of the public schools that all such requests be denied."[59] Less than a year later, the board of commissioners granted a similar request of a Mr. Canavare that Portuguese high school students receive one hour of Portuguese language instruction.[60] Despite the DPI's stated intentions to integrate Asian children into the body of citizens, haole parents questioned whether or not public school teachers spent adequate time on arithmetic, history, and civics, instead allegedly devoting the bulk of the school day to English instruction. In 1914, Alice Sinclair Dodge complained to Governor Walter Frear that her tax dollars supported the latter: "Why should our children not be provided for in the public schools?" Dodge proposed a tuition-free school with free transportation for students and with admission standards that required English fluency. She concluded that "our children ought to have equal rights with the children of non-English speaking peoples [but] . . . do not have it at present."[61] In 1920, the superintendent approved a similar petition of over 400 haole parents, and in the midst of a strike led by Japanese cane workers, Honolulu's Central Grammar School became the first "English Standard School." Despite the superintendent's profession that race and nationality played no role in admission standards, only 5 percent of students at Central in 1925 were Chinese or Japanese, despite representing 60 percent of the total public school population.[62] Cosmopolitan Hawai'i, it seems, had taken cues from Jim Crow.

Simultaneously, the DPI sought to extend its authority over private Japanese language schools that it claimed impeded benevolent haole efforts to make good citizens out of an ethnically and racially diverse school-age population. Japanese parents and community leaders regarded the DPI's position as an attempt to destroy institutional pillars of Japanese life in Hawai'i. The first Japanese language school opened in Hawai'i in 1892 because many of the earliest Issei immigrants intended to return to Japan and sought for their children a Japanese education. By 1910, 140 such schools complemented the public schools that Japanese children attended. With both Buddhist and Christian sponsorship and with support from small tuition fees, donations from childless Issei, and patronage from planters eager to thwart labor strikes, over 7,000 Issei and Nisei children attended these schools.[63] Students studied Japanese language and culture, bowed to the Emperor's portrait, studied the Imperial Rescript on Education, observed major Japanese holidays (and were thus conspicuously absent from public schools), learned calligraphy, and used textbooks approved by the Japanese Ministry of Education.[64] But some Nisei later recalled that their teachers also stressed American ideals, democratic values, and the duties of American citizenship. "We were taught to be loyal and most of all respect our government of the people, for the people, and by the people," Tomayo Kishinani reported to DPI superintendent Vaughan MacCaughey in a 1922 internal survey on Americanization and Japanese language schools. Tsuruno Miyamoto similarly argued that language schools instilled obedience and morality in Nisei children, traits that rendered them model students in the territorial public schools too.[65]

The proliferation of Japanese language schools countered the underrepresentation of Japanese teachers in public schools. In 1906, the DPI did not employ any Japanese teachers and only nine such worked in the islands' private schools. Meanwhile, 3,578 Issei and Nisei children attended public schools, bested only by Hawaiians at 4,045.[66] In 1909, Japanese students comprised 71 percent of the overall increase in public school enrollment, and by 1915, they occupied fully 40 percent of the seats in public schools.[67] At the end of the decade, 98 percent of the 20,651 Japanese students who attended public schools also attended private language schools, and though Japanese public school teachers' numbers grew, they did not keep pace with the number of Nisei students. During and immediately following World War I

FIGURE 9. Graduates of Honomu Japanese Language School, 1925. Courtesy Hawaiʻi State Archives.

haole administrators and territorial legislators increasingly questioned the national loyalty of Nisei, most of whom possessed American citizenship but also remained tied to the language and culture of their parents.[68]

LITIGATING LANGUAGE SCHOOLS

In 1920, the territorial legislature passed Act 30, prohibiting anyone from conducting or teaching in a school in a language other than English or Hawaiian without first obtaining a permit from the DPI. The law stipulated that the DPI only grant permits to operate language schools no more than one hour per day and no more than six days a week to applicants "possessed of the ideals of democracy; knowledge of American history and institutions, and [knowledge of] how to read, write, and speak the English language." Furthermore, the act required that anyone obtaining a permit sign a pledge agreeing to "direct the minds of studies of pupils in said school as will tend to make them good and loyal American citizens." To this end, the law also granted the DPI authority over all curriculum and textbook decisions. As Eileen Tamura has observed, Act 30 served as an unbrokered compromise between Japanese in Hawaiʻi, who hoped to retain autonomous language schools, and mainland Americanizers who, in a 1920 federal survey, recommended the schools' complete abolition.[69]

Secretly, territorial legislators hoped the restrictions on language schools would ultimately destroy them, as the Honolulu Advertising Club also championed in a policy statement submitted to the DPI: "We Therefore Recommend—That the Board of Education adopt as its policy the gradual elimination of language schools as rapidly as may be wise and expedient through the development of an enlarged public school curriculum and lengthened school day." The ad club warned that failure to effectively Americanize children of foreign-born parents would "certainly block Statehood and will probably result in loss of self-government in the Territory." For some haole, the language school issue was one of sovereignty.[70]

Pursuant restrictions appeared to bring the goal of elimination to fruition. The DPI prohibited anyone from attending language schools before the third grade, which placed burdens on working families that relied on language schools for childcare during the working day. In December 1922, four language schools challenged the constitutionality of Act 30 in the Territorial Circuit Court. After a judge found Act 30 constitutional but declared the DPI's regulatory powers invalid, the territory appealed the case to the Territorial Supreme Court. Meanwhile, the legislature sought further restrictions, including annual enrollment fees (Act 171, 1923) and the right of the territory to file suits against noncompliant language school board members or teachers (Act 152, 1925).[71]

Reactions to this series of laws varied, and the DPI attempted to secure broad support from influential haole. Since many immigrant communities conducted language schools on sugar and pineapple plantations, officials appealed to plantation managers to force their workers to accede. Foreign language school supervisor Henry Schwartz implored Pioneer Mill manager Caleb Burns to use his leverage to bring the schools into "harmony with the government." Schwartz recommended that Burns, whose plantation hosted the largest number of Japanese language schools in Hawaiʻi, explain that families and schools required to contribute to a $30,000 legal fund as parties in the lawsuit would be much better off simply paying their annual fees to the DPI. "As long as these people use your land, they should comply with your wishes," concluded Schwartz. Burns promised that after having "talk[ed] these fellows over, [I] finally told them if they did not come into line this coming fall that all donations from the plantation to their school would be stopped."[72]

Schwartz also hoped to enlist the help of Pauwela Pineapple Company manager Worth Aiken to halt the construction of a new language school at Haiku and of James Campsie, the manager at the Hawaiian Agricultural Company at Pahala, the language schools of which had joined the lawsuit in August 1923. Schwartz implored Campsie to challenge the "falsehood and misrepresentation" published in *Hawaii Hochi,* a foremost mouthpiece of support for the Japanese challenge to the language school law. To Aiken, Schwartz even offered use of the public schools for language instruction so long as Japanese residents "were willing to cooperate with the Territory and withdraw from this litigation." Aiken pledged his cooperation but asked Schwartz to personally discuss the matter with the Japanese residents at Haiku. Aiken's lukewarm reception and passive response was typical among plantation managers, many of whom regarded language schools as institutions of stability among Japanese workers similar to provisions for family housing, bonsai gardens, and temples. The schools tied entire families to the land and plantation in ways that low wages and brutal labor conditions could not.[73]

If plantation managers were at best indifferent, Schwartz also communicated directly to parents and officials of Japanese language schools. In an appeal to Mr. T. Toshiyuki of the Central Kona Japanese Language School, Schwartz assured the school committee secretary that its continued litigation against the DPI would likely bring financial ruin on the school: "Kona is not large enough to sustain two or three good schools, and if the law is sustained, the [DPI] will certainly exercise its right to choose one school for the district, and it is not likely to select a school which has been in opposition to the law from its very passage." Schwartz's punitive tone eroded his otherwise latent and reserved contempt for those Japanese communities that would challenge haole authority and its Americanization efforts: "You have a fine opportunity to establish a real American community. I sincerely hope you will think again before you start an enterprise which is certainly to be regarded as an effort to perpetuate alien influences." Governor Farrington concurred with Schwartz: "the residents of the Territory who are now placing themselves in defiance of the educational laws . . . are not only discrediting themselves but are serving as a most unfortunate agency in discrediting the people of their nationality in the general esteem of the American people of the mainland." By threatening closure of the school pending the law's constitutionality, Schwartz seemed decidedly insincere in his desires for a prosperous Japanese American community in Kona.[74]

While it enlisted the support of haole plantation managers and influential Japanese parents, the DPI also hoped to accumulate convincing sociological survey data to justify the elimination of language schools. Superintendent MacCaughey's 1922 survey on the ways that language schools either helped or hindered Americanization overwhelmingly received responses from Nisei public school teachers, which seemed to MacCaughey to lend further credibility to the department's policies.[75] Most respondents argued that language schools prevented Nisei students from learning English more quickly, and several Nisei respondents charged language schools with subversive teachings that prevented Japanese Americans from understanding and executing the duties of good American citizenship. Ruth Fo blamed Buddhism. Hatau Miyake asked rather cynically, "Can a teacher who is a citizen of an alien country, a believer of his own imperial government, who is taught nothing but allegiance to his own country, fidelity to his emperor, and various customs of his fatherland, until recently, change his teachings suddenly to strictly Americanism?" His statement echoed Schwartz's assertions that language school teachers "cannot avoid giving their pupils un-American and sometimes, anti-American ideas."[76] Benjamin Tashiro likewise blamed teachers who have come from Japan ignorant of "the significance of American ideals and institutions" and on Issei parents who, as Japanese subjects, failed to comprehend their children's responsibilities of American citizenship. But Tashiro also assured the superintendent that Nisei "allegiance is staked in America and Japan is beyond their vision."

No doubt many Nisei teachers believed themselves to be fully American in their ideals and in their responsibilities as teachers. But likely also out of a sense of pressure of the haole-dominated administration, some Nisei accommodationists hoped to either garner favor by supporting the position of their employer or at least to avoid being flagged and potentially punished as un-American. Most respondents straddled a fine line between rejection of language schools in ways that seemed to please the administration and affirming the loyalties of Nisei children to the United States.[77]

Despite the DPI's intentions to eliminate or at the very least extend authority over language schools, and despite the supposed support from Nisei public school teachers willing to fall in line, litigants obtained an injunction from a federal court judge in Hawai'i on July 22, 1925. In March 1926, the Ninth Circuit Court of Appeals in San Francisco denied the

Territory's appeal, citing that Act 30 and the ensuing restrictions "abridge[d] privileges and immunities of citizens to deprive them of liberty . . . . You cannot make a good citizen by oppression, or by a denial of constitutional rights." In January 1927, the US Supreme Court upheld the Ninth Circuit decision. However, the Ninth Circuit Court also placed the burden of nonassimilation on the Japanese in Hawai'i, noting, "The Japanese do not readily assimilate with other races, and especially the white race."[78]

The Court's opinion promulgated the friction between constitutional protection of US citizens of foreign parentage and the nativist hysteria of the 1920s. The primary purpose of the innovative 1924 quotas was to maintain tight restrictions on Chinese and Japanese immigration without attracting international charges of discrimination.[79] Legal defeat on the language school question aside, the cosmopolitan rhetoric of haole administrators and teachers, who had seemingly worked so hard to sell the islands' schools as a unique and collective experiment in multiracialism and equal citizenship, now certainly steered a set of educational policies much more in line with prevailing currents of cultural conformity and immigration restriction in California and elsewhere on the mainland. Yet only five years after the court's ruling, colonial officials on the mainland shifted course and reverted back to the harmonious language of cosmopolitanism so prevalent during Woodwell's tenure. In 1932 the US Department of the Interior seized on a University of Hawai'i report to claim that "the sons and daughters of these oriental cane-field workers . . . acquire education with a facility that lags little, if any, behind children of the white races." The report represented a sea change under way in social scientific thinking about heredity, environment, and intelligence that would have significant impacts on the debates about schooling for Mexican Americans and Puerto Ricans during the 1930s (see chapter 6). Interior officials touted the positive effects of territorial schools on "the children of contract laborers, who had remained . . . suppressed . . . through the centuries in their native lands," but who now "bloom out in the public schools of Hawaii . . . and meet the psychological tests as well as do the blonde sons of Nordics." But the "problem," according to the report's authors, was that "first-generation young people born in Hawaii are likely to want to lay aside the cane knife and take up the fountain pen."[80]

Officials had identified not a specifically Hawaiian problem, but one widespread in the United States and its colonies: How best to educate for citizenship those citizens deemed most suited for menial labor? The attempt to eliminate language schools and to push a curriculum of manual training meant to channel the bulk of Hawai'i's nonwhite youth into low-wage, unskilled agricultural and industrial jobs paralleled and indeed informed similar efforts in the US South. African Americans in Atlanta, the subjects of the next chapter, sought equal and adequate public support for black schools, curricular autonomy, and economic opportunities far beyond those envisioned by the city's and region's Jim Crow establishment. In ways similar to Nisei, Chinese, and Hawaiian children and their families, black Atlantans rejected the school board's attempts to open paths to good citizenship that would return them to the plantation fields that their parents and grandparents had worked in bondage.

4

Black Atlanta's Education through Labor

The mill and the forge and coarse loom of the plantation must now give way to the factory and the furnace and such towns must grow as meet the traveler's eye in Connecticut and Pennsylvania. Hence such cities as Atlanta, Columbia, Chattanooga, Knoxville, and Birmingham have sprung into strength, feeling the thrill of new life that followed upon the trying years of first adjustment to the new conditions.[1]

ALBERT PERRY BRIGHAM, *Geographic Influences in American History,* 1903

This nation with its democratic form of government with its allegiance, at least in theory, to liberty and justice for all people, has a peculiarly high mission to fulfill for the world.... And Atlanta University has a peculiar mission within the nation, training the aspiring youth of the Negro race for lives of service; and encouraging sympathetic relations between the people of both races.[2]

ATLANTA UNIVERSITY BULLETIN, *"Inter-racial Co-operation for Human Betterment,"* 1915

IN 1872, EX-SLAVE AND FORMER fourth ward city council representative William Finch called a meeting of African American parents to petition the Atlanta Board of Education for adequate facilities. Finch, who lost his council reelection bid to a white candidate the year before, labored tirelessly to improve the quality of public education, particularly for those students underserved by the city's schools. The petition, brought first before the city council, included among other improvements the demand for a public high school for African Americans. Without justification, the council refused to grant any concessions to the city's black community, concentrated primarily in the third and fourth wards. Finch then took the petition to the school board, which buried the request under a pile of more pressing matters involving repairs and supplies for white schools. The board defended its position on the false premise that Northern aid societies like the American Missionary

Association, which established Atlanta University in 1867, and the Freedmen's Bureau already proved capable of funding black education and did so to the neglect of Southern white children. Black Atlantans would not have access to public secondary education until 1924 and only then after a protracted struggle spearheaded by local black parents, Atlanta University, and the NAACP.[3]

Attempts by Finch, parents, and community organizers in Atlanta to secure or at least allow for the social mobility of their children through public education became embedded in a groundswell of active political and civic engagement on the part of freedmen and women throughout the postwar urban South. In the decades following emancipation, black Southerners created and maintained social and civic institutions to achieve economic gains and access to social and political capital. African Americans in Atlanta and elsewhere did so in the face of staunch white resistance and the retreat of Radical Reconstruction, which officially ended in Georgia in 1871. Despite slavery's demise, black Atlantans, many of whom had migrated to the city from the rural South after 1865, encountered, navigated, and challenged both new and reconstituted forms of racial apartheid and economic repression. Their experiences represent one facet of the broader historical arch of the relationship between public schools and questions of citizenship that informed the lives and decisions of native-born and immigrant nonwhites throughout the United States and its territories. Black Atlantans resisted white efforts to render them colonial subjects within the domestic national space.[4]

Perhaps more than any other New South city, Atlanta's economic, industrial, and population growth was astounding, owing in no small part to its near complete destruction during Union General William T. Sherman's 1864 campaign. During the 1880s, the population climbed from 37,409 to 65,533 by 1890 and then to 89,000 by 1900. It boasted over 200,000 residents by 1920 and became a truly modern city at the center of a regional economy, complete with skyscrapers, streetcars, luxury hotels, restaurants, and a thriving entertainment industry. Transplant industrialists and capitalists that included German-born Jacob Elsas of Atlanta Fulton Bag and Cotton Mill, Tennessee-born cotton broker Samuel Inman, and the infamous Northern Republican Hannibal Kimball whose luxurious Kimball House hotel was financed in large sum by city bonds, became by 1880 the faces, financiers, and primary beneficiaries of Atlanta's explosive commercial growth.[5] The scale and rapidity of urban, social, and economic change that followed over the next four decades involved the hopes, aspirations, struggles, and contestations of Atlanta's

African Americans, who found themselves working, raising families, and building communities amidst a swell of industrial development and white working-class migration from north Georgia and other parts of the Southern Piedmont.[6] segregation of the city of Atlanta.

In 1881, the city played host to the International Cotton Exposition, the first in a series of Southern fairs designed to elevate the region's national profile and highlight its agricultural, industrial, and investment potential.[7] The exposition signaled not only the arrival of Atlanta as the preeminent New South city, it also touted the grandeur of Western science and technology and offered its white patrons a chance at sectional reconciliation to the exclusion of African Americans. Pennsylvania governor Henry Hoyt addressed attendees in civilizational terms: "When I reflect on my citizenship in this great country, I feel that no exposition is tall enough nor broad enough to hold us . . . . It is your business and mine, to add to the welfare of our common country, and to build up American civilization." Kentucky governor Luke Blackburn called for North and South to rebuild "our temple" without "that Ethiopian pillar [of slavery]" and Mississippian H. F. Simroll maintained "the mission of the slaves was accomplished" after having "gone into the swamps of the South and developed her." For leading men at the exposition, slavery in Southern cotton fields had served its purpose, but now it was time for new forms of regional, industrial development. On this national platform, the speakers put forth no comment on the place of African Americans in the New South economy, an issue that they would be unable to ignore when Atlanta hosted a second exposition in 1895.[8]

The oratorical skill and professional fastidiousness of *Atlanta Constitution* managing editor Henry Grady thrust him to the fore of Southern efforts to entice Northern investment for industrial projects. Despite Grady's claims before Northern audiences that the New South order afforded economic opportunities to African Americans, deep-seated beliefs in white supremacy held by many white Atlantans, including Grady, usually prohibited political participation, social integration, and economic mobility.[9] An 1881 exposé in Grady's *Constitution* described in great detail for the paper's assumed white readership "the odor of frying fish—an almost sure sign of a negro lunch house," the "filth and general repulsiveness" of the Beaver Slide neighborhood on Ivy Street, and "Negros of the very worst type" congregating at the Ant Hole on the corner of Ivy and Decatur, where "doubtless many crimes had their conception." Such descriptions fit the common assumptions many whites held about black Atlantans, particularly given that, according to the

Constitution, "the largest proportion of negroes are never really known to us."[10] Though Grady's New South order was visionary and forward-looking, it also required, in the words of Southern historian C. Vann Woodward, "rigid subordination of class conflict . . . to the maintenance of a status quo of a business man's regime identified with white supremacy; and the exclusion of the Negro from political life."[11] But as quickly as white Atlanta sought to enshrine white supremacy through white-only primaries, racial violence, and separate and inferior schools, black Atlanta employed myriad forms of resistance.

Like many of the city's whites in the 1880s, blacks had few antebellum roots in Atlanta. On the eve of the Civil War, the city was home to a slave population of 1,914, or 20 percent of the total population. There were virtually no free blacks in 1860. By 1870, the city's black population had climbed to 10,000, and over 70 percent reported to have migrated from rural Georgia. Almost all were working-class with little property or wealth of which to speak. Migrants from the surrounding states of Tennessee, South Carolina, and Alabama rounded out most of the rest of Atlanta's black communities.[12] Despite Southern roots and native-born status, white supremacy marked freedmen and women as alien and marginal—outside the mainstream of local, regional, and national society and citizenship. In direct resistance to an assigned status as "foreigners within" for African Americans, Native [*they weren't considered citizens*] Americans, and native-born descendants of nonwhite immigrants throughout the United States, Atlanta's black community sought strategies to undermine predetermined notions of belonging and citizenship.[13]

To hear white civic leaders speak about their black fellow citizens, one would assume African American schools had fared quite well and enjoyed the full support of white Atlanta. Twenty years after Finch's petition, Atlanta's superintendent of schools William F. Slaton reported to the city council that black Atlantans had been much appreciative of the public educational opportunities for their children: "The city has given the Negroes substantial aid and assistance in the education of their children, and the thinking men and women of the race appreciate the favor. We have reason to hope that the bread now being cast upon the waters will be gathered up many days hence."[14] The all-white school board and city council collectively asserted, first, that black education was not required of them by law but instead represented a sort of civic charity. According to Slaton, Negro schools were above and beyond the call of duty and outside the purview of the rights of citizens. To city officials, blacks were satisfied with the schools generously provided for them. Second, the school board and other prominent school reformers in Atlanta regarded black schooling as an investment in the future economic growth and social stability of the city. Faced with overwhelming illiteracy rates among black Southerners (and many whites too), New South reformers hoped to promote order, rule of law, morality, and above all industriousness in Atlanta's thriving postbellum economy. Universal education, Slaton purported, was the key to Atlanta's economic prosperity. The city's white professionals and elites hoped that a new kind of subordinate black working class, minimally educated, would labor at the lowest wages and, when necessary, thwart white efforts to organize. In this vein, New South school reformers challenged a long-held Southern planter ideology that literate citizens made poor workers.[15]

But these same white urban elite sought ways to reconstitute the rigid racial hierarchies crafted and codified under slavery, and they grafted them onto a host of social, political, and economic institutions as national reconciliation proceeded along the color line. In one sense, an emphasis on universal education was progressive—a condemnation of an older era in which many adolescents in America learned only basic literacy and arithmetic skills, while slave codes and local laws prohibited enslaved blacks from acquiring any such knowledge. Though the Civil War and Reconstruction eradicated slavery and the legal institutions that undergirded it, academic education eluded many. While most proponents of New South development opposed higher education for African Americans, they also believed that an educated working class could serve the needs of the region's industrialists, investors, planters, and middle-class professionals. In an effort to garner support and funding from the state legislature for public education, Georgia superintendent of education R. L. Glenn argued that public schools could produce a "peaceful, thrifty, and law-abiding" working class capable of turning the state's natural resources into material prosperity. To do so, it required both black subordination and uplift—colonial processes at odds despite Glenn's supposition that they were mutually sustaining.[16]

The Atlanta school board's confidence in their generosity to African Americans was nothing novel in the 1890s. In an 1882 annual report to the Atlanta mayor's office and city council, board president Joseph E. Brown and superintendent Slaton patted themselves on the back for a job well done. Brown described the new Houston Street School, completed in 1881, as "large and convenient," and Slaton heralded the addition of the "well lighted and well ventilated" Negro grammar school, the third of its kind in the city. More importantly though, the opening of the school represented a step forward, in the eyes of white school board members, in the segregation of Atlanta's black population. "This building, suited in every respect for teaching purposes, is the pride of our colored people and an honor to the city. It is officered entirely by colored teachers, who have demonstrated the fact that they understand their own race, and can discipline and teach to the satisfaction of their patrons." Slaton proclaimed that the board had "found the key to the problem of the education of our colored population." But the new schoolhouse did little to solve some of the most pressing needs of African American teachers, parents, and children, who lacked basic supplies and were forced to hold double sessions because of overcrowding. As historian Louis Harlan has described, "the Negro schools occupied the zone between, being kept deliberately poor but not destroyed."[17]

The development of public schools in Atlanta reflected the mutually reinforced polarizations of race and class that informed political battles over municipal services for the benefit of all citizens. Though the establishment of grammar schools met little resistance from the city's elites, wealthy Atlantans expressed ardent opposition to tax-supported high schools they regarded as unnecessary institutions. Since the city's establishment as Terminus in the 1830s—named for the zero milepost of the Western and Atlantic Railroad— the upper class employed private tutors or sent their children to one of the nineteen private academies in the city. As W. E. B. Du Bois would later comment: "education was long regarded as a matter of the private initiative of the rich" in the South.[18] In 1853, the Holland Free School, a public institution, opened for the children of whites who could not afford private school or tutor fees. But state codes against black education prevented free children of color, though small in number, from attending Atlanta's only antebellum public school.[19]

Ex-slaves took the first initiatives at universal public education in the South immediately following the Civil War. "The educational and moral condition of the people will not be forgotten," Freedmen's Bureau general superintendent of schools J. W. Alford remarked in May 1865. Alford advocated not a usurpation of Northern religious and philanthropic efforts to educate black children, but rather the systematization and facilitation of established organizations under the auspices of local governments. These governments were not presided over by white Southerners, but rather by freedmen and white Northerners who succeeded in authorizing public schools for all children in most occupied states.[20] In 1865, leaders of African

American communities throughout the state formed the Georgia Education Association to organize, regulate, and fund black schools. Much to the bewilderment of white philanthropists, many black communities in Georgia and throughout the occupied South preferred to contribute what little money they could to these schools rather than take advantage of white-dominated "free schools" on offer from Northern organizations. In this way, ex-slaves challenged commonly held white assumptions about their apathy toward and incapacity for education and demonstrated their collective existence as a "politically self-conscious social class" that saw literacy as both liberating and necessary for successful participation as citizens in a democratic society.[21]

Following a brief few years immediately after the Civil War during which black Southerners opened and maintained their own schools with the assistance of the Freedmen's Bureau, newly created white school boards in the urban South and their statewide counterparts increasingly assumed the task of regulating, managing, and funding black education as Radical Reconstruction gave way to national reconciliation along the color line. Atlanta's public schools became intrinsically intertwined with Jim Crow segregation, race riots, and lynching—the intersections of law and violence that created a new political landscape but with plenty borrowed from slavery. On one hand, black formal schooling was something new, as most Southern slave codes prohibited the education of slaves. On the other, the paternalism of the antebellum South was "neatly placed within the framework of emancipation." By the 1870s, black Atlantans had little hope of maintaining their own public schools as was possible in the late 1860s and were now forced to navigate a politics of white supremacy that controlled public funding for education.[22] By the 1890s, most Southern states used new or amended constitutions to legalize the subordination and segregation of black Southerners, and for its part, the US Supreme Court enshrined segregation into national law in 1896. Whites "indomitably maintained," in the words of Ulrich B. Phillips, "that [the South] shall be and remain a white man's country."[23]

The Sixth Annual Negro Conference met at Atlanta University in 1901 to outline and address the grave disparities between white and black schools in the postemancipation South. In his report on Negro common schools, Du Bois described black schools in the South as "woefully inadequate." Despite the demands of ex-slaves for basic public education, illiteracy rates remained high. He reported that just under 80 percent of the nation's black population was illiterate in 1870, with Georgia topping the list at 92 percent. Du Bois of course attributed this culture of illiteracy not to black inferiority—as did many of his white counterparts—but to the abundance of antebellum laws prohibiting black education in the South. In Georgia, a series of legal codes enacted in 1770, 1829, and 1833 criminalized black education or the employment of both free and enslaved persons in jobs that might require literacy. Other states maintained similar prohibitions on formal and informal education, and violators risked fines and jail. After emancipation, Southern blacks confronted vestiges of a planters' ideology that regarded state-supported education, particularly for blacks, as a threat to amicable economic and social arrangements. For former slaveholders and transplant industrialists and investors, economic prosperity could return in the wake of the Civil War if they re-galvanized the structures of racial subordination and deference. The New South order both undermined and strengthened black education.[24]

In his declaration that the "problem of the twentieth century is the problem of the color line," Du Bois articulated not a uniquely Southern experience but a national and even global struggle for racial equality. Segregated schools in the South were not an exception to the history of formal education in the United States—easy to dismiss as the vestiges of a backward region and a bygone era of forced labor. Rather, Atlanta's segregated schools constitute a crucial aspect of US domestic and imperial culture at the turn of the century. Superintendent Slaton's assurance that black Atlantans were satisfied with *their* educational facilities preceded the national legalization of Jim Crow in *Plessy v. Ferguson*. As Gary Okihiro has argued, "the schools were powerful instruments in both the shackling and liberating of students' minds, from one point of view, in the historical transition from the total institution of slavery to the era of segregation." Jim Crow was not a Southern phenomenon. It was national policy backed by the authority of the US Supreme Court.[25]

Du Bois was among the first to connect Southern black schools to the broader racial ideologies that at once contradicted and defined American democracy and citizenship. He and the Negro Common School Committee charged the nation with "deliberately rearing millions of our citizens in ignorance and at the same time limiting the rights of citizenship by educational qualifications." While Du Bois and his colleagues certainly recognized that the scale of black illiteracy and inadequate schools in the South overshadowed similar national trends, they nevertheless implicated public schools throughout the entire country in denying to African Americans the right to quality tax-supported education. Du Bois saw segregated education in the South as a localized function of a much more totalizing "new religion of whiteness" that both justified imperialism and protected the borders and

[margin note: 13th Amend, 3/5 of a person = virtually nothing]

privileges of "white men's countries" from people of color.[26] His formulation revealed how deeply the forces of empire penetrated Southern social and civic institutions. In the New South, manual training and industrial education became the hallmarks of white designs on black intellect and advancement— a modern, organized pedagogy that bound together race and class in ways that served the interests of Southern industrialists and Northern investors. It would be implemented not only in work camps and on chain gangs but also in the region's African American normal schools.[27]

INDUSTRIAL EDUCATION AND
BLACK NORMAL SCHOOLS

another way of slavery : of the mind.

Rather than dismantle the institutional gains of postbellum black schooling, many white Southerners embraced a unique education for African Americans that would channel them into low-wage agricultural and industrial jobs. In 1868, the Hampton Normal and Agricultural Institute, founded in Hampton, Virginia, by Samuel Chapman Armstrong, became the first notable means to this end. The son of New England missionaries, Armstrong came of age in Hawai'i where his father's colleague David Lyman ran Hilo Boarding School, and Richard Armstrong became head of the kingdom's Department of Public Instruction. *imperialistic takeover?* The younger Armstrong attended college in New England, and during the Civil War commanded a regiment of African American troops for the Union Army. Armstrong recounted later that his experiences both at Hilo and with the black regiment under his command served as inspirations for Hampton.

Despite its title, Hampton was primarily a training institute for African American common school teachers. Only four students identified themselves as agriculture majors in 1900. According to education historian James Anderson, present misperceptions of Hampton as an industrial school stem from Armstrong's emphasis on manual labor, Christian morality, and "self-help" as the primary means of teacher training. Armstrong's pioneering education model represented and served not the academic or political aspirations of ex-slaves, but rather the continuity of antebellum socioeconomic relationships predicated on subservient black labor. His steadfast belief in the immorality of nonwhite races necessitated their training as manual laborers and domestic workers and their exclusion from political life. Hampton coached aspiring black teachers to espouse an ethic of hard work or the "dignity of labor" throughout the South's black common schools, and school operated on an ideology of uplift through accommodation. Widely acclaimed by both white Southerners and Northern philanthropists as the "Hampton Idea," Armstrong's vision of "Black Reconstruction" sought the marriage of Northern investment and cheap Southern labor through the onus of disenfranchisement, segregation, and economic subservience. Hampton's teacher training program in theory presented white planters, industrialists, and investors the continuity of a deferential, hard-working black laboring class capable of fueling both Southern agriculture and emerging manufacturing sectors in Nashville, Birmingham, and Atlanta.[28]

Hampton's most famous graduate, Booker T. Washington, internalized the Hampton message and founded Tuskegee Normal Institute in Alabama [now Tuskegee University (HBCU)] in 1881. By the time of President Theodore Roosevelt's visit in 1905, Tuskegee enrolled 1,500 students, mostly poor, rural, Southern African Americans. Tuskegee's program mirrored that of Hampton, and each year it sent out small armies of teachers to work in the South's Negro common schools. Washington's infamous "compromise" address at the 1895 Cotton States and International Exposition in Atlanta came to embody conservative black acceptance of "separate but equal" enshrined into national law the next year and vigorously challenged by Du Bois and other intellectuals at Atlanta University. In his address, Washington argued, as he had a year earlier in front of the US House of Representatives appropriations committee that would decide whether or not to provide funding to the exposition's white boosters, that black franchise had been a mistake and that obtaining skills and cultivating habits of work like those taught to Tuskegee's future common school teachers was a more appropriate social and economic plan for the New South and for the United States. Even as Washington discredited the negative stereotypes of African Americans harbored by many white Southerners, he also approved the vision of the New South order held by the city's and state's white elite.[29]

By the turn of the twentieth century the Georgia State Board of Education supported Hampton and Tuskegee methods as progressive political models to ensure a continuous and dependable supply of both unskilled and semiskilled laborers. Fort Valley Industrial School, located approximately 100 miles south of Atlanta and touted by many white Southern progressives as an essential component of racialized economic progress, represented Armstrong's vision for Negro education. Fort Valley and elementary black education ensured a mutually beneficial Southern progress that, to many whites, reflected more

FIGURE 10. Experiment Field, Fort Valley [High and Industrial] School, 1910. Southern Education Foundation Records. Courtesy Atlanta University Center, Robert W. Woodruff Library.

amicable race relations than those of the North. "There is just as much responsibility in the North for the colored man's position as there is in the South," declared Colonel A. K. McClure at a Philadelphia meeting held to garner Northern support for Fort Valley. In seeming complete ignorance of the wave of lynchings that swept the South and the nation from 1900 to 1903 (296 in total), McClure claimed that Southern white familiarity with black Southerners prevented the kind of "mob violence [and] adverse sentiment" prevalent among the Northern white working class.[30]

McClure suggested that the solution to "the menace of negro ignorance" required not only black industrial education in the South but also a more even demographic distribution of black labor across the nation. "When ... the whites of the North are educated up to the point of industrial toleration for the Negro, we will witness ... no undue crowding of sections of the South by the same race. Once the prejudice complained of is dispelled, we shall hear infinitely less about the Negro as a 'problem.'" By implicating national racism in the struggles for Southern economic and educational progress, McClure displaced the burden of racial oppression in order to redeem the white South, and he joined the intentions of both Northern and Southern whites to school the nation's black population for subordinate roles in agriculture and industry. In order to sell this black–white coalition to Northern investors, McClure and the organizers of the Fort Valley school meeting invited Principal J. H.

Torbert to speak, in large part because "he understands the value of an industrial training to his race." At the fundraiser, Torbert exclaimed that "we have got to lift up these people or they will drag the white man down."[31]

Fort Valley was a unique institution, but Georgia's officials embraced manual training as a principal feature for all state-supported schools. Superintendent Glenn's vision of economic progress through public education required not only the control and subordination of future black laborers but also a strong work ethic among working-class whites as well. Glenn sought industrial and agricultural training and, perhaps more importantly, a stronger connection between education and work. "The thought that has been steadily instilled into the minds of our children has been that if they can get an education they can escape hard work," lamented Glenn. In order to combat an increase in discontent among young workers with basic education, Glenn proposed that Georgia's teachers instruct children in a moral work ethic that emphasized character building through manual labor. Glenn's ideal public school graduates would leave with basic reading, writing, and arithmetic skills and an appreciation for work: "The moral character of a man is fixed more by what he can do with his hands, than by what his eye can read out of books .... It is not safe to turn a boy loose upon the world until his moral character as well as his mental habits have been fixed by the training for some useful industry that comes with his hands." If schools instructed working-class whites to be content with their social and economic positions, Georgia's agricultural and industrial leaders could assume that public schools would increase the efficiency and productivity of the workforce and thereby the wealth of the state's elite and professional classes.[32]

Public schooling and manual training for Georgia's black population, however, proved even more prudent for prosperity as it offered the state's elites the opportunity to reinstitute racial hierarchies they believed had worked so well during slavery. Glenn and the state school board drew new hierarchical distinctions between two types of Negroes in Georgia—those raised during slavery and those born since emancipation. According to Glenn, postemancipation education lacked training in deference to authority, thrift, and obedience to the law: "The Negro who was emancipated in 1865 was not wholly uneducated. Association with his white masters and training at hard labor during the early years of his life, gave him a mental discipline and formed habits of industry and thrift .... [T]his class of Negroes is peaceable, law-abiding, respected, and self-respecting."[33] In contrast, Glenn regarded black Georgians born since emancipation, "most of

[whom] have attended public schools," as "lacking in the education they have received." In particular, "it appears to have unfitted them for the only kind of employment open to them here in the South," Glenn concluded. "If the Negro could have had the right kind of manual training, and the right kind of moral training, along with the book learning he has received, my judgment is that the experiment would have resulted much more satisfactorily to all concerned."[34] Glenn articulated a common inclination of whites to lament the transition from the loyal, obedient "darkie" to the supposedly presumptuous "New Negro" whose newfound citizenship and education spawned insolence and an unwillingness to live and work within prescribed racial boundaries.[35]

Other white Georgians, including *Atlanta Constitution* chief editor Clark Howell, believed that black education, broadly conceived, created an imbalance of labor on Georgia's farms and portended the eventual disenfranchisement of white Georgians. Howell warned that new educational voting requirements designed to eliminate black voters would actually have the reverse effect. Many black Georgians, particularly those who resided in towns and cities such as Augusta, Savannah, or Atlanta, sent their children to public school in overwhelming numbers. Estimates from Atlanta suggest that as many as 3,000 black children were denied seats in the grammar schools because buildings had exceeded capacity. Howell also commiserated that many young rural blacks were also vacating menial jobs on Georgia's farms in order to attend school. This dearth of black labor forced young white men to assume agricultural duties and thus "forfeit their educational opportunities." The demise of "practical disenfranchisement" (voter intimidation through threat of violence), he feared, would render "the black vote a controlling force in Georgia as in Reconstruction days." An anxious Howell argued that the education and enfranchisement of blacks, whom he regarded as foreigners, threatened to bring about the demise of the white republic: "While the Negro becomes a full-fledged CITIZEN, the white man, native to the soil and intelligent though unlettered, remains to all intents and purposes an ALIEN."[36]

Howell and others unconsciously saw black public education as a process of reverse colonialism whereby foreign blacks descended upon the New South to subordinate and colonize ordinary whites. Their solution to this perceived crisis was to channel black students into industrial schools. For example, H. L. Keith, supervisor of black vocational schools in Nashville, argued that "every lover of the white race ... should be eager to see the Negro race advanced morally and in the lines of education of the race for its work."

Keith, Howell, Glenn, and others believed that the white South stood to inherit an economic windfall if blacks received training in domestic, industrial, and agricultural service. "The South can be greatly benefited materially . . . by the proper training of the Negro race. The women are the cooks, the nurses, and housemaids of nearly every southern home able to have servants; the Negro men are employed in every occupation in the South," remarked Keith. If black education continued to stress book learning rather than occupational training, the white South would witness not only a shortage of reliable black labor, but also the disenfranchisement of many upwardly mobile whites, forced to occupy jobs vacated by educated African Americans.[37]

Despite the pervasive rhetoric of white Georgia educators, Atlanta's African Americans continued to repel efforts to pigeonhole them into lives of menial labor and economic stasis and reversed the charges of ignorance leveled by white supremacists. As Will Winton Alexander of the Commission on Interracial Cooperation remarked: "an ignorant native white population would be a greater menace to America than an educated Negro population."[38] In Georgia, the most vocal and persistent critique and resistance to the Hampton-Tuskegee model emanated from Atlanta's premier institution for black higher education. Professors and students at Atlanta University, which supplied the bulk of teachers for Atlanta's Negro schools by the mid-1880s, resisted calls by prominent city and state figures to institute manual training and scale back academic courses. In doing so, they led a growing movement among urban Southern blacks that challenged the path to citizenship prescribed for them and instead chose a path that held the promise of political self-awareness, economic vitality, and social mobility.[39]

HIGHER LEARNING AT ATLANTA UNIVERSITY

Both black and white faculty at Atlanta University became deeply critical of Washington and Tuskegee by the 1890s, in part because Washington allowed would-be Northern benefactors to assume that most donations to Tuskegee would support industrial training. His fundraising success meant fewer dollars for other prominent Southern black colleges.[40] Though Atlanta University had its own agricultural and industrial training divisions and advertised itself as such, school officials vocalized their primary mission of providing rigorous academic and teacher training. Unlike Hampton and to a lesser degree Tuskegee, Atlanta University's agricultural and trade divisions

FIGURE 11. Atlanta University Faculty, 1905–6. Du Bois stands back row, second from right. President Bumstead sits third row center-right. Atlanta University Photograph Collection. Courtesy Atlanta University Center, Robert W. Woodruff Library.

offered students practical career skills to supplement its robust academic program rather than compel them to accept social and economic subordination. For example, university officials heralded the work of 1880 graduate Robert L. Smith, who later founded the Farmers' Improvement Society of Texas, as operating "outside of the ordinary lines of effort contemplated by industrial education." In an undated leaflet, likely produced during or after Du Bois's tenure at Atlanta University, university president Horace Bumstead, a white Congregationalist minister and former colored regiment commander like Armstrong, exclaimed: "it seems time to enter a respectful but earnest protest against the doctrine so ardently inculcated by some writers and speakers that industrial education is all that the Negro needs." While Bumstead made clear his intentions not to "depreciate the value of industrial training, which Atlanta University has itself conducted and honored from its earliest years ... furnishing teachers for some of the most important Negro schools in the South," he also channeled Professor Du Bois, who taught at Atlanta University from 1897 to 1910: "it is not enough to make men carpenters— we must also make carpenters men."[41]

Bumstead's evolution of thought on industrial education was likely influenced deeply by African American faculty and students. In 1887, the first year of his tenure as president of Atlanta University, Bumstead paired industrial and academic as twinned means to "secure a well rounded education of head and hand together." He touted the university's industrial training in "carpentry, blacksmithing, and farming" and domestic training in "cooking, sewing, dressmaking, and nursing," but cautioned against those who saw these endeavors as satisfying purely economic motives. "The union of intellectual and industrial education and the systematic thoroughness with which each is carried out, constituted marked features of the work of Atlanta University," he remarked. His solution was to strip industrial training of its profit motive, especially the contracting of student labor to private interests and the economic reliance of the institution on student workers: "the object is education, rather than production, to make students profitable in school, they must be confined to a narrow range of work."[42]

But Bumstead also recognized the utility of industrial education for fundraising. White Northerners and Southerners alike generally concluded that manual training for African Americans constituted a practical path to citizenship. In his 1894 presidential report, Bumstead conceded: "the reduction or suspension of our industrial work would weaken the force of our appeal for funds." Local Secretary Frances Clemmer too appealed to potential benefactors that "Atlanta University has always claimed that there should be no conflict between industrial and the higher education." Clemmer boasted that AU graduates were, by 1905, employed in some twenty industrial institutions. Faced with the realities of economic apartheid and white assumptions about African Americans' incapacity for higher learning, the administration and faculty of Atlanta University continued to jeopardize the institution's financial solvency in order to create capable teachers and informed citizens instead of merely deferential laborers.[43]

Despite the realities of charitable funding allocations for black education, Bumstead tempered his recognition of the necessarily evils of industrial education with an active appeal to higher learning. In their sanctioned letters to potential scholarship donors, Atlanta University students claimed the mantle of professionalization, including Augustus Granville Dill of Portsmouth, Ohio, who announced the "desire to thoroughly fit myself for the profession of teaching by making specialty of mathematics and sciences." Dill reported to donors his intentions to attend Harvard after graduation. Bumstead too wrote to a "dear friend" and likely donor in 1900 that "the good effect of this teaching" like the kind described by Dill "is evident in the Negro communities where Atlanta University graduates have gone, and every known result of the work of this institution shows that it is worthy of the support and co-operation of all Christians who are interested in progress." Three years later, Bumstead further subordinated industrial training as part of the institution's funding appeal: "while giving due attention to industrial training, [Atlanta University] has been especially successful in giving the higher education to the more promising class of Negroes, fitting them, in its normal and college courses, to become teachers and leaders of their race." Bumstead estimated that of living graduates, 63 percent were engaged in "educational and professional work," while "26% more are wives and mothers in a class of homes new among the Negroes."[44]

Atlanta University's normal school sent its graduates into the Negro schools of Atlanta and other Georgia towns and cities. By 1889, 56 of the normal school's 133 graduates since 1873 had worked as teachers in Atlanta, and another 61 of those graduates taught in Negro schools elsewhere in Georgia. AU estimated that those "connected with the Institution" taught over ten thousand black Georgians. The *Boston Herald* reported in 1903 that in Atlanta's largest black public school, which it estimated to serve a thousand pupils, the principal and all but four of the thirteen teachers were Atlanta University graduates, and university officials boasted a library circulation program throughout the city's Negro communities that "at present enjoy no library facilities whatsoever." Unlike Hampton and Tuskegee, the normal school's curriculum more or less mirrored the university's college preparatory program. In 1898, Unitarian minister and former chief editor of the *National Journal of Education* Amory Dwight Mayo reported that of 81 Atlanta University graduates surveyed, only 12 did not work in "learned professions," which included teaching. During the two-year program, students took courses in composition, literature, algebra, bookkeeping, geometry, Latin, geography, history, drawing, music, composition, moral philosophy, botany, physics, astronomy, geology, civil government, and pedagogy. Bumstead noted that not only did students learn "certain branches of knowledge" but also that they did so with the competency to teach them at the high school level. Metal- and wood-working for boys and dressmaking, cooking, and sewing for girls constituted a small component of the university's teacher-training program, and the teachers that then taught in Atlanta's public schools left the normal program with a strong sense of the value of academic learning—not the kind of training that Glenn, Howell, and Armstrong had in mind for African American teachers.[45]

FIGURE 12. Normal School Class of 1893. Atlanta University Photograph Collection—
Groups and Organizations. Courtesy Atlanta University Center, Robert W. Woodruff
Library.

By the late 1880s, Atlanta University's normal school also drew the ire of
white supremacists because it defied Jim Crow norms. In a speech before the
state legislature in July 1889, University of Georgia chancellor William
Ellison Boggs, who regarded black higher education as a threat to the character of a Southern agrarian life rooted in black subservience, described AU's
normal training as "ruinous" to the "destiny of a country" shaped by rural
men and women.[46] AU also found itself at odds with the Georgia Board of
Education, the state house of representatives, and the African Methodist
Episcopal Church, which opened Morris Brown College in Atlanta in 1885.
Since its founding, Atlanta University welcomed white students in all of its
departments, including its grammar (first through fifth grade) and primary
(sixth through eighth grade) departments, though these were phased out by
1899. While most white children who attended Atlanta University were
either the children of professors or "white people of the North as should
desire to patronize the institution," in November 1889, the state legislature
voted overwhelmingly to revoke an $8,000 annual appropriation for Atlanta
University and deliver the funding to Morris Brown College instead, where
its president upheld segregation: "It is inconsistent for the two races to be
educated together. If amalgamation sets in . . . there will not, there cannot,
be peace." The *Atlanta Journal* reported that Bumstead "insisted on the

co-education of the races," and the *Macon Telegraph* lambasted the "notorious connection" between Atlanta University and integrated schooling. Bumstead lobbied the legislature to allow the children of white professors and white Northerners to attend Atlanta University, and agreed not to extend coeducation beyond those exemptions. But the bill passed 107 to 10.[47]

ATLANTA'S NEGRO SCHOOLS

Even if Glenn and Howell's vision of agricultural and industrial growth in the South rested on a moral and obedient black workforce, Atlanta's public schools were not preparing its black population for such a future. The reasons were twofold. First, Atlanta University's normal school graduates, who comprised the majority of Negro school teachers in the city, carried into classrooms a politics of resistance to manual training and Jim Crow. Second, the board of education insisted on providing underfunded, undersized, and understaffed schoolhouses for black students. As Philip Racine has noted, "from the first day of classes in 1872, education for black Atlantans was inferior in every respect to that for whites." When the city council authorized public education at the request of taxpayers, it allotted funding for four white grammar schools, one white boys' high school, one white girls' high school, and two Negro grammar schools. Although school-aged black children outnumbered white counterparts and despite the insistence of Councilman Finch, the school board denied funding for a black high school. Black Atlantans paid tuition at Atlanta University if they wanted their children to receive secondary education. Such disparities found critics not only in black Atlanta but from white school reformers and Southern industrialists as well, although their goals for Negro education varied considerably.[48]

For much of the late nineteenth century, the Atlanta school board insisted that Negro grammar schools were on par and in some cases even superior to the city's white schools. Superintendent Slaton eschewed the charges leveled by Finch and later by Du Bois that public schools continuously underserved black children. Ever ready to sound more progressive in speech than to act in matters of policy, Slaton argued that black education was essential not only to economic progress but also to the integrity of American democracy: "Atlanta has been liberal to her colored population. These Negroes have the same rights before the law as you have, and if they are to have a voice and vote in making the laws of the land, they must be educated, or republican government will be endangered."[49] In 1893, Slaton reasoned that despite the generosity of the school board toward Negro parents and children, an innate black inferiority prevented Atlanta's African American community from ever fully understanding or appreciating the privileges and rights of republicanism: "While we should not demand or expect the same skill in teaching ability, nor the same capacity to learn as is found in the white race . . . their work is in most cases satisfactory." Slaton also noted that while the Atlanta University graduates that comprised nearly 75 percent of the teaching force in Atlanta's Negro schools were "of course . . . not perfect nor up to our standard, still they are the best we have been able to obtain from any sources." The superintendent then touted the school board's financial and material generosity towards the city's African Americans as unparalleled in the New South.[50]

In December 1895, five months before the United States Supreme Court sanctioned national racial segregation in the 1896 landmark case of *Plessy v. Ferguson,* Slaton expounded upon the apparent virtues of "separate but equal." The key to the advancement of black Atlantans, argued Slaton, was the continued employment of black teachers in black schools he considered equal to white schools: "Taught in separate houses, which in all cases are as good as those of the whites, with the same grading, the same class supplies, the same course of study, the Negro has no cause of complaint in this city on account of want of educational facilities." But as tax records reveal, Slaton's definition of equal often strayed far from reality. Atlanta's status as an independent school district allowed it to levy property and business taxes in order to provide public schools that, for whites, were often vastly superior to those located in rural Georgia. In 1908, for example, the city spent all of the $330,000 in local school taxes on white schools and provided Negro schools with only their pro rata share of the state's $65,000 contribution. Black Atlantans paid taxes on over one million dollars of property only to see their required contributions used to subsidize white schools.[51] Though African American organizing afforded state-level victories over proportional distribution of tax revenue, municipal and county school boards ultimately possessed the power to distribute funds. The result was usually the siphoning of black taxpayer dollars into white schools, sometimes even in majority black districts.[52]

Overcrowding also proved detrimental to African American students and teachers. The city council and board of education could not keep pace with Atlanta's exploding population, and beginning in the 1880s, the superintendent and board president complained of insufficient schoolhouse capacity in their annual reports. "Our city is rapidly increasing in population and yet nearly one thousand white children are without places in the schools. [We] now crowd sixty children into a single room," exclaimed board president Hoke Smith. Smith, whose support of black education stressed only rudimentary literacy and manual training, charged the city council with allowing Negro grammar schools to operate in a "deplorable" condition. In 1900, the school board estimated that over half of Atlanta's black school-age population remained without space in the city's five Negro grammar schools. "Can the City of Atlanta afford to allow the Negro children to grow up in ignorance? I do not urge the duty of furnishing higher education to these children, but primary instruction, coupled with manual training, are essential," decried Smith. The future governor, whose racist campaign provided the political fuel for the 1906 Atlanta Race Riot, urged basic black education as a progressive reform to prevent vice, crime, and immorality among the city's lower classes. Minimal education and low-paying but regular employment, Smith hoped, would appease Atlanta's black community and ensure civic peace.[53]

But Smith's proclivity to incite white violence with racist oratory that described African Americans as "savage, vicious, [and] inhuman" undermined his claims that education and jobs would alleviate what he and other whites alleged to be an inherent tendency toward crime and vice among the city's black population.[54] As he campaigned for the governor's seat in the summer of 1906, Smith argued that black political power emboldened black men and threatened the sanctity of white womanhood, and he promised black disenfranchisement through violence if necessary. On September 22, flagrant and erroneous claims about miscegenation and assaults on white women prompted the formation of mobs of white males who proceeded to wage indiscriminate attacks on African Americans in Atlanta's central business district at Five Points and later in the city's peripheral black neighborhoods. The violence left dead thirty-two African Americans and three whites.[55] In the wake of the riot, the state legislature called for a statewide referendum to amend the constitution and enshrine black disenfranchisement. In October 1908, Georgia voters approved the amendment by a two to one margin.[56]

But the Atlanta race riot of 1906 and subsequent constitutional disenfranchisement did little to abate the resolve of black Atlantans to challenge Jim Crow and inadequate municipal services, including public education. If anything, the setbacks strengthened the resistance. The Women's Civic and Social Improvement Committee, a branch of the volunteer Neighborhood

Union founded in 1908 by Lugenia Burns Hope, wife of John Hope of Morehouse College, and other middle-class African American women took up the cause of public schooling in 1913.[57] These reformers sought the alleviation of a host of social and civic problems in which the all-white school board was historically complicit. In 1886 the board had instituted double sessions in black grammar schools as a "temporary" solution to overcrowding and denied community petitions for additional instructors. Teachers, most of whom received their teaching training at Atlanta University, taught one group of students in the morning and another after lunch. The result was overworked and exhausted teachers as well as limited instruction time for students. At Gray Street School for example, nine black teachers instructed 674 students over two daily sessions. At Houston Street School, the self-proclaimed pride of Superintendent Slaton, nine teachers taught 940 students in double sessions. Black teachers received no additional compensation for the extra workload and their salaries remained roughly half those of white teachers. These inequities persisted throughout the first decades of the twentieth century with little attention from the city council budget appropriations committee. While the *Constitution* deemed overcrowding in white schools a "critical situation" that warranted front-page coverage, it made little mention of black double sessions. The school board annually recommended the cessation of double sessions, but the policy continued despite the addition of six more black grammar schools by 1912, and the city council continued to spend the lion's share of local school levies on white schools.[58]

In response, the Women's Committee conducted an extensive six-month survey of Atlanta's twelve black grammar schools. They amassed a body of evidence of the schools' deplorable physical conditions and the impossibility of adequate learning under the conditions of double sessions. For example, its 1913–14 "Survey of Colored Schools" revealed a deficit of 2,061 seats in the city's Negro grammar schools. But rather than simply deliver a report to the school board, likely to either bury it or recommend unsubstantial policy changes, the committee went public by holding mass meetings in churches, allying insurance agents to their cause, and submitting photographs and descriptions to local press outlets. But when the committee did submit their official petition to the school board, including an end to double sessions, improved sanitary conditions, and a new grammar school in south Atlanta, it met with excuses and denial. In November, the board added salt to the wound by proposing to end literary instruction after the sixth grade and to expand industrial training, which the committee decried as

FIGURE 13. Teacher Mary Brook's Class, ca. 1910. Neighborhood Union Collection. Courtesy Atlanta University Center, Robert W. Woodruff Library.

instruction in lesser citizenship. Though the Neighborhood Union mobilized enough African American voters to defeat two school bonds in 1914 and 1915 that excluded appropriations for black schools, double sessions continued.[59]

Not until 1917, when overcrowding in white grammar schools reached critical mass and school officials floated the possibility of double sessions, did white opposition to the policy surface. Superintendent Joseph Wardlaw proposed a temporary measure at Tenth Street School for a one-year double session in three grades until the completion of a new white grammar school. Howell's *Atlanta Constitution* decried the proposal as a "reversion to a policy that is inhumane, barbaric and wholly out of keeping with Atlanta's place and pride." Howell's editorial depicted innocent children trekking to school before dawn and others arriving home well past dark, and public pressure forced the board to rent temporary space rather than institute double sessions. The editorial outraged Atlanta's African American community. While they certainly sympathized with Howell's castigation of the policy, they also received another reminder of their invisibility in public affairs. Black students and teachers had endured double sessions for over thirty years, and white school reformers and the city council continuously refused to acknowledge or alleviate their hardships.[60]

The controversy over double sessions re-energized black Atlantans and mobilized the local NAACP chapter headed by Walter White. White and the NAACP committee on school reform challenged the board's decision to eliminate the seventh grade in black grammar schools. The decision effectively forced the city's black colleges to shoulder the burden of both seventh grade and high school curricula, the latter of which the school board had never provided. White and the NAACP protested the substitution of private schooling for the adequate public education supposedly afforded to all citizens of the city. After a highly politicized fight in which Mayor Asa Candler opposed equal educational opportunities for African Americans, the school board acquiesced to the NAACP and dismissed the motion to abolish the seventh grade. In September 1917, the NAACP succeeded further in its drive for improved black schools. In a letter to the *Constitution,* White outlined the disparate history of black education in Atlanta and demanded the immediate abolition of double sessions. Howell printed the letter in an editorial, and public pressure forced the school board to admit the crippling effect that double sessions had on teaching and learning in black grammar schools.[61]

While the school board's acknowledgment of injustice seemed to be a victory for black Atlantans, double sessions continued as the board then moved decidedly *without* haste to erect new school buildings. In response, the NAACP successfully increased black municipal voter registration from a meager 700 to 3,000 for the school bond elections in 1918 and 1919. School bonds required approval by two-thirds of all registered voters, and the city's black voters could easily defeat bond issues by boycotting the polls. Faced with the inability to fund any schools, black or white, the school board and city council were forced to address the needs of black parents, teachers, and students. In 1921, black Atlantans supported a school bond that funded the construction of eighteen new schools, including four new Negro grammar schools and the first public black high school in the city, which opened three years later.[62]

Public secondary education for African Americans represented an important advance in the history of school reform in Atlanta. But separate and unequal schooling persisted, and it would be another thirty years after Booker T. Washington High School opened its doors until the federal decision to mandate desegregation, which also did not result in educational equality. During the late nineteenth and early twentieth centuries, black school reformers had little choice but to operate within the confines of separation—always adamant in their demands for equal funding and facilities—but usually within the bounds of Jim Crow etiquette and deference. In no small part, the reality or threat of both targeted and indiscriminate forms of racial violence against African Americans reinforced the peculiarly Southern yet broadly American caste system underscored by white supremacy and *Plessy v. Ferguson.* The name of Atlanta's first black public secondary school, Booker T. Washington High School, flew in the face of Hope, Du Bois, White, and even Bumstead who fought not only for equality but also against the system of segregation and accommodation embodied by Washington and Armstrong.[63]

Atlanta's black students and parents continued to face persistent opposition to their demands for adequate public education. In 1921, a minority of white citizens of Atlanta's fourth ward protested mere consideration of a new black grammar school by the school board. A month later, white residents near Fraser Street grammar school demanded that the schoolhouse remain white despite the school board's plans to create a black grammar school. "We concede the right of Negroes to be provided with adequate school facilities, but we do insist that in locating such schools they should not be allowed in white communities," stated fourth ward resident John Roan.[64] Other prominent public officials detested the board's apparent haste in providing a high school for African Americans before addressing the needs of white schools. In the 1924 mayoral race, incumbent James L. Key fought attacks from his opponent Walter Sims that Key had given, in the words of city bond chairman Frank Inman, "royal treatment" to black Atlantans. Sims convinced many white voters that the mayor had forced the construction of the Negro high school before a new white girls' high school could be completed. Despite the inaccuracy of these claims (the building contract for the Negro high school was signed before the board selected the site for the girls' high school), Key lost his reelection bid.[65]

City council tax chairman and future mayor William Hartsfield also charged the school board with undue recklessness in privileging black education over Atlanta's white schools: "The fight I have tried to make is for the hundreds of innocent little grammar-school children and white girls who have been left in ramshackle, temporary buildings, and insanitary firetraps, while unknown to the great majority of people, a great modern four-story Negro high school was being rushed to completion."[66] By the time Washington High opened in September 1924, Atlanta's black students had endured over five decades of inadequate schooling that had, despite the stead-fast work of teachers trained at Atlanta University, prepared many of them for mere literacy and low-wage employment. Segregation meant not simply sepa-rate but also substandard public schools. White Atlantans, either apathetic or outraged, defended the supremacy of white education over that of black children. In doing so, they subscribed to national anxieties among whites over nonwhite social mobility, labor competition, and fitness for republican citizenship. The white South may have born the brunt of charges of inequality and racism from national and international onlookers, but the ideology and practices of Jim Crow traveled far and wide.[67]

Just as segregation became a critical component of nation and empire building by the end of the nineteenth century and was not simply a Southern answer to emancipation, the politics of public education in Atlanta did not hinge solely on Jim Crow and the struggle of African Americans for adequate schools. In June 1921, the Atlanta school board fired Davis Street School principal Julia T. Riordan without specific "dereliction of duty" except that she was an "organizer" and an "agitator." The all-white Atlanta Public School Teachers' Association (APSTA), established in 1905 as Local 89 of the American Federation of Teachers, made no effort to defend Riordan against the board's actions and promptly dismissed her from its membership rolls. Riordan charged the school board, the APSTA, and the Atlanta Federation of Trades with "religious intolerance" and exercising "the right to deny to a Catholic member the privilege which Labor is pledged to secure for every toiler, irrespective of race or of creed."[68] Riordan identified her religion and possibly her Irish background as the grounds on which she was fired as an "outside agitator," the blanket epithet that according to Elna Green has undergirded white Southern conservative responses to abolition, women's rights, civil rights, labor movements, and other kinds of progressive move-ments since the antebellum era.[69]

But Riordan's dismissal as the wrong kind of citizen was a national example and one inseparable from the global interconnections of race and empire. In the decade after World War I, a revival of anti-Catholic violence spearheaded by the Ku Klux Klan and an antiradical campaign championed by the federal government bound together the fates of African Americans with myriad immigrants hailing from diverse origins in Europe, Asia, and Latin America and marked them as outsiders who threatened or eroded Protestant Anglo-Saxon civilization. At the same time, white Southerners were also willing to claim a kind of Americanness for Southern blacks who acquiesced to white demands for subordination and segregation. In the aftermath of the Great War, the Southern Education Association regarded it "appropriate to recall that throughout the period of hostilities the Negro was never suspected of espionage or of sympathy with the enemy, and that he has been wholly indifferent to those movements fostered by radical aliens that aim at the destruction of the American form of government."[70]

Education officials seldom made such blanket statements regarding "new immigrants" from Europe. In New York City, the subject of chapter five and home to immigrants hailing from wildly diverse origins, the school board warned against a complacency of spirit in the Americanization campaigns of the late nineteenth and early twentieth centuries. Given the overwhelming numbers of immigrants from southern and eastern Europe, the New York City Department of Education championed the creation of a young citizenry, foreign in origin, but American in thoughts and values, in order to protect and extend what Anglo Americans regarded as the racially innate attribute of "law and order."[71] In the four decades leading up to the 1924 National Origins Act, which placed strict quotas on immigration from southern and eastern Europe and reaffirmed restrictive laws against immigration from Asia, the language of culture and the science of race became intertwined as New York's European immigrants were afforded the possibility of becoming Caucasian provided that they adopt the kinds of culture norms presumably embraced by native-born white citizens, including the subordination of nonwhites.

5

Becoming White New Yorkers

These immigrant races form colonies, like an invading army, taking section after section of our cities exclusively for themselves; building business on racial lines, coming in contact with practically only the unsuccessful class of Americans. In these districts—city within a city—many foreign customs are observed, and the traditions and prejudices of centuries are perpetuated.[1]

RAYMOND E. COLE, *"The City's Responsibility to the Immigrant,"* 1916

If 750,000 [Negro] slaves in 1795 could furnish us with a problem vital enough to lead to war ... would not the 10,000,000 illiterate and "unable to speak English" immigrants amount to a problem more vital?[2]

ALONZO GRACE, *Immigration and Community Americanization,* 1921

IN ITS 1919 ANNUAL REPORT, the New York City Board of Education surveyed the preceding four decades of formal instruction and declared that "no city in the country has gone further ... in the direction of consciously motivated, systematic training for citizenship." But there was still work to be done. The board reminded and reassured itself, its administrators, and its teachers that efforts to inculcate the school-age population in the ways of American citizenship remained essential to combating perils to national life and identity. It also stressed the uniqueness of the city's multiethnic, multiracial composition, a claim frequently echoed by school officials in Honolulu and San Francisco. "No city needs such training more, for this is no longer an American city, but rather a cosmopolitan city in the process of being Americanized," the board argued. With its hopes tempered by anxiety about an uncertain future in both city and nation, the board warned of "the opposing forces ... ceaselessly at work," percolating throughout the city's immigrant neighborhoods: "the home with alien traditions, alien aspirations ... organizations subversive of law and order, with their public meetings and their street speakers, even competing Sunday and night schools which announce their aim to be 'to offset the vicious teaching of the public school.'" But the board also embraced the opportunities and responsibilities before them—a call to duty in the face of imminent loss of national identity and character and the unstated but perceived dangers of racial and ethnic amalgamation.[3]

Penned in 1919, the board's words told not only of its concerns about assimilating immigrants at home, but also of the anxieties that attended US involvement in World War I and the burden of global leadership that accompanied the peace negotiations at Versailles. Woodrow Wilson predicated his emerging concept of internationalism not only on the expansion of self-government (by which he did not mean a world order free from forms of imperial rule) and cooperation among nations orchestrated by the United States. For Wilson, internationalism also meant the incorporation of national economies into the orbit of increasingly American-led economic globalization. A world "safe for democracy," in the minds of Wilson and his supporters, should also be a world "safe for capitalism."[4] In New York's schools, these twinned tasks fused into attempts at a thorough Americanization of the large non-English-speaking population of European ethnic and national groups and by imparting, through formal instruction, the historical and contemporary wisdom of American leadership in commerce and international politics. When Superintendent William Ettinger wrote to his elementary school superintendents and principals in September 1918 four months after his appointment began, he impressed upon them the need to "convey to the children . . . the real significance of the [Liberty Day] celebration." As he quoted Wilson at length, Ettinger's efforts involved to a significant degree historical interpretations of American expansionism as a process that served in the defense of liberty against autocratic tyranny not unlike that of the Austro-Hungarian, German, and Ottoman empires: "We now know more certainly than we ever knew before why free men brought the great nation and government we love into existence, because it grows clearer and clearer what supreme service it is to be America's privilege to render to the world."[5] The assimilative project at home was increasingly bound to outward projections of American values.

The formal education of New York's new immigrants involved two mutually sustaining processes. The school board's quest to Americanize the progeny of European immigrants involved assimilation—a kind of welcoming of these outsiders into the American polity, labor force, and cultural mainstream. Educators recognized the potential rewards in bolstering the

American industrial machine with docile workers, in creating a semi-informed and predictable electorate, and fitting the children of immigrants with the habits, manners, and patriotic sentiments of Anglo-Americans. And Americanization frequently came at the expense of the new immigrants' linguistic, religious, and other cultural mores. Moreover, *culture* and *ideology* often provided coded, softer substitutes for *race*. The school board's commitment to assimilation also meant the remaking of race—of assigning whiteness to southern and eastern Europeans who, according to the prevailing race science of the day, occupied a space of racial inbetweenness. As natives of Europe, they presumably belonged to the Caucasian race that sat atop racial hierarchies in the pages of geography textbooks. While eugenicists certainly enjoyed popularity among some progressive reformers in the leadup to and after the passage of the National Origins Act in 1924, American racial nationalism, as it unfolded historically, also allowed for assimilation of certain kinds of cultural and racial outsiders.[6] For many European immigrants, Americanization meant becoming white in a cultural sense. Any newcomers who presumably possessed questionable whiteness or appeared to Anglo-Saxon and Nordic Americans to be what David Richards has described as "nonvisibly black" passed through the crucible of race in order to enjoy social acceptance and claim national belonging. At the turn of the twentieth century, the confluence of immigration and empire rendered, according to Matthew Frye Jacobson, "a [fabricated] system of 'difference' by which one might be both white *and* racially distinct from other whites."[7]

Secondly, Americanization involved the inculcation of and adherence to the demands for loyalty that ascendant US nationalism and imperialism required. While school civics courses were designed for a much broader geographic and racial spectrum of schoolchildren that also frequently included nonwhites and native-born whites, New York administrators often tailored their civics curricula to Americanize an increasingly foreign student body of southern and eastern European immigrants. Emphasis on conformity, loyalty, and Americanism increased with the US entry into World War I, and the Bolshevik Revolution fostered a culture of fear and campaigns of absolute Americanism. By combining the traditional function of schools with community transformation and ideological conformity, school men and women became more totalizing in their Americanization efforts. This meant the usurpation of traditional sources of learning for children of immigrant families. As the city school board acknowledged in 1919, the "alien home" represented one of the gravest threats to the health and moral character of the nation. Schools became the first line of defense in a rhetorical and ideological battle in which immigrants and their cultures collectively amounted to an invasion by a foreign power.

Though US involvement in the Great War heightened the specter of immigrant radicalism in New York City, official suspicion of and attempts to Americanize the new immigrants from southern and eastern Europe was already well under way by the time the United States declared war in April 1917. In the 1870s, New York's immigrant population underwent a shift from its longer-standing places of origin in England, Ireland, and Germany to Italy, Poland, Russia, and other parts of southern and eastern Europe. The new immigrants inhabited slums and worked at low-wage industrial jobs previously occupied by Irish and non-Jewish German immigrants. By 1890, the city boasted a population of one and a half million people. Almost 43 percent were foreign-born, and a full 80 percent were either foreign-born or born to immigrant parents. In Brooklyn and the industrial slums of Manhattan's Lower East Side, the city's foreign Jewish population, for example, climbed from 4 to 27 percent of the total, and by 1920, the vast majority came no longer from Germany as they had in the 1880s but primarily from Poland and Russia. By 1900, the new immigration comprised over one-half of all annual immigration to the United States. All told, 22 million immigrants entered the United States between the early 1890s and the mid-1920s, most of them from Europe.[8]

These migration shifts shook the foundations of the 1790 Naturalization Law that, despite its overt exclusion of nonwhites, was decidedly inclusive within the category of white. This inclusiveness made possible nineteenth- and early twentieth-century migrations from Europe and provided legal naturalization, if not cultural assimilation, for almost any European applicant provided they were "free" and "of good character." As such, the whiteness of European newcomers was implicit. But the emergence of scientific racism and social Darwinism underscored new racial formulations that challenged assumptions about the biological unity of the white race in America. By the early 1920s, calls for restriction and exclusion predominated national debates about the racial fitness of immigrants from southern and eastern Europe for democratic participation.[9] Preoccupations with degrees of whiteness and the thorough and rapid assimilation of New York's European immigrants—markedly different from the primary concerns of officials in San Francisco, Hawai'i, and Atlanta—were not simply anxieties produced by the savagery of World War I and the radicalism of the

Bolshevik Revolution. Cultural notions of race informed the politics of Americanization in the city's schools as early as 1880, when the New York school board reported rather inauspiciously that attendance in the city's colored schools was down rather sharply—an average attendance of only 571 throughout the city—"doubtless due mainly to the fact that the doors of all the public schools of [the] city are by law open to the pupils without distinction of color." The board predicted the "gradual absorption . . . of this distinctive or separate class of [colored] schools" and instead focused its energy on the rapid assimilation of an increasingly heterogeneous population of European immigrants. That year's census figures were not lost on board members, who reported that less than one-fifth of the city's population could claim two native-born parents and that, in some classes, fewer than one in ten students heard English at home.[10]

New York's new immigration gave rise and shape to demands from mostly native-born, white, Protestant reformers to scrap the city's purportedly failed experiment with ward control over local schools in favor of centralized management by professional educators and an administration that functioned and thought in business terms. Following a thwarted 1895 attempt by the self-described Committee of Seventy to pass sweeping school centralization measures at the state level—changes adamantly opposed by ward trustees and teachers—school reformers, now led by Columbia philosopher Nicholas Butler and his Citizens Committee for Public School Reform, doubled down on their efforts to wrest control from local wards and usher in what they believed was in both the local and national interest. After a successful vote in the legislature to abolish the ward-trustee system, New York City mayor William Strong sided with the reformers, citing the dangers of local school control in a city "largely impregnated with foreign influences, languages and ideas . . . vast throngs of foreigners" whose "mode of living is repugnant to every American idea." The 1896 school centralization reform bill vested educational authority with a new Board of Superintendents that hired, promoted, and removed teachers and principals and that set curriculum. School centralization was to have dramatic effects on the ways in which those at the helm of the city's public schools shaped discourse on race and immigration and on ideology and empire in the early twentieth century.[11]

But residential divisions between native-born and immigrant communities often rendered assimilation difficult. The 1885 school census, for example, revealed that in the tenth ward, 6,903 of 8,966 students were born in the United States. However, the number of students whose parents were native-born US citizens only reached 603, or just under 9 percent. The tenth ward was home mostly to Polish and Russian immigrants, complemented by a sizable German population. While the Teutonic heritage of non-Jewish German immigrants often allowed them to become Americans without much scrutiny of their whiteness, Jews, Slavs, Italians and others from beyond the regions of northern and western Europe faced a dual transformation of both racial belonging and national allegiance. Educators perceived these tasks as inseparable. Regardless of geographic origin or racial character, school officials sought to exploit this generational divide to distance students from their parents' cultural and linguistic traditions in order to make them presumably more amenable to certain celebrated tenets of American democracy: hard work, responsible civic participation, and loyalty to an orderly state. The children of immigrants could, according to some administrators, be remade in the image of the nation's original white settlers and founders.[12]

Yet belief in the strength of cultural assimilation campaigns was tempered by the discourse of variegated whiteness increasingly prevalent in American academia and that found its way into grammar school curriculum. For example, in a geography transcription one student wrote "thousands of years ago, the white people of Europe were almost savages." His observation revealed that Europe was not a unified continent composed solely of a single civilized white race as many contemporary geography schoolbooks indicated. It not only employed the discourse of civilization but also recognized that certain races or peoples of Europe had not yet reached its higher echelons. "The Russians were the last to become civilized. Turkey is not yet counted as a civilized nation," he concluded. History curricula also confirmed the absence of civilization among certain "races" of Europe. In her lesson outline on "New World Empires," teacher Mary Murphy claimed that by tracing the connections between the United States and Europe, "it was possible for the teacher, starting with the Aryan race, to show the westward progress of civilization into Persia, Greece, Rome, the formation of the English nation and the tendency to move still further westward by crossing the Atlantic to America." The selectivity of these transatlantic migrations, whereby certain people transplanted "civilization" through Aryan and English blood lineage while others (new immigrants) did not, further revealed the unsettled nature of whiteness in New York. According to the prevailing curricula, races retained certain characteristics. Anglo-Saxons, for example, possessed an affinity for civilization and liberty that was coded into their biology and that made them more suitable for self-government in the United States. Others, like

FIGURE 14. They Sang of America. Jewish immigrant children waving tiny US flags while repeating oath of allegiance; at the central school of the Educational Alliance, East Broadway, New York City. Reproduction of drawing by E.V. Nadherny to illustrate H.G. Wells, *The Future in America,* Ch. 9 ("The Immigrant"). Illus. in *Harper's Weekly,* 1906, p. 1205. Courtesy Library of Congress, Prints and Photographs Division, LC-USZ62–44050.

Slavs, Italians, and Russian Jews, had not been endowed with such traits, but with the right kind of training in American schools, could acquire the cultural skills and habits needed for national belonging within the white republic.[13]

REMAKING THE ALIEN HOME

In essence, good citizenship, though still predicated on whiteness, also required a more flexible standard of whiteness that at once defied biological racial formulations and upheld the cultural standards and norms of Anglo-Saxonism so prevalent in notions of national belonging. The mutually sustaining projects of Americanization and language instruction coalesced to produce what Michael Olneck and Clifford Geertz have argued constituted questions of "what cultural forms—what systems of meaningful symbols" would be used to construct, impart, and reshape national identity. Language often evoked emotive responses from native-born Americans, usually Anglos but sometimes others, who perceived non-English speakers as threats to cultural mores. Proponents of Americanization feared the divisive affects that ethnic, non-English speaking groups might have on civic and national character, and they sought conformity of "language, customs, and ways." Administrators and teachers sought to make inroads into immigrant homes and neighborhoods through language instruction. Additionally, industrial capitalism informed this drive for Americanism and for conformity of language. As David Roediger points out, the "'inbetween' consciousness" of many new immigrant workers galvanized them against both native-born favoritism but also against black competition—often in the form of labor strikes. If these immigrants could be solidified as English-speaking whites, complete with a strong sense of American nationalism, they were less prone to collective action. Good patriots made good workers.[14]

Widespread English language education had roots in the 1880s, when some Midwestern and Northeastern cities, New York included, opened night schools for adult immigrants. But working immigrants attended evening courses in low numbers, particularly if English was not necessary on the job or if they eschewed naturalization. In 1880, New York's public schools boasted an enrollment of 18,472 in its evening schools. Though attendance only reached 7,676 that year, the board continued to stress its vitality in assimilating foreign-born adults into the industrial workforce. Beginning in 1906, the board of superintendents created three new grades in the elementary schools, one of which served as a holding area for nonspeakers of English. Immigrant children of all ages entered grade C until they had sufficiently learned enough English to "take up the work of another grade," and grade C teachers were instructed to teach the same lessons used in the adult evening schools. Once assimilated into regular classrooms, foreign-born students would then receive lessons in American history, civics, and patriotism.[15] School administrators joined industry and a host of other agencies including the Bureau of Naturalization, the National Council of Defense, and the National Americanization Committee as primary advocates for Americanization through language training. Industrial leaders also introduced formal English language instruction for immigrant workers. Henry Ford advanced an English-only policy among his factory workers and provided the necessary language training to move toward "100 Percent Americanism." In 1916, the vice president of Packard Motor Company announced to the Committee for Immigrants in America that promotion in their Detroit plant would only be granted to American citizens. In short, the vice president identified the "prerequisite of success [as] American patriotism and American nationalism." While the policy certainly had nativist implications, it at least left open the possibility of economic advancement through Americanization.[16]

In 1881, the New York school board recognized that English language instruction had to date not "been dealt with to the entire satisfaction of the commissioners of education." In particular, the board cited the shortcomings of the Compulsory Education Act (1874), which only mandated attendance for children under the age of fourteen. In the 1870s and 1880s, Northeastern state legislatures passed compulsory school attendance laws with the twinned goals of furthering national cohesion of thought and ideals and alleviating perceived social and moral pressures from what they regarded as an inferior immigrant culture. Most early attendance laws were minimal, and while the laws may have threatened what some parents perceived as their personal right and prerogative to educate their children in ways they saw fit, the new statutes certainly never required adults to attend evening schools to address deficiencies in English.[17]

Yet die-hard reformers in New York hoped that they might expand compulsory attendance at some point in the future, given the trajectories of immigration at the end of the nineteenth century. As the New York school board reported, "the number of people in this city totally ignorant of our language may become so large as to be an element of great danger to municipal prosperity." It offered the large contingent of Italians as evidence "that this is a real and not an imaginary danger," and pushed for increased Americanization through English language instruction for both children and adults. The board warned that if allowed to continue without immediate response from the schools, "there is nothing to hinder similar immigration on the part of other nations equally ignorant of our language, and equally strangers to our habits and customs."[18] By 1885, evening school attendance had decreased to 6,628 total students, but average attendance among those enrolled rose above 30 percent. Still, throughout the early twentieth century, reformers argued that Americanization and language instruction remained in need of significant improvement. Some recognized the essential role of each in reversing what some interpreted as the degeneration of American white racial stock among the country's European population. As University of Wisconsin political economist John R. Commons argued in 1914, cultural and linguistic assimilation could ameliorate the persistence of racial stocks and traits: "Race and heredity may be beyond our organized control; but the instrument of common language is at hand for conscious improvement through education and social environment."[19]

In 1916, the US Bureau of Naturalization issued a call to civic societies to put pressure on school authorities throughout the nation to expand the availability of evening English and civics courses for adult immigrants. The Committee for Immigrants in America reported that of the 13 million foreign-born in the United States, roughly three million could not speak English, and only 38,000 nationwide were enrolled in evening schools. The committee pointed not to refusal on the part of immigrants to learn English but rather to the missed obligation of Americans to assimilate foreigners. The New York superintendent's office responded with plans to advertise evening schools and to extend the authority of the public school directly into homes and neighborhoods.[20] Superintendent William H. Maxwell began employing "visiting teachers" in 1914 who served, under the direction of district superintendents, as liaisons between the home and the school. Visiting teachers were supposed to correct behaviors that frequently fit many progressives' characterizations of children raised in immigrant homes: "unmanageable, nervous, dull, inattentive, over-worked, underfed, poorly clad."

These teachers, sometimes called "home teachers" or "visiting nurses," engaged in "secular missionary work"—efforts to reshape the immigrant home through the inculcation of American standards of living and values. Progressives were quick to report the satisfactory results of home visits and other acts of "willed learning on the part of individuals." For example, in 1916, Joseph Mayper, an editor for Frances Kellor's *Immigrants in America Review*, celebrated the reported success of home teachers on Barren Island in Jamaica Bay off the coast of Brooklyn. "Except for the public school," lamented Mayper, "the [immigrant] community remains an isolated group ... lacking definite aim or purpose." In a collaborative effort with the City Department of Health, public school authorities at Barren Island personally requested the attendance of immigrant men and women in English and civics courses, and furnished English language books, lectures, and moving pictures on patriotism: "The house-to-house work was therefore utilized to arouse among the adults interest in a knowledge of the English language and preparation for American citizenship. Men and women were urged to attend the public evening school, addresses were made before foreign societies, colored posters were put up in various sections of the district, announcements were made by the priest and the co-operation of the employers was secured." For Mayper and the Committee for Immigrants in America, New York's large foreign population necessitated a concerted effort to reach not just schoolchildren but all immigrants. While the public schools played an integral role as the bedrock of the Americanization movement and provided places to teach immigrants, they were more so part of a much broader progressive reform movement that targeted all aspects of immigrant life including health, sanitation, childcare, labor, and recreation. Mayper declared: "the work [at Barren Island] has been constructive and far-reaching and will, no doubt, prove to be of permanent value to the residents and the community and cannot but promote a stable population and a high type of American citizenship."[21]

With the hope that schoolchildren would use their influence to Americanize the city's first-generation immigrants, proponents of adult education continued to play an integral role in the Americanization movement through World War I. In September 1917, the school board appropriated $78,000 for the cause—an investment the board hoped would rectify failed attempts in previous years.[22] In the year following America's entrance into the Great War, the school board unanimously adopted a resolution prohibiting the use of any language other than English in the public schools, except for foreign language instruction. The decision reflected national trends. By 1919, fifteen state legislatures had passed similar prohibitions against foreign languages, including Nebraska, which extended the ban to private and parochial schools as well. As chapter 6 demonstrates, colonial officials in Puerto Rico regularly enforced English as the official language of instruction.

In 1920, board president Anning S. Prall proposed a compulsory Americanization bill aimed specifically at "adult aliens": "We are doing everything possible for children [of foreign born parents] to take back to their homes the story of Americanism. We teach them how to live, love of city, state, and nation. But we must be able to reach the adult more directly." Prall hoped that requiring adults to attend evening classes at the public schools would instill what were, to his mind, distinctly American ideals: respect for authority and love of justice, the latter of which he argued was made a "mockery" in the home countries of many immigrants.[23] Superintendent Ettinger responded with a plan to require upper-grade elementary school students to write letters to their parents informing them of the location of the nearest evening school, hours of operation, and courses offered. Students were then to return the compositions with a parent's signature. Ettinger praised the efforts of children and teachers in spreading Americanism beyond school grounds and regarded "the influence of the school children on their parents" as a crucial mechanism of the Americanization campaign.[24] But throughout the 1910s, the limits of forced Americanization, particularly of immigrant adults, prompted school bureaucrats to experiment with new ways in which to use the schools, particularly to service the needs and demands of industrial capitalism. As Europe descended into war in 1914 and 1915, New Yorkers with a variety of stakes in public schooling debated the introduction of an innovative and self-styled progressive educational model that featured industrial training as one of its alleged benefits. The open battles over the "Gary Plan" revealed how educational policy informed the politics of immigration and Americanization in New York.

THE GARY PLAN

Given the city's large immigrant population, many supporters of the "Gary Plan," including Mayor John Mitchel, touted the innovative educational model as an efficient way to produce active workers and consumers for American industry. The Gary Plan, or "platoon schools" as they were also known, began as the brainchild of school superintendent William A. Wirt of Gary, Indiana. Founded in 1906 by the United States Steel Corporation, Gary quickly grew into a bustling company town, and by 1910, over 63 percent of the school-age population was born of foreign parentage. While considerably smaller than New York, Gary offered a microcosm of the concerns held by many New York school officials and industrialists about the capacity of immigrants to participate in American civic life and to contribute to American industry and the boundlessness of American consumerism. Moreover, the pressures that mass immigration placed on the physical capacity of urban schools lent Wirt a great deal of national credibility among school and city officials concerned with efficiency.

The Gary Plan more or less worked in this way: While half of the students took academic classes like geography and history during the morning, the other half, in yet smaller groups, participated in a variety of specialized activities that included athletics, art, music, dancing, drama, domestic arts, and industrial training. Then the two "platoons," as they became known, switched. Under the plan, student apprentices completed routine building maintenance as part of a school's basic functionality. Proponents argued that the platoon model maximized the use of the school's physical resources and teaching staff. Groups representing opposite sides of progressive educational debates found much to praise about the Gary Plan. It featured a bureaucratic efficiency heralded by corporate capitalists, municipal reformers, and technocrats of the era. Its industrial training program was particularly appealing to the business establishment because it promised to strip labor unions of control over trade apprenticeship. But the Gary Plan also appealed to some leading progressive educational theorists, including John Dewey, who argued that Gary schools promised to prepare children to make "the most intelligent use of their own capabilities and of their environment." Even some political radicals of the period were attracted to its child-centered and hands-on approach to learning. As historians Ronald Cohen and Raymond Mohl have argued, "the Gary schools epitomized two separate and contradictory goals of progressive education."[25]

In 1914, New York's reform mayor John Mitchel introduced the Gary Plan as a solution to financial inefficiency in public education at a time when staffing and construction struggled to keep pace with immigration. He purged the school board of dissenters, especially board president Thomas Churchill, who remained unconvinced of the savings promised by the Gary Plan and who backed a similar homegrown scheme devised by future superintendent William Ettinger that focused primarily on industrial training. Mitchel hired Wirt as a part-time consultant with a salary equal to that of Superintendent William Maxwell. Wirt's charge was to implement and oversee the trial runs at two of the most overcrowded elementary schools in the city, P.S. 45 in the Bronx and P.S. 89 in Brooklyn, ahead of citywide implementation. Meanwhile, Wirt's personal assistant Alice Barrows, a student of Dewey's at Columbia University, labored tirelessly as Mitchel's chief propagandist for the Gary Plan. Barrows reached out to diverse interests in the city including media outlets, religious organizations, labor unions, radical reform groups, universities, business leaders, and immigrant parents. But her efforts, however creative and ambitious, failed to win over the board of superintendents and increasingly, some principals, teachers, parents, and children. Faced with staunch opposition by early 1916, Barrows renewed her campaign by cultivating a veneer of grassroots support from the Gary School League, an organization devoted to "democratic" school reform and mostly composed of Barrow's inner circle of friends. The league published foreign language leaflets, sent speakers into immigrant neighborhoods to drum up political support, organized trips to P.S. 45 to see the plan in action, employed representatives to make home visits in districts where opposition was high, and produced a film series for neighborhood theaters.

When school opened in September 1917, two months ahead of November's municipal elections, Mitchel and Wirt had implemented the Gary Plan in less than 5 percent of the city's schools with mixed results. On the one hand, the Gary schools had increased capacity over their traditional counterparts, which pleased efficiency hawks. On the other hand, critics described the shuffling about of elementary school students between classrooms as disorganized, chaotic, and adverse to focused instruction and learning. The intensive propaganda campaigning on both sides of the issue promised to make school reform the defining issue of the election.[26] Mitchel's most vocal and visible critic was Brooklyn Judge John F. Hylan, the Tammany Hall Democratic mayoral candidate, who promptly played upon the distrust of his working-class constituents for big business. Hylan made it known that Gary supporters, funded and supported by the Rockefeller steel trust, promised to eschew academic learning for industrial training in order to prepare children "only for the mill and the factory," turning them into "wage slaves" and "toilers for the trusts."[27] "If we are to continue a nation of equal rights and equal opportunities to all we must maintain an educational system which gives opportunity for free and equal education of all children," Hylan insisted. A third mayoral challenger, Jewish Socialist candidate Morris Hillquit, also condemned the plan's connections to the Rockefellers and exposed Mitchel's persistent support for the Gary Plan as nothing more than a guise by which to further reduce taxes on the rich. Hylan and Hillquit appealed to the same constituencies, often with the same incendiary anticorporatist rhetoric, but they did so for different reasons. For Tammany, opposition to the Gary Plan offered a path to retake municipal political power. The new mayor had the power to appoint an entirely new board of superintendents. Socialists seemed less motivated by the possibility of political power and more by an ideological challenge to economic inequality. The Gary Plan, they argued, promised to further concentrate wealth in the hands of the privileged few.[28]

Behind both Hylan and Hillquit stood an organized and vocal opposition to the Gary Plan composed of mostly Jewish immigrant parents and students. But this opposition was not a product of either political party, predating the election by two years. Parents were keenly aware that the Gary Plan promised that their children would take their places on the factory and shop floors, and throughout the previous summer, over two hundred parents met regularly to give soapbox speeches and attract support to their cause. They organized debates with school officials, and offered poignant rebuttals to the argument that the Gary Plan balanced industrial training with academics. With the campaign in full swing in mid-October, students, with their parents' support, threatened to strike if the school board did not repeal its decision to lengthen the school day by one hour to make room for military training in the high schools. The United States had declared war on Germany in April and would by December declare war on the Austro-Hungarian Empire. The move by school officials offended both Socialists and other pacifists but also Jewish teenagers who tried to hold jobs after school in order to contribute to their families' income. When Board President Willcox and Superintendent Maxwell finally agreed to meet with high school students, who presented a petition opposing the Gary Plan but also opposing direct action (a strike), the school officials referred the petition to the Committee on High Schools, which had already received the petition and done nothing to respond. Five days later, student strikes swept over the city. Harlem, Yorkville, Brownsville, Flatbush, and Washington Heights saw the most intense action, including speeches, marches, vandalism, clashes with police, and arrests of both parents and students. In Yiddish, street corner orators demanded an end to industrial training and a serious commitment to academic subjects.[29]

The Gary Plan had galvanized Jewish electoral politics. On November 6, Mitchel lost the election to Hylan by a vote of two-to-one. Hillquit garnered only seven thousand fewer votes than Mitchel, the closest margin for any Socialist candidate in a citywide election to that point. Gary Plan supporters seized upon the unrest that preceded Mitchel's defeat to condemn the manipulation of schoolchildren by socialist immigrant parents and political agitators. They charged the International Workers of the World with conspiracy to foment revolutionary unrest in immigrant neighborhoods.[30] Even if they opposed the Gary Plan (which Mayor Hylan promptly dispatched upon taking office), the October strikers also indicated to many school officials that they had not yet succeeded in assimilating and Americanizing the children of immigrants in ways they found satisfactory. The willingness of students to take to the streets revealed proclivities for radical activism. These were not the kinds of upstanding citizens the architects of community civics had imagined. Moreover, as the United States mobilized for the Great War, New York school officials vested themselves with the task of garnering unwavering support for the war effort from parents and children. Their efforts would reshape how the discourses of race and nation impacted debates about immigration from southern and eastern Europe and would further bind the public schools to projects of geopolitical and imperial expansion.

"NO ONE HAS KEPT THE POT MELTING"

A year before the United States declared war on Germany, an editorialist writing in the *Immigration Journal* argued that the American melting pot had exceeded its capacity and could no longer absorb new immigrants. With the frontier closed and the continent conquered, an "army of aliens" threatened "real danger to the country." It was not simply a matter of oppositional cultures but more importantly a matter of numbers. In response, Kellor's *Immigrants in America Review* offered a more sympathetic interpretation: "One cannot tell what the capacity of a melting pot is when the fires are out or at low pressure." Kellor argued that most Italians, Poles, and Bohemians come with the capacity for Americanization, but "America takes so little intelligent thought of using or developing this capacity . . . that the immigrant remains alien in heart and mind." Yet despite Kellor's compassionate stance, her renewed call to arms came to symbolize the dramatic lengths to which many Americanizers were willing to go amidst revolution and global war.[31] Entry into the Great War changed the character of Americanization. Historian Robert Carlson has noted that the war effort "injected an increased tone of suspicion, intolerance, and fear into the campaign," even as Woodrow Wilson, initially hesitant to mobilize for combat, hoped to neutralize political opposition at home. Wilson recast the war as one to extend abroad and defend at home what he considered at once uniquely American *and* universal values of self-government and democratic rule. But wartime government propaganda that rendered Germans savage "Huns," clampdowns on free speech, postwar race riots, the Red Scare, and the 1924 National Origins Act all "revealed that a nasty and coercive Americanism had triumphed," in Gary Gerstle's formulation.[32]

The revitalized politics of fear was not without its critics, including leading educational theorist John Dewey, who struck back at the absolutist Americanization school and desires for racial and cultural conformity, surveillance, and exclusion. Dewey espoused a doctrine of pluralism that defied the logic of Americanism rooted in Protestant Anglo-Saxon traditions, and he openly challenged exclusionists and conformist voices emanating from such organizations as the National Security League, American Protective League, and the Federal Committee on Public Information. But Dewey's intellectual protests were often drowned out by fears of revolution, which antiradicals argued were fomented on shop floors and docks and in textile factories and other industries predominated by southern and eastern European immigrants. Rather than address the political grievances of the laboring classes, many anticommunists argued that inferior racial characteristics prevented immigrant workers from understanding the true value of the American system of free enterprise and private property. They needed to be either coerced into recognizing those values or barred from participation in American life through a more pervasive and restrictive set of immigration laws.[33]

New York's public schools became sites both of the social reform of Dewey and of the watchful investigation of alleged immigrant radicalism espoused by coercive Americanizers. On one hand, the board and superintendent expanded efforts to inculcate Americanism among immigrant students and their families and continued to engage New York's foreign population as future patriots and citizens capable of understanding and fulfilling the duties of self-government. On the other hand, charges of anti-Americanism and Bolshevism against New York's immigrants as well as calls for exclusion emanated from civic societies as well as local, state, and federal government offices. Advocates and detractors of continued immigration from southern and eastern Europe, where Bolshevism and "un-Americanism" had presumably put down their strongest roots, reinforced and recast race in the image of foreignness and alien culture. "Our schools must solve social problems which arise from the complex nature of our population, which includes children and adults of nearly every race," reported the school board. Solving social problems, or eradicating radical un-Americanism, involved not simply political reorientation but also the whitening of one's politics so as to replace all other racially ingrained impulses with Anglo-Saxon values of liberty and free markets.[34]

As the questionability of the whiteness of new immigrants gained momentum in public discourse, protection against anarchism and socialism became central to Americanization in the schools. In particular, teachers stood at the forefront of this ideological defensive line. In 1918, Ettinger charged teachers with the responsibility to "be aggressively patriotic in word and deed ... in furthering all war measures our nation sees fit to enforce." The superintendent made no bones about his contempt for pacifism in the school curriculum: "We want no intellectualized, thin-blooded pacifists, but strong, red-blooded, outspoken Americans who will impress upon their pupils the fact that the Allies are the guardians of civilization."[35] Following the war's conclusion, the school board announced that "no teacher who is not a citizen or a declarant may continue the service after August 31." But citizenship or not, the administration became fixated on the content of classroom instruction. "The teachers of our schools are the guardians of those ideals and traditions which constitute Americanism," exclaimed Ettinger. He called on "patriotic men and women ... to counteract the sinister radicalism" emanating from Europe and from the city's immigrant communities.

But teachers also became the Americanizers' targets, not simply their conduits. Foremost in the minds of school administrators after the Great War was the specter of communism they claimed lurked in the city's immigrant neighborhoods, a fear akin to late nineteenth-century hysteria about the anarchism of militant unions. With evolving plans to exorcise socialism through a combination of surveillance and pedagogy, the Department of Education set in motion an aggressive self-described "patriotic propaganda" campaign and an inspection of the political character of its teaching force. "The Americanism of the mass of teachers cannot be [in question]," Ettinger continued, as he made clear his intentions to cleanse the profession of "vociferous agitators."[36] With the passage of the 1917 immigration law that allowed for the deportation of suspected foreign radicals, school policy aligned rather quickly. In order to ensure that the nation's youth, both native-born and foreign, became staunch opponents of radicalism, school administrators kept watchful eyes on teachers and issued stern formal warnings. "Every member of the teaching and supervising staff is bound, as a matter of contractual and moral obligation, to carry into effect by example and by precept, those ideals of patriotism and civic responsibility," declared Ettinger in February 1919. Following the institution of loyalty oaths and about a month after peace negotiations began at Versailles, he wrote to his teaching staff that "our system has no place for any teacher whose personal convictions make it impossible for him to be a sympathetic expounder of the cherished ideals . . . of our national life." As he seemed fond of doing, Ettinger quoted another official—this time New York education commissioner John Huston Finley: "If a teacher cannot give that unquestioning support of the country that makes his own individual freedom in time of peace possible, his place is not at the school." The superintendent required that principals "make the subject a matter of conference" as well as a "matter of instruction," and assured principals that while he "sincerely deprecate[d] any supervision involving espionage or oppression," the state had bestowed on him and all teachers a "sacred duty" to eschew the expression of views "in conflict with the solemn obligation" of public service.[37]

Ettinger's characterization of radicalism bore racial implications as well. He emphasized the stark difference between the swift and stunning violence of the Bolshevik Revolution and what he saw as "the gradual and orderly changes that have always been characteristic of the development of Anglo-Saxon institutions." Ettinger appealed not only to the stability and inevitability of the progressive American historical narrative, but also implied that nonviolent political and social change was a trait inherent within the racial pedigree of Anglo-Americans. Institutions served as code for racial character. According to this logic, the steady, rational Anglo-American naturally employed democratic change and due process of law. On the other hand, certain European races (and certainly nonwhite races) lacked the cultural or intellectual capacity for self-government unless taught and managed by superior Anglo-Saxons.

But if American schools were Anglo-Saxon institutions, many teachers were not and were suspected of harboring doctrines of subversion and anti-Americanism. In his comprehensive survey of radicalism, Clayton Riley Lusk, New York state senator and head of the Joint Legislative Committee Investigating Seditious Activities, argued that no attempt by state legislatures or the federal government to keep radical teachers of foreign-born students out of public school classrooms and night schools were adequate unless "character" and "loyalty to the institutions of the State and Nation" were the paramount employment qualifications. Lusk reported that certain English teachers in New York schools used "radical and liberal magazines as guides for the discussion of current events," and in response, the committee proposed a bill that required all schoolteachers to obtain a "certificate of good character and of loyalty to the State."[38] The committee's proposal aroused concern about the kind of oversight that the legislature or the school board might employ to enforce loyalty oaths. Ettinger argued that although he did not favor "espionage or oppression," the superintendent's office and the principals of all schools were required to make sure that teachers did not take advantage of "the privacy of the classroom and immaturity of [their] auditors." Lusk gave Ettinger the full support of the committee: "In entering the public school system the teacher assumes certain obligations and must of necessity surrender some of his intellectual freedom."[39]

Lusk also supported less coercive measures of Americanization than the direct oversight of teachers of foreign-born students. These measures comprised a shift from assimilation at all costs to a more nuanced approach along racial lines. The eradication of radicalism remained the first priority, but now Americanizers began to question the necessity of "100 Percent Americanism." Would not the exclusion of certain radical European "races" serve the same purpose? If Asian, black, and other distinctly nonwhite immigrants required subordination and expulsion, so too might certain European nationalities constitute threats to the nation. In *Revolutionary Radicalism*, Lusk included a detailed outline of steps for teachers of citizenship devised by the Young

Men's Christian Association. In its instructions, the YMCA charged its Americanizers with becoming intimately knowledgeable of racial difference: "Fifty varieties! Don't be dismayed . . . . Begin with one nation. Organize work along racial lines. Pass on to another race . . . . Know the mind of a race. When you mix nations, learn which will and which will not mix. Oil and water will not mix; no more will peoples who have racial antipathy and preju- dice. A study of nationality avoids failure."[40] While the YMCA intended its pamphlet as a "how-to" success manual for the would-be Americanizer, it also argued that certain European nationalities were unassimilable because of their racial character. Though Lusk was unspecific about which European nationalities were recalcitrant, his claims of "racial antipathy and prejudice" of immigrants toward one another absolved the Americanizer of racism. If European "races" could not coexist with each other, how could they possibly enrich the American melting pot?

In order to assess whether or not socialism had in fact infiltrated the minds and ideals of the city's schoolchildren, the superintendent's office issued a "War Facts" test. Ettinger assured teachers that the board was not investigat- ing allegations of subversive teaching, and rather that the test would reveal that "a limited number of pupils are in contact with Bolshevism"—likely through the political propaganda available through the foreign language press and less formal institutions prevalent in immigrant communities. "There is no belief," Ettinger assured, "that any teachers alive to their obligations have been teaching with approval of the principles underlying Bolshevism." Instead, the test would be used "only to indicate the measure of the teacher's opportunity and obligation to assist pupils with reference to facts and prob- lems of such vital importance."[41] At the close of the 1918–19 school year, Ettinger's tone was somewhat more congenial. He commended his staff on their attentive guardianship of "those ideals and traditions which constitute Americanism," but nevertheless impressed upon them the urgency with which they must "serve to counteract the sinister radicalism" at work in the city and country: "The dangers to which our national life is exposed, through the contamination of alien revolutionary ideas, measure the exceptional opportunities and also obligations" of teachers.[42]

Yet subsequent actions taken by the board and superintendent's office sug- gested instead a growing suspicion on the part of administrators that teachers were indeed preaching socialism in the public schools, and administrators and even some teachers themselves actively fostered a culture of both top-down and bottom-up policing of the teaching staff. In December 1919, delegates of the Teachers Loyalty League of the Bronx adopted a set of resolutions meant to cultivate a system of self-surveillance whereby teachers were compelled to report any radical ideas or practices held by colleagues. "A teacher cannot through a sense of personal loyalty shut his eyes to the disloyalty of a co-worker," the league's delegation argued. Furthermore, the league sought to restrict teachers from any outside associations or activities deemed un-American: "There is no place in the school system for teachers who believe that because they render service in conformance with the letter of the law during the hours of class room work, it is no concern of the community what their opinions and associations may be outside the school." The league received the hearty endorsement of Superintendent Ettinger.[43]

When reports of "radical teaching" surfaced again in 1920, an Americanization Committee headed by prominent leaders of over thirty organizations, including the Law and Order League, Tammany Hall, and Sons of the Revolution, pressed the board to install stenographers in classrooms to provide evidence of Bolshevist and anarchist propaganda. Committee spokesperson Henry Wood Wise "declared that all efforts to suppress radicalism are handicapped by the fact that sixty percent of . . . the State Department are Socialists and that President Wilson is the most exalted instigator of social revolt in the world." The board did not ultimately take up the recommendation of the Americanization Committee. Instead, it opted for a renewal of loyalty oaths and continued self-regulation. In 1921, the New York state commissioner of education required all supervisors and teachers to take loyalty oaths and obtain loyalty cards or "certification as to moral character." No teacher was allowed to continue teaching after December 31, 1921, without a loyalty certificate.

Ettinger reinforced the necessity of what he called the "ethical standards of the teacher" in a 1923 address before the Schoolmasters' Association in New York City. After reminding his audience that the "cheap radicalism of the soap-box orator and the pernicious propaganda of the oblique-minded parlor socialist" had no place in the public schools, Ettinger turned to the question of "teacher-unionism." As he acknowledged the potential good that might follow increased teacher participation in administrative and pedagogical decision making, Ettinger questioned the efficacy of "class appeal" in what he considered to be a question of democratic school governance separate from the economic concerns of teachers and of American society more broadly: "nothing can be more detrimental . . . than the assumption that the classroom teachers constitute . . . a sort of intellectual proletariat" separate from "a sort of pedagogical capitalistic class constituting the sworn oppressors of the teachers." Such framing, Ettinger argued, contained "the germs common to anarchism or bolshevism." And to demonstrate his solidarity with his subordinates, Ettinger instead promoted teacher professional associations that he argued, falsely, served the same functions as unions, including the redress of workplace grievances and a more inclusive, teacher-driven administration of schools. By no means a despot in his position as superintendent, Ettinger remained committed to the hierarchies of school governance as he eschewed charges of class antagonism and warned against misplaced socialist tendencies among discontented teachers.[44]

Whether of foreign or native origin, New York's teachers were expected to profess to students—and by extension, their families—the absolute necessity of conformity to Anglo-American cultural and political institutions. Taken together, tests of loyalty for both students and teachers and charges of subversive teaching and unionism reveal the parallel tracks of the public school's purge of radicalism and the federal government's socialist witch-hunt spearheaded by Attorney General Mitchell Palmer and a young J. Edgar Hoover. Americanization efforts reached fever pitch during the Red Scare of 1919–20, as authorities charged the nation's immigrants with un-American, subversive activism.[45]

EXCLUSION, EMPIRE, AND PATHS TO WHITENESS

By the early 1920s, many proponents of Americanization championed both conformist assimilation and exclusion. School administrators in New York had worked to erase the "foreignness" of immigrants and replace it with a more familiar, more "American" character. At the same time, a countermovement among the Americanizers emerged rooted less in the need for absolute conformity and more so in the new internationalist visions of American power made possible by an emergent American leadership at Versailles. This frequently involved remaking immigrants in the image of the white settler, citizen, and worker. The transformation of the new European immigrant required that American expansionism, both continental and overseas, become a project that second-generation immigrants in particular could come to recognize as their own. To accomplish this, the New York school board and other public city officials reimagined American historical narratives to meet the immediate postwar diplomatic landscape and national calls for immigration restriction. They turned to the tactics of the civics educators, who sought to bind formal and informal instruction together to produce a totalizing Americanization experience for both native- and foreign-born alike.

The Versailles Treaty was a tenuous peace. Upon his arrival in Paris in December 1918, Wilson informed Italian Foreign Minister Sidney Sonnino and Prime Minister Vittorio Orlando that the 1915 Treaty of London granting Italy sections of Slovenia and Dalmatia—ostensibly to protect Italian minorities against Yugoslav barbarism and terror—was void. British officials charged the Italians with territorial aggrandizement too, even as they themselves sought to expand their imperial authority over the last vestiges of Ottoman rule in the Near East. In May 1919, Orlando and Sonnino left Versailles resigned to the high probability that the other Allied Powers had abandoned earlier promises in order to concede the conference to Wilson and his Fourteen Points. As Orlando addressed the Italian parliament, nationalist forces, predominated by Fascists, protested American cooptation of the peace process. His government did not outlast the month of June, and in September Fascist military leader Gabriele D'Annunzio stormed the city of Fiume, which Orlando had conceded at the last minute to neutrality under the League of Nations. Though D'Annunzio acceded to a temporarily restored Italian democratic government in December 1920, it had become clear to American officials that ethnic nationalism remained a powerful ideological force in Italy and other parts of postwar Europe.[46]

As D'Annunzio solidified his occupation of Fiume in late spring of 1920, New York Governor Alfred Smith declared May 24 "Italy Day." The executive office directed all relevant public departments to hold "suitable exercises commemorative of [Italy's] entry into the World War . . . for the purpose of impressing upon our people the desirability of renewing and cementing the ties of friendship, mutual assistance and amity which have so long existed between the peoples of these two nations." The governor seemed to have both local and international goals. New York's populous Italian immigrant communities, nearly 350,000 mostly in New York City's Lower East Side alone by 1910, presented what some Americanizers considered a nearly insurmountable obstacle to national cohesion, particularly given what most Americanizers saw as racially endowed proclivities to anarchism and antidemocratic revolutionary violence. With the support of the board of education, Smith urged public officials to alleviate animosities that Italian immigrants might harbor in response to Wilson's contemptuous abandonment of Italian demands at the Peace of Paris. Smith hoped to head off any domestic unrest among Italian immigrants and union members and to project a different kind of American authority that bound Italian and American interests together in the service of international peace while still leaving room for nationalistic goals.

And Governor Smith heaped praises on Italy and Italian Americans: "The men of Italian birth have for centuries been leaders in the development of the world . . . . Italy through her valiant son, Christopher Columbus, gave America to the world. She furnished a haven for the down trodden and oppressed and a land of opportunity to the ambitious and energetic." Smith also directed his overtures to principals and teachers, whose job it was to join America's historical founding myths begun under Columbus with the imperatives of American-style democratic rule in Europe following the Great War. In the interest of extending American authority over continental Europe with minimal resistance, particularly from hyper-nationalist forces abroad or anarchist or socialist forces at home, Smith offered Italian immigrants a seat at the founders' table. By doing so, he welcomed Italians as fellow white Americans, even in the midst of forceful Americanization and exclusion campaigns that instead recognized them as labor militants, lesser whites, or even black: "the racial group of Italian inhabitants is fusing with the citizen mass as the second generation grows up and enters business and political life, and bringing gifts of the spirit which America needs."[47]

The department of education sought to extend its commemorative activities beyond the scope of Italian contributions to include all of the city's immigrants, children and adults alike. In September 1921, the school board recalled the recent success of "America's Making," a "civic celebration" of a year prior initiated by the late Franklin K. Lane, former secretary of the interior and "himself an immigrant," and issued calls for a second festival. Ettinger reported receiving over 600 pages of suggestions from students, teachers, administrators, and citizens from all five boroughs "of a highly practical and valuable kind." More importantly, he considered "America's Making" a pivotal moment of "incomparable opportunity" in postwar New York and one in which schoolchildren would play the critical role of transmitters of "the fundamental public school purposes of civic equality, the spirit of brotherhood and good will, the abatement of racial animosities aroused by the World War, a closer relation between public education and the large problems of citizenship." Upon the occasion of an invitation to attend America's Making, President Warren G. Harding remarked that "I have said a good many times

WHERE AMERICA-MAKING
IS A REGULAR BUSINESS

*Forty-Eight Thousand Three Hundred Seventy-Six Posters for America's Making,
Each an Original Design, Have Been Made by Children of the Public Schools*

FIGURE 15. Where America-Making Is a Regular Business. The book of America's Making Exposition, held at the 71st Regiment Armory, New York, October 29–November 12, 1921. Courtesy General Research Division, New York Public Library, Astor, Lenox, and Tilden Foundations.

we of America have no racial entity, and we are making therefore, a people which is born of national aspiration. We are the blend of all peoples in the world."

The celebrations of 1920 and 1921 served as precursors to the cultural gifts movement emerging most prominently after 1924 in which some teachers and children challenged their own racial and religious prejudices by opening spaces in school curricula to celebrate the myriad and diverse contributions of immigrants and racial minorities. Yet in 1921, the New York school board had not wholeheartedly embraced cultural gifts to the abandonment of the melting pot of conformity or exclusionism. The Irish organizing committee, for example, called for the ban of display of any national flags other than the United States, arguing that the purpose of the pageant was not to showcase the "national achievements of the mother countries which have contributed their sons and daughters." When pressed into the service of American nationalism and imperial ambitions couched in the language of internationalism, school administrators tended toward support for conformist Americanism with token interventions that espoused a more inclusive citizenship premised on pluralism.[48]

When administrators embraced pluralism before the National Origins Act, it was usually to advance an imperial framework under the auspices of mutual cooperation and security. In November 1923, acting mayor Murray Hulbert called on New Yorkers to celebrate the 100th anniversary of the Monroe Doctrine. Ettinger immediately obliged. In coordination with the International Pan American Committee, Ettinger gave "assurances" that "everything possible will be done to insure a proper observance in our schools" and committee chair John Barrett, appointed by the late President Harding, praised the "patriotic men and women, boys and girls" for celebrating the "world famous Monroe Doctrine." Barrett reported the participation of "fully tens of millions of other students" across America joining New York City schoolchildren and teachers in recalling the "immortal words of President Monroe" that "saved Mexico, Central and South America, and the Islands of the West Indies" from both "European and Asiatic colonization" and "preserved the democratic form of government throughout the entire western hemisphere."

Likening the southerly republics to children, Barrett noted that there had "grown up" twenty-one independent self-governed states "forming the great and powerful Pan American Union" that conducted "an international commerce valued at nearly twenty billions of dollars." In the wake of the Bolshevik Revolution, it was the capitalist system enforced through American corporate and military power that justly warranted, in Barrett's formulation, "the defense of liberty wherever threatened" and the exercise of "wise American policy." The organizers in New York cast the Monroe Doctrine, as Barrett and national organizers had done, as at once American in origin—a nation of "unexampled progress in industrial life"—and internationalist in scope and meaning "championed by every American whether native or adopted." Not only should citizens of Latin American republics hold "dear" Monroe's principles, but European immigrants in New York might also come to share in the "hope of the world's oppressed."[49]

The inclusiveness of the school board's pageants between the close of the war and 1924 did not prevent, nor did most officials attempt to prevent, the exclusivity of immigration and citizenship enshrined in the National Origins

Act. On May 17, 1924, one week before the National Origins Act became law, descendants of Manhattan's original Dutch settlers celebrated the 300th anniversary of the settlement of New Amsterdam. The *Times* described a process of racial assimilation that unfolded in New York once the Dutch intermarried with successive waves of settlers: "In time the different racial strains were blended, Dutch mixing with Walloon, French and English, and later with the Germans. The common experiences served to strengthen the bonds between them, and made them share a kinship which they did not feel toward their relatives in Europe." The *Times* identified racial assimilation as an essential component of the "epic of America"—wilderness cleared by an amalgam of white frontier settlements and then gradually replaced by civilization "with its schools and churches and industries."[50] The *Times* called for a renewed commitment to national progress modeled on the experiences of Manhattan's first European settlers who "pushed the frontier across the continent from Wall Street to the Golden Gate and laid the foundations of an empire." The daily at once celebrated the role of immigrants in forging the American nation through imperial conquest and restricted such historical acts to those of unquestionable whiteness. The editorial also forecast the trajectories of whiteness following coercive Americanization and immigration restriction. In 1924, as the quota system severely curtailed immigration from southern and eastern Europe—the culmination of four decades of robust racial nationalism whose proponents won a major victory with the Chinese Exclusion Act—newly excluded European "races" already residing in the United States began a process of becoming white. As Matthew Frye Jacobson notes, the National Origins Act represented the "high-water mark of Anglo-Saxon or Nordic supremacy" but also created conditions for the "re-drawing of racial lines" and the ascendency of "monolithic whiteness."[51]

Despite the transformation of the Americanization movement into a crusade against political radicalism, multilingualism, and foreign culture that effectively alienated many of the people it sought to subsume into the American polity and workforce, New York's public schools sustained their efforts to integrate the city's European immigrant children and their families into the American fabric, even if its methods were often coercive and imperialistic in tone. By the time the National Origins Act became law, New York boasted 2 million foreign-born, 2.3 million native-born of foreign parents, and a meager 1.5 million native-born of native parents. School authorities continued to press an agenda of assimilation. "Instruction for naturalization and training in citizenship is a logical part of the public school responsibility," argued the Council on Immigrant Education, as it expressed its gratitude for quota restriction that would "give the public schools a much greater opportunity to teach aliens than in the days when they came here in floods." This was a process by which the "races" of Europe who had, according to the council, swamped New York over the last forty years could at last become "Caucasian" through public education.[52]

Beginning in the 1920s and accelerating through the experiences of the Great Depression and World War II, the "grand" racial taxonomies of black, white, brown, yellow, and red regained their early nineteenth-century salience over the "minor" racial divisions among European nationalities. The New York school board's 1925 annual report revealed the juxtaposition of the persistence of European "racial" divisions and their initial erosion through schooling: "Everybody looks to the public school system for help in solving the social and moral . . . problems of society . . . . In this city the situation is rendered more complex by . . . the fact that our schools must solve special problems which arise from [a] population, which includes children and adults of nearly every race. However, these conditions are not causes for complaint and over-conservatism. Rather are they causes for gratification and progress." The *Times* again invoked America's racial history of whiteness: "In a short time racial consciousness had disappeared. Today the descendants of these early pioneers, though proud of their origin, are utterly unconscious of being anything but Americans." Though it would take the better part of three decades for the popular historical narrative to reflect the contributions of "new immigrants" from Europe, they too came to share in the building of and belief in American democracy. In doing so, they became not only Americans but also whites, and they were consequently granted access to republican citizenship and national belonging often denied to nonwhites, both native- and foreign-born.[53]

Colonial Citizens, Deportable Citizens

In fifty years the vast majority of the people of the United States
will be Latin and not Teutonic. Our future is in the hands of
people who in blood and tradition are alien to the fathers of the
Republic . . . . Yet these adopted children must be taught to love
and venerate the principles of the fathers . . . . Our salvation—
and theirs—is by way of education.[1]

CHARLES WESLEY REED, *"The Comparative Low Standing
of the Public Schools,"* 1911

Alas! Puerto Rico is our problem child. It is our war trophy of
a few years back. It has made a goodly number of Americans
into millionaires—Sugar Kings. It has given headaches to a
few members of Congressional Committees whose business
it is to hear Puerto Rico's pleas for justice and help. It has
given delightful vacations to a few tourists . . . . But by and
large, Puerto Rico just doesn't exist as far as most of us are
concerned.[2]

BELLE BOONE BEARD, *"Puerto Rico—
The Forty-Ninth State?"* 1945

ALMOST AS IF ON CUE, Princeton economist Robert Foerster submitted
to the Department of Labor a report on the racial implications of Latin
American and West Indian immigration to the United States. In 1925, the
year after National Origins quotas took effect, he warned that 90 million
black and brown people "lying south" of the US or on "islands adjacent
thereto" represented a policy issue an order of magnitude greater than the
problem of southern and eastern European immigration that the National
Origins Act supposedly solved. The act had not placed quotas on any nation
in the Western Hemisphere. Having adopted the alarmist language of
Lothrop Stoddard's "rising tide of color" to describe the situation, Foerster
singled out Mexicans as the primary problem with which immigration officials and policymakers must grapple.

Foerster claimed that the postindependence population of Mexico was decidedly less European in its racial attributes and cultural habits than it had been under Spanish rule. "It is entirely fitting, since no confusion will result, to call this [mixed] stock Mexican, but if a color designation is used it is plainly a mistake to continue the common practice [in the United States] of speaking of the stock as white," he argued. His delineation of race foretold the US Census Bureau's 1930 decision to categorize Mexicans as a separate race (from whites). For Foerster, color and race aligned with capacity for civilization and, by extension, capacity for self-government: "no effective democracy resting on universal suffrage can come quickly in a country whose population is still so retrograde as the Mexican in the essential prerequisites of democracy." The anti-imperialists of the post–Civil War era had been correct, he concluded. The racial inferiority of the populations inhabiting the southerly geographic spaces of US imperial desire was[anathema]to the genius of the American democratic experiment.

Education, he continued, hardly solved a biological problem of low intelligence. After calling into question "environmental" considerations of poverty, state violence, and the deleterious effects of New Spain's racial order, Foerster asserted "no degree of education or other social action can effectually overcome the handicap," and even if the "half-breed's position" warranted a study of environmental factors, "the burden of correction may prove very heavy and not necessarily one that can be sustained without great loss." His views often complemented earlier characterizations of Mexicans and Mexican Americans. As California Immigration and Housing officials reported in 1916, "the immigrants of this race seem to have a specific gravity which keeps them at the bottom of the district melting pot . . . . [They are] a primitive people, more Indian than Latin, brought here originally by the [American] corporations for peon labor."[3] In other words, schools for Mexicans in Mexico or the United States were probably a waste of taxpayer money.[4]

While of primary concern, Mexico was not the only target of Foerster's report. He offered a country-by-country analysis of the race stocks of Latin America, and "Porto Rico" appeared in brief. Foerster noted that in 1920, the island's white population was in fact high at 73 percent of 1.3 million, with a black population just under 4 percent and mulattos at around 23 percent. Seemingly heartened that "no *pure* Indian stock has survived until to-day," Foerster warned that "Indian features can still be observed," fueled by migration from neighboring islands. His preoccupation with "Indian features" joined Mexicans and Puerto Ricans as undesirable and dangerous, no matter their legal claims to citizenship.

But more important to this study are the ways in which Foerster described Puerto Rico in relation to the United States. His choice of racial categories aligned with 1920 US census categories to describe immigrants from Latin America not easily identifiable as "negro" or "mulatto." At the time, the Census Bureau classified the racially mixed creole populations of the Americas as white unless visibly identifiable as black and therefore subject to the unwritten one-drop rule. According to the basic racial framework of his report, most Puerto Ricans would make acceptable white citizens should they choose to leave the island for the mainland. Foerster did not level any direct charges of dangerous racial amalgamation or corrosion of democracy against would-be migrants as he did against Mexicans. Implicitly, however, his silence on Puerto Rico's status as a US colony and his statistical analysis of the island's racial composition as part of his larger study of race in Latin America and the Caribbean elided US legal categorizations of most Puerto Ricans as white. In essence, Foerster embedded Puerto Rico within the broader "racial problems involved in immigration from Latin America and the West Indies." Despite the relatively recent imposition of US citizenship via the Jones Act of 1917, he marked Puerto Ricans not as US citizens, white or otherwise, but as prospective immigrants and perpetual foreigners.[5]

The National Origins Act represented a critical turning point for Foerster and other restrictionists of the 1920s. Having blocked the passage of many southern and eastern European "stocks" to the United States, the act allowed free passage from Mexico, Puerto Rico, and other parts of Latin America and the Caribbean, the migrants from which threatened to wrest "control of the future race stock of the United States" from white Americans. "If it is desired to maintain a high average of ability, intelligence, and citizenship no simpler device is at hand than the nonadmission from this time forward of all dubious race elements," Foerster argued. Following decades of US imperial expansion in Puerto Rico, Panama, Cuba, Mexico and other parts of Central and South America and the Caribbean, restrictionists placed the adjacent regions at the center of debates over the fitness of immigrants and American citizens of Mexican and Puerto Rican descent for the duties of US citizenship. In doing so, they trotted out familiar racist arguments and strategies that flipped the colonial relationship and raised the prospect of an impending colonization of the United States by allegedly inferior persons.

This chapter offers what historian Natalia Molina calls a "relational" framework through which to understand the place of Mexicans and Puerto Ricans in American schools, institutions integral to nation- and empire-building projects in the Southwestern states, the Caribbean, and in New York City, where over 45,000 Puerto Ricans resided by 1930. It departs from the previous chapters in two primary ways. First, it more closely examines how schools served as vehicles through which to impose racial and colonial status among multiple national groups—Mexicans and Puerto Ricans—bound to the United States in unequal ways, though certainly familiar to the subjects of the previous chapters. Moreover, it does so with a broader geographic scope in mind. For example, while Chinese and Japanese Americans made similar claims to schooling and citizenship in San Francisco, I have shown how they navigated the politics of immigration and empire within a single school district. Here I demonstrate the interconnectedness of race making and empire building in multiple locations within a single chapter rather than across them.

Second, this chapter extends the book's chronology beyond the National Origins Act. It carries the narrative forward into the thirty-year period between 1924, when Congress enacted landmark immigration restrictions targeting Europeans and Asians, and 1954, when the Immigration and Naturalization Service implemented a massive deportation campaign, racistly dubbed "Operation Wetback." I argue that while older, more established ways of creating "good" citizens continued to shape public education efforts in both states and territories, the period also ushered in a "new regime of 'race-making'" in regard to the education of Latin Americans, especially Mexicans and Puerto Ricans. Forged during the rise of New Deal liberalism and new expectations about state obligations to the basic welfare of its citizens, explanations for poor school performance began to shift, in some cases, from biological race to cultural deficiencies. These novel explanations entrenched, rather than eroded, practices of segregation and Americanization in both colony (Puerto Rico) and metropole (the Southwest). Yet in response, Mexican Americans and Puerto Ricans began to claim greater and more equal access to the privileges of citizenship at the same time that the forces of immigration restriction and colonialism sought their continued repression.

Critical to the relational process of race making were the historical and lived experiences of US empire and the impositions of citizenship. The Treaty of Guadalupe-Hidalgo, which ended military hostilities between the United States and Mexico in 1848, stipulated that Mexicans remaining in the ceded territory one year after the ratification of the treaty and "without having declared their intention to retain the character of Mexicans" automatically became US citizens. Fewer than 3 percent remained Mexican nationals as a result. Similarly, in 1917, Congress conferred US citizenship on all Puerto Ricans born on the island without consultation or referendum from the island's population. As Mae Ngai has argued of the Mexican example, both cases of American citizenship were not consensual or solicited but instead imposed, marking each group as "a conquered population" whose citizenship remained unstable, unfulfilled, and subject to the whims of Congress and the Supreme Court. Histories of US colonialism in Mexico and Puerto Rico then joined an alleged unpreparedness for full citizenship to familiar notions of Indian and black inferiority, challenged their legal and social claims to whiteness, and denied their children access to adequate or equal public schooling.[6]

Though the historical proximity of each school-age population to the actual experience of dispossession, conquest, and forced citizenship differed considerably, both navigated school systems imbued with the racial hierarchies and imperatives of colonial rule. In the Southwest, water diversion projects afforded agribusiness interests command of vast tracts of previously unworkable land, and growers demanded a cheap, malleable, and by the 1930s, deportable immigrant labor force. These new realities permeated debates about the education of Mexican American children, who were often assumed to aspire to or be suited for the transience of seasonal labor. Most Mexican American children in the Southwest attended segregated schools taught or at least administered by Anglo-Americans. Parents and students had little power over curriculum and policy, and thus relied on both proven and unproven strategies of resistance we have seen especially in San Francisco, Hawai'i, and Atlanta. In Puerto Rico, like in Hawai'i, sugar came to dominant the island economy. Both US colonial officials and elite *creoles* sought ways to reform and control workers, thus bringing them into the orbit of US capital. Rural schools quickly became essential to what elite Puerto Ricans imagined as national *regeneración*. By the 1930s, Puerto Ricans made up the majority of the teaching and administrative force in the island's colonial school system. They were able to leverage the importance of racial and national uplift projects among the rural working classes in order to shape and articulate their own visions for Puerto Rico's colonial relationship with the United States.

By bringing these two cases together, we can see how schools and colonialism reciprocated in both uneven and complementary ways, primarily through the processes of immigration restriction and race making. The historical and contemporary imperatives of empire remained at the center of debates over schooling and citizenship after 1924. In the 1930s, as the pains of economic depression generated intensely racist reactions to Mexican immigration and Puerto Rican migration to the mainland, many school officials and teachers in the Southwest kowtowed to their peers at more elite academic and social institutions who claimed that the mental inferiority of Mexican children deemed them unfit to learn in integrated classrooms. In 1935, a scathing report on the inherited intelligence of Puerto Rican schoolchildren in East Harlem, New York, produced a complex set of responses from Puerto Rican educators on the island and migrants in New York that shaped debates over nationalism and statehood before World War II. While elite educators in Puerto Rico denounced the report's findings as racist, some also reinforced US racialized depictions of the island's population by arguing that the "colored" migrants in New York in no way represented the fitness for citizenship of the island's white majority. Mental testing proved to be a primary catalyst for resistance, galvanizing calls for an end to English-only instruction in Puerto Rico and for the collapse of racist segregation of Mexican Americans throughout the Southwest. Despite victories in both cases, empire and education continue to shape the citizenship of both groups.

SCHOOLING CONQUERED CITIZENS
BEFORE THE DEPRESSION

Beginning in the 1830s, the United States extended colonial authority over vast sections of Spain's New World empire. Anglo settlers arrived in Texas in ever-increasing numbers, claimed independence from Mexico in 1836, and presaged the 1846–48 war that ended in Mexico's defeat and cession of over half of its northern territory. Over 90 percent of Mexican nationals living within the ceded territory became by default US citizens. This was, from the outset, a hollow citizenship, and by the outbreak of the Mexican Revolution in 1910 and the subsequent influx of Mexican nationals north of the border, the institutional structures of both school segregation and the Americanization of Mexican children in the Southwest were already in place. The Treaty of Guadalupe-Hidalgo secured US authority over Mexicans living in the newly acquired territories, and though civil and property rights were to warrant protection under the provisions of the treaty, local, state, and territorial practices stripped many of those rights and other privileges of US citizenship. Equal schools were no exception.

As public education expanded in the southwestern states and territories in the last three decades of the nineteenth century, greatly increasing access to institutions previously dominated by Catholic and Protestant authorities, systematic discrimination characterized the experience of Mexican American children.[7] When Mexican communities in the Southwest grew in size and number beginning in the 1890s, as Mexican nationals fled the US-backed economic policies of Porfirio Díaz, Anglo officials segregated Mexican schoolchildren as a matter of practice if not of law. Eighty-five percent of schools in the Southwest were segregated in some form by the mid-1930s. Since most districts did not write segregation into their school codes, residential patterns offered white school authorities plausible deniability of overt discrimination. Consequently, separate schools became part of a broader array of imperial constructions of space that bisected and divided communities according to race and national origin.[8] As more workers and their families left Mexico for the United States in the decade after the revolution, their children encountered public schools that bore the attitudes, symbols, and practices of American imperialism that had spurred their migration from their homeland in the first place. They became joined to, as historian Rodolfo Acuña has described, colonized Mexicans native to the Southwest but excluded from the institutions, privileges, and narratives of American citizenship.[9]

Central to formulations of Mexican foreignness and unfitness for citizenship during the 1910s and 1920s was the image of the dogmatic Mexican nationalist. In the year following the outbreak of the Mexican Revolution, sociologist John Kenneth Turner condemned the southern border crisis as one of overt American aggression against Mexican revolutionary forces. Troubled by the now apparent confirmation of his earlier prediction that the heads of US corporations would use their political leverage to prop up the then thirty-four-year dictatorship of Porfirio Díaz, Turner unintentionally, if sympathetically, implicated Mexicans living north of the border in the revolutionary spirit proliferating to the south: "The confessed purpose [of this intervention by the United States] is to crush the revolution by cutting off the source of its supplies and by preventing patriotic Mexicans residing in the United States from going home to fight for the freedom of their country."[10] Other American observers concluded that given a call to arms against a Mexican government enthralled to US commercial interests, Mexicans in the United States would unequivocally answer that call and threaten to upset the balance of "peaceful" trade between the two countries. In this constructed and repeatedly inscribed scenario, Mexicans were aggressive, bombastic nationalists—Americans, pragmatic economic actors. Conclusions of this variety ignored much deeper historical and imperial connections that tethered the people and governments of the United States and Mexico to each other in unequal ways—a set of relationships with direct implications for questions of Mexican American belonging, citizenship, and education.

Some shared Turner's assumption that though removed from Mexico in a physical sense, migrants and their children, including those born with American citizenship, remained forever tied to the homeland by race, history, and culture. One California governor's report cited the arguments of Americanization teachers who characterized Mexicans as "proud of their country of birth and slow to assimilate." In his 1930 critique of segregated schools, Emory Bogardus argued that Mexicans have "deep and abiding feelings of loyalty" and that because they are "of Latin temperament ... their feelings and emotions are not easily changed," a re-inscription of biological race for the purposes of advancing a liberal education policy.[11] Sociological interviews conducted in 1926 and 1927 seemed to confirm such attitudes. "I would rather die before changing my citizenship," one migrant worker reported to the Social Science Research Council. Another interviewee exclaimed that "if there was a war between Mexico and the United States, I wouldn't go to shoot my own brothers. The Americans wouldn't be foolish enough to give us arms for they know that all the Mexicans would turn against them." These statements suggest an understanding among working-class Mexican immigrants that mutual suspicion, antagonism, and the ability of the more powerful United States to muster military force to protect its economic investments south of the border characterized the US-Mexico relationship.[12]

Between 1910 and 1930, Mexicans constituted the fastest-growing segment of the populations of Arizona, California, Colorado, New Mexico, and Texas. Arizona boasted the highest percentage of its total population at over 25 percent by the time of the 1930 census. By 1927, Mexican and Mexican American children comprised nearly 10 percent of California's public school enrollment, including over 50 percent in Los Angeles, where white residents applied "pressure," according to one school official, to "force a modification" in the school district's principle of nondistinction of race. The district strategically placed "certain neighborhood schools," as they became known, "to absorb the majority of the Mexican pupils" according to patterns of residential segregation. A 1933 US Office of Education report noted that in the case of racially mixed neighborhood schools, Anglos "occasionally move to other neighborhoods, insist on the establishment of separate classes, or . . . acquire a more tolerant attitude toward the situation." Regardless, the report claimed, Mexican children had "special needs" with which many Anglo teachers were ill-equipped to deal, particularly in smaller districts where integration prevailed for budgetary or enrollment reasons. Districts identified these "special needs" primarily in terms of literacy and English language instruction, but also argued that integration had resulted in the development of "unpleasant characteristics" among Mexican children, who bore "little resemblance to the alert, friendly, industrious Mexican children one sees in some [segregated] city schoolrooms where conditions are favorable."[13] In cases of integrated classrooms and schoolhouses, white observers typically found it nearly self-evident that alleged attempts of Mexican children to resist Americanization efforts remained the key stumbling blocks to their transformation into good citizens. As one University of Chicago M. A. candidate noted in her 1926 thesis on integrated San Antonio schools, "Mexican children form their own ball teams and do not want to play with American children. Unless carefully watched, Mexican children speak Spanish."[14] Others similarly blamed the few officials of Mexican descent, where they existed, for failing to provide adequate school buildings.[15]

By the early 1930s, *some* white observers were less convinced of the efficacy of segregating Chicano students. Despite the prevalence of racist claims about Mexican clannishness and self-imposed insularity from the Southwest's Anglo communities, sociological assessments began to reflect a liberal shift to questions about the underlying social and economic causes of the "problem" of Mexican education. In a 1930 report, the California Department of Industrial Relations asserted that low and sporadic wages in the new large-scale industrial and agricultural economies combined with restrictions on property acquisition bred shiftlessness, ignorance, "wretched housing," and in turn an aversion or apathy to formal schooling. But the CDIR also cited racism and nativism as key elements in sustaining such conditions: "we should not expect the Mexicans to be eager to become citizens when they are made to feel that they are persons with whom we do not desire to associate."[16] Others lamented the "unfortunate" nature of race relations between Anglo- and Spanish-Americans, the latter of whom, after "three or four generations are still not well assimilated," one of the central missions of public schooling.

Though these self-described liberals tended to fall back on a supposedly "deep-seated" national loyalty among Mexicans in the United States, racism and nativism served as increasingly prominent variables in sociological assessments of Mexican education and naturalization.[17] Herman Feldman of Dartmouth College described in 1931 the sinister and unethical means by which American "industrialists" in the South and West took advantage of relaxed border enforcement during World War I to commit "violations of the contract-labor law, the literacy test," and to prevent Mexican laborers from seeking higher wages elsewhere under the threat of arrest or deportation.[18] The migrant camps and the primary schools attached to them had become extensions of the security state and the border patrol that increasingly subjected Mexicans to racially and criminally inscribed assumptions about their fitness for national belonging. "Citizenship is disappointing to him," concluded Bogardus in 1934, as "he is still likely to be treated as a Mexican and a foreigner."[19] In other words, eighty years on, neither the American conquest of the Southwest and subsequent American corporate-led modernization of Mexico that prompted large-scale northern migration, nor the schooling of Mexican immigrants and US citizens of Mexican ancestry had transformed Mexicans into Americans.

"THOSE WHO WEAR NECK TIES AND THOSE WHO DON'T"[20]

Like in the Southwest, the expansion of public education was central to the US imperial project in Puerto Rico. Local teachers, administrators, and eventually parents and students shaped debates about the fitness for US citizenship. Following the two-year military occupation that began in 1898, the United States defined Puerto Rico as an "unincorporated territory," a designation that remains today, despite nominal changes in language. There, the US colonial state located military bases, policed and accessed the Panama Canal, and secured lucrative investments in agricultural commodities, especially sugar, which accounted for 60 percent of Puerto Rico's exports by 1945. The Foraker Act of 1900, which served as Puerto Rico's first constitution under US rule, effectively defined Puerto Ricans as colonial subjects, allowing for extremely limited civil government. All laws passed by the Puerto Rican House of Delegates were subject to approval by the US Congress. The Jones Act of 1917 conferred US citizenship on Puerto Ricans and required

FIGURE 16. America's Greatest Gift to Porto Rico—the Public School, Caguas, ca. 1900. Stereograph. Underwood and Underwood. Courtesy Library of Congress, Prints and Photographs Division, FSA / OWI Photograph Collection, LC-USZ62–65597.

military-age males to register for service, but the island's colonial status and prevailing racial ideologies complicated notions of citizenship, which were always defined in relation to the US mainland as "foreign in a domestic sense" and often subject to black / white racial binaries. Nevertheless, American officials demanded support from Puerto Ricans for the US colonial project on the island, and they aggressively promoted schools as institutions through which Puerto Rico would be transformed from an illiterate, impoverished, rural, and poorly governed Spanish colony into a literate, prosperous, and modern American one.

Prevailing narratives of American colonial schooling in Puerto Rico have tended to highlight a sharp dichotomy between US official imperatives for complete Americanization on the one hand and a persistent and assertive nationalist resistance from Puerto Rican teachers, parents, and students on the other. The story goes something like this: In the first two decades of US colonial rule, the Department of Education recruited American teachers to teach and to train local teachers and sent Puerto Rican teachers to the United States for Americanization training. While American recruits were in short supply, the state believed it could rely on the professional and middle-class familiarity of many "local" teachers to advance the Americanization campaign aimed at eradicating Puerto Rican culture, including language and historical memory. According to this narrative, the colonial state was wrong. Many Puerto Rican teachers as well as parents and students refused to accommodate colonialism, particularly its emphasis on a benevolent US imperialism and on English-only education. Instead, they asserted an emergent and collective nationalist identity that eventually bore fruit with the coming of the Cold War. Teachers then, were central to the formation of Puerto Rican nationalism in the first half of the twentieth century, a time when the US colonial state exercised tremendous authority over the island.[21]

But the narrative, historian Solsiree del Moral tells us, is far more interesting and complicated. Rather than a clear case of imperial domination met at every step with local resistance, schooling in Puerto Rico looked more like a kind of negotiated "cultural politics" through which Puerto Rican teachers in particular resisted "racist Americanization" demanded by US officials but also "contribut[ed] to and complement[ed] a broader racial and social uplift project" in which both "elite teachers" and colonial officials shared mutually sustaining vested interests. These negotiations between "intermediate actors" and the colonial state facilitated important changes in the nature of citizenship in Puerto Rico and also led to colonial policy changes in the first half of the twentieth century, including US citizenship for Puerto Ricans born on the island. So while US empire remained intact, negotiated educational practices contributed significantly to Puerto Rico's reformed status as a "Free Associated State" in 1952.[22]

Until the passage of the Jones Act in 1917, US school administrators in Puerto Rico promoted an educational vision that they believed contrasted sharply with Spanish colonial policy on the island. Following the wave of revolutions that swept the Americas in the late eighteenth and early nineteenth centuries, Spain doubled down on its colonies of Cuba and Puerto Rico. Though sugar production declined in Puerto Rico by 1850, coffee generated new forms of labor exploitation in the mountainous highlands. In response to increased migration from Spain and the further consolidation of *peninsulares* privilege, creole Puerto Ricans asserted a novel kind of anticolonial nationalism that included both calls for reform and outright independence. They directed one of their primary critiques of Spanish rule at the lack of attention to education. But creole elites were not without their own class prejudices. While they celebrated working-class culture as the foundation of either a new state or reformed colony, elites also subscribed to racist eugenic formulations of paternalism and social engineering. Common among other creole elites throughout Spanish America, those in Puerto Rico believed that the right kinds of educational and sanitation policies could regenerate the racial health of the island's rural majority. They found both severely lacking in Spanish colonial policy.[23]

When American forces occupied Puerto Rico beginning in late 1898, US officials agreed with creoles that Spanish educational efforts lacked a broad social base and therefore failed as mechanisms for racial regeneration and uplift. As Dr. Tulio Larrínaga, a creole elite and commissioner of Puerto Rico to Washington, DC, reported in 1905: "In the matter of education we have been more fortunate [than in global coffee export markets]. The ablest educators have been sent to Porto Rico. Dr. [Marvin] Brumbaugh," the first appointed commissioner of education in Puerto Rico from 1900 to 1902, "was successful in founding schools there; and he and Professor [Samuel] Lindsay," the island's second commissioner from 1902 to 1904, "were instrumental in establishing there an efficient system of education."[24] Larrínaga was the kind of creole elite that US officials believed they could rely on to promote Americanization policies in Puerto Rico. His account is telling of US efforts to present a specific narrative about schools, chiefly that none of sufficient quality existed under Spanish rule. Thus, the island became a blank slate on which the new imperial power could write school laws, distribute funding, and implement Americanization policies in accordance with its goal of binding Puerto Rico to the United States as a critical economic and strategic colony in the Caribbean.[25]

Larrínaga's description of US colonial schools as "efficient" is also telling of the broader mantra of US education in the early twentieth century. Not only were school budgets to be efficient in the allocation of local, state, and in the case of colonial possessions, federal tax dollars—the vestiges of more conservative nineteenth-century visions of schooling as the obligation of elites and religious institutions only to their progeny and congregations—but schools were also supposed to generate efficiencies among the children of working-class citizens, immigrants, and colonial subjects. Schools, officials argued, instilled values of productivity, patriotism, and social order among society's youngest members and reciprocally strengthened community, nation, and empire. Spanish neglect of Puerto Rico's education needs, American educators charged, was emblematic of a larger Iberian colonial tyranny that contrasted sharply with a more liberal and benevolent US imperial rule. In the end, Americans argued, the Spanish system yielded all kinds of inefficiencies in agricultural production and allocation of municipal resources, and created deep resentment among Puerto Ricans. American rule was to be different.

But Larrínaga's brief 1905 report also criticized colonial restrictions on self-government: "[T]he American Congress did not for the moment care to commit itself [through passage of the Foraker Act of 1900] to any specific form of government that might in the future be an impediment in the enforcement of the general policy of the country . . . . [We] Porto Ricans venture to hope that in the near future the Congress will allow Porto Ricans a larger measure of self-government." Here, in the same document in which he extolled the virtues of US colonial schools, Larrínaga expressed suspicion about Americans' claims that their empire was a different kind than that of Spain. Taken as a whole, his report spoke to the equivocal nature of Puerto Rican resistance in the early twentieth century. Officials like Larrínaga could at once criticize US policy as too restrictive of self-rule and at odds with "the spirit of American institutions" and also praise aspects of US policy, especially its commitment to the creation of a modern system of public instruction. US goals then, in some ways but not others, fit rather well with those of creole elites like Larrínaga, who saw the need for racial and social uplift among working-class, rural Puerto Ricans. As more Puerto Ricans migrated to the metropole in the 1920s, elites would again take up the contradictions of US rule and generate their own in relation to US racial norms.[26]

In the first three decades of the twentieth century, an expanding class of *magisterio* (teachers) challenged US official educational imperatives and asserted their own ideas about the place of schools in Puerto Rico's emerging modernity, even if under the institutional and policy structures of US colonialism. They shared with their US colleagues some ideas about the importance of scientific management, public health, and social engineering to state-building projects, colonial or otherwise. However, elite teachers developed their interpretations of eugenics distinct from mainland practitioners. While many prominent American eugenicists advocated sterilization and segregation as the primary methods by which to engineer racial health, Puerto Rican eugenicists, like their counterparts throughout Latin America, privileged *regeneración* of the national body.

Collectively, *regeneración* involved a threefold makeover of the home, school, and nation. Through schools, elite teachers hoped to train and employ the nation's children as models for parents and future generations in home economics, physical fitness, and agricultural production. And teachers attended their visions for national *regeneración* with modern curriculum custom-designed by the colonial Department of Education. They assigned texts like *Sanitation and Hygiene for the Tropics* (1920) to girls in high school home economics and developed organized sport regiments for boys. Literacy was also central to the *regeneración* plans of Puerto Rican teachers. They concurred with US officials that literacy projects had floundered and pressed those officials for a greater financial and political commitment to expanding education, particularly among the rural poor. Teachers also highlighted high illiteracy rates to critique the shortsighted and ill-conceived plans of the United States to render instruction in English. If the average child attended school for only three years, then it made more sense, teachers argued, to teach in their native Spanish, accelerate reading and writing competency, and leave room for more "practical" instruction. Not only had US colonial administrators pushed for instruction in the wrong language, they had simply not invested enough money, resources, and legal muscle in education. Teachers pressed for compulsory attendance laws and in some cases mandatory night school for illiterate adults, a clear indication that for some the generational shifts occurred too slowly. But these critiques and the absence of others also reaffirmed the colonial project.

As teachers called for practical instruction in Spanish and more teachers and schools, they legitimated US rule by tasking it with fulfilling its pledge to create literate and productive imperial citizens. Elite teachers were more likely to chastise rural parents for an alleged aversion to education than they were to condemn landed rural elites that hired children as cane cutters—labor critical to the colonial export economy that bound the United States and Puerto Rico together in an unequal relationship.[27] These individual and local efforts, teachers believed, would culminate in the regeneration of the health of *la raza,* or "the people," a far more complex social construction than the racial hierarchies of the US imperial state allowed. Indeed, elites employed the term *la raza* to distinguish native Puerto Ricans from American occupiers, including many of the US-born teachers sent to the island to Americanize the teaching force. But in the 1910s and 1920s, their visions for a national community were not direct challenges to American political authority in Puerto Rico. Rather, attempts to implement nationally regenerative projects fit well within the broader goals of the US imperial state, which also sought a more physically and mentally productive, if subordinate, population.[28]

The educational experiences of Mexican Americans and Puerto Ricans through the initial onset of the Great Depression intersected in two key ways. Though separated by fifty years, the colonial expansions of 1848 and 1898 had rendered each population conquered citizens. While both groups possessed legal claims to either birthright or naturalized citizenship, the full exercise of citizenship generated through public education remained elusive. Secondly, many Puerto Ricans and Mexican Americans most impacted by colonial race-making projects did not entirely reject association with US institutions and practices. By the 1920s, Mexican families began to send their US-born children for education in increasing numbers despite segregated schools that taught them their inherited culture was inferior and in need of reform. Meanwhile, Puerto Rican teachers laid claims to citizenship by cultivating their own ideas about racial and social uplift of the rural working class in ways that fit within the prescribed framework of US colonialism. As the final sections demonstrate, colonial citizens sought to expand access to schools for their children amidst heightened calls for their subordination or segregation based on pseudoscientific claims about inferior Mexican and Puerto Rican mental capacity. When many of those children came of age by the late 1930s and early 1940s, they too, like their parents, sought broader social acceptance, upward economic mobility, and the full exercise of citizenship through education.

"POVERTY IS NO SIGN OF MENTAL INFERIORITY"[29]

Beginning in the late 1920s and persisting through the 1930s, intelligence testing became the paramount means of defending the continued segregation of Mexican American students on the one hand, and symbolically challenging Puerto Rican claims to citizenship on the other. In both cases, research teams used mainland school populations that included multiple Mexican American communities in Texas, California, and other southwestern states and the largest contingent of the Puerto Rican diaspora located in New York City. Yet one key difference emerged in the 1930s in regard to these respective testing initiatives. As historian Carlos Kevin Blanton has shown, psychometric testing underwent an important transformation in terms of the "scientific" explanations for the low scores of Mexican American students from the late 1920s through the early 1930s. Rather than rely on race and heredity as the sole basis for conclusions, researchers began to make claims about Mexican "cultural" deficiencies, especially English language illiteracy. Thus, Blanton contends, school administrators continued to segregate Mexican American children, only now they did so on "pedagogical, not racial, grounds." But in East Harlem, the research team commissioned by the Special Committee on Immigration and Naturalization of the New York State Chamber of Commerce found racial heredity to be the sole factor contributing to the low scores of Puerto Rican students. The team used their findings to generate popular support for "the symbolic as [well] as actual exclusion" of Puerto Rican citizens and other Caribbean immigrants, whose hybrid racial identities bucked the American color line but who also allegedly introduced a foreign "Negro" element into the citizenry, adjacent to a growing, politically active African American population in Harlem no less. When examined in relation to one another, both cases of intelligence testing attest to the variety of attempts to use schools to affect changes to immigration and colonial policies in a period when immigrants and colonial subjects were forging their own expressions of citizenship and defying subjugation based on race and national origin.[30]

The intelligence tests used in Mexican American schools during the 1920s represented the accumulation of revisions of the work of French psychologist Alfred Binet. In 1916, Lewis Terman of Stanford University expanded the Binet-Simon Revision test that measured "mental age" to include adults, and the US Army soon used the Stanford-Binet Intelligence Scale to measure the mental capacities of soldiers entering World War I. Despite having failed to conduct any of his own research on the matter, Terman alleged that feeble-mindedness pervaded "Spanish-Indian and Mexican families" and that schooling did little to correct inherited deficiencies. He did, however, argue that they could still become efficient workers, a mantra that fit rather well within pedagogical approaches in African American, Native American, and Hawaiian schools. Terman's test soon began to proliferate throughout school districts in the United States and its colonial territories.[31] As the numbers of both first- and second-generation Mexican immigrants increased during the 1920s, complementing the numbers of Mexican American families native to the Southwest, intelligence testing became the primary means through which school officials justified continued segregation for the purposes of "special" instruction. School bureaucrats in California, for example, derived from intelligence tests that Mexican American children carried to school the burden of "retardation" measurable anywhere from two to four grade levels. These designations had important impacts on secondary school enrollment. When and if Mexican American students reached the eighth grade, many were already sixteen years old, the age at which school attendance became voluntary. Many including Terman recommended that schooling for Mexican American students beyond the eighth grade be vocational in nature, and a host of academic studies emerged to support claims that while Mexicans made hard workers, they lacked the intellectual capacity for democratic citizenship.[32]

It was primarily the racial science of eugenics, so instrumental in the passage of the National Origins Act, that informed assumptions about the mental inferiority of Mexican Americans. But by the late 1920s, some social scientists began to entertain the notion that race alone could not be the sole determinant of intelligence testing outcomes. Even as eugenic arguments persisted, some who tested Mexican American students began to attribute poor performance not only to race but also to environment. Walter Dearborn, director of the Psycho-Educational Clinic at Harvard University, for example, opposed intelligence measurement on the basis of racial heredity alone: "When we fully realize the power of the home, of the school, and of the more general cultural environment . . . we can hardly interpret the findings of the tests in regard to different racial groups as evidence of hereditary intelligence alone."[33] As one education graduate student at the University of Southern California concluded in 1938, "the home life of the Mexican child was very poor. There was little or no educational background," and "ideals of honesty, morality, and cleanliness were extremely different from those of the average American family."[34] The sea change was part of a broader sociological reinterpretation of the plight of Mexican Americans, immigrants, and other minorities in the Southwest, as researchers, school administrators, and teachers increasingly saw socioeconomic and cultural differences as legitimate and logical reasons for cycles of menial labor and poor performance in school. Yet by framing poor test scores within the context of "home life" and "ideals" and by moving away from hardline racist arguments about innate mental capacity, these new scholars were not necessarily embracing or celebrating cultural pluralism per se. They still saw Mexican American homes and values as problems to be reformed and overcome.

Consequently, the shift in methodological interpretation did not signal revisions to school policies, nor did it suppress continued calls for tighter border control and immigration restriction measures. Indeed the two often converged, according to a 1934 University of Southern California study, which found that many public school teachers in the state also favored restriction. Though they claimed to represent "the most loyal friends that Mexicans have in the United States" and served as "excellent spokesmen for the Mexicans' needs," sociologist Emory Bogardus asserted that schoolteachers lamented that Mexicans in the United States were already living far below "American" standards. Citing the "adverse effects of migratory labor and transient living conditions," teachers claimed, "under present conditions, 'Americans' are not adequately providing for the Mexicans." According to the authors of the survey, the Mexican populations of the Southwest retained an alleged Indian transience and needed to be brought under the control and supervision of the state through settlement projects and other means of assimilation, including separate education that addressed their unique challenges.[35] Authors of a relatively sympathetic Texas school survey concurred that "if it were possible to control the movements of Mexicans across the border ... it would do much to relieve the school situation in many communities."[36] Until Anglos accepted Mexicans, not simply as part of the economic order but also as part of the American social fabric, and until Mexicans attempted to reform their habits of mind and body as the schools were struggling to do, restrictive immigration policies and a more militarized southern border allegedly offered the only means of keeping the problem from intensifying.

Given that few serious measures on the order of magnitude of the National Origins Act were likely to present themselves in the mid-1930s, school administrators and teachers doubled down on segregation, which could now draw authority from both eugenic hardliners who saw little potential in Mexican American students and the sociologists and psychologists who now folded cultural factors into their analysis. Even the most liberal theorists and practitioners of educational testing in the 1930s continued to see bilingualism not as an asset to be cultivated but instead as a problem to be isolated, evaluated, and remedied. As George I. Sánchez of the New Mexico Department of Education put it in 1932: "bilingualism, over and above its environmental attributes, is a handicap acting not only upon language expression and language understanding but upon more intricate psychological processes. At the very least it presents an extra obstacle in the learning process of foreign-language children."[37] No longer positing that the new "achievement" tests measured innate mental ability, researchers now claimed that poor performance was primarily the result of "language deficiency," and when administered in Spanish, Mexican American students demonstrated "normal mentality," as the author of one Texas curriculum handbook put it.[38] In sum, the new sociology did little to address the continued segregation of Mexican American children. It simply offered a more liberal interpretation of lower test scores that proved more palatable to a growing coalition of New Deal liberals during the 1930s who came to lead important social and political movements that emphasized "positive rights" and an active state tasked with protecting those rights, including access to public education. But most white liberals usually failed to challenge in substantive ways the realities of the color line that defined schooling in the 1930s for not just Mexican Americans but other minority groups as well.[39]

Moreover, new cultural sensitivities within the testing movement were not exactly harbingers of the end of eugenic arguments proffered by the architects of the National Origins Act. As over 45,000 Puerto Ricans made homes in New York City by the early 1930s, eugenicists affiliated with the New York State Chamber of Commerce challenged the right of Puerto Rican metropolitan migration on the grounds that the migrants' innate mental inferiority presented insurmountable obstacles to their participation in democratic society. Consequently, the intelligence tests administered to Puerto Rican schoolchildren in East Harlem in 1935 reinvigorated popular and official deliberations both on the island and in the metropole about the colonial status of Puerto Rico and the fitness of its inhabitants for US citizenship.

Two shifts, one political and the other demographic, redefined education in Puerto Rico and of Puerto Ricans in the United States in the 1920s. First, experienced elite Puerto Rican teachers replaced many US officials in the Department of Education. This newfound bureaucratic power enabled advocates of *regeneración* to further the goal of transforming rural children into healthy, literate, and productive members of *la raza*. Elite educators and their US collaborators hired, trained, and staffed physical education programs intended to revitalize the physical and moral health of the island's rural population, still 78 percent of the total in 1920. They secured donations from landowners for public recreation spaces, and attempted, with limited success, to get rural parents to buy into the intrinsic and modern value of new physical education regimens. Local teachers held physical education and literacy, the latter of which generated more popular support among rural parents than the former, as twinned projects designed to create a healthy and productive *Puerto Rican* citizenry, not simply second-class colonial subjects of the United States in possession of a hollow citizenship. Yet the launch of the initiatives from within the colonial Department of Education reinforced many of the same goals held by US educators for Puerto Rico, even if Puerto Rican teachers and administrators defined them as local progressive initiatives independent of US rule.[40]

Second, by 1930, approximately 53,000 Puerto Ricans lived in the United States, a tenfold increase from 1910. Citizenship afforded easier migration, and in the 1920s, stagnant sugar exports prompted many more Puerto Ricans to seek employment on the mainland or other parts of the US empire. The vast majority of Puerto Rican migrants settled in New York City, with smaller communities emerging in Florida and in Hawai'i, where sugar planters were eager to exploit new colonial labor pools in efforts to undermine the exercise of US citizenship of an emerging Nisei majority. In New York, members of the *colonia* opened businesses, worked as laborers, formed social organizations, and created alliances with local Tammany Democrats, trading votes for support on issues important to the island, including federal hurricane relief aid and a resolution to the question of sovereignty. Many Puerto Rican New Yorkers were well aware that the Insular Government's policies hindered rather than advanced economic and social progress. As the Great Depression contracted economies across the globe in the 1930s and triggered a return of some Puerto Ricans to the island, immigration restrictionists, who seemed to have reached the apex of their legislative power with the National Origins Act, redirected much of their rhetorical and academic energy toward the exclusion of Puerto Rican US citizens from the mainland. They redeployed the arguments of eugenicists dedicated to cultivating superior racial traits and stymieing the proliferation of allegedly inferior ones.[41]

The debates over the biological intelligence of Puerto Rican schoolchildren in New York informed national discussions about the imperial status of Puerto Rico and the Philippines in the mid-1930s. Congressional approval of the Tydings-McDuffie Act in March 1934 set the Philippines on a ten-year track toward independent self-government and simultaneously reclassified Filipinos as foreign nationals subject to National Origins quota restrictions, though agribusiness interests often lobbied successfully for more substantial flows of cheap labor, especially to Hawaiian sugar plantations. The escalation of New Deal federal assistance coincided, decidedly not coincidentally, with the high point of Puerto Rican nationalism before World War II, and the migrant community in the United States, or *colonia,* found themselves at the center of debates about the colonial status of Puerto Rico and their own status as American citizens of the diaspora. Were they, as Lorrin Thomas has asked, "foreigners with US citizenship, immigrant-citizens but not Americans"? Antonio Barcelo of the Puerto Rican Liberal Party condemned American citizenship as serving "no other purpose than [for Puerto Ricans] to seize it and hurl it in the faces of those who humiliate us."[42]

After the Harlem riots in the spring of 1935, when African American and Puerto Rican residents protested police brutality, substandard housing, unemployment, and racial inequality, at times in solidarity and at others times at cross purposes, eugenicists Clairette P. Armstrong, Edith M.

Achilles, and Mervin J. Sacks subjected 159 Puerto Rican students at Public School 57 in East Harlem to psychometric intelligence testing. The Special Committee on Immigration and Naturalization of the New York State Chamber of Commerce commissioned the study under the leadership of John B. Trevor, a colleague of Harry H. Laughlin, the leading researcher at the Eugenics Records Office at Cold Springs Harbor, New York—regarded by historians as the most influential eugenicist voice in matters of immigration restriction during the 1920s. The results, in retrospect, were unsurprising given the individuals involved.

In the previous year, Armstrong, who worked as the psychologist for the City of New York Children's Court, revealed her career-long motives in a refutation of studies conducted by J. B. Maller and Harry Shulman on juvenile delinquency and intelligence. Of particular importance to Armstrong was the omission of "nationality origins" in Maller and Shulman's analyses: "The common denominator of delinquency and crime, by and large is low-grade immigration .... Of the approximately 12,000 children arraigned yearly in the Children's Court, fewer than a fifth are second-generation American-born white.... These children are also far below the average public school child in intelligence." Armstrong couched her arguments in the language of a "clash of civilization," whereby "intellectually dull immigrants thrust into our complicated, highly organized civilization are unable to adjust their likewise intellectually dull offspring to the exigencies of such environment." Why, she extolled, "should the United States continue to admit immigrants who lower standards of education any more than the schools should undertake to educate the chimpanzee?" Her rhetorical question echoed the calls of Foerster in 1925 for the cessation of regular academic education for Mexicans and other inferior immigrants. Eugenicists found such efforts futile.

Given the successful implementation of strict quotas on Asians and southern and eastern Europeans as part of the National Origins Act, the unspoken targets of Armstrong's vitriol were very likely migrants from Latin America and the Caribbean, including Mexicans and Puerto Ricans. As a potential solution save wholesale immigration restriction that included colonial citizens in Puerto Rico, the Philippines, and other insular possessions, Armstrong prescribed "lower standards of education for the lowgrade immigrant offspring," including "more special classes of a manual nature requiring less of the pupil" and "some ethical training" in order to mitigate what she perceived as a problem of rampant delinquency among nonwhite immigrant youth.[43]

A little over a year later and in no uncertain terms, the committee charged that Puerto Rican children in New York were "very inferior" to the control groups: "But few bright or even average Puerto Ricans were found." They recommended that because "the majority of Puerto Rican children are so low in intelligence . . . they require education of a simplified, manual sort, preferably industrial, for they cannot adjust in a school system emphasizing the three R's." In their report, the committee certainly singled out Puerto Rican schoolchildren as a particularly pernicious threat to the character of the American citizenry but also argued that Puerto Ricans "[added] greatly to the already tremendous problem of intellectually subnormal school retardates of alien parentage." They concluded that there was simply no possibility for assimilation of Puerto Rican children, who "were helping to turn the tide back to a lower stage of progress."[44]

Puerto Rican leaders both in New York and on the island contested the committee's findings, but did so for both overlapping and divergent reasons. M. Rios Ocana, secretary of the Puerto Rican Casino of Brooklyn, challenged the researchers, especially Sacks, "to go to Puerto Rico to make a complete investigation of the mental qualifications of our people." Ocana highlighted the duality of Puerto Rican identity and citizenship: "We Puerto Ricans are in a state of transition. We feel that we have to leave behind the theories of the old Spanish culture and absorb the new spirit of American ideals"—a position in some ways at odds with many colonial elites in Puerto Rico, including teachers and school administrators. But, Ocana lamented, "if, in spite of our attitude, we are forever condemned to a position of inferiority, then we will have no other alternative [but] to follow the ideals of a minority of Puerto Ricans who preach complete separation from the United States." Ocana understood the relationship between island and diaspora as both a political and cultural kinship that was in flux—shaped in particular by American formulations of racial and national identity and by US imperial prerogatives. If, Ocana hoped, Americans came to recognize Puerto Ricans as the rightful citizens and patriotic Americans that he claimed they were, Puerto Rican nationalism would remain largely symbolic and exist rather safely within the framework established by the US colonial state. However, Ocana feared, if the tide of American racism toward Puerto Ricans failed to ebb, then independence was the only logical solution.[45]

In his retort, Sacks attempted to clarify the committee's intentions with regard to Puerto Ricans residing on the island and "the Puerto Rican colony in New York City": "It was never our intention to condemn an entire race on the basis of our findings, for this would be extremely unscientific," Sacks declared. He defended the usefulness of the Army Individual Performance Test for its ability to reveal "individual differences relatively free from the effects of environment" and reiterated the committee's principal research questions: "Is this New York group of Puerto Ricans representative of children in Puerto Rico?" and "Does Puerto Rico export to New York mostly her lowest strata and worst mental levels?" The original report challenged the findings of an earlier study, in which the researchers attributed comparatively inferior intelligence of Puerto Ricans in Hawai'i to the overrepresentation of the "most undesirable strata" among the migrant population. On the question of exporting the "lowest strata," Armstrong and company argued: "this at least, is hardly probable." In other words, the children tested in New York were absolutely representative of the mental capacity of the island's population and condemned to intellectual inferiority by virtue of their race.[46]

Bureaucratic and cultural elites in Puerto Rico expressed outrage at the report, primarily because it claimed that all Puerto Ricans were illiterate, poor, burdens to the state, and unfit for citizenship. Rafael Menendez Ramos, commissioner of agriculture within the colonial government, objected on the grounds that the "committee's conclusions will be used by interests hostile to the island to injure relations with the Washington government." Ramos sought a preservation of Puerto Rico's colonial ties to the United States, which meant that he could claim protection over destitute members of the diaspora "faced with the difficulties of a new language and a new environment" from racist charges while he simultaneously disowned working-class migrants in East Harlem as unrepresentative of the island's more prosperous and literate classes. His formulation was indicative of the kinds of contradictory responses leveled against the Armstrong report from both island and metropole. The editors of the Puerto Rican daily *El Mundo* too charged the research team with ignoring environmental factors and blasted John B. Trevor, the committee's chairman, as "consistently 'anti-immigrant.'" *El Mundo*'s critique was particularly indicative of the contested and ambiguous nature of US citizenship for Puerto Ricans, despite the Jones Act. As colonial citizens, Puerto Ricans were not in fact immigrants, and were free to move between island and mainland. But the daily also articulated a kind of Puerto Rican citizenship and belonging, which cast migrants, in the language of the Supreme Court's 1901 decision in *Downes v. Bidwell,* as "foreign in a domestic sense" in relation to the mainland United States. *El Mundo*'s refutation then, was both a challenge to popular assumptions about Puerto Ricans in the United States as foreign-born and thus immigrants and a boon to the assertions of the Armstrong team that Puerto Ricans comprised a separate "national" and "racial" group.[47]

Perhaps the most significant and meticulous response to the committee's report came from Puerto Rico's assistant commissioner of education. Published in the *Porto Rico School Review* in 1936 and distributed in official pamphlet format by the Department of Education, Pedro Cebollero first and foremost rejected the committee's intentions to restrict Puerto Rican "immigration" to the United States on the rather obvious grounds that Puerto Ricans were already US citizens and therefore not immigrants in the least. Yet like Ramos, Cebollero also denounced the intelligence study of a sector of the New York diaspora as wholly unrepresentative of the island's population. His challenge sustained earlier contradictions among elite educators on the island in relation to continued US imperial claims, especially constructions of race and class. The assistant commissioner pointed out that the 1930 US census defined the island's population as 74 percent white, while Armstrong, Achilles, and Sacks had tested "colored" students at a rate of 76 percent—a reversal of racially constructed US figures for the island. Moreover, Cebollero dismissed the team's collection of data about parents' welfare relief and employment status as "inconsequential," stating that a more thoroughgoing attention to occupation and therefore social status was absolutely essential to psychological analyses of intelligence. Though better versed in the sociology of class than of race, Cebollero's rebuttal nevertheless relied on colonial elite formulations of race and class that, in this case, more neatly aligned with the racial rationale of the Armstrong study than Cebollero admitted.

While Cebollero was not a convinced eugenicist of the Anglo-American stripe and he accused the New York team of neglecting relevant class factors, he still understood race and class in Puerto Rico as mutually sustaining. In Puerto Rico, one's status as "colored" usually (but not always) corresponded to lower socioeconomic status, a correlation that reinforced Cebollero's own privilege. He accepted the primary logic of the study that "all results show the negro decidedly inferior to the white on standard intelligence tests." He simply dismissed the assertion that the test group was in any way representative of racial proportions present among the island's population. In this regard, Cebollero did not reject but in fact reinforced US imperial objectives abroad informed by formulations of race at home. An elite, self-described white, liberal creole like himself—dedicated to the pursuit of public education—actually had less in common with the black working classes Cebollero professed to uplift than with the social scientists he now accused of unscientific methods and unscrupulous and unlawful aims to restrict the free movement of Puerto Rican US citizens.[48]

Ironically, in his preoccupation with the overrepresentation of "colored" Puerto Ricans in the Armstrong sample, Cebollero failed to notice that Armstrong and her team had not hung their conclusions about Puerto Rican inferiority on any alleged blackness. Nevertheless, in his repudiation, the assistant commissioner articulated a Puerto Rican "national" identity emergent in the 1930s that increasingly employed elite *creole* understandings of the relationship between race and class to construct historical differences "between diaspora and nation." Cebollero questioned not the assumed racial logic of the report but instead the "representativeness" of the sample group and therefore the "authenticity" of the diaspora. Though migrant children in New York were in most cases only a generation removed, many prominent island elites regarded them, like earlier Puerto Rican migrants to Hawai'i's cane fields, as having degenerated from their Latin roots by adopting the habits and mores of Anglo-Saxon civilization.[49] In the 1930s, the proponents and indeed some detractors of intelligence testing had helped to reinforce the colonial status of Mexican Americans and Puerto Ricans. The shift from eugenic to cultural explanations of poor test scores affirmed rather than questioned the logic of Mexican American school segregation. The stark eugenics of the Armstrong report created outrage among Puerto Ricans on the island and in the metropole, but elite educators on the island bolstered rather than contested the racial logic of the results by claiming that the diaspora in New York simply did not represent the island's white majority.

The Armstrong report had come amidst two key developments in the 1930s that would transform Mexican American and Puerto Rican politics through the 1940s. First, in the Southwest, the postrevolutionary generation of US-born Mexicans came of age, and they began to forge a political outlook that included both an embrace of the possibilities of public education and a confrontational challenge to the inequalities inherent in most school systems that they and their peers attended. Mexican Americans began to assert their identity as US citizens while guarding their parents' cultural roots from anti-immigrant attacks. Their efforts were instrumental in the dismantling of *de jure* segregation by the late 1940s, but ultimately failed to stem the tide of popular violence and state-sponsored repatriation and deportation programs that targeted both new immigrants and Mexican Americans. Second, imbued by a surging nationalist politics during the mid-1930s, Puerto Rican parents and students also began to demand not the dismantling of the US educational apparatus or the colonial state on the island, but instead expanded access to schools. They supported the emergent Partido Popular Democrático (PPD, Popular Democratic Party) led by populist Luis Muñoz Marín, whose social justice campaign included agrarian reform and expanded access to rural schools, but also an emphasis on the mutual responsibilities between citizens and the colonial state. It was within this populist political framework that parents and students articulated a new vision for education. Their demands centered on expanded access to public schooling, which for poor rural families often carried with it prohibitive expenses for transportation, clothing, shoes, books, and lunch.

As the colonial state struggled to meet the demands for reciprocation between citizen and state, local elites in the Department of Education advocated for significant modifications to Americanization policies, especially English language instruction, that for decades had not granted Puerto Ricans possibilities for upward social and economic mobility. However, arguably one of the most influential educational elites of the 1940s, Cebollero, by then dean of the College of Education at the University of Puerto Rico, sought to scale back English instruction not because it represented an oppressive colonial policy but instead because English was simply impractical for those schoolchildren destined for a life of toil in the fields or in housework. Cebollero recommended that manual training replace English instruction in the primary grades, a change that would further institutionalize the colonial relationship that afforded his elite social status. His recommendation of a new language policy came amidst a groundswell of calls from rural parents and teachers who sought not manual training that reinforced their current stations in life, but instead an education that carried with it the possibility of liberation from field and domestic work. Theirs was a different vision for colonial citizenship than that of elites like Cebollero. However, because parents and students appealed to school officials for expanded access, they too implicitly recognized the legitimacy of the colonial state, which they argued should do a better job of meeting the needs of the masses.[50] Though independent in their respective methods and goals, both Mexicans and Puerto Ricans inaugurated concerted and persistence challenges to educational inequality during the 1930s and 1940s that advanced their claims to upward mobility and a fuller exercise of their citizenship.

FIGURE 17. Young sons of resettlers in an outdoor class of the agricultural school. La Plata project, Puerto Rico. Courtesy Library of Congress, Prints and Photographs Division, FSA / OWI Photograph Collection, LC-DIG-fsa-8b30542.

A POLITICS OF RESISTANT ACCOMMODATION

When social psychologists began to interpret low intelligence test scores as the result of Mexican American cultural deficiencies in the early 1930s, they did so not to dismantle segregation for Mexican American children but instead to justify its continuation. In 1931, 85 percent of California districts, for example, reported separate "Mexican" schools complete with all of the trappings of inferior education for Native and African Americans: high teacher-student ratios, lower per pupil expenditures, few (and often racist) books, unsafe school buildings, lack of extracurricular activities, and high dropout rates. At "Mexican" schools, manual training prevailed as the primary curriculum, as most school officials and teachers believed Mexican children possessed few abilities or aspirations beyond agricultural and domestic employment.[51]

In response, communities throughout the Southwest mounted legal challenges in the midst of record repatriation and deportation efforts totaling one-third of the Mexican population in the United States. Though overruled upon appeal, a Texas court ruled in *Independent School District v. Salvatierra* (1930–31) that the Del Rio school district violated the state constitution that only permitted segregated schools between white and "colored" children. The subsequent appellate court decision aligned with the new social psychology of cultural shortcomings and promptly restored segregation on "educational grounds," citing English language deficiencies of Mexican students. Separate schools, Anglo educators insisted, were critical to the Americanization of Mexican children. But in *Alvarez v. Lemon Grove School District* (1931), a California superior court judge challenged this rationale, arguing that "separate facilities for Mexican American students were not conducive toward their Americanization and retarded the English-language development of the Spanish-speaking children." Until 1931, children in Lemon Grove attended an integrated grammar school, but in January the school district built a separate school in the barrio for Mexican American students. Shoddily and hastily constructed, the building drew the ire of local residents, who referred to the barn-like structure as *La Caballeriza* (the stable). The school and the livestock reference were not unique in Southern California. Locals in Orange, in neighboring Orange County, referred to the Sycamore Street School as "The Barn" for similar reasons. Shortly after it opened, parents and students boycotted the Lemon Grove school and immediately sought legal recourse for the eighty-five students impacted by the school board's decision.[52] In the early 1930s, Judge Claude Chambers's decision in favor of the plaintiffs represented a resounding victory for local Mexican American parents and schoolchildren who defied the flawed logic of cultural deficiency as a rationale for separate schools. Implicitly though, the judge challenged not the scheme of Americanization but instead the means through which forced assimilation was best carried out. The case remained locally isolated with no national implications until 1947.

In the intervening years, the second generation of Mexican Americans, many of whose parents had left behind revolutionary violence and US imperialism south of the border, grew into political awareness and activism. In 1934, high school students in Los Angeles founded the Mexican American

FIGURE 18. Students at Sycamore School, also known as "The Barn," West Sycamore Avenue and North Lemon Street, Orange, California, 1925. Courtesy Local History Collection, Orange Public Library.

Movement, a youth-led organization dedicated to "the progress of Mexican American people through education." In 1938, MAM began to publish the English-language *Mexican Voice* through which it articulated to Chicano youth throughout Southern California the central importance of education and personal responsibility. MAM members regarded themselves as the proof that a commitment to education generated upward socioeconomic mobility and diminished racial prejudice from Anglo-Americans. That MAM members, most of whom were bilingual, published the *Mexican Voice* in English attested to their desire and willingness to integrate into the broader society. However, as historian George J. Sánchez notes, MAM members often suffered from naivete and tended to reduce the problem of widespread racial discrimination against Mexican Americans to a simple dearth of collective Chicano knowledge. Most Mexican American children still faced segregated schooling, and dropout rates were high. But "exaggerated optimism" aside, MAM represented an important challenge to earlier claims that Mexicans in the United States possessed allegiance to a foreign and often antagonistic Mexican government and thus remained culturally and politically inassimilable. Indeed, the very point of MAM's activism was to demonstrate the willingness of Mexican American youth to assimilate—and at times even conform to—Anglo norms, and at the same time to proclaim proudly one's Mexican cultural heritage. But by the late 1930s and early 1940s, MAM struggled to win over Chicano youth who grew increasingly disillusioned by continued school segregation, protracted social discrimination, racial violence, and the stalled prosperity of the New Deal.[53]

Despite the turmoil of the early 1940s, MAM's clarion calls for young Mexican Americans to embrace education did gain traction following the war. By 1945, many Southern Californians who had comprised the target audience for MAM's original calls to embrace public education now had children of their own. These young parents either became politically active or continued the activism of their youth in order to attack segregated schools and other forms of discrimination. Through new political organizations including the GI Forum and the Community Service Organization and older ones like the League of United Latin American Citizens (LULAC), parents protested official resistance to school integration in Ontario, Santa Ana, Riverside, San Bernardino, and other districts in Southern California. Their activism created the political conditions for legal challenge to segregation. In 1945, Gonzalo Méndez, a naturalized US citizen, and his Puerto Rican–born wife Félicitas, along with four other families, brought suit against the Garden Grove, Santa Ana, El Modena, and Westminster school districts in Orange County. Two years later, the US Ninth Circuit Court upheld the decision of Judge Paul McCormick in which he found that segregated schools for Mexican children violated the equal protection clause of the Fourteenth Amendment. The suit, supported by the ACLU and the NAACP among others, had direct implications for the 1954 decision of California governor–turned–Supreme Court justice Earl Warren in *Brown v. Board of Education.*[54]

The victory over *de jure* school segregation in California aside, significant obstacles to full acceptance as either native-born or naturalized US citizens remained deeply embedded in the politics of agribusiness, immigration, and border patrol. Mexican Americans had continually demonstrated their desire for full engagement with the responsibilities of citizenship only to become ensnared in repatriation and deportation schemes throughout the Southwest. Nor were Mexican Americans united in their views of continued immigration from Mexico and its implications for their own national belonging in the United States. Shortly after the *Méndez* decision was handed down, George Isidore Sánchez issued a rather alarmist report titled "Wetbacks" to the Advisory Committee for the Study of Spanish Speaking People at the University of Texas where he taught from 1940 until his death in 1972. Sánchez, a vigorous challenger of school segregation in the 1930s and 1940s, did so because he believed that separate schools hindered the Americanization of Mexican American children. Indeed LULAC, the organization for which he served as president from 1941 to 1942, explicitly excluded non–US citizens from membership.

Sánchez found in the "Wetback Invasion" a problem of more far-reaching importance than mere school segregation. The brief report described the "evil effects and devastating repercussions that derive from . . . a hundred thousand to half a million homeless wanderers—men, women, and children without legal status, without skills, without knowledge of our ways and customs, without protection, without opportunity to improve their condition." While seemingly sympathetic at times to the treacherous and dangerous existence of undocumented farmworkers, Sánchez primarily portrayed "contraband labor" as "the focal point from which flow social poisons that manifest themselves in symptoms of various kinds: disorganized, migratory populations; segregated schools; hostilities and tensions; political apathy; economic waste; peonage; and a divided citizenry." His formulation was at its core rather simple: "Wetbacks" dragged down wages for all workers, degraded social and sanitary conditions throughout communities, and forced citizens like him to bear the burden of both welfare relief and discrimination.

It is unlikely that Sánchez would have agreed with Robert Foerster that Mexican immigrants constituted a racial problem. But he certainly concurred with the Princeton economist that federal and state authorities needed to curtail immigration from Mexico. In particular, Sánchez felt that "wetbacks," foreign to both "Spanish- and English-speaking [Texans] alike," threatened the power and privilege of his American citizenship. But Sánchez's very use of the term "wetback" carried with it elements of both criminalization and racialization. First popularized during the 1920s and 1930s to describe "peon" laborers recruited by large-scale farmers, its application expanded by the 1940s and 1950s as a racialized stereotype applied to both immigrants and Mexican Americans alike. Sánchez seems to have been indifferent or insensitive to this in his report, even if he did implicate the owners of large agribusinesses throughout the Southwest in the maintenance of a brutal labor system dependent on threats of deportation, union repression, and government collusion to sustain high profits.

Five years after Sánchez issued his "Wetbacks" report, the INS initiated a massive roundup of suspected illegal immigrants throughout the Southwest. The agency boasted over one million deportations between June and September of 1954. In the midst of or soon after the deportations subsided, many Mexican Americans initially opposed to the Bracero guest-worker agreement between the United States and Mexico and certainly to "wetback" labor realized that the McCarran-Walter Act of 1952, which greatly expanded the authority of the INS to deport and denaturalize US citizens, was "devastating Mexican American families" throughout the Southwest.[55] The new immigration regime of the early 1950s had further bound together the fortunes of Mexican immigrants and Mexican Americans by eliding citizenship in favor of race. As Los Angeles journalist Ruben Salazar wrote of a recent high school dropout in 1962: "Though he looks like a Mexican, Pablo [Mendez] is not. He's an American, but doesn't think of himself as one, and in many respects is not looked upon as one by non-Mexican-Americans."[56]

As Mexican Americans pushed for integrated schools and for assimilation on their own terms, sometimes to the disdain and detriment of more recent migrants from Mexico, administrators, teachers, parents, and students in Puerto Rico too struggled to negotiate the terms of their US citizenship in relation to public schooling. Though contentious since the initial US occupation, the language of instruction in the public schools—English or Spanish—took on heightened importance in debates about Americanization and empire in the late 1930s and 1940s. While American officials including President Franklin Roosevelt found English instruction absolutely imperative for US citizenship, Puerto Rican administrators vied for a more practical approach to language that took into account the realities of the rural working classes. Though not immediately concerned with the issue of language, rural parents and students too made claims on the promise of upward mobility and economic security that a new generation of colonial school officials allied with the PPD made with increasing regularity.

In 1945, Pedro Cebollero, by then (as mentioned earlier) dean of the College of Education at the University of Puerto Rico, published *A School Language Policy for Puerto Rico*. On the eve of the wave of decolonizations that would sweep away most European empires after World War II, his report was at once a history of language instruction under US rule, a global survey of language policies in the colonial schools of other (European) empires, and a political tract that challenged the overarching assumptions of the US colonial state about the best ways to Americanize the island's subjects. Cebollero called for a reformed policy that met "the needs of the people whom the educational policies are intended to serve."[57] In his survey, Cebollero wrote that from the outset the American colonial regime had "forced [English] upon the schools" as a "permanent addition" to a wrongheaded colonial policy, subject to the "whim of the administrator in office or the pressure of dissatisfied patrons or teachers." He recalled the failures and shortsightedness of previous administrations, particularly those led by American commissioners.[58] While the island's first commissioner favored the use of Spanish in elementary instruction and English in secondary schools, Brumbaugh also regarded English as an integral component of Americanization: "In almost every city of the island, and at many rural schools, the children meet and salute the flag as it is flung to the breeze . . . . The pupils then sing America, Hail Columbia, The Star Spangled Banner, and other patriotic songs. The marvel is that they sing them in English. The first English many of them know is the English of our national songs."[59] From 1905 to 1913, Commissioner Roland Falkner attempted a comprehensive enforcement of English-only in all grades and all courses except Spanish. The administration tied the renewal of teaching certificates and salary increases to the acquisition of skills in English language instruction, required teachers to take examinations in English, and adopted English language textbooks for classroom use. The results, Cebollero reported, were disastrous. Local teachers and parents protested the overemphasis on English instruction to the neglect of a "rounded education" and to the detriment of students' "mental and physical health."

Not until 1934, in Cebollero's estimation, did Puerto Rico have a reasonable language instruction policy: "with the exception of José Padín [1930–37], no commissioner of education ever gave adequate consideration to the real needs of the people." A Hoover appointee and the first education commissioner of Puerto Rican birth, Padín reinstated Spanish as the language of instruction for grades one through eight. But in 1937, the chair of the Senate Committee on Insular Affairs forced Padín's resignation, arguing that an overall lack of knowledge of English among Puerto Ricans had contributed to recent political violence, including the Ponce Massacre of March 1937 when colonial police fired on militant nationalist marchers, killing eighteen. The new appointee, José Gallardo, reinstated English as a language of instruction alongside Spanish. On his watch, the Department of Education hired more American English teachers, purchased more English language books, and appointed supervisors throughout rural districts to ensure that local teachers adhered to the new policy. Gallardo's policy was not of his own making, however. In April 1937, President Roosevelt handed down his charge to the new commissioner in no uncertain terms: "It is an indispensable part of the American policy that the coming generation of American citizens in

Puerto Rico grow up with complete facility in the English tongue. It is the language of our nation. Only through the acquisition of this language will Puerto Rican Americans secure a better understanding of American ideals and principles." Though Roosevelt gave lip service to "the usefulness of the rich Spanish cultural legacy of the people," he implored Gallardo to equip "the American citizens of Puerto Rico" with English literacy so that they might take advantage of "the unique historical circumstance which has brought to them the blessings of American citizenship." The president called on insular schools to begin to teach English "at once with vigor, purposefulness, and devotion."[60]

Cebollero opposed Roosevelt's position, but not because he was a nationalist. As an elite within the island's educational bureaucracy, Cebollero owed his status to the continuation of the US–Puerto Rican colonial relationship. What Cebollero sought was neither independence nor statehood, but instead a reformed colonial state that attended to local particularities of language and culture. For example, he regarded the coincidence of popular protests against English-only policies with the rise of "nationalistic propaganda in Puerto Rico" during World War II as detrimental to the advance of what he considered a more evenhanded and collaborative school language policy that included both Spanish and English: "The confusion that originated at the time has survived with so much vigor that even to this day it is almost impossible to take an honest, intellectual position on this question, on the strength of pedagogical reasons, without being accused of siding with one or the other of the political tendencies." Cebollero found Roosevelt's charge that Puerto Rican schoolchildren become bilingual simply impractical—failing to account for the socioeconomic complexities of the island.[61]

Versed in the populist language of Muñoz Marín, Cebollero proposed a language instruction policy for the public schools that "adapted to the majority of the children for whom the schools exist": "To conclude that English is equally necessary for the peasant who works in the coffee plantations . . . and the business man engaged in import and export trade in San Juan is obviously absurd," he remarked. Cebollero's appeal to the practical educational needs of the rural working classes and to the reciprocal obligations between the colonial state and its citizens demonstrated that at least some elites within the educational bureaucracy were now listening to the demands of the parents and students who constituted the working poor. Even so, Cebollero remained attentive to older, enduring elite visions for colonial citizenship in which he and his peers, not the working classes, defined the relationship between Puerto Rico and the United States. His recommendations better complemented the outlook of US colonial officials whose primary concern was the maintenance of a profitable agricultural export economy, which required a minimally educated rural citizenry that was respectful of and deferential to US authority. An impractically educated working class with hopes and aspirations beyond the realities of the cane fields might challenge the colonial status quo, thus threatening the social and political capital possessed by Cebollero and his fellow elites. Cebollero, like most of his counterparts on the mainland, sought not "equality of education" but instead hoped to give "the kind and amount of education from which [schoolchildren] will most profit in view of their ability and their probable length of stay in school." His desire to work within the structures of the colonial state revealed the limits of his populism. The rural masses for whom he claimed to know best may have also found English impractical, but they also eschewed the kinds of manual training Cebollero prescribed in favor of a more well-rounded curriculum that could advance their economic prospects.[62]

By the time Cebollero's language policy went to press, rural parents and teachers were already mobilizing for increased access to schools. They came to expect a more robust educational infrastructure capable of enabling them to achieve their social and economic aspirations. Their demands fit within the PPD's "modernizing" project, which culminated in the establishment of the Free Associated State (*Estado Libre Asociado,* ELA), whereby island leadership renegotiated the terms of its relationship to the United States in the midst of increasing local and international pressure to address questions of sovereignty during the era of global decolonization. As del Moral argues, the ELA was a "modern reinterpretation of the traditional colonial relationship," the formal approval of which came to represent a new era of popular democratic will and debate among the island's constituents. On the international stage and before the American public, ELA supporters intended to show that the relationship between the United States and Puerto Rico "could no longer be defined as strictly colonial."[63]

A modern and more accessible school system quickly became one the cornerstones of this reformed vision. In the 1940s, the Department of Education built and opened more schools, hired more teachers, and staffed classes for adults through community extension programs, all with an eye to promoting ELA definitions of citizenship. In 1949, the department established a Central Scholarship Committee to receive applications and render decisions regarding financial aid to the working poor, most of whom could not afford the added costs of schooling that included books, clothing, transportation, and lunch. While some students applied for scholarship money, which the commissioner's office was always too slow to disperse, others flooded the offices of the Department of Education with requests for very specific forms of assistance that in their estimation would allow them to continue to attend school—food; a pair of shoes; a shirt; books. Students and their parents, who also wrote letters on behalf of sons and daughters, sought not charity but rather official reciprocity from the colonial state. If the state claimed as part of its mandate to prepare the island's population for American citizenship, then it needed to safeguard the rights of children to attend school in order to become productive citizens.

Ultimately, the ELA could not keep its promise of free and full access to schools for all of the working poor. Though it doled out one thousand scholarships each year, many students who were unable to secure financial support "likely made the difficult and painful decision to withdraw from school."[64] As was the case in the Southwest after *Méndez,* reinterpretations of the US–Puerto Rico colonial relationship ultimately failed to create the kinds of citizens imagined by either Roosevelt or the thousands of poor children and parents who implored the state for meager financial assistance in order to attend school. But it was not for lack of trying. Despite the rhetoric of expanded access, of equal and integrated schooling, or of reciprocation between state and citizen, the economic imperatives of empire remained paramount. In Puerto Rico and the Southwest, coffee and cotton, sugar and sugar beets, made different kinds of claims on citizens and immigrants than those made by administrators and teachers.

Epilogue

KNOWLEDGE AND CITIZENSHIP

IN THE TWENTY-FIRST CENTURY, neo-restrictionists continue to call into question the belonging and citizenship of nonwhite groups while they pursue draconian border enforcement policies of the variety practiced and lauded by Maricopa County, Arizona sheriff Joe Arpaio and his supporters.[1] And questions of race, empire, and citizenship have recently, as they have in the past, pervaded the realm of public education. In May 2010, Arizona governor Jan Brewer signed into law a bill banning ethnic studies programs in public schools. HB 2281 targeted Tucson Unified School District's acclaimed Mexican American Studies, or *La Raza* program in a 65 percent Latino district. Despite the program's availability to students of all ethnic backgrounds, the bill prohibited schools from offering courses that "promote the overthrow of the United States government, promote resentment toward a race or class of people, are designed primarily for pupils of a particular ethnic group, or advocate ethnic solidarity instead of the treatment of pupils as individuals." Districts or charter schools on notice for failing to comply with the law would shoulder 10 percent funding cuts each month by the Arizona Department of Education. Tucson Unified School District stood to lose $15 million annually in state funding if *La Raza* continued.[2]

The following year, newly elected Arizona superintendent of public instruction John Huppenthal promptly cancelled Tucson's ethnic studies program, citing, in addition to its supposed violation of HB 2281, its Marxist origins, methodologies, and undercurrents: "The designers of the Mexican American Studies classes explicitly say in their journal articles that they're going to construct Mexican American Studies around this Marxian framework with a predominantly ethnic underclass, the oppressed, being—filling out that Marxian model and a predominantly Caucasian class filling out the role of the oppressor. It really is so simplistic . . . and a lot of things, very unhealthy," Huppenthal asserted in a 2012 debate with Richard Martinez, the attorney representing students and teachers demanding *La Raza*'s reinstatement. The anticommunist fervor among school officials of the post–WWI period had not subsided with the passage of quota restrictions on European immigrants . . . or with the end of the Cold War.[3]

Supporters of HB 2281 hailed what they considered to be the new law's commitment to racial equality and individualism. A gubernatorial spokesperson argued that "public school students should be taught to treat and value each other as individuals and not be taught to resent or hate other races or classes of people."[4] In an open letter to the citizens of Tucson written three years before HB 2281's passage, Huppenthal's predecessor Tom Horne, the law's architect and long-standing champion, outlined his adamant opposition to ethnic studies. He cited his "participation" in the 1963 March on Washington where he claimed to have internalized Dr. Martin Luther King Jr.'s call for judgment based on character, not skin color—a philosophy affronted by ethnic studies, argued Horne. The outgoing education secretary later relayed his civil rights credentials in a 2010 debate with Georgetown sociologist Michael Eric Dyson on CNN's *Anderson Cooper 360°*, shortly after the law's passage and in the midst of Horne's successful run for state attorney general. Dyson decried Horne's theft of King's legacy and the candidate's obfuscation of King's steadfast commitment to direct confrontation of racial injustice, which Dyson noted was the express and essential purpose of ethnic studies. In his earlier letter, Horne enumerated "personal observations" of ethnic studies students acting "rudely and in defiance of authority," actions he "believe[d] the students did not learn . . . at home, but from their *Raza* teachers." In particular, Horne claimed that in 2007, a group of students walked out on a speech by Deputy Superintendent Margaret Dugan intended to refute a "prior allegation made to the student body that 'Republicans Hate Latinos.'" Horne also cited the case of Hector Ayala, a Mexican-born English teacher at Cholla High School, who allegedly reported that the director of Cholla's *Raza* program accused Ayala of being a "white man's agent" and "taught a separatist political agenda."[5]

Horne saved his most damning critique for *La Raza*'s textbooks. Paolo Freire's *Pedagogy of the Oppressed* (1970), which Horne incorrectly cited as "the pedagogy of oppression," besieged the true place of America in the world as the land of opportunity. Ignoring or more likely sidestepping the political storm of "illegal" immigration brewing in Arizona, Horne claimed that "most of these students' parents and grandparents came to this country, legally, because this is the land of opportunity . . . if they work hard they can achieve their goals. They should not be taught that they are oppressed." Horne's assumption that all Arizonan families of Mexican descent were at some point immigrants to the United States belied the history of American empire, whereby many Mexican nationals became US citizens whether they liked it or not. They had not come to the United States. The United States had come to them.

Horne also named Rodolfo Acuña's *Occupied America* (1988) and Carlos Jimenez's *The Mexican-American Heritage* (1994) as textbook examples of rife anti-Americanism in Tucson's ethnic studies curriculum. Acuña, Horne claimed, lauded historical Chicano figures who incited their brethren to "kill the gringo," while Jimenez, whose book was "paid for by American taxpayers . . . [gloated] over the difficulty we are having controlling our border." Horne's earlier circumvention of the border question as it applied to older Chicano generations collided with his acknowledgment of the twenty-first-century "difficulty" in regulating immigration, revealing his rhetorical ability to find fault, even criminality, among Chicano youth without expressly saying so. In early 2012, Tucson Unified School District issued a list of banned books used in the now illegal ethnic studies curriculum.[6]

Horne's letter and the statute in which it culminated failed to escape the criticism of activists progressive on issues of education, immigration, and racial justice. Sean Arce, director of TUSD's Mexican American Studies Department, decried the provisions of the law as not only "outlandish" but simply inapplicable to the program's daily curriculum. "We don't do those things," Arce told the *Arizona Daily Star,* in direct contradiction to Horne's claims that ethnic studies promoted ethnic insularity and fostered resentment toward whites. The Tucson school board later fired Arce in April 2013 for his ongoing and outspoken resistance to HB 2281.[7] Tucson Democrats urged not just the protection of Mexican American Studies, the only high school program of its kind in the entire country, but also the expansion of its critical pedagogical approach "to include more ethnicities and cultures throughout Arizona." All the while, the most ardent Tea Party supporters of HB 2281, a bill that allegedly guarded against attempts to overthrow the US government, waged political battles against the Obama administration's authority in the state. In 2012, the legislature reintroduced and passed "cherished nullification legislation" demanding that the federal government "relinquish control over publicly owned land" in Arizona. The hypocrisy could not have been more blatant.[8]

The backlash against HB 2281 did not just include school officials like Arce or local politicians. On May 12, 2010, police arrested fifteen Arizonans protesting Horne's brainchild outside the state house. Kim Dominguez, a *La Raza* alumnus and one of those arrested, told *Democracy Now!*'s Amy Goodman and Juan Gonzalez that "if anything is promoted in the [ethnic studies] classes, it's solidarity among humanity, not any—between any ethnic group." Isabel Garcia, co-chair of the Tucson-based Coalition for Human Rights, placed the ethnic studies ban in a broader context. Three weeks before the passage of HB 2281, Governor Brewer signed Senate Bill 1070, directing state and local law enforcement to "determine the immigration status" of any person for which an officer has "reasonable suspicion . . . that the person is an alien" and to arrest "without a warrant" but with "probable cause to believe that the person has committed any public offense that makes the person removable from the United States." Garcia described the situation of Latino Arizonans as "untenable": "Police officers are enforcing [SB 1070] left and right. And even individuals, just civilians, feel free to make racist comments, to question anybody that looks brown." Garcia also spoke of the historical role of US empire in fomenting the new restrictions: "It's a pretty amazing thing here, considering the history, especially of this particular region. All of this was Mexico. It was Tohono O'odham lands. It was the other Indian lands. The Mexican Lands. And here we are being subjected to a law of racial profiling."[9]

Contrasts between HB 2281 supporters like Brewer, Horne, and Huppenthal and detractors like Dominguez, Garcia, and Dyson reveal public education's entanglement with the forces and institutions of citizenship and empire in American politics. And both sides have continued to appeal to history. Horne's embrace of King's character content catchphrase as the beginning of racism's supposed demise contradicts and challenges Garcia's contention that ethnic studies in particular, but school curriculum in general, should require students to think critically about the stark, deeper historical and contemporary realities of racism and empire in the United States. In March 2013, a district court declared in *Maya Arce v. John Huppenthal* that subsection three of HB 2281, which banned courses "designed for pupils of a particular ethnic group," was "unconstitutionally overbroad" but argued that it was severable from the remainder of the law. In January 2015, the US Ninth Circuit Court of Appeals in San Francisco heard oral arguments from Erwin Chemerinsky, dean of the University of California, Irvine School of Law and lead counsel representing Maya Arce and her father, Sean Arce, challenging the constitutionality of the remainder of HB 2281. On July 7, the court allowed the challenge to proceed to trial. The panel led by Judge Jed Rakoff argued that "it is undisputed that the statute's enactment and enforcement has had a disparate impact on Mexican American students" and "given that 'officials acting in their official capacities seldom, if ever, announce on the record that they are pursuing a particular course of action because of their desire to discriminate against a racial minority' . . . the legislative history . . . and the sequence of events . . . leading to its enactment reasonably suggest an intent to discriminate." The panel found particularly troubling the likelihood that HB 2281 "threatens to chill the teaching of ethnic studies courses that may offer great value to students" without "furthering the legitimate pedagogical purpose of reducing racism." As this book goes to press, a trial date has yet to be set.[10]

Schools have long served as places where the political battles waged by adults over immigration policy, imperial expansion, and racial inequality have impacted the conditions in which, how, and what children learn and know about the United States and their myriad hierarchical places in it. Horne's discomfort with addressing the oppressive dimensions of American power recalls the tone of school historians of more than a century ago that stressed the opportunities that US expansion supposedly afforded to its subjects. According to these authors, US imperialism carried with it democratizing and civilizing elements that instructed and elevated inferior populations both at home and abroad. Imperial projects not only targeted Hawaiians, Puerto Ricans, and Filipinos, but also African, Asian, and Mexican Americans, as well as dubiously white southern and eastern Europeans. Through the processes first of conquest, then of education, these groups of children became different and unequal varieties of American citizens.

Horne also seems to have internalized the rather naïve notion that all individuals are treated equally under US law and that schools ought to teach students that everyone's citizenship carries the same kinds of access, rights, and privileges. As we have also seen, the industrial schools established by the first New England missionaries in Hawai'i not only shaped the future of the islands' territorial schools that sought to prepare children for menial field and domestic labor, but also became models for Native and African American instruction on the mainland. School officials in New York City also sought to prepare the children of southern and eastern European immigrants for lives of obedience to industrial production and to the imperatives of US imperialism. Many parents and children openly rejected the former in particular by the 1910s. Supporters and practitioners of segregation from California to Georgia claimed that the separate education of the races was good for all involved. It allegedly provided Chinese, Japanese, Mexican, and African Americans space to cultivate skills best suited to their prescribed stations in life, free from higher order thinking with which they were presumably ill equipped to deal. In separate schools, they could learn to become the kinds of "good" citizens prescribed by hierarchies of race and economic imperatives of empire.

And yet at the same time, many school officials throughout the nation seemed wholeheartedly, like Horne, to accept the notion that the public school was the great equalizer at a time when profound changes—immigration and empire—dramatically reshaped politics, economics, and society. Writing in the *California Educational Review* in 1891, Merrill Edward Gates pressed for basic instruction in the functions of American government because "any male citizen of suitable age may become a legislator or an office holder, while every citizen has an appreciable influence upon the political life of his neighborhood."[11] Though women were excluded in this formulation, Gates placed the individual political actor at the center of American political life. Many of Gates's contemporaries disagreed, and instead advocated for community civics as a way to deemphasize individual activism in favor of social and political conformity. But while their methods differed, both ultimately agreed that the nation's public schools should serve to alleviate the growing pains of geopolitical expansion and industrialization. Horne, in his appeal to King, seems to have internalized and reconciled these contradictory visions for American education as well.

HB 2281 and SB 1070 are not simply examples of the latest subjection to historical whitewashing, immigration restriction, and unequal forms of imperial citizenship of a particular racial group. Nor do they stand as aberrations in an otherwise (and imagined) postracial America. Instead, the laws are symptomatic of an inability and unwillingness in mainstream politics to address the historically enduring and resilient nature of race and empire in American schools and the broader society for which schools prepare citizens. Yet Maya Arce, Korina Lopez, and Nicholas Dominguez, the plaintiffs in the original case against HB 2281, along with their diverse and numerous supporters, invoke the persistence displayed by their historical predecessors—students and parents—who demanded an education that prepared them not for social marginalization and economic subservience but for recognition, national belonging, and the full exercise of American citizenship.

NOTES

INTRODUCTION: GOOD CITIZENS

1. Circular, Office of the Superintendent of Public Instruction to the Superintendents and Teachers of the Schools of California, July 20, 1892, 2A-1-11, San Francisco Unified School District Records, San Francisco History Center, San Francisco Public Library, San Francisco, CA. Hereafter SFH 3; Cecilia O'Leary, *To Die For: The Paradox of American Patriotism* (Princeton: Princeton University Press, 1999), 157–67.

2. Quoted in Jackson Lears, *Rebirth of a Nation: The Making of Modern America, 1877–1920* (New York: HarperCollins, 2009), 168. Also see Robert Rydell, *All the World's a Fair: Visions of Empire at American International Expositions, 1876–1916* (Chicago: University of Chicago Press, 1984).

3. The book's subtitle derives from Waddy Thompson's 1913 *Primary History of the United States* in which he argued that a reverence for pioneers, presidents, inventors, and generals would guide children along a singular "path of good citizenship." The path that Thompson described was almost certainly intended for native-born white males, and his textbook recounted the lives of national figures most often invoked to stir patriotism and a deep reverence for the nation's past and present progress. See Waddy Thompson, *Primary History of the United States* (Boston: D.C. Heath, 1913), iii.

4. Elizabeth Cohen, *Semi-Citizenship in Democratic Politics* (New York: Cambridge University Press, 2009), 2; Linda Kerber, "The Meanings of Citizenship," *Journal of American History* 84, 3 (Dec. 1997): 833–54.

5. The role of modern public schools in the training of citizens has a rich historiography. But few works bring together the tropes of empire, immigration, and race as I propose here. Nor do many examine extensively the entangled relationship between the construction of narratives and knowledge about US imperial expansion in curricula on the one hand and localized policies of segregation, exclusion, or Americanization on the other in the creation of tiered citizenships. For recent work on US imperialism and education, see Solsiree Del Moral, *Negotiating Empire:*

The Cultural Politics of Schools in Puerto Rico, 1898–1952 (Madison: University of Wisconsin Press, 2013); Sarah Manekin, "Spreading the Empire of Free Education, 1865–1905" (PhD diss., University of Pennsylvania, 2009); A. J. Angulo, *Empire and Education: A History of Greed and Goodwill from the War of 1898 to the War on Terror* (New York: Palgrave Macmillan, 2012); Lisa Jarvinen and Richard Garlitz, eds., *Teaching America to the World and the World to America: Education and Foreign Relations since 1870* (New York: Palgrave Macmillan, 2012). The literature on schools and immigration and / or race is far more extensive, though most employ more locally defined contexts or address the experiences of a particular group of immigrants or cultural or racial outsiders. Important and relatively recent examples include Jeffrey Mirel, *Patriotic Pluralism: Americanization Education and European Immigrants* (Cambridge: Harvard University Press, 2010); Jacqueline Fear-Segal, *White Man's Club: Schools, Race, and the Struggle of Indian Acculturation* (Lincoln: University of Nebraska Press, 2007). Standards particularly germane to the case studies included in this volume include Eileen Tamura, *Americanization, Acculturation, and Ethnic Identity: The Nisei Generation in Hawai'i* (Urbana: University of Illinois Press, 1994); Charles Wollenberg, *All Deliberate Speed: Segregation and Exclusion in California Schools, 1855–1975* (Berkeley: University of California Press, 1976); James Anderson, *The Education of Blacks in the South, 1860–1935* (Chapel Hill: University of North Carolina Press, 1988); Bernard J. Weiss, ed., *American Education and the European Immigrant, 1840–1940* (Urbana: University of Illinois Press, 1982); Aida Negrón de Montilla, *La americanización en Puerto Rico y el sistema de instrucción pública, 1900–1930* (San Juan: Editorial de la Universidad de Puerto Rico, 1998).

6. Paul Kramer, "Power and Connection: Imperial Histories of the United States in the World," *American Historical Review* 116, 5 (Dec. 2011): 1349.

7. As Michael Katz notes in his important 1971 study, schools functioned as "imperial institutions designed to civilize the natives ... designed to reflect and confirm the social structure that erected them." See Katz, *Class, Bureaucracy, and Schools: The Illusion of Educational Change in America* (New York: Praeger, 1971), xvi.

8. On contested notions of modern school reform and governance, particularly as it informed socioeconomic opportunity, see David Tyack, *The One Best System: A History of American Urban Education* (Cambridge: Harvard University Press, 1974); Lawrence A. Cremin, *The Transformation of the School: Progressivism in American Education, 1876–1957* (New York: Alfred A. Knopf, 1961); Meyer Weinberg, *A Chance to Learn: The History of Race and Education in the United States* (New York: Cambridge University Press, 1977); William J. Reese, *Power and the Promise of School Reform: Grass-roots Movements during the Progressive Era* (Boston: Routledge and Kegan Paul, 1986); Tracy Steffes, *School, Society, and State: A New Education to Govern Modern America, 1890–1940* (Chicago: University of Chicago Press, 2012).

9. Cohen, *Semi-Citizenship in Democratic Politics,* 14. Also see Evelyn Nakano Glenn, *Unequal Freedom: How Race and Gender Shaped American Citizenship and Labor* (Cambridge: Harvard University Press, 2002), 18–55; Natalia Molina,

How Race Is Made in America: Immigration, Citizenship, and the Historical Power of Racial Scripts (Berkeley: University of California Press, 2014); Linda Bosniak, *The Citizen and the Alien* (Princeton: Princeton University Press, 2006).

10. Thompson, *Primary History of the United States,* iii.

11. On degrees of Americanization and tensions between racial and civic nationalism, see Mirel, *Patriotic Pluralism;* Gary Gerstle, *American Crucible: Race and Nation in the Twentieth Century* (Princeton: Princeton University Press, 2001). Guadalupe San Miguel, Jr. and Richard Valencia's notions of additive (the inculcation of Anglo-American values) and subtractive (the active discouragement of an immigrant group's original culture) Americanization are also instructive here. See San Miguel, Jr., and Valencia, "From the Treaty of Guadalupe-Hidalgo to *Hopwood:* The Educational Plight and Struggle of Mexican Americans in the Southwest," *Harvard Educational Review* 68, 3 (Fall 1998): 358.

12. On the relationship among race, immigration, and empire in US history, see Matthew Frye Jacobson, *Barbarian Virtues: The United States Encounters Foreign Peoples at Home and Abroad, 1876–1917* (New York: Hill & Wang, 2000); Paul Spickard, *Almost All Aliens: Immigration, Race, and Colonialism in American History and Identity* (New York: Routledge, 2007); James T. Campbell, Matthew Pratt Guterl, and Robert G. Lee, eds., *Race, Nation, and Empire in American History* (Chapel Hill: University of North Carolina Press, 2007).

13. Katz, *Class, Bureaucracy, and Schools;* Olivier Zunz, *Making America Corporate, 1970–1920* (Chicago: University of Chicago Press, 1990), 1–4; Alan Trachtenberg, *The Incorporation of America: Culture and Society in the Gilded Age* (New York: Hill & Wang, 2007 [1982]), ix; Martin Sklar, *The Corporate Reconstruction of American Capitalism, 1890–1916: The Market, The Law, and Politics* (New York: Cambridge University Press, 1988), 78–85; Jacobson, *Barbarian Virtues,* 13–97.

14. Jacobson, *Barbarian Virtues,* 3–9; Sklar, *The Corporate Reconstruction of American Capitalism,* 78–85. For the reciprocal nature of colonialism and education in the example of the Philippines, see Ann Paulet, "To Change the World: The Use of American Indian Education in the Philippines," *History of Education Quarterly* 47, 2 (May 2007): 173–202; Paul Kramer, *The Blood of Government: Race, Empire, the United States and the Philippines* (Chapel Hill: University of North Carolina Press, 2006), 168–70, 201–3. Kramer reveals how American-run schools in the Philippines became the "defining metaphor" for the US colonial state: "tutelary and assimilationist."

15. Most classic and recent accounts of the period mark the end of Reconstruction and the end of World War I as temporal bookends and stress themes of reunion between North and South, industrial growth, and expansive state power. As important as these processes are, 1882 and 1924 provide a framework that positions race, immigration, and empire at the center of Gilded Age and Progressive Era historical narratives and allow us to better understand the entanglements of immigration and empire. For important examples of the former, see Lears, *Rebirth of a Nation;* Nell Irving Painter, *Standing at Armageddon: The United States, 1877–1919* (New York: W.W. Norton, 1987); Robert Wiebe, *The Search for Order,*

1877–1920 (New York: Hill & Wang, 1967). Jacobson's *Barbarian Virtues* stands as the most prominent exception.

16. On the transatlantic exchange of people, ideas, and institutions, see Daniel Rodgers, *Atlantic Crossings: Social Politics in a Progressive Age* (Cambridge: Belknap Press of Harvard University, 2000). Important recent work that embeds Pacific histories of migration, border control, and nation building within both US and global historical narratives include Adam McKeown, *Melancholy Order: Asian Immigration and the Globalization of Borders* (New York: Columbia University Press, 2008); Marilyn Lake and Henry Reynolds, *Drawing the Global Colour Line: White Men's Countries and the International Challenge of Racial Equality* (New York: Cambridge University Press, 2008); Erika Lee, *At America's Gates: Chinese Immigration during the Exclusion Era, 1880–1943* (Chapel Hill: University of North Carolina Press, 2003).

17. Molina, *How Race Is Made in America,* 20–21.

18. Lisa Lowe, *Immigrant Acts: On Asian American Cultural Politics* (Durham, NC: Duke University Press, 1996), 5.

19. Paul Kramer's recent review essay speaks to the growing richness and enormous potential of the imperial as a primary category of analysis in United States history. See Kramer, "Power and Connection." Also see Alfred McCoy and Francisco Scarano, eds., *Colonial Crucible: Empire in the Making of the Modern American State* (Madison: University of Wisconsin Press, 2009); Amy Kaplan, *The Anarchy of Empire in the Making of US Culture* (Cambridge: Harvard University Press, 2002).

20. An important recent exception is Steffes, *School, Society, and State.*

21. J. Stuart Foster, "The Struggle for American Identity: Treatment of Ethnic Groups in United States History Textbooks," *History of Education* 28, 3 (1999): 254. On the textbook industry and competing national narratives, especially between North and South, see Joseph Moreau, *Schoolbook Nation: Conflicts over American History Textbooks from the Civil War to the Present* (Ann Arbor: University of Michigan Press, 2003), 26–91. Also see Adam Shapiro, *Trying Biology: The Scopes Trial, Textbooks, and the Antievolution Movement in American Schools* (Chicago: University of Chicago Press, 2013).

22. Lake and Reynolds, *Drawing the Global Colour Line;* James Belich, *Replenishing the Earth: The Settler Revolution and the Rise of the Anglo World, 1783–1939* (New York: Oxford University Press, 2009).

23. Elmer Miller, "Education Value of Geography Study," *Bulletin of the American Bureau of Geography* 1, 1 (March 1900), 7–8.

24. Robert F. Foerster, *The Racial Problems Involved in Immigration from Latin America and the West Indies to the United States* (Washington: Government Printing Office, 1925).

25. School Board Newspaper Scrapbook Clipping (hereafter SBNSC), *San Francisco Call,* December 2, 1906, 7–99, SFH 3.

26. SBNSC, *San Francisco Chronicle,* March 3, 1907, 7–99, SFH 3; Eiichiro Azuma, *Between Two Empires: Race, History and Transnationalism in Japanese*

America (New York: Oxford University Press, 2005); Eileen Tamura, "Asian Americans in the History of Education," *History of Education Quarterly* 41, 1 (Spring 2001): 58–59. The standard overviews for California remain Wollenberg, *All Deliberate Speed;* Irving G. Hendrick, *The Education of Non-Whites in California, 1849–1970* (San Francisco: R & E Research Associates, 1977).

27. Noriko Asato, "Mandating Americanization: Japanese Language Schools and the Federal Survey of Education in Hawai'i," *History of Education Quarterly* 43, 1 (Spring 2003): 34–35, 37–38.

28. A. D. Mayo, "Report of Atlanta University", n. d., Atlanta University Collection, Series 7, Box 4, Folder 1, Auburn Avenue Research Library on African American Culture and History, Atlanta-Fulton Public Library System. Hereafter cited as AUC. Southern connections to schooling in Hawai'i appear in Gary Okihiro, *Island World: A History of Hawai'i and the United States* (Berkeley: University of California Press, 2008), 98–134.

29. Newspaper clippings, *Atlanta Journal,* November 2, 1889, *August Chronicle,* July 12, 1889, 7-2-26, AUC.

30. Rachel St. John, *A Line in the Sand: A History of the Western US-Mexico Border* (Princeton: Princeton University Press, 2011), 202.

31. "JW Proposal Board Committee for Curriculum Review," Jeffco Public Schools Board of Education website, September 18, 2014, accessed September 25, 2014, www.boarddocs.com/co/jeffco/Board.nsf/goto?open&id=9NBUKW7 C6977.

32. Arizona Revised Statute § 15-112.

33. Jonathan Zimmerman, *Whose America? Culture Wars in the Public Schools* (Cambridge: Harvard University Press, 2002).

CHAPTER 1: GEOGRAPHY, HISTORY, AND CITIZENSHIP

1. Calvin Kendall and George Mirick, *How to Teach the Fundamental Subjects* (Boston: Houghton Mifflin, 1915), 224.

2. Department of the Interior, Bureau of Education, "The Social Studies in Secondary Education," Bulletin no. 28 (Washington: Government Printing Office, 1916), 9.

3. Paris Exposition of 1900, Board of Education Exhibition, Series 235, Records of the New York City Board of Education. Hereafter RNYCBE.

4. See John Willinsky, *Learning to Divide the World: Education at Empire's End* (Minneapolis: University of Minnesota Press, 1998); Martin Lewis and Kären Wigen, *The Myth of Continents: A Critique of Metageography* (Berkeley: University of California Press, 1997).

5. Horace Tarbell, *Introductory Geography* (New York: Werner School Book, 1900 [1896]), 51.

6. On Americanization and whiteness, see David Roediger, *Working toward Whiteness: How America's Immigrants Became White* (New York: Basic Books,

2005); Matthew Frye Jacobson, *Whiteness of a Different Color: European Immigrants and the Alchemy of Race* (Cambridge: Harvard University Press, 1998).

7. American Book Company Advertisement, "Leading Geographies," in Sidney Marsden Fuerst, James A. O'Donnell, and Marie L. Bayer, eds., *New York Teachers' Monographs* 11, 1 (March 1909), ii; Ginn & Company Advertisement, "Famous Textbooks in Geography," *Bulletin of the American Bureau of Geography* 1, 2 (June 1900): 201; Susan Schulten, *The Geographical Imagination in America, 1880–1950* (Chicago: University of Chicago Press, 2001), 93.

8. Peter Novick, *That Noble Dream: The "Objectivity Question" and the American Historical Profession* (New York: Cambridge University Press, 1988), 61.

9. Albert Bushnell Hart, "Imagination in History," *American Historical Review* 15, 2 (Jan. 1910): 242; *Journal of the New York State Teachers' Association* 6, 1 (Feb. 1919); Hart, *New American History* (New York: American Book, 1921), 643; Albert Bushnell Hart, *Essentials in American History* (New York: American Book, 1905), 568–69; Novick, *That Noble Dream*, 111; *The Study of History in Schools: Report to the AHA by the Committee of Seven* (New York: MacMillan, 1899), 74, quoted in Novick, *That Noble Dream*, 72.

10. Julie Reuben, "Beyond Politics: Community Civics and the Redefinition of Citizenship in the Progressive Era," *History of Education Quarterly* 37, 4 (Winter 1997): 399.

11. Horace Tarbell and Martha Tarbell, *Complete Geography* (New York: American Book, 1899), 17; "Werner School Book Company Advertisement for the 'New Geography,'" in *Michigan School Moderator* 10, 7 (Dec. 1899): 224. Horace Tarbell served as superintendent of Providence, Rhode Island public schools until 1902 and co-authored the 1895 "Report of the Committee of Fifteen" for the National Education Association of the United States. In 1897, Martha Tarbell became the first woman to receive a PhD (in German Studies) from Brown University.

12. Michael Adas, "From Settler Colony to Global Hegemon: Integrating the Exceptionalist Narrative of the American Experience into World History," *American Historical Review* 106, 5 (Dec. 2001): 1692–94.

13. Ralph Tarr and Frank McMurry, *Home Geography and the Earth as a Whole* (New York: MacMillan, 1901), 121; Maturin Ballou, *Foot-prints of Travel, Or Journeyings in Many Lands* (Boston: Ginn, 1889), 23; Fanny E. Coe, *The World and Its People, Book IV: Our American Neighbors* (New York: Silver, Burdett, 1899), 161; Tarbell and Tarbell, *Complete Geography,* 17. On the shift from description to scientific analysis in school geography in the late nineteenth century, see Schulten, *The Geographical Imagination in America,* 109–40.

14. William Morris Davis, *Elementary Physical Geography* (Boston: Ginn, 1903), 332.

15. Tarr and McMurry, *Home Geography,* 121–22.

16. Albert Perry Brigham, *Commercial Geography* (Boston: Ginn, 1911), 403, 412–13.

17. Mytton F. Maury, *Physical Geography* (New York: University Publishing, 1893), 116.

18. Maury, *Physical Geography,* 117; Gary Gerstle, "Theodore Roosevelt and the Divided Character of American Nationalism," *Journal of American History* 86, 3 (Dec. 1999): 1280–1307.

19. Aristide Zolberg, *A Nation by Design: Immigration Policy in the Fashioning of America* (Cambridge: Harvard University Press, 2006), 199–201.

20. Maury, *Physical Geography,* 116–117; Mytton F. Maury, *Maury's Manual of Geography* (New York: University Publishing, 1892), 98. Also see Ralph Tarr and Frank McMurry, *Advanced Geography* (New York: Macmillan, 1907 [1900]), 37; William Swinton, *Primary Geography* (New York: Ivison, Blakeman, Taylor, 1881), 21; Frank McMurry and A. E. Parkins, *Elementary Geography* (New York: Macmillan, 1921), 230–31.

21. Ellsworth Huntington and Sumner Cushing, *Principles of Human Geography* (New York: John Wiley & Sons, 1922 [1920]), 256–57, 261.

22. Ellen Churchill Semple, *Influences of Geographic Environment* (New York: Henry Holt, 1911), 608, 622–24.

23. Swinton, *Primary Geography,* 13.

24. Swinton, *Primary Geography,* 18–19, 21.

25. Tarr and McMurry, *Advanced Geography,* 34–35. Also see *Harper's Introductory Geography* (New York: Harper Bros., 1877), 41; Augustus Mitchell, *Mitchell's New Primary Geography* (Philadelphia: J. H. Butler, 1878), 26; Fanny Coe, *Our American Neighbors* (New York: American Book, 1889), 51–52.

26. William Brewer, *Warren's New Physical Geography* (Philadelphia: E. H. Brewer, 1890), 93.

27. Albert Perry Brigham and Charles McFarlane, *Essentials of Geography* (New York: American Book, 1921), 51.

28. Richard Ellwood Dodge, "Albert Perry Brigham," *Annals of the Association of American Geographers* 20, 2 (June 1930): 55–56; Ballou, *Foot-prints of Travel,* 8–10; Davis, *Elementary Physical Geography,* 371.

29. *Harper's Introductory Geography,* 37; Tarr and McMurry, *Home Geography,* 179.

30. Davis, *Elementary Physical Geography,* 372.

31. Wallace Atwood, *New Geography* (Boston: Ginn, 1920), 277, 304.

32. Atwood, *New Geography,* 304.

33. Atwood, *New Geography,* 304.

34. Albert Bushnell Hart, "The Historical Opportunity in America," *American Historical Review* 4, 1 (Oct. 1898): 2.

35. Albert Bushnell Hart, *We and Our History: A Biography of the American People* (New York: American Viewpoint Society, 1923), 230.

36. For example, see Emerson David Fite, *History of the United States* (New York: Henry Holt, 1916), 315.

37. For school history treatments of Native Americans and settler colonialism, see Hart, *We and Our History,* 39, 48; Thomas F. Donnelly, *Barnes' Primary History of the United States* (New York: American Book, 1899), 12; John Fisk, *A History of the United States for Schools* (Boston: Houghton, Mifflin, 1899), 1–18; Thomas Wentworth

Higginson, *Young Folks' History of the United States* (New York: Longmans, Green, 1901), 1; John Bach McMaster, *A School History of the United States* (New York: American Book, 1897), 66–70; Waddy Thompson, *A History of the United States* (Boston: D.C. Heath, 1904), 270; Charles Morris, *Elementary History of the United States* (Philadelphia: J.B. Lippincott, 1909), 58; Hart, *Essentials in American History*, 22–28; Samuel Eagle Forman, *Advanced American History* (New York: Century, 1914), 533; Henry Elson, *School History of the United States* (New York: Macmillan, 1912), 24–26, 27–30; L.A. Field, *A Grammar School History of the United States* (New York: American Book, 1897), 22–23; Edward Eggleston, *A First Book in American History* (New York: American Book, 1899), 10, 12–14, 16, 25; Nathaniel Wright Stephenson, *An American History* (Boston: Ginn, 1913), 1; William Mace, *A Beginner's History* (Chicago: Rand McNally, 1921), 13; Charles Beard and William Bagley, *The History of the American People* (New York: MacMillan, 1918, 1920), vi, 39–41, 461, 464.

38. For examples, see Higginson, *Young Folks' History of the United States,* 258; Thompson, *A History of the United States,* 275; David Saville Muzzey, *An American History* (Boston: Ginn, 1920), 444; David Montgomery, *The Leading Facts of American History* (Boston: Ginn, 1920), 217. On the changing nature of the Monroe Doctrine, see Jay Sexton, *The Monroe Doctrine: Empire and Nation in Nineteenth-Century America* (New York: Hill & Wang, 2011). Eliga Gould has argued that the Monroe Doctrine was not a rejection of European empire, but rather an attempt to engage with European states on equal footing as an imperial power. See Eliga Gould, *Among the Powers of the Earth: The American Revolution and the Making of a New World Empire* (Cambridge: Harvard University Press, 2012), 210–17.

39. Novick, *That Noble Dream,* 111–12.

40. Beard and Bagley, *History of the American People,* 241–43; William Appleman Williams, *The Tragedy of American Diplomacy* (New York: W.W. Norton, 1972), 18–58.

41. Fite, *History of the United States,* 493–94; John Latane, *History of the United States* (Boston: Allyn & Bacon, 1926), 526; Eric T.L. Love, *Race over Empire: Racism and US Imperialism, 1865–1900* (Chapel Hill: University of North Carolina Press, 2004), 27–72; Sexton, *The Monroe Doctrine,* 163–65.

42. Muzzey, *An American History,* 207–8. For discussions of right-wing attacks on Muzzey's Anglophilia as it pertained to his treatments of the American Revolution and War of 1812, see Gary B. Nash, Charlotte Crabtree, and Ross E. Dunn, *History on Trial: Culture Wars and the Teaching of the Past* (New York: Knopf, 1997), 26–32.

43. Walter Nugent, "The American Habit of Empire: The Case of Polk and Bush," *Western Historical Quarterly* 38, 1 (Spring 2007): 4–24.

44. Fite, *History of the United States,* 277–78.

45. Beard and Bagley, *The History of the American People,* 92.

46. Allen Thomas, *A History of the United States* (Boston: D.C. Heath, 1899), 241–42.

47. For Hart's outlook on race, see Novick, *That Noble Dream,* 75, 82–83.

48. Thomas, *A History of the United States*, 241–42; Albert Bushnell Hart, *School History of the United States* (New York: American Book, 1920), 297. Also see Hart, *New American History*, 342, 346; Reginald Horsman, *Race and Manifest Destiny: The Origins of American Racial Anglo-Saxonism* (Cambridge: Harvard University Press, 1981), 250.

49. Muzzey, *An American History*, 275, 279–80.

50. Zimmerman, *Whose America?*, 55–56.

51. Fite, *History of the United States*, 424.

52. Fite, *History of the United States*, 315.

53. Muzzey, *An American History*, 461; Fite, *History of the United States*, 470–71.

54. Mace, *A Beginner's History*, 354–55.

55. Muzzey, *An American History*, 451; Thomas Schoonover, *Uncle Sam's War of 1898 and the Origins of Globalization* (Lexington: University Press of Kentucky, 2003).

56. Montgomery, *The Leading Facts of American History*, 383.

57. Hart, *School History of the United States*, 450–51; Mace, *A Beginner's History*, 357–59.

58. Hart, *School History of the United States*, 450; Montgomery, *The Leading Facts of American History*, 382; Beard and Bagley, *The History of the American People*, 552–54; Fite, *History of the United States*, 483–84.

59. Mace, *A Beginner's History*, 357–59.

60. On race and anti-imperialist arguments regarding the Philippines, see Love, *Race over Empire*, 159–95.

61. Kramer, *The Blood of Government*, 1–2.

62. Muzzey, *An American History*, 458–60.

63. Hart, *New American History*, 643; Hart, *Essentials in American History*, 568–69.

64. Jasper McBrien, *America First: Patriotic Readings* (New York: American Book, 1916), 5–6.

65. Merrill Edwards Gates, "What the School Owes the State," in *California Educational Review* (San Francisco: Educational Review Publishing, 1891), 10.

66. For examples, see Caspar T. Hopkins, *A Manual of American Ideas, Third Revised Edition* (San Francisco: H. S. Crocker, 1887), 11; Board of Education, *Annual Report*, 1881, p. 44, Series 22, RNYCBE.

67. On the training of nonwhites and the "new immigrant" for industrial and factory work, see Stephen Meyer, "Adapting the Immigrant to the Line: Americanization at the Ford Factory, 1914–1921," *Journal of Social History* 14, 1 (Autumn 1980): 67–82; James Barrett, "Americanization from the Bottom-Up: Immigration and the Remaking of the Working Class in the United States, 1880–1930," *Journal of American History* 79, 3 (Dec. 1992): 996–1020; Fear-Segal, *White Man's Club*; Donald Spivey, *Schooling for the New Slavery: Black Industrial Education, 1868–1915* (Westport, CT: Greenwood, 1978).

68. Reuben, "Beyond Politics," 399–401.

69. For example, see Samuel Eagle Forman, "The Aim and Scope of Civics," *School Review* 11, 4 (Apr. 1903): 289. In 1887, Forman graduated from Dickinson College in Carlisle, Pennsylvania, site of the Carlisle Indian School. He authored four civics textbooks and four history textbooks. Forman's *Advanced Civics* (first edition, 1905) represented the old guard in school civics and was adopted in several major urban school systems, including Chicago public schools in 1906. See "Report to Adopt Text Book in Civics Amended," Proceedings of the Chicago School Board, 1906, p. 727, Chicago Public Library, Chicago, IL.

70. Michael Kammen, *Mystic Chords of Memory: The Transformation of Tradition in American Culture* (New York: Alfred Knopf, 1991), 244.

71. Circular, Charles L. Barrington to Principals, October 20, 1898, 2A1-11, SFH 3.

72. Circular, Memorial Day Committee to the Children of the Public Schools, May 19, 1903, 2A1-11, SFH 3. On the origins and politics of Memorial Day, particularly its co-opting by white reconciliationists in the late nineteenth century, see David Blight, *Race and Reunion: The Civil War in American Memory* (Cambridge: Belknap Press of Harvard University, 2001).

73. Benedict Anderson, *Imagined Communities: Reflections on the Origin and Spread of Nationalism* (New York: Verso, 2006 [1981]), 144. On the US war in the Philippines, see Kramer, *The Blood of Government.*

74. Georgia Department of Education, *Annual Report* (Atlanta: Department of Education, 1917), 19–20.

75. National War-Savings Committee to School Superintendents and Teachers of California, April 15, 1918, 2A1-16, SFH 3.

76. Special Circular No. 6, October 8, 1917, 512: 23, RNYCBE.

77. Special Circular No. 2, September 25, 1918, 512: 23, RNYCBE.

78. John Higham, *Strangers in the Land: Patterns of American Nativism, 1865–1920* (New Brunswick: Rutgers University Press, 2002), 242–50.

79. Georgia Department of Education, *Annual Report,* 1917, 33.

80. "Report to the President, Cabinet, and Congress of the United States," Series VII, Box 7, Folder 2: Reports, Neighborhood Union Collection, Archives and Special Collections, Robert Woodruff Library, Atlanta University Center, Atlanta, GA. Hereafter, NUC.

81. Roncovieri and Dohrmann to Citizens of San Francisco, November 16, 1922, 2A1-20, SFH 3.

82. For both the legal and popular interpretations of whiteness for Mexicans, Turks, and Asian Indians in the United States, see discussions of *In re Rodriguez,* and *United States v. Thind* in Ian F. Haney-Lopez, *White by Law: The Legal Construction of Race* (New York: New York University Press, 1996), 61, 79–109. On the potential whiteness of Russians and other eastern Europeans, see Roediger, *Working toward Whiteness;* Jacobson, *Whiteness of a Different Color;* Jacobson, *Roots Too: White Ethnic Revival in Post–Civil Rights America* (Cambridge: Harvard University Press, 2006).

83. Higham, *Strangers in the Land,* 138–39.

84. Robert Ward, "Our New Immigration Policy," *Foreign Affairs* 3, 1 (Sep. 15, 1924): 99–100, 103.

85. Jacobson, *Whiteness of a Different Color,* 3–4, 90–92.

86. O'Leary, *To Die For,* 244–45.

CHAPTER 2: VISIONS OF WHITE CALIFORNIA

1. Muzzey, *An American History,* 296.

2. New York Department of Education, *Course of Study and Syllabus, Short Unit and Naturalization Course for the Evening Elementary Schools, The City of New York, 1922* (New York: Stillman Appellate Printing, 1922), 9.

3. Circular, Andrew Jackson Moulder to Principals, April 1, 1886, 2A-1-8, SFH 3.

4. Ibid.; Samuel F. Black, *Seventeenth Biennial Report of the Superintendent of Public Instruction* (Sacramento: A.J. Johnson, State Superintendent Printing, 1896), 97.

5. Copy of Preamble to Budget Recommended by the Board of Education, 1913, 2A-1-15, SFH 3.

6. McKeown, *Melancholy Order,* 8.

7. Barbara Berglund, *Making San Francisco American: Cultural Frontiers in the Urban West, 1846–1906* (Lawrence: University Press of Kansas, 2007), 4–5, 8–9. On the idea of cosmopolitanism, see Pheng Cheah, "Cosmopolitanism," *Theory, Culture, and Society* 23, 2–3 (2006): 486–96; Pnina Werbner, "Vernacular Cosmopolitanism," *Theory, Culture, and Society* 23, 2–3 (2006): 496–98.

8. Lowe, *Immigrant Acts,* 5.

9. Quoted in Ronald Takaki, *Strangers from a Different Shore: A History of Asian Americans* (New York: Little, Brown, 1989), 80–82; McKeown, *Melancholy Order,* 58.

10. Tomás Almaguer, *Racial Fault Lines: The Historical Origins of White Supremacy in California* (Berkeley: University of California Press, 1994), 38.

11. Wollenberg, *All Deliberate Speed,* 8–11, 13–14, 21–27; Hendrick, *The Education of Non-Whites in California,* 17–24. Section 1669 of the 1874 California school code required local school boards to admit black and Indian children to white schools should boards fail or choose not to provide separate schools.

12. Frank Van Nuys, *Americanizing the West: Race, Immigrants, and Citizenship, 1890–1930* (Lawrence: University Press of Kansas, 2002), 33.

13. Ballou, *Footprints of Travel,* 8–10.

14. Yong Chen, *Chinese San Francisco, 1850–1943* (Stanford: Stanford University Press, 2000), 54–69.

15. California State Senate Special Committee on Chinese Immigration, *Chinese Immigration,* 15.

16. Chen, *Chinese San Francisco,* 56–57.

17. G. B. Densmore, *The Chinese in California, Description of Chinese Life in San Francisco. Their Habits, Morals, and Manners* (San Francisco: Pettit & Russ, 1880), 117–18.

18. Quoted in Gary Okihiro, *Margins and Mainstreams: Asians in American History and Culture* (Seattle: University of Washington Press, 1994), 159.

19. Wollenberg, *All Deliberate Speed*, 31–34.

20. Stuart Creighton Miller, *The Unwelcome Immigrant: The American Image of the Chinese, 1785–1882* (Berkeley: University of California Press, 1969).

21. Lears, *Rebirth of a Nation*, 73, 99; Alexander Saxton, *The Indispensable Enemy: Labor and the Anti-Chinese Movement in California* (Berkeley: University of California Press, 1971), 113–15; Jacobson, *Barbarian Virtues*, 77; Najia Aarim-Heriot, *Chinese Immigrants, African Americans, and Racial Anxiety in the United States, 1848–1882* (Urbana: University of Illinois Press, 2003), 189–90; Diana L. Ahmad, *The Opium Debate and Chinese Exclusion Laws in the Nineteenth-Century American West* (Reno: University of Nevada Press, 2007), 4–5; Almaguer, *Racial Fault Lines*, 168–74.

22. *Constitution, Rules and By-Laws for subordinate camps of California Encampment, Order of Caucasians* (Sacramento: H. A. Weaver, 1876), 3.

23. *Debates and Proceedings of the Constitutional Convention of the State of California convened at the city of Sacramento, Saturday, September 28, 1878* (Sacramento: State Printing Office, 1881), 677, 679, 1238; Aarim-Heriot, *Chinese Immigrants, African Americans and Racial Anxiety in the United States*, 191–92.

24. California State Senate Special Committee on Chinese Immigration, *Chinese Immigration*, 7.

25. Andrew Gyory, *Closing the Gate: Race, Politics, and the Chinese Exclusion Act* (Chapel Hill: University of North Carolina Press, 1998), 1–2, 15–16.

26. "Chinese Exclusion," Speech of George C. Perkins of California, in the Senate of the United States, Wednesday, November 1, 1893 (The Provisions of the New Chinese Law), Washington, 1893, p. 2, Chinese in California Collection, Bancroft Library, University of California Berkeley, Digital Library, accessed October 8, 2013, doi: F870.C5.P4.

27. *Sacramento Daily Record-Union*, October 10, 1884; Wendy Rouse Jorae, *The Children of Chinatown: Growing Up Chinese American in San Francisco, 1850–1920* (Chapel Hill: University of North Carolina Press, 2009), 115; Wollenberg, *All Deliberate Speed*, 29; Okihiro, *Margins and Mainstreams*, 159–60.

28. The amendment remained in effect through the Japanese school exclusion crisis of 1906–7 and the Gentlemen's Agreement. See *School Law of California* (Sacramento: State Printing Office, 1913), 80.

29. Wollenberg, *All Deliberate Speed*, 43–44.

30. Circulars, Babcock to Principals, April 28, 1896, 2A-1-9, SFH 3; Langdon to Principals, April 16, 1903, September 13, 1904, 2A-1-11, SFH 3; Webster to Principals, November 11, 1908, 2A-1-12, SFH 3; Roncovieri to Principals, January 9, 1912, 2A-1-13, SFH 3.

31. Roger Daniels, *The Politics of Prejudice: The Anti-Japanese Movement in California and the Struggle for Japanese Exclusion* (Berkeley: University of California Press, 1962), 3, 6–8, 15–16.

32. SBNSC, *San Francisco Bulletin*, November 1, 1906, 7–99, SFH 3; Lake and Reynolds, *Drawing the Global Colour Line*, 175–76. I am grateful to the official at

the San Francisco School Board who compiled, apparently in real time, an extensive scrapbook of mostly local but also state and national newspaper articles that covered the school exclusion crisis in detail.

33. SBNSC, *San Francisco Chronicle*, December 24, 1908, 7–101, SFH 3.

34. SBNSC, *San Francisco Bulletin*, November 1, 1906, 7–99, SFH 3.

35. Yuji Ichioka, *The Issei: The World of the First Generation of Japanese Immigrants, 1885–1924s* (New York: Free Press, 1988), 3, 7–8, 27, 38–39.

36. Quoted in Ichioka, *The Issei*, 39.

37. Azuma, *Between Two Empires*, 19.

38. Quoted in Ichioka, *The Issei*, 10.

39. Azuma, *Between Two Empires*, 17–22; Ichioka, *The Issei*, 51–52; M. Browning Carrott, "Prejudice Goes to Court: The Japanese and the Supreme Court in the 1920s," *California History* 62, 2 (Summer 1983): 122.

40. Azuma, *Between Two Empires*, 17–22; Akira Iriye, *Pacific Estrangement: Japanese and American Expansion, 1897–1911* (Cambridge: Harvard University Press, 1972), 131; Lake and Reynolds, *Drawing the Global Colour Line*, 179–81; Belich, *Replenishing the Earth*, 49.

41. Quoted in Daniels, *The Politics of Prejudice*, 21.

42. Daniels, *The Politics of Prejudice*, 20–21, 26–28.

43. *Proceedings of the Asiatic Exclusion League, San Francisco, April 1908* (New York: Arno Press, 1977), 15.

44. Daniels, *The Politics of Prejudice*, 31–33.

45. Circular, Secretary E. C. Leffingwell to Principals, October 13, 1906, 2A-1-12, SFH 3; *Report of the Superintendent of Schools and Board of Education, San Francisco, Cal. for the Fiscal Years 1906–1907 and 1907–1908* (San Francisco: Neal Publishing, 1908), 17.

46. Mae Ngai, *Impossible Subjects: Illegal Aliens and the Making of Modern America* (Princeton: Princeton University Press, 2004), 23.

47. SBNSC, *San Francisco Call*, November 3, 1906, 7–99, SFH 3. On Japanese and Issei notions of race and racial superiority both in Japan and United States, see Azuma, *Between Two Empires*, 83–84, 214.

48. SBNSC, *San Francisco Call*, November 15, 1906, 7–99, SFH 3.

49. SBNSC, *San Francisco Call*, October 23, 1906, *San Francisco Examiner*, November 2, 1906, 7–99, SFH 3.

50. SBNSC, *San Francisco Examiner*, November 2, 1906, 7–99, SFH 3; Lake and Reynolds, *Drawing the Global Colour Line*, 173–74; Jacobson, *Whiteness of a Different Color*, 227–29.

51. Theodore P. Ion, "The Japanese School Incident at San Francisco from the Point of View of International and Constitutional Law," *Michigan Law Review* 5, 5 (Mar. 1907): 328, 330, 341.

52. Edwin Maxey, "Exclusion of Japanese Children from the Public Schools of San Francisco," *Yale Law Journal* 16, 2 (Dec. 1906): 92–93.

53. James D. Richardson, ed., *A Compilation of the Messages and Papers of the Presidents, Volume X* (New York: Bureau of National Literature, 1913), 7433–36;

Daniels, *The Politics of Prejudice*, 38–39; Wollenberg, *All Deliberate Speed*, 60–61. On Roosevelt's twinned nationalisms, see Gerstle, "Theodore Roosevelt and the Divided Character of American Nationalism," 1280–307.

54. SBNSC, *San Francisco Chronicle*, December 5, 1906, 7–99, SFH 3.

55. Theodore Roosevelt and Victor Metcalf, *Message from the President of the United States transmitting the Final Report of Secretary Metcalf on the Situation Affecting the Japanese in the City of San Francisco, Cal* (San Francisco: R & E Research Associates, 1971 [reprint]), 17–19; Daniels, *The Politics of Prejudice*, 40.

56. Nichibei Shinbunsha, *Zaibei Nihonjin Nenkan* (San Francisco: Nichibei Shinbunsha, 1908), 202–4. I am indebted to Eiichiro Azuma and Emily Anderson for assistance with this Japanese language source.

57. Daniels, *The Politics of Prejudice*, 40.

58. Azuma, *Between Two Empires*, 27–29, 31, 38–40; Ichioka, *The Issei*, 146–48.

59. SBNSC, *San Francisco Bulletin*, December 6, 1906, 7–99, SFH 3.

60. SBNSC, *San Francisco Call*, December 7, 1906, reprinted from *Sacramento Union*, 7–99, SFH 3.

61. SBNSC, *San Francisco Call*, December 1, 1906, 7–99, SFH 3.

62. SBNSC, *Berkeley Daily Gazette*, November 15, 1906, 7–99, SFH 3.

63. Quoted in SBNSC, *San Francisco Chronicle*, March 9, 1907, 7–99, SFH 3.

64. *Report of the Superintendent*, 17; Daniels, *The Politics of Prejudice*, 41.

65. SBNSC, *Berkeley Daily Gazette*, November 15, 1906, 7–99, SFH 3; Aarim-Heriot, *Chinese Immigrants, African Americans, and Racial Anxiety in the United States*, 69. On white popularization of hyper-sexualized freedmen and their perceived threat to white womanhood, see Hannah Rosen, *Terror in the Heart of Freedom: Citizenship, Sexual Violence, and the Meaning of Race in the Postemancipation South* (Chapel Hill: University of North Carolina Press, 2009), 172–73, 196–202; Gail Bederman, *Manliness and Civilization: A Cultural History of Gender and Race in the United States, 1880–1917* (Chicago: University of Chicago Press, 1995), 46–48, 142–43.

66. SBNSC, *San Francisco Chronicle*, February 19, 1907, *San Francisco Call*, February 26, 1907, *San Francisco Examiner*, February 27, 1907, 7–99, SFH 3.

67. SBNSC, *San Francisco Chronicle*, January 9, 1907, *San Francisco Call*, January 10, 1907, 7–99, SFH 3.

68. SBNSC, *San Francisco Chronicle*, March 9, 1907, 7–99, SFH 3.

69. SBNSC, *San Francisco Examiner*, March 10, 1907, 7–99, SFH 3.

70. Azuma, *Between Two Empires*, 64–65.

71. Ngai, *Impossible Subjects*, 39–40; State Board of Control of California, *California and the Oriental: Japanese, Chinese, and Hindus, Report of State Board of Control of California to Gov. Wm. D. Stephens* (Sacramento: California State Printing Office, 1922), 8.

72. Ngai, *Impossible Subjects*, 42; David Yoo, *Growing Up Nisei: Race, Generation, and Culture among Japanese Americans in California, 1924–1949* (Urbana: University of Illinois Press, 2000), 22–23.

73. Ngai, *Impossible Subjects,* 49.

74. "Japan's Secret Policy, Her Immigrants and American Born Citizens Using Their Position to Aid Japan, the Startling Statement of a Japanese Professor at the University of California," *Sacramento Bee,* November 1920, Japanese Pamphlets, vol. 2, California State Library Digital Collection, accessed October 3, 2013, http://archive.org/details/japanesepamphlet02cali; Azuma, *Between Two Empires,* 127–28, 133–34, 138.

75. Ichioka, *The Issei,* 207–10.

76. Department of the Interior, *The Public School System of San Francisco, California,* Bulletin 1917, no. 46 (Washington: Government Printing Office, 1917), 560–61.

77. Juichi Soyeda and Tadao Kamiya, "A Survey of the Japanese Question in California" (San Francisco: Japan Society of America, 1913), 16, Japanese Pamphlets, vol. 1, California State Library Digital Collection, accessed October 1, 2013, http://archive.org/details/japanesepamphlet01cali.

CHAPTER 3: HAWAIIAN COSMOPOLITANS AND
THE AMERICAN PACIFIC

1. Ernest A. Mott-Smith, *Report of the Minister of Public Instruction to the President of the Republic of Hawaii for the Biennial Period ending December 31st, 1899* (Honolulu: Hawaiian Gazette, 1900), 5.

2. Atkinson's report included in Sanford B. Dole, *Report of the Governor of the Territory of Hawaii to the Secretary of the Interior* (Washington: Government Printing Office, 1903), 66.

3. William Woodwell to W. J. Leavitt, July 1, 1881, 261-16-4; D. D. Baldwin to C. R. Bishop, July 2, 1881, 261-16-8, Records of the Hawaii Department of Education. Hereafter RHDE.

4. Cheah, "Cosmopolitanism," 486, 488.

5. *Hawaiian Gazette,* November 15, 1907, 2.

6. Comparative Table of the Nationality of Pupils Attending School in the Territory of Hawai'i for the Years 1896–1906; Table, Nationality of Public School Children by Island, December 31, 1906, 231-54-19, RHDE; Christine Skwiot, *The Purposes of Paradise: US Tourism and Empire in Cuba and Hawai'i* (Philadelphia: University of Pennsylvania Press, 2010), 73; Edward Beechert, *Working in Hawai'i: A Labor History* (Honolulu: University of Hawai'i Press, 1985), 147. On Portuguese as a separate class of Caucasian from haole, see James A. Geschwender, Rita Carroll-Seguin and Howard Brill, "The Portuguese and Haoles of Hawai'i: Implications for the Origin of Ethnicity," *American Sociological Review* 53, 4 (Aug. 1988): 515–27; Romanzo Adams, *Interracial Marriage in Hawai'i: A Study of the Mutually Conditioned Processes of Acculturation and Amalgamation* (New York: MacMillan, 1937), 119–20.

7. Skwiot, *The Purposes of Paradise,* 4–6, 50–51; Henry Nash Smith, *Virgin Land: The American West as Symbol and Myth* (Cambridge: Harvard University

Press, 1950); Alexander Saxton, *The Rise and Fall of the White Republic* (New York: Verso, 1990).

8. *Honolulu Bulletin,* January 3, 1908. To be sure, many prominent haole continued to issue calls for settlement by Anglo-Saxons. For example, see then former governor Sanford Dole's editorial in the *Hawaiian Gazette,* May 24, 1907, in which he called for the "introduction of persons from the mainland who have acquired by long residence and particularly by inheritance and position the qualities of citizenship."

9. Tamura, *Americanization, Acculturation, and Ethnic Identity,* xiii–xv.

10. Archibald Alexander, quoted in Mary Frances Morgan Armstrong and Samuel Chapman Armstrong, *Richard Armstrong: America, Hawaiʻi* (Hampton, VA: Normal School Steam Press, 1887), 11, 17; Edith Armstrong Talbot, *Samuel Chapman Armstrong: A Biographical Study* (New York: Doubleday, 1904), 4; Richard Armstrong to Caroline Armstrong, October 6, 1844, in *Richard Armstrong,* 64.

11. Okihiro, *Island World,* 108.

12. Jonathan Kay Kamakawiwoʻole Osorio, *Dismembering Lāhui: A History of the Hawaiian Nation to 1887* (Honolulu: University of Hawaiʻi Press, 2002), 26–27, 44–47, 50–51.

13. Benjamin O. Wist, *A Century of Public Education in Hawaii, 1840–1940* (Honolulu: Hawaii Educational Review, 1940), 63–64, 76. The Board of Commissioners became the Board of Education in 1865.

14. Okihiro, *Island World,* 103–4; Carl Kalani Beyer, "Manual Training and Industrial Education for Hawaiians," *Hawaiian Journal of History* 38 (2004): 18.

15. Talbot, *Samuel Chapman Armstrong,* 4.

16. Quoted in Okihiro, *Island World,* 117.

17. Samuel Chapman Armstrong, "Reminiscences," in *Richard Armstrong,* 91, 99.

18. Skwiot, *The Purposes of Paradise,* 31–32; Beechert, *Working in Hawaiʻi,* 47, 61; Gary Okihiro, *Cane Fires: The Anti-Japanese Movement in Hawaiʻi, 1865–1945* (Philadelphia: Temple University Press, 1991), 9.

19. Quoted in Rob Wilson, "Exporting Christian Transcendentalism, Importing Hawaiian Sugar: The Trans-Americanization of Hawaiʻi," *American Literature* 72, 3 (Sept. 2000): 530.

20. Sally Engle Merry, *Colonizing Hawaiʻi: The Cultural Power of Law* (Princeton: Princeton University Press, 2000), 131–32.

21. Merry, *Colonizing Hawaiʻi,* 125–26; Takaki, *Strangers from a Different Shore,* 45.

22. Noenoe K. Silva, *Aloha Betrayed: Native Hawaiian Resistance to American Colonialism* (Durham, NC: Duke University Press, 2004), 122, 126; Ralph S. Kuykendall, *The Hawaiian Kingdom, Volume III, 1874–1893: The Kalākaua Dynasty* (Honolulu: University of Hawaiʻi Press, 1967), 470–74; Osorio, *Dismembering Lāhui,* 243.

23. Osorio, *Dismembering Lāhui,* 244; Silva, *Aloha Betrayed,* 126.

24. Christen Tsuyuko Sasaki, "Pacific Confluence: Negotiating the Nation in Nineteenth Century Hawaiʻi" (PhD diss., University of California, Los Angeles, 2011), 77–78, 81–82, 85–86.

25. William D. Alexander, *Biennial Report of the President of the Board of Education to the Legislature of the Republic of Hawaii, 1894–1895* (Honolulu: Hawaiian Gazette, 1896), 6–7.

26. Mott-Smith, *Report of the Minister of Public Instruction, 1899,* 4–5.

27. Okihiro, *Cane Fires,* 13–17.

28. *Honolulu Republican,* May 25, 1901.

29. Ibid.

30. *Honolulu Republican,* May 25, 1901; Skwiot, *The Purposes of Paradise,* 51. Figures from 1901 indicate that white American and European students made up 9 percent of enrollment in public and private schools. Since whites disproportionately attended private schools, public schools figures were likely considerably lower. Figures from 1906 place white (American) public school numbers at only 3 percent. See *Honolulu Republican,* June 16, 1901; *Hawaiian Gazette,* November 15, 1907.

31. Alatau Atkinson, copy of *Report of the Superintendent to the Governor of the Territory of Hawaii,* 33–38, 261-54-18, RHDE.

32. Report of Vocational Committee, February 25, 1913, 235–10, RHDE.

33. Report of the Superintendent to the Governor, July 30, 1915, 261-54-21, RHDE.

34. Biennium Report for period ending December 31, 1918, 261-54-23, RHDE.

35. Ibid.; Report of the Superintendent to the Governor, July 30, 1915, 261-54-21, RHDE.

36. Hugh Tucker to Willis Pope, January 8, April 21, 23, 24, 1912, 261-53-22, RHDE.

37. Tucker to Pope, May 11, 22, 1911, 261-53-20, RHDE.

38. Atkinson, duplicate copy of *Report to the Governor,* 54-55, 261-54-18, RHDE; James Davis, duplicate copy of *Report to the Acting-Governor, 1905,* 27, 261-54-18, RHDE.

39. Report on the Girls' Industrial School, August 1, 1909—April 1, 1910, 235-10-1; "Report of the Girls' Industrial School, 1905," 261-54-19, RHDE.

40. Sterritt to Kinney, November 24, 1914; Sterritt to DPI, December 8, 1914, 235-10-1, RHDE.

41. Atkinson, "Education and the Public Schools," in George Carter, *Report of the Governor of the Territory of Hawaii to the Secretary of the Interior* (Washington: Government Printing Office, 1904), 35; Atkinson, copy of *Report to the Governor,* 53–54, 261-54-18, RHDE.

42. Atkinson, in Carter, *Report of the Governor,* 28.

43. Sanford Dole, *Report of the Governor of the Territory of Hawaii to the Secretary of the Interior* (Washington: Government Printing Office, 1902), 30, 41, 73–74; Charles McCarthy, *Report of the Governor of the Territory of Hawaii to the Secretary of the Interior* (Washington: Government Printing Office, 1919), 59.

44. Thomas M. Gibson to Pope, July 11, 1910, 261-53-20, RHDE.

45. Tucker to Pope, November 14, 1910, 261-53-20, RHDE.

46. Enrollment Chart for Boys' Industrial School, n.d., 261-53-20; Letter, Tucker to Pope, April 1, 1913, 261-53-23; Letter, Pope to Tucker, October 5, 1911, 261-53-21, RHDE.

47. George Carter, *Report of the Governor of the Territory of Hawaii to the Secretary of the Interior* (Washington: Government Printing Office, 1906), 6.

48. Beechert, *Working in Hawai'i,* 170; Industrial School Boys Employed by Kahuku Plantation Company during July 1910, 261-53-20; Unsigned Letter to Governor Lucius Pinkham, March 17, 1914, 261-54-21, RHDE.

49. *Honolulu Star-Bulletin,* November 22, 1915; Kinney to Brown, December 2, 1915, 261-54-13, RHDE.

50. Charles McCarthy, *Report of the Governor of the Territory of Hawaii to the Secretary of the Interior* (Washington: Government Printing Office, 1920), 64; US Department of the Interior, Bureau of Education, *A Survey of Education in Hawaii,* Bulletin no. 16 (Washington: Government Printing Office, 1920), 32, quoted in Okihiro, *Cane Fires,* 139.

51. *Hawaiian Gazette,* November 19, 1907.

52. *Hawaiian Gazette,* November 15, 1907.

53. Beechert, *Working in Hawai'i,* 89, 186–87; Okihiro, *Cane Fires,* 93–96. For migration numbers and a discussion of the limits of statistical accuracy, see Tamura, *Acculturation, Americanization, and Ethnic Identity,* 22–30.

54. For arrivals and departures by race and national origin between 1905 and 1916, see Beechert, *Working in Hawai'i,* 132.

55. Okihiro, *Cane Fires,* 39, 83; Beechert, *Working in Hawai'i,* 174–75, 191–92, 197, 214–15, 243–44; Kramer, *The Blood of Government,* 397–98.

56. Tamura, *Acculturation, Americanization, and Ethnic Identity,* 128.

57. "Butler Sends Forceful Message Showing Islands' Need of Labor," *Maui News,* September 27, 1921.

58. Quoted in Tamura, *Acculturation, Americanization and Ethnic Identity,* 126.

59. Board of Commissioners, Minutes, June 3, 1911, 235-10, RHDE.

60. Board of Commissioners, Minutes, May 25, 1912, 235-10, RHDE.

61. Dodge to Frear, June 7, 1913, 261-54-21, RHDE.

62. Okihiro, *Cane Fires,* 139–40.

63. Tamura, *Acculturation, Americanization, and Ethnic Identity,* 146–47.

64. John Hawkins, "Politics, Education, and Language Policy: The Case of Japanese Language Schools in Hawaii," *Amerasia* 5, 1 (1978): 42.

65. Responses to MacCaughey Survey, "Americanizing of Hawaii's Young People," 1922, 316-6-3, RHDE.

66. Report, October 15, 1906, 261-54-19, RHDE.

67. Report, June 30, 1909, 261-54-20; *Report of the Superintendent to the Governor,* June 30, 1915, 261-54-21, RHDE.

68. Tamura, *Acculturation, Americanization, and Ethnic Identity,* 146–147.

69. Territorial Legislature, *Laws of the Territory of Hawaii Passed by the Eleventh Legislature, Special Session, 1920* (Honolulu: Honolulu Advertising Publishing, 1921), 31–32; Tamura, *Acculturation, Americanization, and Ethnic Identity,* 147–49.

70. Honolulu Ad. Club, "Suggested Policy and Program: Foreign Language School Question," 316-1-2, RHDE.

71. Hawkins, "Politics, Education, and Language Policy," 45–46.

72. Schwartz to Burns, June 15, 1925, Burns to Schwartz, June 16, 1925, 316-1-4B; Schwartz to Campsie, August 22, 1923, 316-1-5C, RHDE.

73. Schwartz to Aiken, June 25, 1924; Aiken to Schwartz, July 3, 1924, 316-1-1A, RHDE.

74. Schwartz to Toshiyuki, June 2, 1924, 316-1-5C, Farrington to Schwartz, August 16, 1923, 316-2-2, RHDE.

75. Vaughan MacCaughey to Principals, Circular: "Americanizing Hawaii's Young People," October 16, 1922, 316-6-3, RHDE. Records do not reveal whether the DPI only sent the survey to public schools that employed teachers of Japanese descent or whether the overwhelming number of responses simply came from Nisei teachers. Given that Nisei made up only a small minority of public school teachers, the former seems more likely.

76. Henry Schwartz, "A Survey of the Language School Situation in Hawaii: An Essay Read before the Honolulu Social Science Club," March 2, 1925, 7, 316-6-4, RHDE.

77. MacCaughey, "Americanizing Hawaii's Young People."

78. *Farrington, Territorial Governor, et al. v. T. Tokushige et al.,* 11 Fed. 710 (9th Cir. 1926), quoted in Yoshihide Matsubayashi, "The Japanese Language Schools in Hawaii and California, 1892–1941" (PhD diss., University of San Francisco, 1984), 175–77. The Ninth Circuit decision was based in part on previous decisions, including *Meyer v. Nebraska* and *Bartels v. Iowa,* that struck down nativist attempts to eliminate the teaching of foreign languages. See Tamura, *Acculturation, Americanization, and Ethnic Identity,* 149–50.

79. On the intricacies of the quota system, see McKeown, *Melancholy Order,* 331–35.

80. U.S. Department of the Interior, *Hawaii and Its Race Problems* (Washington: Government Printing Office, 1932), 117–19.

CHAPTER 4: BLACK ATLANTA'S EDUCATION
THROUGH LABOR

1. Albert Perry Brigham, *Geographic Influences in American History* (Boston: Ginn, 1903), 192–93.

2. *Atlanta University Bulletin,* series II, no. 20, July 1915, "Inter-Racial Cooperation for Human Betterment," 7, 27-1, AUC Catalogues and Bulletins, 1867–1933, Atlanta University Published and Printed Materials, Archives Research Center, Robert Woodruff Library, Atlanta University Center, Atlanta, GA. Hereafter AUPPM.

3. Charles Strickland, "The Rise of Public Schooling and the Attitude of Parents: The Case of Atlanta, 1872–1897," in *Schools in Cities: Consensus and Conflict in*

American Educational History, ed. Ronald Goodenow and Diane Ravitch (New York: Holmes and Meier, 1983), 249–62; Eugene Watts, "Black Political Progress in Atlanta, 1868–1895," *Journal of Negro History* 59, 3 (July 1974): 273; Jennifer Lund Smith, "The Ties That Bind: Educated African-American Women in Post-Emancipation Atlanta," in *Georgia in Black and White: Explorations in the Race Relations of a Southern State, 1865–1950,* ed. John Inscoe (Athens: University of Georgia Press, 1994), 96.

4. Strickland, "The Rise of Public Schooling and the Attitude of Parents," 249–62; C. Vann Woodward, *The Strange Career of Jim Crow* (New York: Oxford University Press, 1974).

5. Clifford Kuhn, *Contesting the New South Order: The 1914–15 Strike at Atlanta's Fulton Mills* (Chapel Hill: University of North Carolina Press, 2001), 11, 14, 34–35; *Atlanta Constitution,* May 5, 1885.

6. Allison Dorsey, *To Build Our Lives Together: Community Formation in Black Atlanta, 1875–1906* (Athens: University of Georgia Press, 2004), 27–28.

7. Ruth Winton, "Negro Participation in Southern Expositions, 1881–1915," *Journal of Negro Education* 16, 1 (Winter 1947): 34.

8. Hannibal Kimball, *Report of the Director-General of the International Cotton Exposition* (New York: D. Appleton, 1882), 154, 174–75, 220.

9. Edward Ayers, *The Promise of the New South: Life after Reconstruction* (New York: Oxford University Press, 1992), 21.

10. Franklin Garrett, *Atlanta and Environs: A Chronicle of Its People and Events, Volume II* (Athens: University of Georgia Press, 1969), 25–26.

11. C. Vann Woodward, *Tom Watson: Agrarian Rebel* (New York: Oxford University Press, 1963), 165–66.

12. Dorsey, *To Build Our Lives Together,* 17–18, 57; William Harris, "Work and Family in Black Atlanta, 1880," *Journal of Social History* 9, 3 (Spring 1976): 320.

13. Kim Cary Warren, *The Quest for Citizenship: African American and Native American Education in Kansas, 1880–1935* (Chapel Hill: University of North Carolina Press, 2010), 2–3; Lowe, *Immigrant Acts,* 5.

14. Atlanta Board of Education, *Annual Report* (Atlanta: Jas. P. Harrison, 1892), 647.

15. Anderson, *The Education of Blacks in the South,* 80–81.

16. Georgia Department of Education, *Annual Report,* 1899, 6.

17. Atlanta Board of Education, *Annual Report* (Atlanta: Jas. P. Harrison, 1882), 5, 8; Louis Harlan, *Separate and Unequal: Public School Campaigns and Racism in the Southern Seaboard States, 1901–1915* (Chapel Hill: University of North Carolina Press, 1958), 8.

18. W. E. B. Du Bois, "Cultural Missions of Atlanta University" *Phylon* 3, 2 (1942): 105.

19. Philip Noel Racine, "Atlanta's Schools: A History of the Public School System, 1869–1955" (PhD diss., Emory University, 1970), 2–3. Racine's dissertation remains the most comprehensive history of the development of Atlanta's public schools through the watershed *Brown v. Board of Education* Supreme Court

decision in 1954 mandating, with varying degrees of success, the integration of public schools throughout the United States.

20. J. W. Alford, Circular No. 2, May 19, 1865, quoted in Du Bois, "The Negro Common School," 23, 37.

21. Anderson, *The Education of Blacks in the South,* 11–12, 15–18.

22. Guiss Griffis Johnson, "Southern Paternalism toward Negroes after Emancipation," *Journal of Southern History,* 23, 4 (Nov. 1957), 483.

23. Ulrich B. Phillips, "The Central Theme of Southern History," *American Historical Review* 34, 1 (Oct. 1928): 31. Also see Lears, *Rebirth of a Nation,* 129–31; Blight, *Race and Reunion.*

24. W. E. B. Du Bois, "The Negro Common School," in *Atlanta University Publications,* No. 6 (New York: Arno Press and *New York Times,* 1969 [1901]), 17–18; Anderson, *The Education of Blacks in the South,* 2.

25. Okihiro, *Island World,* 130; Gerstle, *American Crucible,* 37.

26. W. E. B. Du Bois, E. J. Penney, and T. J. Bell, *Proceedings of the Sixth Atlanta Conference* (New York: Arno Press and *New York Times,* 1969 [1901]), ii; Lake and Reynolds, *Drawing the Global Colour Line,* 247–49.

27. On the reconstitution of forced labor in the postbellum period, see Douglas Blackmon, *Slavery by Another Name: The Re-Enslavement of Black Americans from the Civil War to World War II* (New York: Doubleday, 2008).

28. Anderson, *The Education of Blacks in the South,* 33–37; Okihiro, *Island World,* 98–134.

29. Robert Norrell, *Up from History: The Life of Booker T. Washington* (Cambridge: Belknap Press of Harvard University, 2009), 8–9, 121–28.

30. *Atlanta Constitution,* May 25, 1903; "Lynchings by year and race," accessed August 1, 2013, www.law.umkc.edu/faculty/projects/ftrials/shipp/lynchingyear.html.

31. *Atlanta Constitution,* May 25, 1903.

32. Georgia State Board of Education, *Annual Report,* 1898, 13–14; Anderson, *The Education of Blacks in the South,* 80.

33. Georgia State Board of Education, *Annual Report,* 1898, 10.

34. Georgia State Board of Education, *Annual Report,* 1898, 11–12.

35. Kaplan, *The Anarchy of Empire,* 79–80.

36. *Atlanta Constitution,* January 28, 1906, A4; *Atlanta Constitution,* February 8, 1906, 6.

37. *Atlanta Constitution,* September 26, 1917, 96.

38. Will Winton Alexander, "The Race Situation in America," VII-10–28: Gate City Free Kindergarten, NUC.

39. Mary S. Hoffschwelle, *The Rosenwald Schools of the American South* (Gainesville: University Press of Florida, 2006), 119–20.

40. Norrell, *Up from History,* 97.

41. *Bulletin of Atlanta University* 104 (Nov. 1899), 1; Atlanta University Leaflet No. 9, Series 1, Box 1, Folder 5, Atlanta University Collection, Auburn Avenue Research Library on African American Culture and History, Atlanta-Fulton Public Library System.

42. Newspaper clipping, *Philadelphia Echo,* April 1887, 7-2-26, AUC.

43. President's Report, 1894, 2-1-9, AUC; Frances Clemmer to potential benefactors, March 1905, Series 4, Box 21, Folder: Circulars, News Items, and Financial Appeals, 1899–1907, Atlanta University Presidential Records. Hereafter AUPR.

44. Augustus Granville Dill to donors, Horace Bumstead to "dear friend," January 9, 1900, Series 4: Horace Bumstead Records, Box 20, Folder: Student letters to donors of scholarships, 1898–1904, AUPR; Horace Bumstead, Funding Appeal, n. d., Series, 4, Box 21, Folder: Circulars, News Items, and Financial Appeals, 1899–1907, AUPR.

45. *Catalogue of the Officers and Students of Atlanta University* (Atlanta: Mutual Printing, 1890), 6–9, 25–36, 34; Newspaper clipping, *Boston Herald,* January 26, 1903, Frances B. Clemmer to potential benefactors, December, 1905, Series 4: Horace Bumstead Records, Box 21, Folder: Circulars, News Items and Financial Appeals, 1899–1907, AUPR; A. D. Mayo, *Report of Atlanta University,* 7-4-1, AUC; *Philadelphia Echo,* April 1887, AUC.

46. Newspaper clipping, *Augusta Chronicle,* July 12, 1889, 7-2-26, AUC.

47. Newspaper clippings, *Atlanta Journal,* November 2, 1889, *Macon Telegraph,* July 11, 1889, 7-2-26, AUC. Atlanta University discontinued its elementary grades in 1894 and its sixth, seventh, and eighth grades in 1899. In 1904, it established the Oglethorpe Practice School, which offered grades kindergarten through fourth, as an extension of the normal school, but AU did not consider these children to be enrolled students. See Horace Bumstead, "Negro Colleges in Atlanta Georgia," 1908, William B. Matthews Papers, Box 1, Folder 10, Archives Division, Auburn Avenue Research Library.

48. Racine, "Atlanta's Schools," 33. According to the school census of 1882, Atlanta had 10,554 children of school age, 53 percent of whom were white and 47 percent of whom were black. Yet white grammar schools outnumbered those of blacks by 6 to 3. See Atlanta Board of Education, *Annual Report,* 1885, 9.

49. Atlanta Board of Education, *Annual Report,* 1891, 17.

50. Atlanta Board of Education, *Annual Report,* 1895, 17; William F. Slaton, "Testimony of Southern Officials," Series 5: E. T. Ware, Box 33, Folder 18: General Education Board, AUPR.

51. *Atlanta Constitution,* October 13, 1909, 6; Edgar A. Toppin, "Walter White and the Atlanta NAACP's Fight for Equal Schools, 1916–1917," *History of Education Quarterly* 7, 1 (Spring 1967): 7.

52. Hoffschwelle, *The Rosenwald Schools of the American South,* 17.

53. Atlanta Board of Education, *Annual Report,* 1899, 20.

54. Thomas Deaton, "Atlanta During the Progressive Era" (PhD diss., University of Georgia, 1969), 170.

55. Gregory Mixon, *The Atlanta Riot: Race, Class and Violence in a New South City* (Gainesville: University of Florida Press, 2005), 1.

56. Alton Hornsby, Jr., *Black Power in Dixie: A Political History of African Americans in Atlanta* (Gainesville: University of Florida Press, 2009), 34–35.

57. Hornsby, *Black Power in Dixie,* 41.

58. Atlanta Board of Education, *Annual Report,* 1899, 32; Atlanta Board of Education, *Annual Report,* 1912, 20–22; *Atlanta Constitution,* November 22, 1914, 1.

59. "Survey of Colored Schools," 1913–1914, Series VII, Box 7, Folder 1, NUC; Jacqueline Rouse, *Lugenia Burns Hope: Black Southern Reformer* (Athens: University of Georgia Press, 1989), 73–78.

60. Quoted in Toppin, "Walter White," 12–13.

61. *Atlanta Constitution,* September 28, 1917; Toppin, "Walter White," 9–10, 13–14.

62. Toppin, "Walter White," 15–16.

63. Toppin, "Walter White," 16. For an analysis of schools and the limits of desegregation in Atlanta immediately after the *Brown* decision, see Kevin Kruse, *White Flight: Atlanta and the Making of Modern Conservatism* (Princeton: Princeton University Press, 2005), 161–79.

64. *Atlanta Constitution,* December 1, 1921, 7; *Atlanta Constitution,* January 11, 1922.

65. *Atlanta Constitution,* September 18, 1924, 7.

66. *Atlanta Constitution,* March 2, 1924, 2; *Atlanta Constitution,* August 26, 1924, 3.

67. Joan Pope Melish, "The Racial Vernacular: Contesting the Black / White Binary in Nineteenth-Century Rhode Island," in *Race, Nation and Empire in American History,* ed. Campbell, Guterl, and Lee, 17–39.

68. Julia T. Riordan to Mary Barker, December 19, 1921, Box 2008, Folder 1, Mary Barker, 1921–1940, Series 1: Correspondence, 1919–1971, Atlanta Education Association Records, L1975–31, Southern Labor Archives, Special Collections and Archives, Georgia State University, Atlanta, GA.

69. Elna C. Green, "Hidden in Plain View: Eugene Poulnot and the History of Southern Radicalism," *Florida Historical Quarterly* 84, 3 (Winter 2006): 349.

70. The Trustees of the John F. Slater Fund, Occasional Papers, no. 24, "Five Letters of the University Commission on Southern Race Questions," (Charlottesville, VA: Michie, 1927), 13, 1-11-2, Southern Education Records, Archives and Special Collections, Robert Woodruff Library, Atlanta University Center, Atlanta, GA.

71. *Annual Report of the Superintendent of Schools,* 1919, 25, Series 401, RNYCBE.

CHAPTER 5: BECOMING WHITE NEW YORKERS

1. Raymond E. Cole, "The City's Responsibility to the Immigrant," *Immigrants in America Review* 1, 2 (June 1915): 36.

2. Alonzo G. Grace, *Immigration and Community Americanization* (Minneapolis: ACME Printing & Publishing, 1921), 12.

3. Department of Education, *Annual Report,* 1919, p. 25, Series 201: Annual Report of the Department of Education, 1899–1965, RNYCBE.

4. Trygve Throntveit, "The Fable of the Fourteen Points: Woodrow Wilson and National Self-Determination," *Diplomatic History* 35, 3 (June 2011): 446; Thomas Bender, *A Nation among Nations: America's Place in World History* (New York: Hill & Wang, 2006), 242–45; Michael Hunt, *The American Ascendancy: How the United States Gained and Wielded Global Dominance* (Chapel Hill: University of North Carolina Press, 2007), 45, 60–61; Cyrus Veeser, *A World Safe for Capitalism: Dollar Diplomacy and America's Rise to Global Power* (New York: Columbia University Press, 2007). Also see Victoria de Grazia's treatments of the "Market Empire" and "democracies of consumption" in *Irresistible Empire: America's Advance through Twentieth-Century Europe* (Cambridge: Belknap Press of Harvard University, 2005).

5. Circular, William Ettinger to Superintendents and Principals, September 26, 1918, Series 512: 5, RNYCBE.

6. Nell Irving Painter, *The History of White People* (New York: Norton, 2010), 311–26.

7. Roediger, *Working toward Whiteness*, 10; David Richards, *Italian American: The Racializing of an Ethnic Identity* (New York: New York University Press, 1999), 2; Jacobson, *Whiteness of a Different Color*, 6.

8. Diane Ravitch, *The Great School Wars: New York City, 1805–1973, A History of the Public Schools as Battlefield of Social Change* (New York: Basic Books, 1974), 108; Stephen F. Brumberg, *Going to America, Going to School: The Jewish Immigrant Public School Encounter in Turn-of-the-Twentieth Century New York City* (New York: Praeger, 1986), 3; Mirel, *Patriotic Pluralism*, 13.

9. Jacobson, *Whiteness of a Different Color*, 38.

10. Board of Education, *Annual Report*, 1885, p. 120, Series 22, RNYCBE.

11. Ravitch, *The Great School Wars*, 138–39, 144–45, 156–58, 161. William Strong, quoted in Ravitch, *The Great School Wars*, 158.

12. Board of Education, *Annual Report*, 1885, p. 22, Series 22, RNYCBE.

13. Paris Exposition of 1900, Board of Education Exhibition, 1900, Series 235, RNYCBE; Jacobson, *Whiteness of a Different Color*, 5.

14. Michael Olneck, "Americanization and the Education of Immigrants, 1900–1925," *American Journal of Education* 97, 4 (Aug. 1989): 400, 402; Clifford Geertz, *The Interpretation of Cultures* (New York: Basic Books, 1973), 243; US Department of Labor, Bureau of Naturalization, *Federal Textbook on Citizenship Training, Part III: Our Nation* (Washington: Government Printing Office, 1926), 207; Raymond Tatalovich, *Nativism Reborn?: The Official English Language Movement and the American States* (Lexington: University of Kentucky Press, 1995), 2; Roediger, *Working toward Whiteness*, 122–30.

15. Teachers' Council Committee on School Records and Statistics, *Digest of Matter of Current Value from Circulars issued by the City Superintendent of Schools, 1902–1915* (New York: Boys' Vocational School, 1915), p. 88, Series 511, RNYCBE.

16. Higham, *Strangers in the Land*, 234–39, 244, 246–47; Board of Education, *Annual Report*, 1880, Series 22, RNYCBE; "Americanization by Industry," *Immigrants in America Review*, April, 1916, 11.

17. Steffes, *School, Society, and State*, 123–124.

18. New York City Board of Education, *Annual Report*, 1881, Series 22, RNYCBE.

19. John R. Commons, *Races and Immigrants in America* (New York: Macmillan, 1914), 20.

20. "Keep the Schools Open," *Immigrants in America Review*, April, 1916, 8; Francis Kellor, "Straight America," *Immigrants in America Review*, July, 1916, 14.

21. Special Circular No. 13, William H. Maxwell to District Superintendents and Principals, February 3, 1914, Series 512, Box 23, RNYCBE; Joseph Mayper, "Americanizing Immigrant Homes," *Immigrants in America Review*, July, 1916, 54–56, 59–60.

22. *New York Times,* September 10, 1917.

23. Mirel, *Patriotic Pluralism*, 60; *New York Times,* July 4, 1920; Pedro A. Cebollero, *A School Language Policy for Puerto Rico* (San Juan: Imprenta Baldrich, 1945), 9–10.

24. Circular no. 2, Ettinger to District Superintendents and Principals, September 15, 1920, Circular no. 4, September 22, 1921, 512: 23, RNYCBE.

25. Ronald D. Cohen and Raymond A. Mohl, *The Paradox of Progressive Education: The Gary Plan and Urban Schooling* (Port Washington, NY: National University Publications, 1979), 5–7. Dewey quoted on page 6.

26. Cohen and Mohl, *The Paradox of Progressive Education*, 35–50.

27. Quoted in Cohen and Mohl, *The Paradox of Progressive Education*, 51.

28. *New York Times,* September 8, 1917; Cohen and Mohl, *The Paradox of Progressive Education*, 51–52, 61–63.

29. The details of the strikes are meticulously documented in Melissa Weiner, *Power, Protest, and the Public Schools: Jewish and African American Struggles in New York City* (New Brunswick: Rutgers University Press, 2010), 47–51.

30. Cohen and Mohl, *The Paradox of Progressive Education*, 60–61.

31. W. W. Husband, ed., "The Problem of Americanization," *Immigration Journal* 1, 2 (April 1916): 21; Frances Kellor, ed., "The Capacity of the Melting Pot," *Immigrants in America Review* 2, 1 (April 1916): 14.

32. Robert Carlson, "Americanization as an Early Twentieth-Century Adult Education Movement," *History of Education Quarterly* 10, 4 (Winter 1970): 453–54; Gerstle, *American Crucible*, 89, 100; Gary Gerstle, "Liberty, Coercion, and the Making of Americans," *Journal of American History* 84, 2 (Sept. 1997): 530–31.

33. Thomas D. Fallace, "The Racial and Cultural Assumptions of the Early Social Studies Educators, 1901–1922," in *Histories of Social Studies and Race, 1865–2000*, ed. Christine Woyshner and Chara Bohan (New York: Palgrave Macmillan, 2012), 43–45.

34. New York City Superintendent of Schools, *Annual Report*, 1925, p. 41, Series 401, RNYCBE; Otis L. Graham Jr. and Elizabeth Koed, "Americanizing the Immigrant, Past and Future: History and Implications of a Social Movement," *Public Historian* 15, 4 (Autumn 1993): 30.

35. William Ettinger, *Address to the Teachers of New York City, September 20, 1918* (New York: Boys Vocational School, 1918), 12; *New York Times,* September 29, 1918.

36. Special Circular no. 1, September 28, 1919, Circular, Ettinger to Principals of all Schools and Directors of Special Branches, May 1, 1920, Circular No. 8, November 19, 1921, 512: 23, RNYCBE.

37. Circular, February 22, 1919, 512: 23, RNYCBE.

38. Clayton Riley Lusk, *Revolutionary Radicalism: Its History, Purpose and Tactics* (Albany, NY: J. B. Lyon, 1920), 2340, 2343.

39. Circular from the Office of the Superintendent of Schools, February 22, 1919, 512: 23, RNYCBE; Lusk, *Revolutionary Radicalism*, 2343.

40. Lusk, *Revolutionary Radicalism*, 3027.

41. General Circular No. 33, June 25, 1919, 512: 23, RNYCBE; Carlson, "Americanization as an Early Twentieth-Century Adult Education Movement," 454–55.

42. General Circular no. 33, June 25, 1919, 512: 23, RNYCBE.

43. General Circular no. 5, December 15, 1919, 512: 23, RNYCBE.

44. Ettinger, "The Ethical Standards of the Teacher," in *Ten Addresses Delivered before Associate and District Superintendents of the New York City Schools and Other Professional Bodies* (New York: Stillman Appellate Printing), 90–91, 93.

45. Circular No. 8, November 19, 1921, 512: 23, RNYCBE; *New York Times,* April 29, 1920; Hunt, *The American Ascendancy,* 67.

46. Margaret MacMillan, *Peacemakers: The Paris Peace Conference of 1919 and Its Attempts to End War* (London: John Murray, 2001), 123, 292–96, 307–9.

47. General Circular no. 19, Ettinger to Principals, May 21, 1920, 512: 23, RNYCBE; *New York Times,* May 23, 1920; Spickard, *Almost All Aliens,* 187–189.

48. General Circular no. 4, Ettinger to District Superintendents and Principals, September 22, 1921, 512: 23, RNYCBE; *New York Times,* February 13, 1921, February 17, 1921, October 16, 1921; Diana Selig, *Americans All: The Cultural Gifts Movement* (Cambridge: Harvard University Press, 2008), 185.

49. General Circular no. 12, Ettinger to District Superintendents and Principals, November 27, 1923, 512: 23, RNYCBE.

50. *New York Times,* May 18, 1924; *New York Times,* November 10, 1924.

51. *New York Times,* May 18, 1924; Higham, *Strangers in the Land,* 323; Jacobson, *Whiteness of a Different Color,* 93; Jacobson, *Roots Too,* 36–42.

52. *New York Times,* July 14, 1924.

53. New York City Superintendent of Schools, *Annual Report,* 1925, p. 41, 401, RNYCBE; Jacobson, *Whiteness of a Different Color,* 92; *New York Times,* May 18, 1924.

CHAPTER 6: COLONIAL CITIZENS,
DEPORTABLE CITIZENS

1. Charles Wesley Reed, "The Comparative Low Standing of the Public Schools of San Francisco and Their Improvement," Address before the Commonwealth Luncheon, September 16, 1911, 2A-31-6, SFH 3.

2. Belle Boone Beard, "Puerto Rico: The Forty-Ninth State?" *Phylon* 6, 2 (2nd Qtr. 1945): 105.

3. *Second Annual Report of the Commission of Immigration and Housing of California* (Sacramento: State Printing Office, 1916), 143.

4. Foerster, *The Racial Problems Involved in Immigration from Latin America and the West Indies to the United States*, 1, 11, 14, 48; Ian F. Haney-López, *Racism on Trial: The Chicano Fight for Justice* (Cambridge: Belknap Press of Harvard University, 2003), viii. From 1940–70, the Census Bureau counted Mexicans as whites, repealing its 1930 decision to classify Mexicans as a separate race. In 1960, the census enumerated them as "white persons of Spanish surname." This presented legal problems for lawyers attempting to demonstrate historical discrimination based on race. See Haney-López, *Racism on Trial*, 42–45.

5. Foerster, *The Racial Problems Involved in Immigration from Latin America and the West Indies to the United States*, 38–39 (emphasis added); Ngai, *Impossible Subjects*, 98; Lorrin Thomas, *Puerto Rican Citizen: History and Identity in Twentieth-Century New York City* (Chicago: University of Chicago Press, 2010), 6.

6. Molina, *How Race Is Made In America*, 2–3; Treaty of Guadalupe-Hidalgo, Article VIII, February 2, 1848, accessed April 8, 2015, http://avalon.law.yale.edu/19th_century/guadhida.asp; Ngai, *Impossible Subjects*, 51.

7. San Miguel and Valencia, "Guadalupe-Hidalgo to *Hopwood*," 354, 357.

8. Gilbert González, *Chicano Education in the Era of Segregation* (Cranbury, NJ: Associated University Presses, 1990), 21.

9. Rodolfo Acuña, *Occupied America: The Chicano's Struggle toward Liberation* (San Francisco: Canfield Press, 1972), 146.

10. John Kenneth Turner, *Barbarous Mexico* (Chicago: Charles H. Kerr, 1910), 6.

11. State of California, *Mexicans in California: Report of Governor C. C. Young's Mexican Fact-Finding Committee* (San Francisco: Department of Industrial Relations, 1930), 72; Emory Bogardus, "The Mexican Immigrant and Segregation," *American Journal of Sociology* 36, 1 (July 1930): 77.

12. Manuel Gamio, *The Life Story of the Mexican Immigrant* (Chicago: University of Chicago Press, 1931), 126, 269.

13. Annie S. Reynolds, "The Education of Spanish-Speaking Children in Five Southwestern States," Bulletin 11, Office of Education (Washington: Government Printing Office, 1933), 6, 10–11; Charles Wollenberg, "*Mendez v. Westminster:* Race, Nationality, and Segregation in California Schools," *California Historical Quarterly* 53, 4 (Winter 1974): 319.

14. Eunice Elvira Parr, "A Comparative Study of Mexican and American Children in the Schools of San Antonio, Texas" (MA thesis, University of Chicago, 1926), 50.

15. Reynolds, "The Education of Spanish Speaking Children," 13.

16. State of California, *Mexicans in California*, 72, 125.

17. Emory S. Bogardus, *The Mexican in the United States* (Los Angeles: University of Southern California Press, 1934), 10.

18. Herman Feldman, *Racial Factors in American Industry* (New York: Harper Bros., 1931), 104–5.

19. Bogardus, *The Mexican in the United States,* 78.

20. Luis Muñoz Marín quoted in Carey McWilliams, *Brothers under the Skin* (New York: Macmillan, 1951), 214.

21. Negrón de Montilla, *La americanización en Puerto Rico y el sistema de instrucción pública;* McWilliams, *Brothers under the Skin,* 211; Solsiree del Moral, *Negotiating Empire: The Cultural Politics of Schools in Puerto Rico, 1898–1952* (Madison: University of Wisconsin Press, 2013), 6–11, 49–50.

22. Del Moral, *Negotiating Empire,* 17–18, 152–53.

23. Del Moral, *Negotiating Empire,* 28–33.

24. Tulio Larrínaga, "Conditions in Porto Rico," *Annals of the Academy of Political and Social Science* 26 (July 1905): 56.

25. Del Moral, *Negotiating Empire,* 46–47, 55.

26. Larrínaga, "Conditions in Porto Rico," 56. Born in Puerto Rico in 1847 and educated as a civil engineer in the United States, Larrínaga's foray into politics began in 1898. After six years of US rule during which he served as assistant secretary of the interior and as a member of the House of Delegates, he joined the Unionist Party, founded in 1904, whose leadership pressed for greater political autonomy. It was then he was elected commissioner of Porto Rico, and in his 1905 report, he exposed what he saw as waffling on the part of the US Congress in regard to the status of Puerto Rico. See United States House of Representatives, "Tulio Larrínaga," in *Biographical Directory of the United States Congress,* accessed March 20, 2015, http://bioguide.congress.gov/scripts/biodisplay.pl?index=L000102.

27. Del Moral, *Negotiating Empire,* 96–97, 101–3.

28. Del Moral, *Negotiating Empire,* 77, 79: Elise Mae Willsey, *Course of Study in Home Economics for the Elementary and High Schools of Porto Rico* (San Juan: Department of Education, 1923), 13. On US eugenic projects in Puerto Rico, see Laura Briggs, *Reproducing Empire: Race, Sex, Science, and U.S. Imperialism in Puerto Rico* (Berkeley: University of California Press, 2002). For an example of the overlap between local elites and US colonial officials, see Victor S. Clark et al., *Puerto Rico and Its Problems* (Washington, DC: Brookings Institution, 1930), 72–77.

29. M. Rios Ocana, "Puerto Rican 'Inadequacy,'" *New York Times,* February 21, 1936.

30. Carlos Kevin Blanton, "From Intellectual to Cultural Deficiency: Mexican Americans, Testing, and Public School Policy in the American Southwest, 1920–1940," *Pacific Historical Review* 72, 1 (Feb. 2003): 41; Thomas, *Puerto Rican Citizen,* 85; del Moral, *Negotiating Empire,* 138.

31. Quoted in Blanton, "From Intellectual to Cultural Deficiency," 43.

32. For example, see Don T. Delmet, "A Study of the Mental and Scholastic Abilities of Mexican Children in the Elementary School" (MA thesis, University of Southern California, 1928); Blanton, "From Intellectual to Cultural Deficiency," 47–48, 50; Wollenberg, "*Mendez v. Westminster,*" 322.

33. Walter Dearborn, *Intelligence Tests: Their Significance for School and Society* (Boston: Houghton Mifflin, 1928), 132–33.

34. William Nathan Wilson, "An Analysis of the Academic and Home Problems of the Pupils in a Mexican Junior High School" (MS thesis, University of Southern California, 1938), 14.

35. Bogardus, *The Mexican in the United States,* 84.

36. George A. Works, *Texas Educational Survey Report, Volume I: Organization and Administration* (Austin: Texas Educational Survey Commission, 1925), 243–44.

37. George I. Sánchez, "Group Differences and Spanish-Speaking Children: A Critical Review," *Journal of Applied Psychology* 16, 5 (Oct. 1932): 550.

38. Quoted in Blanton, "From Intellectual to Cultural Deficiency," 54, 59.

39. Thomas, *Puerto Rican Citizen,* 95; Gary Gerstle, "The Protean Character of American Liberalism," *American Historical Review* 99 (Oct. 1994): 1044–45, 1068–69.

40. Del Moral, *Negotiating Empire,* 104, 106–7, 119.

41. *New York Times,* March 23, 1931; del Moral, *Negotiating Empire,* 120–21. The figures for the Puerto Rican diaspora vary widely. For a discussion, see Thomas, *Puerto Rican Citizen,* 24.

42. Thomas, *Puerto Rican Citizen,* 3; *New York Times,* January 31, 1935.

43. Clairette P. Armstrong, "Low-Grade Newcomers Held Common Denominator of Some of our Crime and Social Misfits," *New York Times,* April 22, 1934; del Moral, *Negotiating Empire,* 126.

44. Clairette P. Armstrong, Edith M. Achilles, and Mervyn J. Sacks, *A Report of the Special Committee on Immigration and Naturalization of the Chamber of Commerce of the State of New York Submitting a Study on Reactions of Puerto Rican Children in New York City to Psychological Tests* (New York: Special Committee on Immigration and Naturalization, Chamber of Commerce of the State of New York, 1935), 5, 7–8.

45. M. Rios Ocana, "Puerto Rican 'Inadequacy,'" *New York Times,* February 21, 1936.

46. Mervin Sacks, "Puerto Rican Children: Results of Group Study Here Intended to Apply Locally," *New York Times,* February 19, 1936; Armstrong, Achilles, and Sacks, *Report of the Special Committee,* 8; S. D. Porteus and M. E. Babcock, *Temperament and Race* (Boston: Badger, 1926).

47. *El Mundo,* February 10, 1936, quoted in *New York Times,* February 11, 1936; *Downes v. Bidwell,* 182 U.S. 244 (1901); Kaplan, *Anarchy of Empire,* 1–22; del Moral, *Negotiating Empire,* 132.

48. Cebollero's response to the Armstrong study is meticulously analyzed by del Moral in *Negotiating Empire,* 140–48.

49. Del Moral, *Negotiating Empire,* 140–41; Thomas, *Puerto Rican Citizen,* 86–87.

50. Del Moral, *Negotiating Empire,* 150–53, 158–69.

51. San Miguel, Jr., and Valencia, "Guadalupe-Hidalgo to *Hopwood*," 370–72; Vicki Ruiz, "South by Southwest: Mexican Americans and Segregated Schooling, 1900–1950," *OAH Magazine of History* (Winter 2001): 24–25.

52. San Miguel, Jr., and Valencia, "Guadalupe-Hidalgo to *Hopwood*," 374–75; Ruiz, "South by Southwest," 25.

53. Sánchez, *Becoming Mexican American*, 255–57, 259–60, 264–65. Sánchez has meticulously documented the activism of the second generation in Los Angeles before World War II, a scholarly intervention that challenges more commonly held assumptions that the Chicano rights movement commenced only after the war. Also see David Gutiérrez, *Walls and Mirrors: Mexican Americans, Mexican Immigrants, and the Politics of Ethnicity* (Berkeley: University of California Press, 1995), 136–38.

54. Wollenberg, "*Méndez v. Westminster*," 325; Ruiz, "South by Southwest," 25–26. As governor, Warren signed the 1947 California law repealing all state mandated segregation.

55. George I. Sánchez and Lyle Saunders, *Wetbacks: A Preliminary Report to the Advisory Committee for the Study of Spanish Speaking People* (Austin: University of Texas, 1949), 1, 8, 16–17; Molina, *How Race Is Made In America*, 113–14. David Gutiérrez has shown that most Mexican Americans were not as ideologically driven as Sánchez in their positions on Mexican immigrants, undocumented or otherwise. See Gutiérrez, *Walls and Mirrors*, 143–51.

56. Ruben Salazar, *Border Correspondent: Selected Writings, 1955–1970* (Berkeley: University of California Press, 1995), 70.

57. Cebollero, *A School Language Policy*, 74.

58. Cebollero, *A School Language Policy*, 2–3.

59. Martin Brumbaugh, *Report of the Commissioner of Education* (San Juan: Department of Education, 1901), 361–76, quoted in Cebollero, *A School Language Policy*, 9–10.

60. Cebollero, *A School Language Policy*, 74; José Gallardo, *Annual Report of the Commissioner of Education, 1937–38* (San Juan: Bureau of Supplies, Printing, and Transportation, 1938), 34–35; Bonnie Urciuoli, *Exposing Prejudice: Puerto Rican Experiences of Language, Race, and Class* (Boulder, CO: Westview Press, 1996), 49. Roosevelt's letter to Gallardo was reprinted in the *New York Times*, April 18, 1937.

61. Cebollero, *A School Language Policy*, 10–14.

62. Cebollero, *A School Language Policy*, 84–85.

63. Del Moral, *Negotiating Empire*, 153–54.

64. Del Moral, *Negotiating Empire*, 158–69, 177.

EPILOGUE: KNOWLEDGE AND CITIZENSHIP

1. On Sheriff Joe Arpaio, see Jeff Biggers, *State Out of the Union: Arizona and the Final Showdown over the American Dream* (New York: Nation Books, 2012).

2. Prohibited Courses; Discipline; Schools, Arizona House Bill 2281 (2010).

3. "Debating Tucson School District's Book Ban after Suspension of Mexican American Studies Program," *democracynow.org,* January 18, 2012, accessed September 4, 2014, www.democracynow.org/2012/1/18/debating_tucson_school_districts_book_ban.

4. Julianne Hing, "Arizona Gov. Brewer Signs Ethnic Studies Ban into Law," *colorlines.com,* May 12, 2010, accessed September 4, 2014, http://colorlines.com /archives/2010/05/arizonas_gov_brewer_signs_ethnic_studies_ban_into_law .html.

5. Tom Horne, "An Open Letter to the Citizens of Tucson," June 11, 2007, reprinted in Valerie Strauss, "Why Arizona Targeted Ethnic Studies," *washington-post.com,* May 25, 2010, accessed September 4, 2014, http://voices.washingtonpost .com/answer-sheet/civics-education/why-arizona-targeted-ethnic-st.html. Strauss linked to the letter "prominently posted" on the Arizona Department of Education's website. The letter is no longer there. CNN, "Ethnic Studies Ban Racist?" *YouTube* video, 12:19, May 13, 2010, www.youtube.com/watch?v=TgvOdD5bVsg; *Arce v. Douglas,* 13–15657, 13–15760 F. 6, 9 (9th Cir. July 7, 2015), accessed August 11, 2015, http://cdn.ca9.uscourts.gov/datastore/opinions/2015/07/07/13-15657.pdf. Diane Douglas was elected superintendent in 2014 and thus her name has replaced Huppenthal in subsequent legal proceedings.

6. Horne, "An Open Letter to the Citizens of Tucson," 2007.

7. Alexis Huicochea, "TUSD: Bill Won't Alter Ethnic Studies, Horne: Measure Sent to Brewer Is Aimed at District," *Arizona Daily Star,* May 4, 2010, accessed September 4, 2014, http://tucson.com/news/local/education/article_8d522665 -3753-5221-9b64-45c72b426777.html.

8. Quoted in Biggers, *State Out of the Union,* xxi, 6–7.

9. Arizona Revised Statute § 11–1051, 2010.

10. "Fighting Arizona's Attack on Ethnic Studies—*Maya Arce et al. v. John Huppenthal et al.,*" *Seattle University School of Law,* accessed April 30, 2015, www.law.seattleu.edu/centers-and-institutes/korematsu-center/arizona-ethnic-studies-case; "13–15657, 13–15760 Maya Arce v. John Huppenthal," YouTube video, 43:35, posted by "The United States Court of Appeals for the Ninth Circuit," January 12, 2015, www.youtube.com/watch?v=Oj9Xl_zhdsc; *Arce v. Douglas,* 13–15657, 13–15760, 17, 33.

11. Gates, "What the School Owes the State," 10.

WORKS CITED

ARCHIVES AND COLLECTIONS

Atlanta Public School Archives. Atlanta, GA.
  Atlanta Board of Education Papers.
Auburn Avenue Research Library. Atlanta, GA.
  Atlanta University Collection.
  William B. Matthews Papers.
Bird Library Special Collections. Syracuse University. Syracuse, NY.
  American Book Company Collection.
  Mytton Maury Papers.
Chicago Public Library. Chicago, IL.
  Municipal Reference Collection.
Hawaii State Archives. Honolulu, HI.
  Records of the Department of Education.
New York City Department of Records / Municipal Archives. New York, NY.
  Records of the New York City Board of Education.
Robert Woodruff Library. Atlanta University Center. Atlanta, GA.
  Atlanta University Photographs Collections.
  Atlanta University Presidential Records.
  Neighborhood Union Collection.
  Southern Education Archives.
San Francisco History Center. San Francisco Public Library. San Francisco, CA.
  San Francisco Unified School District Records.
Southern Labor Archives. Georgia State University. Atlanta, GA.
  Atlanta Education Association Records.

Atlanta Constitution
Berkeley Daily Gazette
Boston Herald
Hawaiian Gazette
Honolulu Bulletin
Immigrants in America Review
The Immigration Journal
New York Times
Sacramento Union
San Francisco Bulletin
San Francisco Call
San Francisco Chronicle
San Francisco Examiner
San Francisco Globe

GOVERNMENT DOCUMENTS

Alexander, William D. *Biennial Report of the President of the Board of Education to the Legislature of the Republic of Hawaii, 1894–1895*. Honolulu: Hawaiian Gazette, 1896.

Arizona Revised Statute § 11-1051, 2010.

Atlanta Board of Education. *Annual Report*. Atlanta: Jas. P. Harrison, 1882.

———. *Annual Report*. Atlanta: Jas. P. Harrison, 1892.

Black, Samuel F. *Seventeenth Biennial Report of the Superintendent of Public Instruction*. Sacramento: A. J. Johnson, State Superintendent Printing, 1896.

California State Senate Special Committee on Chinese Immigration. *Chinese Immigration: The Social, Moral and Political Effect of Chinese Immigration. Policy and Means of Exclusion. Memorial of the Senate of California to the Congress of the United States, and an Address to the People of the United States*. Sacramento: State Printing Office, 1877.

Carter, George. *Report of the Governor of the Territory of Hawaii to the Secretary of the Interior*. Washington: Government Printing Office, 1904, 1906.

Commission of Immigration and Housing of California. *Second Annual Report of the Commission of Immigration and Housing of California*. Sacramento: State Printing Office, 1916.

Constitution, Rules and By-Laws for subordinate camps of California Encampment, Order of Caucasians. Sacramento: H. A. Weaver, 1876.

Debates and Proceedings of the Constitutional Convention of the State of California convened at the city of Sacramento, Saturday, September 28, 1878. Sacramento: State Printing Office, 1881.

Department of the Interior. *The Public School System of San Francisco, California*, Bulletin 1917, no. 46. Washington: Government Printing Office, 1917.

Dole, Sanford B. *Report of the Governor of the Territory of Hawaii to the Secretary of the Interior*. Washington: Government Printing Office, 1903.

McCarthy, Charles. *Report of the Governor of the Territory of Hawaii to the Secretary of the Interior*. Washington: Government Printing Office, 1919, 1920.

Mott-Smith, Ernest A. *Report of the Minister of Public Instruction to the President of the Republic of Hawaii for the Biennial Period ending December 31st, 1899*. Honolulu: Hawaiian Gazette, 1900.

Prohibited Courses; Discipline; Schools, Arizona House Bill 2281. 2010.

Report of the Superintendent of Schools and Board of Education, San Francisco, Cal. for the Fiscal Years 1906–1907 and 1907–1908. San Francisco: Neal Publishing, 1908.

Reynolds, Annie S. "The Education of Spanish-Speaking Children in Five Southwestern States," Bulletin 11, Office of Education. Washington: Government Printing Office, 1933.

Roosevelt, Theodore and Victor Metcalf. *Message from the President of the United States transmitting the Final Report of Secretary Metcalf on the Situation Affecting the Japanese in the City of San Francisco, Cal.* San Francisco: R & E Research Associates, 1971 [reprint].

State Board of Control of California. *California and the Oriental: Japanese, Chinese, and Hindus, Report of State Board of Control of California to Gov. Wm. D. Stephens*. Sacramento: California State Printing Office, 1922.

State of California. *Mexicans in California: Report of Governor C. C. Young's Mexican Fact-Finding Committee*. San Francisco: Department of Industrial Relations, 1930.

Territorial Legislature, *Laws of the Territory of Hawaii Passed by the Eleventh Legislature, Special Session, 1920*. Honolulu: Honolulu Advertising Publishing, 1921.

US Department of the Interior, Bureau of Education. *A Survey of Education in Hawaii*, Bulletin 16. Washington: Government Printing Office, 1920.

US Department of Labor, Bureau of Naturalization. *Federal Textbook on Citizenship Training, Part III: Our Nation*. Washington: Government Printing Office, 1926.

Works, George A. *Texas Educational Survey Report, Volume I: Organization and Administration*. Austin: Texas Educational Survey Commission, 1925.

BOOKS AND ARTICLES

Aarim-Heriot, Najia. *Chinese Immigrants, African Americans, and Racial Anxiety in the United States, 1848–1882*. Urbana: University of Illinois Press, 2003.

Acuña, Rodolfo. *Occupied America: The Chicano's Struggle toward Liberation*. San Francisco: Canfield Press, 1972.

Adams, Romanzo. *Interracial Marriage in Hawai'i: A Study of the Mutually Conditioned Processes of Acculturation and Amalgamation*. New York: MacMillan, 1937.

Adas, Michael. "From Settler Colony to Global Hegemon: Integrating the Exceptionalist Narrative of the American Experience into World History." *American Historical Review* 106, 5 (Dec. 2001): 1692–94.

Ahmad, Diana L. *The Opium Debate and Chinese Exclusion Laws in the Nineteenth-Century American West*. Reno: University of Nevada Press, 2007.

Almaguer, Tomás. *Racial Fault Lines: The Historical Origins of White Supremacy in California*. Berkeley: University of California Press, 1994.

Anderson, Benedict. *Imagined Communities: Reflections on the Origin and Spread of Nationalism*. New York: Verso, 2006 [1981].

Anderson, James. *The Education of Blacks in the South, 1860–1935*. Chapel Hill: University of North Carolina Press, 1988.

Angulo, A. J. *Empire and Education: A History of Greed and Goodwill from the War of 1898 to the War on Terror*. New York: Palgrave Macmillan, 2012.

Armstrong, Clairette P., Edith M. Achilles, and Mervyn J. Sacks. *A Report of the Special Committee on Immigration and Naturalization of the Chamber of Commerce of the State of New York Submitting a Study on Reactions of Puerto Rican Children in New York City to Psychological Tests*. New York: Special Committee on Immigration and Naturalization, Chamber of Commerce of the State of New York, 1935.

Armstrong, Mary Frances Morgan and Samuel Chapman Armstrong. *Richard Armstrong: America, Hawai'i*. Hampton, VA: Normal School Steam Press, 1887.

Asato, Noriko. "Mandating Americanization: Japanese Language Schools and the Federal Survey of Education in Hawai'i." *History of Education Quarterly* 43, 1 (Spring 2003): 10–38.

Atwood, Wallace. *New Geography*. Boston: Ginn, 1920.

Ayers, Edward. *The Promise of the New South: Life after Reconstruction*. New York: Oxford University Press, 1992.

Azuma, Eiichiro. *Between Two Empires: Race, History, and Transnationalism in Japanese America*. New York: Oxford University Press, 2005.

Ballou, Maturin. *Foot-prints of Travel, Or Journeyings in Many Lands*. Boston: Ginn, 1889.

Barrett, James. "Americanization from the Bottom-Up: Immigration and the Remaking of the Working Class in the United States, 1880–1930." *Journal of American History* 79, 3 (Dec. 1992): 996–1020.

Beard, Belle Boone. "Puerto Rico: The Forty-Ninth State?" *Phylon* 6, 2 (2nd Qtr. 1945): 105–17.

Beard, Charles and William Bagley. *The History of the American People*. New York: MacMillan, 1920 [1918].

Bederman, Gail. *Manliness and Civilization: A Cultural History of Gender and Race in the United States, 1880–1917*. Chicago: University of Chicago Press, 1995.

Beechert, Edward. *Working in Hawai'i: A Labor History*. Honolulu: University of Hawai'i Press, 1985.

Belich, James. *Replenishing the Earth: The Settler Revolution and the Rise of the Anglo-World, 1783–1939*. New York: Oxford University Press, 2009.

Bender, Thomas. *A Nation among Nations: America's Place in World History*. New York: Hill & Wang, 2006.

Berglund, Barbara. *Making San Francisco American: Cultural Frontiers in the Urban West, 1846–1906*. Lawrence: University of Kansas Press, 2007.

Beyer, Carl Kalani. "Manual Training and Industrial Education for Hawaiians." *Hawaiian Journal of History* 38 (2004): 1–34.

Biggers, Jeff. *State Out of the Union: Arizona and the Final Showdown over the American Dream*. New York: Nation Books, 2012.

Blackmon, Douglas. *Slavery by Another Name: The Re-Enslavement of Black Americans from the Civil War to World War II*. New York: Doubleday, 2008.

Blanton, Carlos Kevin. "From Intellectual to Cultural Deficiency: Mexican Americans, Testing, and Public School Policy in the American Southwest, 1920–1940." *Pacific Historical Review* 72, 1 (Feb. 2003): 39–62.

Blight, David. *Race and Reunion: The Civil War in American Memory*. Cambridge: Belknap Press of Harvard University, 2001.

Bogardus, Emory S. "The Mexican Immigrant and Segregation," *American Journal of Sociology* 36, 1 (July 1930): 74–80.

———. *The Mexican in the United States*. Los Angeles: University of Southern California Press, 1934.

Bosniak, Linda. *The Citizen and the Alien* (Princeton: Princeton University Press, 2006.

Brewer, William. *Warren's New Physical Geography*. Philadelphia: E.H. Brewer, 1890.

Briggs, Laura. *Reproducing Empire: Race, Sex, Science, and US Imperialism in Puerto Rico*. Berkeley: University of California Press, 2002.

Brigham, Albert Perry. *Geographic Influences in American History*. Boston: Ginn, 1903.

———. *Commercial Geography*. Boston: Ginn, 1911.

——— and Charles McFarlane. *Essentials of Geography*. New York: American Book, 1921.

Brumberg, Stephen F. *Going to America, Going to School: The Jewish Immigrant Public School Encounter in Turn-of-the-Twentieth Century New York City*. New York: Praeger, 1986.

Campbell, James T., Matthew Pratt Guterl, and Robert G. Lee, eds. *Race, Nation and Empire in American History*. Chapel Hill: University of North Carolina Press, 2007.

Carlson, Robert A. "Americanization as an Early Twentieth-Century Adult Education Movement." *History of Education Quarterly* 10, 4 (Winter 1970): 440–64.

Carrott, M. Browning. "Prejudice Goes to Court: The Japanese and the Supreme Court in the 1920s." *California History* 62, 2 (Summer 1983): 122–38.

Cebollero, Pedro A. *A School Language Policy for Puerto Rico*. San Juan: Imprenta Baldrich, 1945.

Cheah, Pheng. "Cosmopolitanism." *Theory, Culture, and Society* 23, 2–3 (2006): 486–96.

Chen, Yong. *Chinese San Francisco, 1850–1943*. Stanford: Stanford University Press, 2000.

Clark, Victor S., et al., *Puerto Rico and Its Problems*. Washington, DC: Brookings Institution, 1930.

Coe, Fanny. *Our American Neighbors*. New York: American Book, 1889.

———. *The World and Its People, Book IV: Our American Neighbors*. New York: Silver, Burdett, 1899.

Cohen, Elizabeth. *Semi-Citizenship in Democratic Politics*. New York: Cambridge University Press, 2009.

Cohen, Ronald D. and Raymond A. Mohl. *The Paradox of Progressive Education: The Gary Plan and Urban Schooling*. Port Washington, NY: National University Publications, 1979.

Cole, Raymond E. "The City's Responsibility to the Immigrant." *Immigrants in America Review* 1, 2 (June 1915): 36–41.

Commons, John R. *Races and Immigrants in America*. New York: Macmillan, 1914.

Cremin, Lawrence A. *The Transformation of the School: Progressivism in American Education, 1876–1957*. New York: Alfred A. Knopf, 1961.

Daniels, Roger. *The Politics of Prejudice: The Anti-Japanese Movement in California and the Struggle for Japanese Exclusion*. Berkeley: University of California Press, 1962.

Davis, William Morris. *Elementary Physical Geography*. Boston: Ginn, 1903.

De Grazia, Victoria. *Irresistible Empire: America's Advance through Twentieth-Century Europe*. Cambridge: Belknap Press of Harvard University, 2005.

Dearborn, Walter. *Intelligence Tests: Their Significance for School and Society*. Boston: Houghton Mifflin, 1928.

Deaton, Thomas. "Atlanta during the Progressive Era." PhD diss., University of Georgia, 1969.

Del Moral, Solsiree. *Negotiating Empire: The Cultural Politics of Schools in Puerto Rico, 1898–1952*. Madison: University of Wisconsin Press, 2013.

Delmet, Don T. "A Study of the Mental and Scholastic Abilities of Mexican Children in the Elementary School." MA thesis, University of Southern California, 1928.

Densmore, G. B. *The Chinese in California, Description of Chinese Life in San Francisco. Their Habits, Morals, and Manners*. San Francisco: Pettit & Russ, 1880.

Dodge, Richard Ellwood. "Albert Perry Brigham." *Annals of the Association of American Geographers* 20, 2 (June 1930): 55–62.

Donnelly, Thomas F. *Barnes' Primary History of the United States*. New York: American Book, 1899.

Dorsey, Allison. *To Build Our Lives Together: Community Formation in Black Atlanta, 1875–1906*. Athens: University of Georgia Press, 2004.

Du Bois, W. E. B. "Cultural Missions of Atlanta University." *Phylon* 3, 2 (1942): 105–15.

————, E. J. Penney, and T. J. Bell. *Proceedings of the Sixth Atlanta Conference.* New York: Arno Press and *New York Times,* 1969 [1901].

Eggleston, Edward. *A First Book in American History.* New York: American Book, 1899.

Elson, Henry. *School History of the United States.* New York: Macmillan, 1912.

Ettinger, William L. *Ten Addresses Delivered before Associate and District Superintendents of the New York City Schools and Other Professional Bodies.* New York: Stillman Appellate Printing, 1923.

Fear-Segal, Jacqueline. *White Man's Club: Schools, Race, and the Struggle of Indian Acculturation.* Lincoln: University of Nebraska Press, 2007.

Feldman, Herman. *Racial Factors in American Industry.* New York: Harper Bros., 1931.

Field, L. A. *A Grammar School History of the United States.* New York: American Book, 1897.

Fisk, John. *A History of the United States for Schools.* Boston: Houghton Mifflin, 1899.

Fite, Emerson David. *History of the United States.* New York: Henry Holt, 1916.

Foerster, Robert F. *The Racial Problems Involved in Immigration from Latin America and the West Indies to the United States.* Washington: Government Printing Office, 1925.

Forman, Samuel Eagle. "The Aim and Scope of Civics." *School Review* 11, 4 (Apr. 1903): 288–94.

————. *Advanced Civics: The Spirit, the Form, and the Functions of the American Government.* New York: Century, 1912.

————. *Advanced American History.* New York: Century, 1914.

Foster, J. Stuart. "The Struggle for American Identity: Treatment of Ethnic Groups in United States History Textbooks." *History of Education* 28, 3 (1999): 251–78.

Fuerst, Sidney Marsden, James A. O'Donnell, and Marie L. Bayer, eds. *New York Teachers' Monographs* 11, 1 (Mar. 1909).

Gamio, Manuel. *The Life Story of the Mexican Immigrant.* Chicago: University of Chicago Press, 1931.

Garrett, Franklin. *Atlanta and Environs: A Chronicle of Its People and Events, Volume II.* Athens: University of Georgia Press, 1969.

Gates, Merrill Edwards. "What the School Owes the State." In *California Educational Review.* San Francisco: Educational Review Publishing, 1891.

Geertz, Clifford. *The Interpretation of Cultures.* New York: Basic Books, 1973.

Gerstle, Gary. "The Protean Character of American Liberalism." *American Historical Review* 99, 4 (Oct. 1994): 1043–73.

————. "Liberty, Coercion, and the Making of Americans." *Journal of American History* 84, 2 (Sept. 1997): 524–58.

————. "Theodore Roosevelt and the Divided Character of American Nationalism." *Journal of American History* 86, 3 (Dec. 1999): 1280–1307.

————. *American Crucible: Race and Nation in the Twentieth Century.* Princeton: Princeton University Press, 2001.

Geschwender, James A., Rita Carroll-Seguin, and Howard Brill. "The Portuguese and Haoles of Hawai'i: Implications for the Origin of Ethnicity." *American Sociological Review* 53, 4 (Aug. 1988): 515–27.

Glenn, Evelyn Nakano. *Unequal Freedom: How Race and Gender Shaped American Citizenship and Labor.* Cambridge: Harvard University Press, 2002.

González, Gilbert. *Chicano Education in the Era of Segregation.* Cranbury, NJ: Associated University Presses, 1990.

———and Raúl Fernando. "Empire and the Origins of Twentieth-Century Migration from Mexico to the United States." *Pacific Historical Review* 71, 1 (Feb. 2002): 19–57.

Goodenow, Ronald and Diane Ravitch, eds. *Schools in Cities: Consensus and Conflict in American Educational History.* New York: Holmes and Meier, 1983.

Gould, Eliga. *Among the Powers of the Earth: The American Revolution and the Making of a New World Empire.* Cambridge: Harvard University Press, 2012.

Grace, Alonzo G. *Immigration and Community Americanization.* Minneapolis: ACME Printing & Publishing, 1921.

Graham Jr., Otis L. and Elizabeth Koed. "Americanizing the Immigrant, Past and Future: History and Implications of a Social Movement." *Public Historian* 15, 4 (Autumn 1993): 24–49.

Green, Elna C. "Hidden in Plain View: Eugene Poulnot and the History of Southern Radicalism." *Florida Historical Quarterly* 84, 3 (Winter 2006): 349–82.

Gutiérrez, David. *Walls and Mirrors: Mexican Americans, Mexican Immigrants, and the Politics of Ethnicity.* Berkeley: University of California Press, 1995.

Gyory, Andrew. *Closing the Gate: Race, Politics, and the Chinese Exclusion Act.* Chapel Hill: University of North Carolina Press, 1998.

Haney-López, Ian F. *White by Law: The Legal Construction of Race.* New York: New York University Press, 1996.

———. *Racism on Trial: The Chicano Fight for Justice.* Cambridge: Belknap Press of Harvard University, 2003.

Harlan, Louis. *Separate and Unequal: Public School Campaigns and Racism in the Southern Seaboard States, 1901–1915.* Chapel Hill: University of North Carolina Press, 1958.

Harper's Introductory Geography. New York: Harper Bros., 1877.

Harris, William. "Work and Family in Black Atlanta, 1880." *Journal of Social History* 9, 3 (Spring 1976): 319–30.

Hart, Albert Bushnell. "The Historical Opportunity in America." *American Historical Review* 4, 1 (Oct. 1898): 1–20.

———. *Essentials in American History.* New York: American Book, 1905.

———. "Imagination in History." *American Historical Review* 15, 2 (Jan. 1910): 227–51.

———. *School History of the United States.* New York: American Book, 1920.

———. *New American History.* New York: American Book, 1921 [1917].

———. *We and Our History: A Biography of the American People.* New York: American Viewpoint Society, 1923.

Hawkins, John. "Politics, Education, and Language Policy: The Case of Japanese Language Schools in Hawaii." *Amerasia* 5, 1 (1978): 39–56.

Hendrick, Irving G. *The Education of Non-Whites in California, 1849–1970.* San Francisco: R & E Research Associates, 1977.

Higginson, Thomas Wentworth. *Young Folks' History of the United States.* New York: Longmans, Green, 1901.

Higham, John. *Strangers in the Land: Patterns of American Nativism, 1865–1920.* New Brunswick: Rutgers University Press, 2002.

Hoffschwelle, Mary S. *The Rosenwald Schools of the American South.* Gainesville: University Press of Florida, 2006.

Hopkins, Caspar T. *A Manual of American Ideas, Third Revised Edition.* San Francisco: H. S. Crocker, 1887.

Hornsby, Jr., Alton. *Black Power in Dixie: A Political History of African Americans in Atlanta.* Gainesville: University of Florida Press, 2009.

Horsman, Reginald. *Race and Manifest Destiny: The Origins of American Racial Anglo-Saxonism.* Cambridge: Harvard University Press, 1981.

Hsu, Madeline Y. *Dreaming of Gold, Dreaming of Home: Transnationalism and Migration between the United States and South China, 1882–1943.* Stanford: Stanford University Press, 2000.

Hunt, Michael. *The American Ascendancy: How the United States Gained and Wielded Global Dominance.* Chapel Hill: University of North Carolina Press, 2007.

Huntington, Ellsworth and Sumner Cushing. *Principles of Human Geography.* New York: John Wiley & Sons, 1922 [1920].

Ichioka, Yuji. *The Issei: The World of the First Generation of Japanese Immigrants, 1885–1924.* New York: Free Press, 1988.

Inscoe, John, ed. *Georgia in Black and White: Explorations in the Race Relations of a Southern State, 1865–1950.* Athens: University of Georgia Press, 1994.

Ion, Theodore P. "The Japanese School Incident at San Francisco from the Point of View of International and Constitutional Law." *Michigan Law Review* 5, 5 (Mar. 1907): 326–43.

Iriye, Akira. *Pacific Estrangement: Japanese and American Expansion, 1897–1911.* Cambridge: Harvard University Press, 1972.

Jacobson, Matthew Frye. *Whiteness of a Different Color: European Immigrants and the Alchemy of Race.* Cambridge: Harvard University Press, 1998.

————. *Barbarian Virtues: The United States Encounters Foreign Peoples at Home and Abroad, 1876–1917.* New York: Hill & Wang, 2000.

————. *Roots Too: White Ethnic Revival in Post–Civil Rights America.* Cambridge: Harvard University Press, 2006.

Jarvinen, Lisa and Richard Garlitz, eds. *Teaching America to the World and the World to America: Education and Foreign Relations since 1870.* New York: Palgrave Macmillan, 2012.

Johnson, Guion Griffis. "Southern Paternalism toward Negroes after Emancipation." *Journal of Southern History* 23, 4 (Nov. 1957): 483–509.

Jorae, Wendy Rouse. *The Children of Chinatown: Growing Up Chinese American in San Francisco, 1850–1920*. Chapel Hill: University of North Carolina Press, 2009.

Kammen, Michael. *Mystic Chords of Memory: The Transformation of Tradition in American Culture*. New York: Alfred Knopf, 1991.

Kaplan, Amy. *The Anarchy of Empire in the Making of US Culture*. Cambridge: Harvard University Press, 2002.

Katz, Michael B. *Class, Bureaucracy, and Schools: The Illusion of Educational Change in America*. New York: Praeger, 1971.

Kendall, Calvin and George Mirick. *How to Teach the Fundamental Subjects*. Boston: Houghton Mifflin, 1915.

Kerber, Linda. "The Meanings of Citizenship." *Journal of American History* 84, 3 (Dec. 1997): 833–54.

Kimball, Hannibal. *Report of the Director-General of the International Cotton Exposition*. New York: D. Appleton, 1882.

Kramer, Paul. *The Blood of Government: Race, Empire, the United States, and the Philippines*. Chapel Hill: University of North Carolina Press, 2006.

———. "Power and Connection: Imperial Histories of the United States in the World." *American Historical Review* 116, 5 (Dec. 2011): 1348–91.

Kruse, Kevin. *White Flight: Atlanta and the Making of Modern Conservatism*. Princeton: Princeton University Press, 2005.

Kuhn, Clifford. *Contesting the New South Order: The 1914–15 Strike at Atlanta's Fulton Mills*. Chapel Hill: University of North Carolina Press, 2001.

Kuykendall, Ralph S. *The Hawaiian Kingdom, Volume III, 1874–1893: The Kalākaua Dynasty*. Honolulu: University of Hawai'i Press, 1967.

Lake, Marilyn and Henry Reynolds. *Drawing the Global Colour Line: White Men's Countries and the International Challenge of Racial Equality*. New York: Cambridge University Press, 2008.

Larrínaga, Tulio. "Conditions in Porto Rico." *Annals of the Academy of Political and Social Science* 26 (July 1905): 55–56.

Latane, John. *History of the United States*. Boston: Allyn & Bacon, 1926.

Lears, Jackson. *Rebirth of a Nation: The Making of Modern America, 1877–1920*. New York: HarperCollins, 2009.

Lee, Erika. *At America's Gates: Chinese Immigration during the Exclusion Era, 1882–1943*. Chapel Hill: University of North Carolina Press, 2003.

Lewis, Martin W. and Kären E. Wigen. *The Myth of Continents: A Critique of Metageography*. Berkeley: University of California Press, 1997.

Love, Eric T. L. *Race over Empire: Racism and US Imperialism, 1865–1900*. Chapel Hill: University of North Carolina Press, 2004.

Lowe, Lisa. *Immigrant Acts: On Asian-American Cultural Politics*. Durham, NC: Duke University Press, 1996.

Lusk, Clayton Riley. *Revolutionary Radicalism: Its History, Purpose and Tactics*. Albany: J. B. Lyon, 1920.

Mace, William H. *A Beginner's History*. Chicago: Rand McNally, 1921.

———— and Edwin P. Tanner. *Old Europe and Young America*. Chicago: Rand McNally, 1915.

MacMillan, Margaret. *Peacemakers: The Paris Peace Conference of 1919 and Its Attempts to End War*. London: John Murray, 2001.

Manekin, Sarah. "Spreading the Empire of Free Education, 1865–1905." PhD diss., University of Pennsylvania, 2009.

Matsubayashi, Yoshihide. "The Japanese Language Schools in Hawaii and California, 1892–1941." PhD diss., University of San Francisco, 1984.

Maury, Mytton F. *Maury's Manual of Geography*. New York: University Publishing, 1892.

————. *Physical Geography, Revised Edition*. New York: University Publishing, 1893.

Maxey, Edwin. "Exclusion of Japanese Children from the Public Schools of San Francisco." *Yale Law Journal* 16, 2 (Dec. 1906): 90–93.

McBrien, Jasper L. *America First: Patriotic Readings*. New York: American Book, 1916.

McCoy, Alfred and Francisco Scarano, eds. *Colonial Crucible: Empire in the Making of the Modern American State*. Madison: University of Wisconsin Press, 2009.

McKeown, Adam. *Melancholy Order: Asian Migration and the Globalization of Borders*. New York: Columbia University Press, 2008.

McMaster, John Bach. *A School History of the United States*. New York: American Book, 1897.

McMurry, Frank and A. E. Parkins. *Elementary Geography*. New York: Macmillan, 1921.

McWilliams, Carey. *Brothers under the Skin*. New York: Macmillan, 1951.

Merry, Sally Engle. *Colonizing Hawai'i: The Cultural Power of Law*. Princeton: Princeton University Press, 2000.

Meyer, Stephen. "Adapting the Immigrant to the Line: Americanization at the Ford Factory, 1914–1921." *Journal of Social History* 14, 1 (Autumn 1980): 67–82.

Michigan School Moderator 10, 7 (Dec. 1899): 197–224.

Miller, Elmer. "Education Value of Geography Study." *Bulletin of the American Bureau of Geography* 1, 1 (Mar. 1900): 7–8.

Miller, Stuart Creighton. *The Unwelcome Immigrant: The American Image of the Chinese, 1785–1882*. Berkeley: University of California Press, 1969.

Mirel, Jeffrey. *Patriotic Pluralism: Americanization Education and European Immigrants*. Cambridge: Harvard University Press, 2010.

Mitchell, Augustus. *Mitchell's New Primary Geography*. Philadelphia: J. H. Butler, 1878.

Mixon, Gregory. *The Atlanta Riot: Race, Class, and Violence in a New South City*. Gainesville: University of Florida Press, 2005.

Molina, Natalia. *How Race Is Made in America: Immigration, Citizenship, and the Historical Power of Racial Scripts*. Berkeley: University of California Press, 2014.

Montgomery, David. *The Leading Facts of American History*. Boston: Ginn, 1920.

Moreau, Joseph. *Schoolbook Nation: Conflicts over American History Textbooks from the Civil War to the Present.* Ann Arbor: University of Michigan Press, 2003.

Morris, Charles. *Elementary History of the United States.* Philadelphia: J. B. Lippincott, 1909.

Muzzey, David Saville. *An American History.* Boston: Ginn, 1920.

Nash, Gary B., Charlotte Crabtree, and Ross E. Dunn. *History on Trial: Culture Wars and the Teaching of the Past.* New York: Knopf, 1997.

Negrón de Montilla, Aida. *La americanización en Puerto Rico y el sistema de instrucción pública, 1900–1930.* San Juan: Editorial de la Universidad de Puerto Rico, 1998.

Ngai, Mae. *Impossible Subjects: Illegal Aliens and the Making of Modern America.* Princeton: Princeton University Press, 2004.

Norrell, Robert. *Up from History: The Life of Booker T. Washington.* Cambridge: Belknap Press of Harvard University, 2009.

Novick, Peter. *That Noble Dream: The "Objectivity Question" and the American Historical Profession.* New York: Cambridge University Press, 1988.

Nugent, Walter. "The American Habit of Empire: The Case of Polk and Bush." *Western Historical Quarterly* 38, 1 (Spring 2007): 4–24.

O'Leary, Cecilia. *To Die For: The Paradox of American Patriotism.* Princeton: Princeton University Press, 1999.

Okihiro, Gary. *Cane Fires: The Anti-Japanese Movement in Hawai'i, 1865–1945.* Philadelphia: Temple University Press, 1991.

———. *Margins and Mainstreams: Asians in American History and Culture.* Seattle: University of Washington Press, 1994.

———. *Island World: A History of Hawai'i and the United States.* Berkeley: University of California Press, 2008.

Olneck, Michael. "Americanization and the Education of Immigrants, 1900–1925: An Analysis of Symbolic Action." *American Journal of Education* 97, 4 (Aug. 1989): 398–423.

Osorio, Jonathan Kay Kamakawiwo'ole. *Dismembering Lāhui: A History of the Hawaiian Nation to 1887.* Honolulu: University of Hawai'i Press, 2002.

Painter, Nell Irving. *Standing at Armageddon: The United States, 1877–1919.* New York: W. W. Norton, 1987.

———. *The History of White People.* New York: Norton, 2010.

Parr, Eunice Elvira. "A Comparative Study of Mexican and American Children in the Schools of San Antonio, Texas." MA thesis, University of Chicago, 1926.

Paulet, Ann. "To Change the World: The Use of American Indian Education in the Philippines." *History of Education Quarterly* 47, 2 (May 2007): 173–202.

Phillips, Ulrich B. "The Central Theme of Southern History." *American Historical Review* 34, 1 (Oct. 1928): 30–43.

Porteus, S. D. and M. E. Babcock, *Temperament and Race.* Boston: Badger, 1926.

Racine, Philip Noel. "Atlanta's Schools: A History of the Public School System, 1869–1955." PhD diss., Emory University, 1970.

Ravitch, Diane. *The Great School Wars: New York City, 1805–1973, A History of the Public Schools as Battlefield of Social Change.* New York: Basic Books, 1974.

Reese, William J. *Power and the Promise of School Reform: Grass-roots Movements during the Progressive Era.* Boston: Routledge and Kegan Paul, 1986.

Reuben, Julie. "Beyond Politics: Community Civics and the Redefinition of Citizenship in the Progressive Era." *History of Education Quarterly* 37, 4 (Winter 1997): 399–420.

Richards, David. *Italian American: The Racializing of an Ethnic Identity.* New York: New York University Press, 1999.

Richardson, James D., ed. *A Compilation of the Messages and Papers of the Presidents, Volume X.* New York: Bureau of National Literature, 1913.

Rodgers, Daniel. *Atlantic Crossings: Social Politics in a Progressive Age.* Cambridge: Belknap Press of Harvard University, 2000.

Roediger, David. *Working toward Whiteness: How America's Immigrants Became White.* New York: Basic Books, 2005.

Rosen, Hannah. *Terror in the Heart of Freedom: Citizenship, Sexual Violence and the Meaning of Race in the Postemancipation South.* Chapel Hill: University of North Carolina Press, 2009.

Rouse, Jacqueline. *Lugenia Burns Hope: Black Southern Reformer.* Athens: University of Georgia Press, 1989.

Ruiz, Vicki. "South by Southwest: Mexican Americans and Segregated Schooling, 1900–1950." *OAH Magazine of History* (Winter 2001): 23–27.

Rydell, Robert. *All the World's a Fair: Visions of Empire at American International Expositions, 1876–1916.* Chicago: University of Chicago Press, 1984.

Salazar, Ruben. *Border Correspondent: Selected Writings, 1955–1970.* Berkeley: University of California Press, 1995.

San Miguel, Jr., Guadalupe and Richard Valencia. "From the Treaty of Guadalupe-Hidalgo to *Hopwood:* The Educational Plight and Struggle of Mexican Americans in the Southwest." *Harvard Educational Review* 68, 3 (Fall 1998): 353–412.

Sánchez, George I. "Group Differences and Spanish-Speaking Children: A Critical Review." *Journal of Applied Psychology* 16, 5 (Oct. 1932): 549–58.

——— and Lyle Saunders. *Wetbacks: A Preliminary Report to the Advisory Committee for the Study of Spanish Speaking People.* Austin: University of Texas, 1949.

Sánchez, George J. *Becoming Mexican American: Ethnicity, Culture, and Identity in Chicano Los Angeles, 1900–1945.* New York: Oxford University Press, 1994.

Sasaki, Christen Tsuyuko. "Pacific Confluence: Negotiating the Nation in Nineteenth Century Hawai'i." PhD diss., University of California, Los Angeles, 2011.

Saxton, Alexander. *The Indispensible Enemy: Labor in the Anti-Chinese Movement in California.* Berkeley: University of California Press, 1971.

———. *The Rise and Fall of the White Republic.* New York: Verso, 1990.

Schoonover, Thomas. *Uncle Sam's War of 1898 and the Origins of Globalization.* Lexington: University Press of Kentucky, 2003.

Schulten, Susan. *The Geographical Imagination in America, 1880–1950.* Chicago: University of Chicago Press, 2001.

Selig, Diana. *Americans All: The Cultural Gifts Movement.* Cambridge: Harvard University Press, 2008.

Semple, Ellen Churchill. *Influences of Geographic Environment.* New York: Henry Holt, 1911.

Sexton, Jay. *The Monroe Doctrine: Empire and Nation in Nineteenth-Century America.* New York: Hill & Wang, 2011.

Shapiro, Adam. *Trying Biology: The Scopes Trial, Textbooks, and the Antievolution Movement in American Schools.* Chicago: University of Chicago Press, 2013.

Shinbunsha, Nichibei. *Zaibei Nihonjin Nenkan.* San Francisco: Nichibei Shinbunsha, 1908.

Silva, Noenoe K. *Aloha Betrayed: Native Hawaiian Resistance to American Colonialism.* Durham, NC: Duke University Press, 2004.

Sklar, Martin. *The Corporate Reconstruction of American Capitalism, 1890–1916: The Market, The Law, and Politics.* New York: Cambridge University Press, 1988.

Skwiot, Christine. *The Purposes of Paradise: US Tourism and Empire in Cuba and Hawai'i.* Philadelphia: University of Pennsylvania Press, 2010.

Smith, Henry Nash. *Virgin Land: The American West as Symbol and Myth.* Cambridge: Harvard University Press, 1950.

Spickard, Paul. *Almost All Aliens: Immigration, Race, and Colonialism in American History and Identity.* New York: Routledge, 2007.

Spivey, Donald. *Schooling for the New Black Slavery: Black Industrial Education, 1868–1915.* Westport, CT: Greenwood, 1978.

St. John, Rachel. *A Line in the Sand: A History of the Western US-Mexico Border.* Princeton: Princeton University Press, 2011.

Steffes, Tracy. *School, Society, and State: A New Education to Govern Modern America, 1890–1940.* Chicago: University of Chicago Press, 2012.

Stephenson, Nathaniel Wright. *An American History.* Boston: Ginn, 1913.

Swinton, William. *Primary Geography.* New York: Ivison, Blakeman, Taylor, 1881.

Talbot, Edith Armstrong. *Samuel Chapman Armstrong: A Biographical Study.* New York: Doubleday, 1904.

Tamura, Eileen. *Americanization, Acculturation, and Ethnic Identity: The Nisei Generation in Hawai'i.* Urbana: University of Illinois Press, 1994.

———. "Asian Americans in the History of Education: An Historiographical Essay." *History of Education Quarterly* 41, 1 (Spring 2001): 58–71.

Takaki, Ronald. *Strangers from a Different Shore: A History of Asian Americans.* Boston: Little, Brown, 1998.

Tarbell, Horace. *Introductory Geography.* New York: Werner School Book Company, 1900 [1896].

———and Martha Tarbell. *Complete Geography.* New York: American Book, 1899.

Tarr, Ralph. *Home Geography and the Earth as a Whole.* New York: MacMillan, 1901.

——— and Frank McMurry. *Advanced Geography.* New York: Macmillan, 1907 [1900].

Tatalovich, Raymond. *Nativism Reborn?: The Official English Language Movement and the American States.* Lexington: University of Kentucky Press, 1995.

Thomas, Allen C. *A History of the United States.* Boston: D. C. Heath, 1899 [1893].

Thomas, Lorrin. "How They Ignore Our Rights as American Citizens: Puerto Rican Migrants and the Politics of Citizenship in the New Deal Era." *Latino Studies* 2 (2004): 140–59.

———. *Puerto Rican Citizen: History and Political Identity in Twentieth Century New York City.* Chicago: University of Chicago Press, 2010.

Thompson, Waddy. *Primary History of the United States.* Boston: D. C. Heath, 1913.

———. *A History of the United States.* Boston: D. C. Heath, 1919, [1904].

Throntveit, Trygve. "The Fable of the Fourteen Points: Woodrow Wilson and National Self-Determination." *Diplomatic History* 35, 3 (June 2011): 445–81.

Toppin, Edgar A. "Walter White and the Atlanta NAACP's Fight for Equal Schools, 1916–1917." *History of Education Quarterly* 7, 1 (Spring 1967): 3–21.

Trachtenberg, Alan. *The Incorporation of America: Culture and Society in the Gilded Age.* New York: Hill & Wang, 1982.

Turner, John Kenneth. *Barbarous Mexico.* Chicago: Charles H. Kerr, 1910.

Tyack, David. *The One Best System: A History of American Urban Education.* Cambridge: Harvard University Press, 1974.

Urciuoli, Bonnie. *Exposing Prejudice: Puerto Rican Experiences of Language, Race, and Class.* Boulder, CO: Westview Press, 1996.

Van Nuys, Frank. *Americanizing the West: Race, Immigrants, and Citizenship, 1890–1930.* Lawrence: University of Kansas Press, 2002.

Veeser, Cyrus. *A World Safe for Capitalism: Dollar Diplomacy and America's Rise to Global Power.* New York: Columbia University Press, 2007.

Ward, Robert. "Our New Immigration Policy." *Foreign Affairs* 3, 1 (Sept. 15, 1924): 99–111.

Warren, Kim Cary. *The Quest for Citizenship: African American and Native American Education in Kansas, 1880–1935.* Chapel Hill: University of North Carolina Press, 2010.

Watts, Eugene. "Black Political Progress in Atlanta, 1868–1895." *Journal of Negro History* 59, 3 (July 1974): 268–86.

Weinberg, Meyer. *A Chance to Learn: The History of Race and Education in the United States.* New York: Cambridge University Press, 1977.

Weiner, Melissa. *Power, Protest, and the Public Schools: Jewish and African American Struggles in New York City.* New Brunswick: Rutgers University Press, 2010.

Weiss, Bernard J., ed. *American Education and the European Immigrant, 1840–1940.* Urbana: University of Illinois Press, 1982.

Werbner, Pnina. "Vernacular Cosmopolitanism." *Theory, Culture, and Society* 23, 2–3 (2006): 496–98.

Wiebe, Robert. *The Search for Order, 1877–1920.* New York: Hill & Wang, 1967.

Williams, William Appleman. *The Tragedy of American Diplomacy.* New York: W. W. Norton, 1972.

Willinsky, John. *Learning to Divide the World: Education at Empire's End.* Minneapolis: University of Minnesota Press, 1998.

Willsey, Elise Mae. *Course of Study in Home Economics for the Elementary and High Schools of Porto Rico.* San Juan: Department of Education, 1923.

Wilson, Rob. "Exporting Christian Transcendentalism, Importing Hawaiian Sugar: The Trans-Americanization of Hawai'i." *American Literature* 72, 3 (Sept. 2000): 521–52.

Wilson, William Nathan. "An Analysis of the Academic and Home Problems of the Pupils in a Mexican Junior High School." MS thesis, University of Southern California, 1938.

Winton, Ruth. "Negro Participation in Southern Expositions, 1881–1915." *Journal of Negro Education* 16, 1 (Winter 1947): 34–43.

Wist, Benjamin O. *A Century of Public Education in Hawaii, 1840–1940.* Honolulu: Hawaii Education Review, 1940.

Wollenberg, Charles. *All Deliberate Speed: Segregation and Exclusion in California Schools, 1855–1975.* Berkeley: University of California Press, 1976.

———. "*Mendez v. Westminster:* Race, Nationality, and Segregation in California Schools." *California Historical Quarterly* 53, 4 (Winter 1974): 317–32.

Woodward, C. Vann. *Tom Watson: Agrarian Rebel.* New York: Oxford University Press, 1963.

———. *The Strange Career of Jim Crow.* New York: Oxford University Press, 1974.

Woyshner, Christine and Chara Bohan, eds. *Histories of Social Studies and Race, 1865–2000.* New York: Palgrave Macmillan, 2012.

Yoo, David. *Growing Up Nisei: Race, Generation, and Culture among Japanese Americans in California, 1924–1949.* Urbana: University of Illinois Press, 2000.

Zimmerman, Jonathan. *Whose America? Culture Wars in the Public Schools.* Cambridge: Harvard University Press, 2002.

Zolberg, Aristide R. *A Nation by Design: Immigration Policy in the Fashioning of America.* Cambridge: Harvard University Press, 2006.

Zunz, Olivier. *Making American Corporate, 1870–1920.* Chicago: University of Chicago Press, 1990.

WEBSITES

CNN. "Ethnic Studies Ban Racist?" *YouTube* video. 12:19. May 13, 2010. www.youtube.com/watch?v=TgvOdD5bVsg.

"Debating Tucson School District's Book Ban after Suspension of Mexican American Studies Program," democracynow.org, January 18, 2012. Accessed September 4, 2014. www.democracynow.org/2012/1/18/debating_tucson_school_districts_book_ban.

Hing, Julianne. "Arizona Gov. Brewer Signs Ethnic Studies Ban into Law," *Colorlines.com.* May 12, 2010. Accessed September 4, 2014. http://colorlines

.com/archives/2010/05/arizonas_gov_brewer_signs_ethnic_studies_ban_into_
law.html.

Horne, Tom. "An Open Letter to the Citizens of Tucson." June 11, 2007. Reprinted
in Valerie Strauss, "Why Arizona Targeted Ethnic Studies," *washingtonpost.com,*
May 25, 2010. Accessed September 4, 2014. http://voices.washingtonpost.com
/answer-sheet/civics-education/why-arizona-targeted-ethnic-st.html.

Huicochea, Alexis. "TUSD: Bill Won't Alter Ethnic Studies, Horne: Measure Sent
to Brewer Is Aimed at District," *Arizona Daily Star,* May 4, 2010. Accessed September
4, 2014. http://tucson.com/news/local/education/article_8d522665
-3753-5221-9b64-45c72b426777.html.

Jeffco Public Schools. "JW Proposal Board Committee for Curriculum Review,"
Jeffco Public Schools Board of Education website, September 18, 2014. Accessed
September 25, 2014. http://www.boarddocs.com/co/jeffco/Board.nsf/goto?open
&id=9NBUKW7C6977.

Treaty of Guadalupe-Hidalgo, Article VIII, February 2, 1848. Accessed April 8,
2015, http://avalon.law.yale.edu/19th_century/guadhida.asp.

United States House of Representatives. "Tulio Larrínaga," in *Biographical Directory
of the United States Congress.* Accessed March 20, 2014. http://bioguide
.congress.gov/scripts/biodisplay.pl?index=L000102.

INDEX

Page references followed by fig. *indicate an illustration.*

Central Pacific Railroad, 58–59
Central Scholarship Committee (Puerto Rico), 208–9
Chambers, Claude, 201
Chemerinsky, Erwin, 215
Chinatown (San Francisco), 56–59, 61–63, 66, 67*fig.*
Chinese Americans, 52, 56–58
Chinese Exclusion Act (1882), 54; and becoming white, 171; debates surrounding, 6; extensions/expansions of, 10–11, 60–61, 65, 230n28; and Hawaiian anti-Chinese movement, 92; importance of, 3; Jim Crow anticipated by, 6; passage/terms of, 60; racial restrictions repealed, 14; support for, 61; white nationalists' role in, 10; and the "yellow peril," 63, 79
Chinese immigrants, 52–56, 95. *See also* Chinese Exclusion Act
Chinese language teaching, 51–52, 58, 82–83
Cholla High School (Tucson), 212
Churchill, Thomas, 157
Citizens Committee for Public School Reform, 149
citizenship: alternative paths to, 4, 9; as Americanization, 106; Asians excluded from (*see under* California); and the dignity of labor, 107; educational qualifications for, 125; forced, 176–77, 213; haole on, 88, 106, 234n8; via Hawai'i schools, 94, 97; via higher education, 12; and knowledge, 211–17; via manual training, 9, 13, 131, 133; of Mexicans, 176–78, 182, 198–99; national loyalty as requirement for, 80–82; of Native Americans, 6; progress and prosperity via, 1, 9; of Puerto Ricans, 14, 175, 177, 182–84, 195–97, 196.193; semi-citizenship, 2; unequal paths to, 1–3, 9, 13, 219n3; and whiteness, 3–4, 150–51, 172 (*see also* New York City schools). *See also* geography, history, and civics; naturalization
City of New York Children's Court, 194
civics. *See* geography, history, and civics
civil rights movement, 14, 49, 143

Civil War (United States), 12, 92, 121–26
Clemmer, Frances, 133
Cohen, Elizabeth, 2
Cohen, Ronald, 157
Cold War, 184, 212
Cole, Raymond E., 145
Columbus, Christopher, 168
Columbus Day, 1
commemoration rituals, 44–45
Commission of Immigration and Housing (CSCIH), 80–81
Committee for Immigrants in America, 154
Committee of Seventy, 149
Commons, John R., 153
Community Service Organization, 203
Complete Geography (the Tarbells), 20
Compulsory Education Act (New York, 1874), 153
Coolidge, Calvin, 48
cosmopolitan unity, 85. *See also under* Hawai'i
Cotton States and International Exposition (Atlanta, 1895), 127
Council on Immigrant Education, 171–72
creole elites, 177, 184–86, 197–98
CSCIH (Commission of Immigration and Housing), 80–81
Cuba, 29, 39, 92, 184
Cuban revolution, 30
cultural gifts movement, 169
Cushing, Sumner: *Principles of Human Geography,* 24

Dana, Richard, 37
Daniels, Roger, 73
D'Annunzio, Gabriele, 167
D. Appleton, 8
Davis, James, 100
Davis, William Morris, 18, 21, 24, 28
Dearborn, Walter, 190
dekasegi migrants, 64, 73
dekasegi-shosei (Japanese student-laborers), 64
delinquency, 194
del Moral, Solsiree, 184, 208
democracy: American, tenets of, 150; black education's importance to, 136–37; in

Europe following World War I, 168; a world safe for, 45, 146

Denman, James, 57–58

Densmore, G. B., 57

Department of Public Instruction (DPI; California), 51

Department of Public Instruction (DPI; Hawai'i). *See* DPI (Department of Public Instruction; Hawai'i)

Dewey, John, 157, 160–61

Díaz, Porfirio, 179

Digennaro, Charles, 16–17

Dill, Augustus Granville, 133–34

Dodge, Alice Sinclair, 110

Dohrmann, F., Jr., 47

Dole, Sanford, 234n8

Dominguez, Kim, 214

Dominguez, Nicholas, 216–17. *See also* HB 2281

Douglas, Diane, 249n5

Downes v. Bidwell, 196–97

DPI (Department of Public Instruction; California), 51

DPI (Department of Public Instruction; Hawai'i), 84–85, 97–104, 106, 126; and the HSPA, 109–10; Japanese language schools opposed by, 89, 107, 110–15, 237n75; on modernization, Americanization, and civilizing, 87; schools under supervision of, 11, 94, 101–3, 110–11; Supreme Court suit against (1927), 11, 82, 89; textbooks/curricula supervision of, 111–12

Du Bois, W. E. B., 123–27, 132, 132*fig.*, 136, 142

Dugan, Margaret, 212

Dyson, Michael Eric, 212, 214

Educational Alliance school (New York City), 151*fig.*

ELA (*Estado Libre Asociado;* Free Associated State; Puerto Rico), 184, 208–9

Elsas, Jacob, 119

English language education, 152

English-only movement: Americanization via, 9, 12; in "Mexican" schools, 13; in New York City, 12, 152, 155; in Puerto Rico, 155, 178, 183–84, 187, 205–7

English proficiency, 82

ethnic studies, 14, 211–17, 249n5

Ettinger, William, 146, 155, 157, 161–66, 168, 170

eugenic arguments/eugenicists, 59–60, 147, 184, 186, 190–95, 197–98

Eugenics Records Office, 194

evolutionary science, 17, 20–21, 22

exceptionalizing difference, modes of, 2

factories, 4–5, 118, 152, 158, 160

Falkner, Roland, 206

Farmers' Improvement Society of Texas, 132

Farrington, Wallace, 110, 114

Fascists, 167

Federal Committee on Public Information, 160

Fickert, Charles, 68–69

Filipino immigrants, 7, 193

Finch, William, 118–19, 121, 136

Finley, John Huston, 162

Fite, Emerson, 33, 35–37, 39–40

flag drills, 44*fig.,* 48

Flood, Noah, 55

Fo, Ruth, 115

Foerster, Robert, 173–75, 194, 204

Foraker Act (1900), 182, 185–86

Ford, Henry, 152

foreign miners' license tax, 54

Forman, Samuel Eagle: *Advanced Civics,* 228n69

Fort Valley Industrial School (Georgia), 127–29, 128*fig.*

Fourteen Points, 167

Fourteenth Amendment's equal protection clause, 62, 203

Fraser Street grammar school (Atlanta), 142

Free Associated State (*Estado Libre Asociado;* ELA; Puerto Rico), 184, 208–9

Freedmen's Bureau, 118–19, 123–24

Freire, Paolo: *Pedagogy of the Oppressed,* 15, 212–13

Frye, Alexis Everett, 18–19

Fugitive Slave Act (1850), 61

Furuseth, Andrew, 78–79

Gallardo, José, 206–7
Garcia, Isabel, 214
Gary (Indiana), 156–57
Gary Plan, 156–59
Gary School League, 157
Gates, Merrill Edward, 41–42, 216
Geary Act (1892), 10–11, 61, 65
Geertz, Clifford, 151
Gentlemen's Agreement (1909), 11, 72–73, 79, 81, 89, 106–7, 230n28
geography, history, and civics, 16–49; and American exceptionalism, 17–18, 29, 43; American histories of imperial expansion, 29–41, 38*map*, 226n38; and blood mixture/miscegenation, 26; civics/politics of patriotism, 41–49, 44*fig.*, 228n69; and climate, 16–17, 21–22, 24, 26–28; community civics, 19–20, 42–43; and empire vs. republic, 28; geographic determinism, 27; and Native Americans, 27–28, 31; overview of, 9–10, 16–20; patriotic, 19; racial/imperial metageographies, 20–29, 25*map;* and savagery vs. civilization, 20–21, 28; scientific, 18–22; and settlers/natives/immigrants/colonial subjects, 31–32; textbooks/courses on civics, 19–20, 41–43, 228n69; textbooks on geography, 18–19, 21–22; textbooks on history, 19. *See also* textbooks
Georgia: ban on black education in, 123, 125; black labor shortage in, 130–31; black voters in, 130, 141; illiteracy among blacks in, 124; Radical Reconstruction in, 119. *See also* Atlanta schools
Georgia Department of Education, 46–47
Georgia Education Association, 123–24
Georgia State Board of Education, 127, 135–37
Gerstle, Gary, 160
Gibson, Thomas, 102
GI Forum, 203
Gilded Age, 5–6, 60, 221n15
Ginn & Company, 8, 18–19
Glenn, R. L., 122, 129–31, 134, 136
gold rush, 52
Gould, Eliga, 226n38

Government English School (Pahala, Hawai'i), 85
Grace, Alonzo, 145
Grady, Henry, 120–21
Grant, Madison, 59–60
Gray Street School (Atlanta), 139
Great Depression, 172, 178, 187, 193
Great War. *See* World War I
Green, Elna, 143
Guadalupe-Hidalgo, Treaty of, 176–79
Gutiérrez, David, 248n55
Gyory, Andrew, 61

Hampton Normal and Agricultural Institute (Virginia), 12, 88, 91–92, 126–27, 131
haole (Hawaiian-born whites): on citizenship, 88, 106, 234n8; cosmopolitan rhetoric of, 116; on manual training, 96, 103–4; in ministry positions, 90–91, 93–94; on Nisei, 106–8; on the Portuguese, 87; racial ideology of, 11–12, 89, 103–4; schools under supervision of, 86–87, 89, 94 (*see also* DPI); vs. US whites and nonwhite Hawaiians, 96
Hapai, Mike, 99–100, 104
Harding, Warren G., 109, 168–70
Harlan, Louis, 123
Harlem riots (1935), 193–94
Harper Brothers, 8
Hart, Albert Bushnell, 29, 35–36, 39; *New American History,* 19, 40–41; *School History of the United States,* 19, 36; *We and Our History,* 30
Hartsfield, William, 142
Havlock, May, 77
Hawai'i: Americanization of, 86–88, 106–7, 109, 111, 115; American missionaries in, 37, 87; cane workers in, 11, 87, 92–93, 107–10; Chinese in, 92–93, 106, 109; constitutional convention debates in (1894), 93–94; cosmopolitanism of, 11, 53, 84–86, 94, 111; exports from, 92; Filipinos in, 108–9; Japanese in, 89, 92–93, 106–12, 108*fig.;* labor shortages in, 109; Nisei in, 89, 106–12, 115, 237n75; pineapple canning/growing in, 105–6, 114; Portuguese in, 87, 108–9; preserva-

tion laws in, 103; Puerto Ricans in, 108–9, 196, 198; as a republic, 93–94, 96; statehood granted to, 14; sugar industry in, 92, 95, 98, 100–110, 113–14; US annexation of, 87–88, 94–97; US empire in, 6, 84, 86–88; US–Hawaiian kingdom trade, 92; voting rights in, 93–94; white establishment in (*see* haole); white population of, 87–88. *See also* Hawai'i schools

Hawai'i American Legion, 109

Hawaiian Sugar Planters' Association (HSPA), 108–10

Hawai'i Board of Education, 53

Hawai'i Board of Industrial Schools, 101, 105

Hawaii Hochi, 114

Hawai'i schools, 85–117; Americanization via, 88–89; Chinese, 94; citizenship via, 94, 97; DPI supervision of, 11, 94, 101–3, 110–11; English language in, 88–89, 94–95, 110–12 (*see also* Act 30); Hawaiian language in, 94, 112; Hawaiian monarchy's control over education, 90; Hilo Boarding School, 88, 90–92, 104, 126; Japanese children in, 106–12, 112*fig.;* Japanese teachers in, 111, 115, 237n75; Lahainaluna School, 89, 97–99; amid land dispossession and annexation, 87–88, 90–91, 93–96; litigation surrounding language schools in, 112–17, 237n75, 237n78; manual training emphasized in, 84–85, 88–91, 95–99, 106, 116–17, 215–16; New England missionary origins of, 87, 89–93, 215–16; overview of, 83–89, 234n8; racial order in, 53; reform schools, 11, 99–101, 106 (*see also* Waiale'e Boys' Industrial School); vocational, 97–99, 105–6; Waiale'e Boys' Industrial School, 11, 89, 99–106, 102*fig.,* 105*fig.;* Waiale'e Girls' Industrial School, 100–101; white children in, 86–87, 96, 235n30

Hayes, Everis A., 10

Hayes, Rutherford B., 60

Haymond, Creed, 56–57, 60

HB 2281 (Arizona), 211–17, 249n5

Higher Wages Association, 108

Hillquit, Morris, 158–59

Hilo Boarding School (Hawai'i), 88, 90–92, 104, 126

history and geography. *See* geography, history, and civics

History of the United States (A. C. Thomas), 35–36

Holland Free School (Atlanta), 123

Honolulu Advertising Club, 113

Honolulu Reform School, 11, 100

Honolulu Star-Bulletin, 105

Honomu Japanese Language School (Hawai'i), 112*fig.*

Hoover, J. Edgar, 166

Hope, John, 46–47

Hope, Lugenia Burns, 46–47, 138–39

Horne, Tom, 212–16

Houston Street School (Atlanta), 122–23, 139

Howell, Clark, 130–31, 134, 136, 140–41

Hoyt, Henry, 120

HSPA (Hawaiian Sugar Planters' Association), 108–10

Hulbert, Murray, 170

Huli, Joseph, 99–100, 104

Huntington, Ellsworth, 21; *Principles of Human Geography,* 24

Huppenthal, John, 14, 211–12, 214–15

Hurley, Jennie, 61–62

Hylan, John F., 158–59

Imamoto, Soichi, 103

Immigrants in America Review (Kellor), 154, 160

Immigration and Naturalization Service (INS), 176, 204–5

Immigration Journal, 159–60

immigration laws/policies: and Americanization, 3, 6; deportation of foreign radicals, 162; Geary Act, 10–11, 61, 65; Immigration Act (1924), 48; McCarran-Walter Act, 205; quotas, 116; restrictionism in debates about, 18; Senate Bill 1070, 214. *See also* Chinese Exclusion Act; National Origins Act

Imperial Chinese Consulate (San Francisco), 61–62

imperialism, historiography/overview of, 2, 219–20n5

Larrínaga, Tulio, 185–86, 246n26
Latane, John, 33
Latin America and the Monroe Doctrine, 32–33
Latin America immigrants, 7, 173, 175. *See also* Mexicans
Laughlin, Harry H., 194
Law and Order League, 165
The Leading Facts of American History (Montgomery), 39–40
League of Nations, 167
League of United Latin American Citizens (LULAC), 203–4
Leavitt, J. W., 85
Lemon Grove school (California), 201
liberalism, 32, 176, 182, 191–92
Liberty Loans, 45–46
Lili'uokalani, Queen, 93
Lincoln, Abraham, 8
Lindsay, Samuel, 185
Lininoe, Willie, 100
Lippincott's Gazetteer, 70
London, Treaty of, 167
Lopez, Korina, 216–17. *See also* HB 2281
Los Angeles Mexicans, 180–81, 202–3, 248n53
Louisiana's sugar economy, 92
Lowe, Lisa, 53
Lowery, E. G., 86–88, 106
loyalty oaths/cards, 162–63, 165–66
LULAC (League of United Latin American Citizens), 203–4
Lusk, Clayton Riley, 163–64
Lyman, David, 90, 96, 104, 126
lynchings, 47, 76, 124, 128

MacArthur, Walter, 65–66
MacCaughey, Vaughan, 111, 115, 237n75
Mace, William, 39–40
MacMillan, 8
Macon Telegraph, 135–36
Maka'āinana (people of the land), 90–91
Maller, J. B., 194
MAM (Mexican American Movement), 201–3
Manhattan, 148
Martinez, Richard, 212
Marxism, 211–12

Maury, Matthew Fontaine, 23
Maury, Mytton: *Physical Geography,* 23–24
Maxey, Edwin, 71
Maxwell, William H., 154, 157, 159
Maya Arce v. John Huppenthal, 214–15. *See also* HB 2281
Mayo, Amory Dwight, 134
Mayper, Joseph, 154–55
McBrien, Jasper, 41
McCarran-Walter Act (1952), 205
McCarthy, Charles, 101
McClatchy, V. S., 81
McClure, A. K., 128–29
McDougal, John, 54
McKeown, Adam, 52
McMaster, John Bach, 19
McMurray, Frank, 25*map,* 26
Meiji period/elites (Japan), 64–65, 79
melting pot, 18, 48, 159–66, 169
Méndez, Gonzalo and Félícitas, 203
Méndez v. Westminster, 203, 209
Metcalf, Victor, 69–73
The Mexican-American Heritage (Jimenez), 213
Mexican American Movement (MAM), 201–3
Mexican Americans'/Puerto Ricans' school experiences, 173–209; Americanization efforts, 181, 183–84, 201; bilingualism, 191, 207; and citizenship, 187–89, 192; discrimination/segregation, 177–81, 188–89, 191, 198, 200, 202–4; English-only instruction, 183–84, 199, 205; and eugenic arguments/eugenicists, 184, 186, 190–95, 197–98; during the Great Depression, 187, 193; imperialistic attitudes/symbols/practices, 179; and the INS deportation campaign, 176, 204–5; intelligence of Puerto Rican children, report on, 178; intelligence testing, 188–98, 200; literacy projects, 186–87, 192; manual training, 194–95, 199–201, 208; Mexican schools, 200–201; overview/background of, 13–14, 173–78; physical education programs, 192; and politics of resistant accommodation, 200–209, 248nn53,55; and poverty perceived as sign of mental

Mexican Americans *(continued)*
inferiority, 188–99; scholarships, 208–9; "special needs" of Mexican children, 181; vocational training, 189; "wetback," use of term, 176, 203–4
Mexican American Studies program (*La Raza* program, Tucson), 14, 211–14
Mexican Revolution, 178–80
Mexicans: in Arizona, 180, 213; English language illiteracy among, 188; immigrant population in the Southwest, 180–81; as Mexican vs. white, 174, 245n4; national loyalty of, 179–80, 182, 202; perceived as inferior, 34–35, 174–75, 178, 188, 190; perceived as undesirable/deportable, 7, 13, 48–49, 173–75, 199, 201; politics of Mexican-Americans, 198–99, 201–2; racist reactions to Mexican immigrants, 178; US citizenship of, 176–78, 182, 198–99; "wetback," use of term, 176, 203–4. *See also* Mexican Americans'/Puerto Ricans' school experiences
Mexican Voice, 202
Mexican War (1846–48), 17, 34–37, 178
Mexico, 177–78, 182
Meyer v. Nebraska, 237n78
migrant laborers, 177
Miller, Elmer, 9–10
Mirick, George, 16
miscegenation, 26, 138
missionary party (Hawai'i), 93
mission schools. *See under* Hawai'i schools
Mitchel, John, 156–59
Miyakawa, Matsuji, 68–69, 75
Miyake, Hatau, 115
Miyamoto, Tsuruno, 111
Mohl, Raymond, 157
Mōʻī (paramount chief or monarch), 91
Molina, Natalia, 176
"Mongolian" as a racial category, 67–70, 79
Monroe, James, 33–34, 170
Monroe Doctrine, 17, 32–34, 37, 170, 226n38
Montgomery, David Henry: *The Leading Facts of American History*, 39–40
Morris Brown College (Atlanta), 135
Mott-Smith, Ernest A., 84–85, 88, 94–95
Moulder, Andrew, 50–51, 61–62

Mukai, Frank, 77, 78*fig.*
El Mundo, 196–97
Muñoz Marín, Luis, 199, 207
Murphy, Mary, 150
Muzzey, David Saville: *An American History*, 34, 36–37, 38*map*, 39, 50

NAACP (National Association for the Advancement of Colored People), 12, 119, 141, 203
Namalu, David, 103
National Americanization Committee, 152
National Association for the Advancement of Colored People. *See* NAACP
National Council of Defense, 152
nationalism, racial, 68
National Origins Act (1924): Anglo-Saxonism represented by, 171; as coercive Americanism, 160; eugenic arguments' role in, 59–60, 147, 190, 192; events leading to, 82; exclusivity of, 60–61, 170–71; and the Gentlemen's Agreement, 11; goals of, 4, 48; immigration from southern/eastern Europe curtailed by, 13; importance of, 3; Latin America/Caribbean not covered by, 175; Mexican Americans'/Puerto Ricans' school experiences after (*see* Mexican Americans'/Puerto Ricans' school experiences); quota system of, 4, 6–7, 10, 14, 144, 171, 173, 193–94
National Security League, 160
National War-Savings Committee, 45
Native Americans, 6, 27–28, 31, 121
nativists: Anglo-Saxonism of, 80–81; as anti-Japanese, 75, 106; on assimilation, 13, 80–82, 116; hysteria of, 107, 116; on integrated schools, 88; role in Americanization campaigns, 107
naturalization: for Chinese immigrants, 52, 95; for European immigrants, 148; for Japanese immigrants, 70–72, 95; language requirements for, 94
Naturalization Act (1790), 49, 54, 148
Nebraska, English-only instruction in, 155
Negro Common School Committee, 125
Neighborhood Union (Atlanta), 46–47, 138–40

peninsulares privilege, 184
Perkins, George C., 61
Phelan, James Duval, 65–66
Philippines: American colonial schools in, 5, 221n14; self-government for, 193; as a US colony, 39–40, 44
Phillips, Ulrich B., 124
Physical Geography (Mytton Maury), 23–24
Pinkham, Lucius, 104
platoon model of education (Gary Plan), 156–59
Platt Amendment (1901), 39
Plessy v. Ferguson (1896), 6, 54, 124–25, 137, 142
pluralism, 160, 170, 190
Poe, Palea, 99
politics of resistant accommodation, 200–209, 248nn53,55
Polk, James K., 36
Ponce Massacre (Puerto Rico, 1937), 206
Pope, Willis T., 99–100
Portuguese language schools/courses, 110
positive rights, 191
PPD (Partido Popular Democrático; Popular Democratic Party; Puerto Rico), 199, 205, 208
Prall, Anning S., 155
Principles of Human Geography (Huntington and Cushing), 24
progressives, 5–6, 143, 154–55, 221n15
Prussia, 32, 39
P.S. 45 (the Bronx), 157
P.S. 57 (East Harlem), 193–94
P.S. 89 (Brooklyn), 157
public education, 4. *See also* schools
Puerto Ricans: of the diaspora vs. the nation, 198; as "foreigners within," 7; in Hawai'i, 108–9, 196, 198; illiteracy among, 187; nationalism of, 193, 195, 199, 206–7; in New York City, 176, 188–89, 192–93, 195–96, 198; perceived as inferior, 175, 178, 188, 192, 195–96; perceived as undesirable/deportable, 48–49, 174–75; politics of, 199, 205, 208; racist reactions to Puerto Rican immigrants, 178; US citizenship of, 14, 175, 177, 182–84, 195–97, 196.193; as

white, 175. *See also* Mexican Americans'/Puerto Ricans' school experiences
Puerto Rico: agricultural school in, 200*fig.*; Americanization in, 185; coffee industry in, 184; constitution of, 182; creole elites in, 177, 184–86, 197–98; English-only instruction in, 155, 178, 183–84, 187, 205–7; as a Free Associated State, 184, 208–9; modernization of, 208; public schools in, 183–87, 183*fig.*; race and class in, 197–98; racial composition of, 174–75, 197; *regeneración* of, 177, 186–87, 192; self-government for, 185–86, 246n26; social justice campaign in, 199; as a Spanish colony, 184–85; Spanish language instruction in, 206–7; statehood considered for, 173, 178; sugar industry in, 177, 182, 184; as an unincorporated territory, 182; as a US colony, 39–40, 175, 177–78, 182–87, 193, 195–96, 199, 207–9

race/racism: and the American melting pot, 18, 48, 159–66, 169; Anglo-Saxonism, 34–35, 37, 40, 95, 143, 151, 161–63; anti-Chinese racism, 58–59 (*see also under* California); blood mixture/miscegenation, 26, 138; characteristics of races, 150–51; civilization and race, 150; and climate zones, 21–22; Darwinian schematics of, 27; debates about race/nation/law, 68–74; degrees of whiteness, 148–49, 172; and domesticity, in the press, 74–80, 78*fig.*; geographic distribution of races, 25*map*, 27; Mexican inferiority, assumptions of, 34–35, 174–75, 178, 188, 190; Mexican vs. white, 174, 245n4; "negro"/"mulatto" identification, 175; one-drop rule, 175; Puerto Rican inferiority, assumptions of, 175, 178, 188, 192, 195–96; racial assimilation, 171; racial instinct, 71; racial strain of nationalism, 68; racial taxonomies, 172; scientific racism, 52, 59, 66, 148 (*see also* eugenic arguments/eugenicists); struggle for equality, 125; violence against blacks, 47, 76, 124, 128, 142; whiteness of European races, 49, 150–51; white

supremacy, 5, 12, 29, 120–21, 124–26, 135; and white womanhood, protection of, 76–77, 138. *See also* Caucasians
Racine, Philip Noel, 136, 238–39n19
radicalism, 148, 161–63, 166
Radical Reconstruction, 119, 124
railroad building, 5–6
Rakoff, Jed, 215
Ramos, Rafael Menendez, 196
la raza (the people), 187, 192
La Raza program (Mexican American Studies program, Tucson), 14, 211–14
Reciprocity Treaty (1875), 92
Reconstruction, 6, 8, 33, 122, 124, 130, 221n15
Red Scare (1919–20), 166
Reed, Charles Wesley, 173
Restarick, Henry, 106–7
Rethinking Columbus, 15
Reuben, Julie, 19
Richards, David, 147
Richards, William, 90
Richardson, William, 75–76
Riordan, Julia T., 143
Roan, John, 142
Rockefeller steel trust, 158
Roediger, David, 152
Roncovieri, Alfred, 47, 66
Roosevelt, Franklin, 205–7, 209
Roosevelt, Theodore: on alien races, 76; on Japanese naturalization, 71–72; on the racial classification of the Japanese, 69–70; racial nationalism of, 72; on segregated schooling for Japanese students, 11, 63, 71, 74, 77; on US–Japanese relations, 72, 74, 79; visit to Tuskegee, 127
Root, Elihu, 74
Russia, 32

Sacks, Mervin J., 193–96
Sacramento Union, 75
Salazar, Ruben, 205
Sánchez, George I., 191, 203–4, 248n55
Sánchez, George J., 202, 248n53
San Francisco: anti-Japanese violence in, 66–67; Chinese in, 55–57 (*see also* Chinatown); importance as a port, 52;

Japanese in, 72–73; racial/ethnic diversity in, 52; trade with Asia, 51; as an urban center, 52. *See also* San Francisco schools
San Francisco Bulletin, 74
San Francisco Chronicle, 72
San Francisco earthquake (1906), 66
San Francisco Examiner, 70, 77
San Francisco schools, 50–84; adult evening school, 55; Asian children segregated in, 10–11, 53, 67–75, 86, 88 (*see also* Japanese exclusion crisis); and Asian exclusion's origins, 53–63, 230n28; black children segregated in, 54–55, 229n11; Chinese exclusion from, 50–51; and debates about race/nation/law, 68–74; and empire/exclusion, 53, 80–84; and the Japanese exclusion crisis (1906–7), 63–68, 67*fig.,* 70–72, 80, 83, 86, 230n28, 230–31n32; Oriental school in Chinatown, 57–58, 61–63, 66, 67*fig.,* 72; overview of, 50–53; "separate but equal" schools, 54–55, 62, 71, 77, 229n11
SB 1070 (Arizona), 214, 216
Schmitz, Eugene, 66, 75–77
schoolbooks. *See* textbooks
School History of the United States (Hart), 19, 36
A School Language Policy for Puerto Rico (Cebollero), 205–6
schools: as Anglo-Saxon institutions, 162–63; attendance laws, 153; citizenship paths for white students in, 3–4 (*see also* New York City schools); coeducational, 75; empire building via, overview of, 2, 5, 7–8, 14, 220n7; ethnic studies in, 14, 211–17, 249n5; historical interpretations in, 14–15, 211–14 (*see also* geography, history, and civics); and immigration/race, historiography of, 220n5; integration of, 12, 203, 238–39n19; local/regional (*See* Atlanta schools; Hawai'i schools; New York City schools; San Francisco schools); Mexican Americans'/Puerto Ricans' experiences in (*see* Mexican Americans'/Puerto Ricans' school experiences); "separate but equal," 127, 137, 141–42 (see also *Plessy v.*

schools *(continued)*
Ferguson); social studies curriculum/
civics courses in, 7, 10, 16; vocational,
97–99, 105–6, 130, 189. *See also* segregated schools
Schwartz, Henry, 113–15
scientific management, 4, 186
segregated schools, 2, 216; in Atlanta,
135–44 (*see also* Atlanta schools); in
California, 201, 203, 248n54 (*see also*
San Francisco schools); ended by *Brown
v. Board of Education*, 12, 238–39n19;
legal challenges to, 203; under *Plessy v.
Ferguson*, 6, 54, 125, 137, 142; in San
Francisco, 54–55, 229n11; as "separate
but equal," 54–55, 62, 71, 77, 229n11; in
Texas, 201. *See also* English-only movement; Jim Crow policies/laws
segregation: end of, 14, 141; residential,
180–81
Semple, Ellen Churchill, 21; *Influences of
Geographic Environment*, 24
Sherman, William T., 119
Shulman, Harry, 194
Simroll, H. F., 120
Sims, Walter, 142
Sixth Annual Negro Conference (Atlanta
University, 1901), 124
Skwiot, Christine, 97
Slaton, William F., 121–23, 125, 136–37, 139
slavery: education of slaves/ex-slaves, 122–
24; US, end of, 36–37, 119, 122
Smith, Alfred, 167–68
Smith, Hoke, 138
Smith, Robert L., 132
Smith, Walter Maxson, 95–97
social Darwinism, 17, 148
social engineering, 184, 186
socialism, 158–59, 161–62, 164, 166
Sonnino, Sidney, 167
Sons of the Revolution, 165
the South: ban on black education in,
123–25; paternalism of, 124; race riots/
lynchings in, 124, 128, 138; segregation
in, 124–26 (see also *Brown v. Board of
Education*; *Plessy v. Ferguson*); white
supremacy in, 124–26. *See also* Atlanta;
Atlanta schools; Georgia

Southern Education Association, 144
Southern fairs, 120
Soyeda, Juichi, 83
Spanish-American War, 17, 37, 40
Spanish conquest/colonialism, 30, 32, 39,
184–85
Special Committee on Immigration and
Naturalization (New York State Chamber of Commerce), 188–89, 194
Spencer, Herbert, 17, 22
Stanford-Binet Intelligence Scale, 189
Sterritt, Sadie, 100–101, 104
Stoddard, Lothrop, 173
Stout, Arthur B., 76–77
Strong, William, 149
Stuart, C. V., 59
sugar cane workers' strike (Hawai'i, 1909),
101–2, 108
sugar cane workers' strike (Hawai'i, 1920),
108–9
sugar plantations, 92, 98, 100–110, 113–14
Supreme Court: *Brown v. Board of Education*, 12, 203, 238–39n19; *Downes v.
Bidwell*, 196–97; Hawai'i DPI suit, 11,
82, 89; *Plessy v. Ferguson*, 6, 54, 124–25,
137, 142; ruling on Japanese language
schools, 116
survival of the fittest, 17, 22
Swett, John, 62
Swinton, William, 24, 26
Sycamore Street School (Orange, Calif.),
201, 202*fig.*

Tammany Hall, 158, 165
Tape family, 61–62
Tarbell, Horace and Martha, 22, 224n11;
Complete Geography, 20
Tarr, Ralph, 18, 25*map*, 26
Tashiro, Benjamin, 115
Teachers Loyalty League of the Bronx,
164–65
Tea Party, 213
Teller Resolution (1898), 39
Telles, George, 99
Telles, Martin, 99–100, 104
Tenth Street School (Atlanta), 140
Terman, Lewis, 189
Texas, 34, 36, 201

World War I (Great War) *(continued)*
democracy in Europe following, 168;
fear of communism during, 13, 162; fear
of immigrant radicalism during, 148;
impact on Americanization, 160;
pacifism about, 161; US entry into, 18,
32–33, 41, 98, 147–48, 155, 158–59,
159–60
World War II, 172

Yasuhara, K., 68–69
YMCA (Young Men's Christian Association), 163–64
Young, John P., 66
Young Men's Christian Association
(YMCA), 163–64
Young Men's Research Club (Hawai'i),
95–96
Yukichi, Fukuzawa, 65